Assia Djebar
In Dialogue with Feminisms

FRANCO
POLY
PHONIES 3

Collection dirigée par/
Series editors:

Kathleen Gyssels
et/and
Christa Stevens

Assia Djebar
In Dialogue with Feminisms

Priscilla Ringrose

Amsterdam - New York, NY 2006

The author would like to thank Jean-Louis Augé, chief curator of the Musée Goya, Castres, France for his generosity in providing the image of Marcel Briguiboul's painting *Femme de la tribu des Ouad Sidi-Aysee* for the cover page.

Cover design: Pier Post

The paper on which this book is printed meets the requirements of 'ISO 9706: 1994, Information and documentation - Paper for documents - Requirements for permanence'.

Le papier sur lequel le présent ouvrage est imprimé remplit les prescriptions de "ISO 9706:1994, Information et documentation - Papier pour documents - Prescriptions pour la permanence".

ISBN: 90-420-1739-2
©Editions Rodopi B.V., Amsterdam - New York, NY 2006
Printed in The Netherlands

For my tribe Daniel, Miriam, Juliette, Christy and Philip

with thanks to Professor Sissel Lie and Dr Keith Aspley

Introduction

Dialogic Spaces

> Ideology 'acts' or 'functions' in such a way that it 'recruits' subjects among the individuals ... by that very precise operation which I have called interpellation or hailing, and which can be imagined along the lines of the most commonplace everyday police[man] (or other) hailing: 'Hey, you there!'[1]

The image of Althusser's individual walking along the street only to be startled by this unexpected call conjures up the compelling and compulsive effect of certain ideologies on the individual. Taking his analogy further, Althusser claims that when the call rings out "one individual (nine times out of ten it is the right one) turns round, believing/suspecting/knowing that it is for him", recognising that "it is really 'he' who is meant by the hailing."[2] By this "mere one-hundred-and-eighty-degree physical conversion", he becomes a subject.[3] Those who do not respond to the verbal call or ideological wolf whistle, who are not recruited by (the) ideology as "good subjects" are simply relegated by Althusser to the status of "bad subjects."[4]

The first impetus for this book came when I visualised Assia Djebar walking along a street, and in the distance three French feminists trying to attract her attention.[5] Each one in turn calls out. Does she turn around? Is it merely a question of turning around, or walking on unperturbed, or can I fudge Althusser's imagery by imagining her stopping for a moment to talk to her interpellators?

My original intention was to assess how far Djebar had been interpellated by feminist thinking, in order to categorise her, in Althusser's terminology, as a "good" or "bad" subject, a "good" or "bad" feminist. However the analogy of the "ideological" policeman, a figure of authority and power, "arresting" his subject would imply a hierarchical relationship between writer and theorist. The second image, *of two subjects talking together* on Althusser's street, suggests a more egalitarian relationship:

---

[1] Louis Althusser, "Ideology and Ideological State Apparatuses" (1969). In *Lenin and Philosophy and Other Essays*, trans. Ben Brewster (London: NLB, 1971), p. 55.
[2] Ibid., p. 56.
[3] Ibid., p. 55.
[4] Ibid., p. 55.
[5] My usage of the term "French feminists" is discussed later in this chapter.

> ... je dis que l'essentiel, *c'est qu'il y ait deux femmes, que chacune parle, et que l'une raconte ce qu'elle voit à l'autre*. La solution se cherche dans des rapports de femmes. J'annonce cela dans mes textes, j'essaie de le concrétiser dans leurs constructions, avec leurs miroirs multiples.
>
> ... I say that what is essential *is that there should be two women, that each of them should speak and tell the other what she sees*. The solution is to be found in relations between women. I proclaim this in texts, I try to give concrete expression to this in the way I structure them, with their multiple mirrors.[6]

Djebar's comment above, proffered in the wildly different context of the problem of Algerian women (the quote is preceded by "Quand je me pose des questions sur les solutions à trouver pour les femmes dans des pays comme le mien..." [When I ask myself questions about the solutions to be found for women from countries such as mine...] inadvertently points to another solution, the one I have come up with in this book – namely to put women in relation with each other. Echoing Djebar's words, in each of the chapters of this book, there are two women (Djebar and a succession of feminist theorists), each of whom speaks, and each of whom "tells the other what she sees."

My aim is to match the Djebar's novels with the works of a selection of feminist writers and to "make their texts talk to each other." I expect the meeting between them to be productive, to create a new space in which common sympathies and differences can be established. And finally, I expect the result to be mutually illuminating, and in particular, to promote a better understanding of Djebar's work.

Christiane Makward provides what could perhaps be construed as "etiquette" for the way feminist critics should ideally approach *textes féminins*.[7] For her, this approach coincides with feminist attentiveness to its object as described by Hélène Cixous in *La Venue à l'écriture*: "Celle qui regarde avec le regard qui reconnaît, qui étudie, respecte, ne prend pas, ne griffe pas, mais attentivement, avec un doux acharnement, contemple et lit, caresse, baigne, fait rayonner l'autre."[8]

---

[6] Mildred Mortimer, "Entretien avec Assia Djebar, écrivain algérien", *Research in African Literatures*, 19:2 (1988), pp. 197-205, p. 205. My translation. [My emphasis]

[7] Christiane Makward, "Nouveau regard sur la critique féministe en France", *Revue de l'Université d'Ottowa*, 50:1, pp. 47-54, p. 49. Quoted in Gayle Greene and Coppélia Kahn, "Feminist Scholarship and the Social Construction of Woman", in Gayle Greene and Coppélia Kahn (eds), *Making a Difference: Feminist Literary Criticism* (London and New York: Routledge, 1985), p. 94.

[8] Hélène Cixous (in collaboration with Annie Leclerc and Madeleine Gagnon), *La Venue à l'écriture* (Paris: UGE, 10/18, 1977), p. 56.

This "soft" approach militates against the temptation to "stuff" such texts into the theoretical machinery, a pitfall I hope to sidestep by means of a dialogical approach: "Judging a writer on the basis of her service to feminism is as bad as judging her 'according to her looks.'"[9]

Joanna Griffith's wry comment points to the dangers of reducing literature to ideology, or in my case of reducing literature to literary theories. Rather than judging Djebar "according to her looks", I hope to follow Makward's advice and to observe her (in dialogue with others) with a gaze "that recognises, that studies [and] that respects", although I cannot promise to go as far as to caress, bathe and make her gleam.[10] But I must confess that, on several occasions, I am compelled to abandon ship, to seize Djebar's text and make my mark.

In conclusion, the aim of this book is to create dialogues between Djebar's texts and the theoretical works of a selection of feminist writers (Leila Ahmed, Hélène Cixous, Luce Irigaray, Julia Kristeva and Fatima Mernissi) in order to evaluate how much Djebar's work has in common with these different feminisms. The aim is not to try to prove whether or not Djebar has been *influenced* by specific theorists (in any case, Djebar has claimed not to have read Kristeva, whereas we know that she is familiar with Cixous[11]), but rather to show at what point what Djebar describes as "my own kind of feminism"[12] runs in parallel with these other feminisms, as well as demonstrating at what points they move apart. But before explaining my choice of a feminist approach to Djebar's œuvre, and more specifically, the particular selection of feminist thinkers I refer to, I will give a brief introduction to Assia Djebar and her œuvre.

A Sister to Sagan?

Born in the coastal city of Cherchell in 1936, Assia Djebar (*née* Fatima-Zohra Imalhayène) is Algeria's most renowned and prolific

---

[9] Joanna Griffiths referring to Erica Jong's book *What Do Women Want?* (London: Bloomsbury, 1999) in Guardian Weekly, Feb 21, 1999.
[10] Hélène Cixous, *La Venue à l'écriture,* p. 56, trans. Deborah Jenson, "Coming to Writing", in Deborah Jensen (ed), *Coming to Writing and Other Essays* (Cambridge, MA: Harvard University Press, 1991), p. 51.
[11] The first fact I established in a brief conversation I held with Djebar at the ASCALF conference, London, in 1997, the second is evident by Djebar's use of an epigraph from *La Jeune née.*
[12] Clarisse Zimra, "Woman's Memory Spans Centuries: An Interview with Assia Djebar", Afterword to Assia Djebar, *Women of Algiers in their Apartment,* trans. Marjolijn de Jager, (Charlottesville/London: University of Virginia Press, 1992), p. 175.

woman novelist and film-maker. I will let Clarisse Zimra take up her story:

> In 1957 a young unknown burst on the French literary scene with an insolently sensual story written on a dare. *La Soif* had everything: beautiful females, well-off males, fast cars, lazy days at the beach, and, to top it off, a botched abortion resulting in death. Its author, the proper daughter of a Moslem civil servant, was not quite twenty years old. To the Parisian pundits, the resemblance to young Françoise Sagan's 1954 scandalous *Bonjour tristesse* published by the same press [Julliard] was unmistakable.[13]

Assia Djebar's "self-indulgent bourgeois stories" (*La Soif* was soon followed by *Les Impatients*, 1958) attracted nothing but praise from the French press, eager to jump on an example of the successful implementation of "leur mission civilisatrice", and equal contempt from Algerian revolutionaries for whom these stories "did nothing to advance the cause of national liberation."[14] Djebar would nevertheless prove her political commitment during the War of Independence, a time which for her brought exile, first to Tunisia where she took a degree in history, then to Morocco. This period also signalled her entry into a more politicised literary output, producing two novels, *Les Enfants du nouveau monde* (1962) and *Les Alouettes naïves* (1967) "works that even the most intransigent revolutionaries would consider 'ideologically correct.'"[15] She did not return to Algeria until 1962, the year of independence, when she took up a post at the University of Algiers, and went on to produce a collection of verse, *Poèmes pour l'Algérie heureuse* (whose publication by the state publishing house, SNED, was an unmistakable sign of "official favour").[16] In 1969, she stopped publishing and there followed a ten-year period of near silence.[17]

---

[13] Clarisse Zimra, "Writing Woman: The Novels of Assia Djebar", *Substance: A Review of Literary Criticism*, 21:3 (1992), pp. 68-84, p. 68.
[14] Ibid., p. 68.
[15] Ibid., p. 68.
[16] Ibid., p. 69.
[17] Twenty-two years later Djebar would admit to the *real* reason for this silence: "Je sais que j'ai souvent dit avant que mon silence avait à voir avec ma relation problématique au langage [to the French language]. C'est ce que j'ai prétendu principalement pour qu'on me laisse en paix. Mais vos questions me forcent à reconsidérer et je suis persuadée qu'il y avait quelque chose d'autre au fond de moi. Je sais, par exemple, que j'ai dû attendre jusqu'à *L'Amour, la fantasia* pour être à même de prendre en charge mon écriture, pour être capable d'inscire mon moi profond dans mon oeuvre." *Women of Algiers in their Apartment*, trans. Marjolijn de Jager (Charlottesville/London: University of Virginia Press, 1992), pp. 159-211. Quoted in Sonia Assa-Rosenblum, "M'introduire dans ton histoire: Entrée des

Introduction

Djebar's return to public life came in 1979 with the production of her first film *La Nouba des femmes du Mont Chenoua*, which received first prize at the Venice film festival. Her return to narrative "life" and entry into the international stage came in 1980, with *Femmes d'Alger dans leur appartement*, a collection of short stories which "heralded a change in the thematic and stylistic nature of her writing."[18] Published by "des femmes", it signalled a "new concern with women's words and women's voices: the aural manifestation of a female solidarity."[19]

> *Femmes d'Alger* représenta le saut dans la modernité scriptive déclenché par le ferment philosophique et féministe des années de théâtre à Paris d'une part (débuts des années soixante-dix) et de l'autre (fin des années soixante-dix) par le retour au pays et l'expérience sur le tas de l'oralité...[20]

Since then Djebar has published three semi-autobiographical works, *L'Amour, la fantasia* (1985), *Ombre sultane* (1987) and *Vaste est la prison* (1995), as part of an Algerian quartet, but interrupted this particular literary trajectory to produce *Loin de Médine* (1991), a novel about the origins of Islam, which she felt compelled to write in response to rising fundamentalism in Algeria. Then came *Le Blanc de l'Algérie* (1996), a direct and impassioned reaction to the Algerian civil war, and a tribute to the works and deaths of well-known writers, intellectuals, and thinkers (including Franz Fanon, Albert Camus, Mouloud Mammeri, Kateb Yacine, Jean Amrouche and Abdelkader Alloula). This novel represents another violent rupture in her literary trajectory, written after she was shaken by the murder, in Oran, of Abdelkader Alloula, her brother-in-law, childhood friend and a respected theatre director and playwright.

Le Blanc de l'Algérie was closely followed by a collection of short stories, *Oran langue morte* (1997), a novel, *Les Nuits de Strasbourg* (1997), a collection of essays, *Ces voix qui m'assiègent* (1999), and her latest novels, *La femme sans sépulture* (2002) and *La Disparition de la langue française* (2003).

---

narrateurs dans *L'Amour, la fantasia* d'Assia Djebar", *Etudes Francophones*, 12:2 (1977), 67-80, p. 69.
[18] Patricia Geesey, "Women's Worlds: Assia Djebar's *Loin de Médine*", in Kenneth W. Harrow (ed.), *The Marabout and the Muse: New Approaches to Islam in African Literature* (Portsmouth, NH: Heinemann, 1996), pp. 40-50, p. 40.
[19] Ibid., p. 40.
[20] Clarisse Zimra, "Comment peut-on être musulmane?", *Notre Librairie*, 118, Nouvelles Écritures Féminines 2: Femmes d'ici et d'ailleurs (July-September 1994), pp. 57-63, p. 57.

Djebar has been awarded a number of literary prizes, including the Neustadt Prize for Contributions to World Literature (1996), the Marguerite Yourcenar Prize (1997) the prestigious Friedenspreis des Deutschen Buchhandels (1997) and the International Prize of Palmi (1998). All this is a long way from the most enduring and much-quoted autobiographical image in Djebar's œuvre, that of the little girl walking hand in hand with her schoolteacher father, who allowed her to sit in on a class full of boys, at a time when Algerian girls did not normally receive an education.[21] It is not for nothing that years later, in an interview with Lise Gauvin, Djebar declares that: "Donc le féminisme, chez nous, enfin l'émancipation des femmes, est passé par l'intercession des pères" [For us then, feminism or the liberation of women was associated with the intercession of fathers].[22]

Approaches to Djebar's œuvre

The multifaceted *œuvre* of Assia Djebar lends itself to a variety of theoretical approaches. Its engagement with colonial history and multiple references to colonial artistic and literary texts has made it a popular object of postcolonial criticism.[23] Its commitment to giving voice to what Gayatri Spivak has called "the gendered subaltern" means that it could equally well lend itself to a Marxist critique.[24] The stated autobiographical aims of several of the works, combined with Djebar's ambiguity towards self-disclosure, allows for interpretations based on autobiographical theory.[25] Similarly, the considerable use of intertexts from colonial and Islamic history could call for a generic approach, while the blurring of the historical and the autobiographical in several novels would permit a reading from the perspective of genre criticism. However, given Djebar's commitment to privileging the experience and voice of women in her novels, her work has most

---

[21] "Fillette arabe allant pour la première fois à l'école, un matin d'automne, main dans la main du père." Assia Djebar, *L'Amour, la fantasia* (Casablanca: EDDIF, 1992), p. 15.
[22] Lise Gauvin, "Assia Djebar, territoires des langues: entretien", *Littérature – L'Ecrivain et ses langues*, 101 (February 1996), pp. 73-87, p. 81.
[23] See for example Clarisse Zimra, "Disorienting the Subject in Djebar's *L'Amour, la fantasia*", *Yale French Studies*, 87 (1995), pp. 149-70.
[24] Gayatri Spivak, "Acting Bits/Identity Talk", in Kwame Anthony Appiah and Henry Louis Gates, Jr (eds), *Identities* (Chicago: University of Chicago Press, 1995), pp. 147-81, pp. 147-48.
[25] Mildred Mortimer, "Assia Djebar's Algerian Quartet: A Study in Fragmented Autobiography", *Research in African Literatures*, 28: 2 (1997), pp. 102-17.

Introduction

consistently been approached from a feminist perspective and here again a range of feminisms have been drawn on.[26]

Feminist antipathy towards notions of category and indeed theory problematises the very concept of categorizing the spectrum of feminist literary theories. However, within academia, various attempts at creating various "schools of feminisms" have been made. But these attempts draw immediate attention to the difficulty of distinguishing between theoretical approaches, especially if you take account of the fluidity and borrowings between different disciplines. This is obvious in the case of feminist anthologies, which range feminist theory under intellectual traditions such as Feminism and Marxism, Feminism and Freudianism, Feminism and Existentialism, Enlightenment Liberal Feminism.[27] In some quarters, the dividing line between feminisms has been drawn between what can be considered to be the arbitrary category of national barriers, creating a fissure between Anglo-American and French feminisms. Others make distinctions based on a combination of national and theoretical positions, singling out Anglo-American, materialist and poststructuralist feminisms.[28] I will use this latter categorization to illustrate various possible feminist approaches to Djebar's work, and to explain my particular choice of Western feminist theorists (Cixous, Irigaray and Kristeva) who fall within the poststructuralist camp. I will subsequently deal with the Arab scholars, Fatima Mernissi and Leila Ahmed.[29]

Whereas poststructuralist feminist approaches are more focused on discourse and representation, "Anglo-American feminism is generally more interested in history, whether literal history (accounts of lived experiences of people in the world) or literary history or both, and

---

[26] For a selection of such approaches, see Laurence Huughe, "Ecrire comme un voile: The Problematics of the Gaze in the Work of Assia Djebar", *World Literature Today*, 70:4 (1996), pp. 867-876; Valérie Budig-Markin, "La Voix, l'historiographic: Les dernières œuvres d'Assia Djebar", in Ginette Adamson and Jean-Marc Gouanvic (eds), *Francophonie Plurielle* (Québec. Hurtubise HMH, 1995); Katherine Gracki, "Writing violence and the violence of writing in Assia Djebar's Algerian quartet", *World Literature Today*, 70:4 (1996), pp. 835-43; Monique Gadant, "La permission de dire 'je': Réflexions sur les femmes et l'écriture à propos d'un roman d'Assia Djebar, *L'Amour, la fantasia*", *Peuples Méditerranéens*, 48-49 (July-December 1989), pp. 93-105.
[27] See Josephine Donovan, *Feminist Theory* (New York: Continuum, 1993).
[28] See Michael Groden and Martin Kreiswirth (eds), http://www.press.jhu.edu/books/ hopkins_guide_to_literary_theory/ *The John Hopkins Guide to Literary Theory and Criticism*, 1997.
[29] Because of the brevity of this overview of approaches, simplifications and generalisations are inevitable.

focuses more on the interaction of texts with the extratextual world."[30] Early Anglo-American feminist criticism (up to the mid-70s) was centred on women's experiences as encountered in female fictional characters, on the responses of women readers and on the devices and themes deployed by women writers. American-based periodicals such as *Signs*, which conformed to this experiential vein, wanted its audience to "fix and grasp a sense of the totality of women's lives and the realities of which they have been a part."[31] Theoretical borrowings from history, sociology and psychology became crucial to this enterprise. Collections published in the late 1970s reinforced the extra-referential approach, which drew on women's experience of specific historical periods. Art was examined as "the product of a particular cultural milieu, sometimes embodying a society's most deeply held convictions, sometimes questioning these values, sometimes disguising an artist's own ambivalence with regard to these matters."[32] In addition to their interest in the material, social and gendered conditions of authors' lives, feminist critics of this period focused on challenging the masculine bias of literary canons and on rehabilitating women's literature.

In a similar mode, the concept of gynocritics, formalised by Elaine Showalter, attempts to "construct a female framework for the analysis of women's literature [and] to develop new models based on the study of female experience, rather than to adapt male models and theories."[33] Gynocritics' main contribution can be measured in terms of its ambition to construct female social histories, while its empirical methods and preference for close textual analysis (reminiscent of New Criticism) belie its anti-theoretical pretensions.[34]

---

[30] Robyn R. Warhol and Diane Price Herndl (eds), *Feminisms: An Anthology of Literary Theory and Criticism* (New Brunswick: Rutgers University Press, 1997), p. xv.
[31] Catharine R. Stimpson, "Editorial", *Signs* 1:1 (1975), pp. v-viii, p. v.
[32] Arlyn Diamond and Lee R. Edwards (eds), *The Authority of Experience* (Amherst: University of Massachusetts, 1977), pp. ix-x.
[33] Elaine Showalter, "Towards a Feminist Poetics", in Elaine Showalter (ed.), *The New Feminist Criticism: Essays on Women, Literature and Theory* (London: Virago, 1985), pp. 125-143, p. 131.
[34] Bonnie Kime Scott, "Feminist Theory and Criticism: 2. Anglo-American Feminisms", in *The John Hopkins Guide to Literary Theory and Criticism*, pp. 1-6, p. 3.

Despite being a reticent autobiographer,[35] Djebar leaves enough traces of her own experiences in her texts to allow for an Anglo-American style examination of the author as product of "a particular cultural milieu." Djebar's upbringing was atypical since she was afforded educational opportunities (thanks to her schoolteacher father) that were unusual for a young Algerian girl of her era. From an Anglo-American critical perspective, this means that a study of "the author's ambivalence towards her social milieu" could be located at the intersection of Djebar's desire to relate to the intimate world of Algerian women, from which her education separates her on the one hand, and her denunciation of the patriarchal values, which construct the repressive boundaries of that world, on the other.

Djebar's own approach could equally well be interpreted in "gynocritical terms." She too attempts to construct female social histories, drawing on historical sources to recreate the lives of the Arab women - such as those who lived in the early Islamic period. However, this interpretation is problematic, for Djebar's initiative is on the whole not so much centred around the everyday lives of *ordinary* women but around specific incidents in the lives of *extraordinary* women of this period. In her evocation of the Algerian War of Independence, however, she privileges the histories of ordinary women veterans of that era, using "ethnographic methods" (transcripts of interviews with these women) to give voice to their experiences. Nevertheless, historical contextualisation and interpretation take second place to literary extrapolations. The transcribed testimonies are devoid of specific historical and spacial markers and are followed by impressionistic, lyrical rewritings of these women's experiences described in Djebar's own language.

Material feminism is another cross-current within feminist literary theory from which Djebar's work could be examined. This type of approach was initially characterised by the attempt to synthesise feminist politics with Marxist analyses. More recently, materialist feminists have moved beyond the boundaries of traditional Marxist and socialist formulations, analysing the position of women not only

---

[35] Gayatri Chakravorty Spivak, "Three Women's Texts and Circumfession", in Alfred Hornung and Ernstpeter Ruhe (eds), *Postcolonialism and Autobiography* (Amsterdam: Rodopi, 1998), pp. 7-22, p. 10. Spivak states here that Djebar concurred with her observation that the latter's autobiographical work, *L'Amour, la fantasia*, "was [about] a withheld autobiography."

in terms of relations of "production and private property",[36] but also in terms of psychoanalytically based theories of sexuality and gender: "In keeping with subsequent developments within the women's movements, the materialist feminist problematic has extended to questions of race, nationality or ethnicity, lesbianism and sexuality, cultural identity, including religion, and the very definition of power."[37] Eschewing traditional literary concerns with issues of canon, form, genres and authorship and *œuvre*, materialist feminists now tend to ground their critical positions in political theory, psychoanalysis and sociology.[38] For many materialist critics, literary questions are therefore contingent rather than central: "Politics comes first ... since literature and art help constitute social life but do not determine it."[39]

Djebar's work is open to criticism from the materialist camp. While her writing engages with relations of power, whether in the context of the colonial period, post-Independence political structures, patriarchal social norms, familial relations or religious authority, her criticism of the asymmetries of political structures and social and familial gender inequalities is implicit rather than explicit. Djebar's work does not advocate direct political action nor does it explicitly address the material needs of her contemporaries. Nevertheless, her work has been "adopted" by the Marxist feminist critic Gayatri Spivak, who hails its engagement with the gendered subaltern as of particular value to the autobiographical project.[40]

The last group of feminist critics I will address are poststructuralist feminists (such as Kristeva, Cixous and Irigaray), whose focus on discourse, representation and on the constructedness of subjectivity lay them open to criticism from a materialist feminist perspective. Their approach can be characterised by Barbara Johnson's apt formulation: "The question of gender is a question of language."[41] In the most general terms, their thinking proceeds from

---

[36] Donna Landry and Gerald MacLean, "Feminist Theory and Criticism: 4. Materialist Feminisms", in *The John Hopkins Guide to Literary Theory and Criticism*, pp. 1-6, p. 1.
[37] Ibid., p. 1.
[38] Ibid., p. 1.
[39] Ibid., p. 2. Donna Landry and Gerald MacLean here point in particular to the perspective of Michèle Barrett, referring to her work, *Women's Oppression Today: Problems in Marxist Feminist Analysis* (London/New York: Verso, 1980), revised ed., *Women's Oppression Today: The Marxist/Feminist Encounter* (1988).
[40] Gayatri Spivak, "Acting Bits/Identity Talk", pp. 147-48.
[41] Barbara Johnson, *A World of Difference* (Baltimore: John Hopkins University Press, 1987), p. 37. Quoted in Diane Elam, "Feminist Theory and Criticism: 4.

Introduction 17

the premises of Lacanian psychoanalysis and adopts or adapts the methods of Derridean deconstruction (although some poststructuralist feminist such as Monique Wittig reject deconstructive approaches altogether):

> [Poststructuralist feminism] take as its starting point the premise that gender difference dwells in language rather than in the referent... In placing their emphasis on language, however, these feminists are not suggesting a sort of linguistic or poetic retreat into a world made only of words. Rather, language intervenes so that "materiality" is not taken to be a self-evident category, and language itself if understood as radically marked by the materiality of gender. The poststructuralist focus on language thus raises fundamental questions that extend beyond matters of usage.[42]

The common enemy of post-structuralist feminists is patriarchal discourse, whose ethical and political underpinnings they seek to expose. This feature emerges in their readings of Western literary, philosophical and psychoanalytical texts. The approach of one group of post-structuralist feminists (such as Michèle Le Doeuff, Barbara Johnson, Julia Kristeva and Luce Irigaray) aims at unmasking the political determinations of such discourses and at disrupting the power structures that underlie them. Other post-structuralist feminists, such as Monique Wittig and Cixous, prefer to develop an alternative non-phallogocentric discourses instead of the strategy of subversive readings. Cixous turns to fiction and envisages *une écriture féminine* as a bisexual political act which privileges the expression of *voice*, and which opens up the possibility of changing the symbolic order. As well as publishing close to fifty novels and plays, Cixous has produced some more theoretical essays such as *La Jeune née*. Her work has engaged the literary texts of James Joyce, Edgar Allan Poe, and Clarice Lispector,[43] deconstructed Greek, Latin and Egyptian mythology[44] and taken up specific instances of political struggle in the Third World.[45]

Materialist Feminisms", in *The John Hopkins Guide to Literary Theory and Criticism*, pp. 1-6, p. 1.
[42] Diane Elam, "Feminist Theory and Criticism: 3. Poststructuralist Feminisms", pp. 1-6, p. 1.
[43] *L'Exil de James Joyce ou l'art du remplacement* (Paris: Grasset, 1969); *Prénoms de personne* (Paris: Seuil, 1974); *Vivre l'orange* (Paris: des femmes, 1975).
[44] *Illa* (Paris: des femmes, 1980); *Le Livre de Promethea* (Paris: Gallimard, 1983); *La* (Paris: Gallimard, 1976).
[45] *L'Histoire terrible mais inachevée de Norodom Sihanouk, roi du Cambodge* (Paris: Théâtre du Soleil, 1985); *L'Indiade ou L'Inde de leurs rêves* (Paris: Théâtre du Soleil, 1987).

Whereas the common enemy of poststructuralist feminists is patriarchal discourse, the common concern of the *early* works of three writers I draw on most extensively (Cixous, Kristeva and Irigaray) is their revalorization of the maternal and the feminine, and in particular of "*the archaic force of the pre-oedipal*"[46] through the medium of language. I would argue that it is this specific common denominator that brings these early French feminist texts (published in the 1970s and 1980s) into a productive dialogue with the novels of Djebar that I will examine (published in the 1980s and 1990s). This is because Djebar as a pioneering Arab "feminist" novelist, writing in a strongly patriarchal Algerian-Islamic context, relates most closely to this *early* desire to revalorize the maternal as the necessary first step in changing the status and image of Arab women, and for her, as for Cixous, Kristeva and Irigaray, language is the favoured medium to achieve this change.

According to Marie-Claude Hurtig, Michèle Kail and Hélène Rouch, current debates within feminism in France have gone beyond earlier preoccupations with female specificity and difference (although it must be noted that Kristeva has always distanced herself from "difference" feminism, while sharing some of its preoccupations): "Durant les deux ou trois dernières décennies, la formulation des problématiques s'est ainsi transforméee: de l'étude de la différence sexuelle et de celle de la catégorie 'autre' – les femmes – on est passé à l'étude des *rapports entre les sexes*, dans le double sens de rapport social et de relation conceptuelle. Loin d'être un simple retournement, cette évolution a représenté un changement radical de perspective: d'une attention portée aus sexes et à leurs caractéristiques – les sexes étant envisagés comme des "entités séparées" mais de fait seule l' "entité" femme étudiée – à un intérêt pour le sexe et les catégories qu'il sous-tend, c'est-à-dire pour le principe même de la *catégorisation par sexe.*"[47]

The new debates within the new waves of French feminism have also eclipsed the revolutionary ideals of the 1970s. Many of the earlier French feminist writings (and this is especially true in the case of Cixous) were based on the premise that alternative and subversive writings would not only challenge patriarchal discourse, but would also bring about a revolution in the patriarchal socio-symbolic order. Although these revolutionary ideals now seem outdated (in the way

---

[46] Elizabeth Grosz, *Jaques Lacan: A Feminist Introduction* (London: Routledge, 1990), p. 149.
[47] Marie-Claude Hurtig, Michèle Kail and Hélène Rouch (dir.), *Sexe et genre: De la hiérarchie entre les sexes*, (Paris: CNRS Editions, 2003), p. 11.

that the feminist "conversations" of the 1970s and early 1980s, which attempted to bring feminism into dialogue with Marxism do), many important questions raised by these "pioneering" works continue to generate new debates about the relationship between power and discourse, about the symbolic significance of the body and about the ways in which the sex and gender systems are constructed and transgressed.

Before enlarging on the concept of the revalorization of the maternal and its relevance to Djebar's *œuvre*, I will address some wider issues related to the work of the triad of thinkers who have collectively come to be known as "the French feminists." This appellation has come under fierce attack from feminists such as Christine Delphy.[48] Delphy states that the term "French feminism" was in fact "made in the USA."[49] She believes that Anglo-American feminists have coined the phrase to denote a number of very selective extracts from a small group of unrepresentative thinkers. Moreover, she considers two of them (Cixous and Kristeva) to be outside the feminist debate in France altogether.[50] This, she claims, makes a mockery of "the real history" of feminist political activism and theoretical thinking in France.[51]

But more controversially, Delphy claims that French feminism is more than unrepresentative, it simply does not exist at all – it is an American chimera, a forced conjoining of a series of fragments of texts peremptorily selected from the texts of a group of very diverse thinkers, upon whom a unjustifiable common agenda has arbitrarily been imposed (she then proceeds to equate French feminism with the Anglo-American authors "responsible" for its invention, rather than with the "product" itself). This, she maintains, is a political move made in the interests of an unconscious American pro-essentialist manifesto. In other words, she believes that the "underlying essentialism" of the selected fragments taken to be "French feminism" has an unconscious attraction for an American feminist audience. This group, she claims, while defending French feminist thinking against charges of essentialism, is secretly reassured by its covert biologism.[52]

In any case, the charges of essentialism that have raged around these authors are open to interpretation. Cixous' strategy of referring

---

[48] See Christine Delphy, "L'Invention du 'French Feminism': une démarche essentielle", in *L'Ennemi principal* (Paris: Syllepse, 2001).
[49] Ibid., p. 320.
[50] Ibid., p. 321.
[51] Ibid., p. 325.
[52] Ibid., p. 347-48.

to bodily analogies, rather than colluding with the biologism of Freud, can be seen to reflect a notion of femininity and feminine writing based not on a given essence of male and female characteristics, but on culturally achieved conventions. Both Irigaray's and Cixous' use of multiple references to the body can be interpreted as a means of using "biological metaphors and images of woman already prevalent in Western discourse in order to produce a new discourse that does not *see* sexual difference as a question of pure anatomical difference."[53] Kristeva's emphasis on marginality (rather than on femininity or femaleness) allows us to view the repression of the feminine in terms of positionality (as marginal) rather than on essences.

Although some of Delphy's arguments, such as the exclusivity implied by the term "French feminism", cannot be denied, her claim that the "selection" of texts by Kristeva, Cixous and Irigaray cited by Anglo-American feminists are both unrepresentative (of both their own works and of feminist theory from France as a whole) and irrelevant (to the French and international feminist scene) are exaggerated. In any case, Delphy does not take into account the fact that most of the works of Cixous, Kristeva and Irigaray are easily accessible in English and that these critics do not therefore rely on a "few theoretical fragments" to make their case about French feminism. Furthermore, Delphy also falls into the trap of misrepresenting Anglo-American feminist critics, by treating them as a unified whole and generalizing about their intellectual tendencies.

I use the term French feminists as a practical way of referring to this group of francophone authors whose work is commonly identified with the appellation "French feminism", who have been influential in the development of feminist theory and criticism both in France and in Western academia in general, and whose ideas, while extremely diverse, nevertheless have some clearly identifiable common denominators (which will be dealt with later in this Introduction).

In two of the chapters in this book I refer to theorists (Mernissi and Ahmed) outside the fold of French feminism. This theoretical extension was necessitated by the limitations of a Western feminist perspective when discussing socio-sexual norms found within an Islamic frame of reference, whether in a historical or a contemporary context. In Djebar's treatment of the women of early Islam, this specific historical context opened up a dialogue with other branches of feminist scholarships outside French feminism, and with Arab

---

[53] Diane Elam, "Feminist Theory and Criticism: 3. Poststructuralist Feminisms", pp. 1-6, p. 2.

feminist historical scholarship in particular. Therefore, in one of the following chapters (In Dialogue with Feminisms: *Loin de Médine*), the textual approach I primarily adhere to is combined with an extra-referential approach that aims at deconstructing some of the ideological contradictions inherent in *Loin de Médine*.

Novelistic Choices and Theoretical Perspectives

The corpus selected from Djebar's *œuvre* for the purposes of this book comprises the four novels that were written within the ten year period (1985-1995), corresponding not so much to Djebar's feminist period, but rather to a period when her work has been in constant dialogue with feminism. These four novels followed her watershed collection of short stories, *Femmes d'Alger dans leur appartement*, the work which first marked her out not only as a writer of international stature, but also as a writer of "feminist" credentials. According to Clarisse Zimra, Djebar referred to *Femmes d'Alger dans leur appartement* "among all [her] books, [as] the one most in dialogue with [French] feminism."[54] I suggest that the dialogue with feminism begun in *Femmes d'Alger dans leur appartement* is sustained and elaborated in these succeeding four novels. Each of the chapters of this book creates a dialogic space between a novelistic text and the *oeuvre* of one (or two) feminist scholar(s) I have already alluded to:

L'Amour, la fantasia – Julia Kristeva
Vaste est la prison – Hélène Cixous
Ombre sultane – Luce Irigaray, Fatima Mernissi
Loin de Médine – Leila Ahmed, Fatima Mernissi

Three of these novels (*L'Amour, la fantasia*, *Ombre sultane* and *Vaste est la prison*) are semi-autobiographical works that form part of the Algerian quartet. The fourth, *Loin de Médine*, represents an interruption in the autobiographical trajectory[55] and an entry into

---

[54] Clarisse Zimra refers here to Djebar's response to the following question put to her by Zimra in a private interview: "Was your choice of a maverick [at the time] French feminist publisher deliberate?" See Clarisse Zimra, "Disorienting the Subject in Djebar's *L'Amour, la fantasia*", *Yale French Studies*, 87 (1995), pp. 149-70, p.151.
[55] Gayatri Spivak inventively locates a "cryptic autobiographical figure living in that history", suggesting that the only totally imaginary figure in the novel, Habiba (translated by Spivak as "the friend") is in fact Djebar ("habibi Assia Djebar", literally my beloved Assia Djebar – strictly habibti – Spivak inadvertently uses the masculine form here).

"Arab-Islamic cultural-political spaces."[56] As Clerc (quoting Djebar) explains, the decision to write *Loin de Médine* was purely circumstantial:

> Face à cette actualité menaçante [the Algerian riots of 1989], la romancière suspend l'écriture de *Vaste est la prison*: 'J'ai alors pris la décision d'écrire *Loin de Médine*. Avec *L'Amour, la fantasia* j'avais acquis un savoir-faire entre l'Histoire et le roman. Je me suis donc dit qu'il fallait que j'utilise cet acquis pour raconter les premiers temps de l'Islam du point de vue des femmes; j'ai senti que les intégristes allaient revenir en force et monopoliser la mémoire islamique.'

> Confronted with these threatening events [the Algerian riots of 1989], the writer [Djebar] postpones the completion of *So vast the prison*: "It was then that I decided to write *Far from Medina*. By writing *Fantasia: An Algerian Cavalcade*, I acquired a certain expertise in the interplay between history and the novel. So I told myself that I should use this know-how to tell the story of the beginnings of Islam, from the point of view of the women of the time; I had the feeling that the fundamentalists were going to come back with a vengeance and monopolise the history of Islam."[57]

Although this novel marks an interruption of the semi-autobiographical mode, and an entry into the Islamic arena, *Loin de Médine*, as Djebar's words above indicate, nevertheless continues the dialogue with both French and Arab feminisms.

Voices Searching amongst Open Graves

These four novels are all introduced in full in each of the four main chapters. So at this stage, before explaining my choice of theoretical perspective in relation to each novel, it would be useful to give a general comparative overview of these works, starting with a quotation from the celebrated collection of short stories that immediately preceded them:

> – Je ne vois pour les femmes arabes qu'un seul moyen de tout débloquer: parler, parler sans cesse d'hier et d'aujourd'hui, parler entre nous, dans tous les gynécées, les traditionnels et ceux des H.L.M. Parler entre nous et regarder. Regarder dehors, regarder hors des murs et des prisons!... La femme-regard et la femme-voix ... La voix qui cherche dans les tombeaux ouverts!

---

[56] Winifred Woodhull, "Feminism and Islamic Tradition", *Studies in 20th century literature*, 17:1 (1993), pp. 27-44, p.27.
[57] Interview with Sophie Bonnet in *Les Inrockuptibles*, October 1995, pp. 59-60. Quoted in Jeanne-Marie Clerc, *Assia Djebar: écrire, transgresser, résister* (Paris: L'Harmattan, 1997), p. 116. My translation.

Introduction

> "For Arabic women I see only one single way to unblock everything: talk, talk without stopping, about yesterday and today, talk among ourselves, in all the women's quarters, the traditional ones as well as those in the housing pojects. Talk among ourselves and look. Look outside, look outside the walls and the prisons! ... The voice that is searching in the opened tombs."[58]

This passage sets the tone for the novels which I examine, where "women speak out not only as individuals but also blend their voices to form a polyphonic chorus that will resist the pressure to return to what Djebar elsewhere has identified as a state of silence imposed by the heritage of cultural tradition and colonialism."[59] Here Djebar not only signals a move from the personal to the collective voice, but also a return to the gory past - "La voix qui cherche dans les tombeaux ouverts" [The voice that is searching in the opened tombs] could well be Djebar's own voice, which in the next novel, *L'Amour, la fantasia*, will cry out the pain of "les aïeules mortes" [dead matriarchs], in a tribute to the women sacrificed to the violent desires of the colonisers.

To the quest to restitute women's voices begun in *Femmes d'Alger dans leur appartement*, *L'Amour, la fantasia* adds two further ambitions, the re-examination of colonial history or restoration of a "more genuine" Algerian national identity (the book provides an Algerian perspective on both the French invasion of Algeria and the Algerian War of Independence) *and* the insertion of the autobiographical voice, an ambitious target even, it seems, for Djebar:

> First, I had to figure a way to move back and forth between the past and the present. Second, I had to figure out a way to navigate between the world of men and the world of women. And then, as you know, I suddenly found my answer: I thought of the interwoven polyphony of all the women's voices in *Nouba* [*La Nouba des femmes du Mont Chenoua*]. They formed a chorus – a choir in which I wanted to plunge myself, but without completely dissolving, losing my own sense of self. I wanted to remain myself, yet become one of their voices. At that precise moment I discovered how to write my quartet: I had to re-enter my own autobiography.[60]

And thus *L'Amour, la fantasia* was born, an autobiographical or rather semi-autobiographical novel in which Djebar starts off by

---

[58] Assia Djebar, *Femmes d'Alger dans leur appartement* (Paris: des femmes, 1980), p. 68, trans. Marjolijn de Jager, *Women of Algiers in their Apartment* (Charlottesville/London: University of Virginia Press, 1992), p. 50.
[59] Patricia Geesey, "Women's Worlds: Assia Djebar's *Loin de Médine*", p. 41.
[60] Clarisse Zimra, "When the Past Answers our Present – Assia Djebar Talks about *Loin de Médine*", *Callaloo*, 16:1 (1993), pp. 116-31, p. 124-5. The interview with Djebar included in this article is translated into English (the original French is not provided).

juxtaposing autobiographical and historical chapters (dealing with the French invasion) in counterpoint, and ends by joining her own voice to a whole chorus of women's voices, whose aural testimonies recall the War of Independence. This solution on the level of form brought to light another familiar problem, that of writing resistance in the language of the coloniser, the language of the enemy, "the language of murder, blood and gore"[61], a problem that Djebar attempts to address by "arabising" her French.

While the quest for national/historical identity is dropped in the succeeding novel, *Ombre sultane*, the principle of *female plurality* developed in *L'Amour, la fantasia* resurfaces here, as Djebar explores the *doubling of feminine identities* that is central to the novel's message of female sisterhood and solidarity. *Ombre sultane* tells the story of two women, the emancipated Isma and the traditional Hajila, who have both been married to the same man. Djebar recounts how Isma match-makes her ex-husband with the hapless, illiterate Hajila, and charts the trajectory of a relationship between the two women as a journey that begins in ambiguity and ends in solidarity.

Apart from feminine plurality, another aspect of *L'Amour, la fantasia* finds expression in *Ombre sultane*, albeit in a different form: war. In *Ombre sultane* war is re-enacted, this time in the relationship between the sexes: "In *A Sister* [*A Sister to Sheherazade*, English title of *Ombre sultane*] Djebar describes her [Isma's] relationship with her husband in terms of war (barricades, defiance, confrontation) … Likewise, Hajila, through Isma's narrative voice, describes her first sexual experience with her husband in terms of struggle, battle, and resistance."[62]

Although the story of Isma and Hajila appears to depart from the original autobiographical intent of the quartet, similarities can be discerned between the past experiences of Isma (as described in *Ombre sultane*), and those of the adolescent Djebar (as described in *L'Amour, la fantasia*), giving autobiographical resonances to what at first reading appears to be a fictional story. Less predictably, a more sombre note of similarity is struck between the narrator of *Vaste est la prison* and the other protagonist in *Ombre sultane*, the timid, uneducated Hajila, as the terrifying experience Hajila suffers when her husband tries to blind her is repeated in Part 1 of *Vaste est la prison*, where, according to Gracki, "Djebar courageously reveals and writes

---

[61] Ibid., p.128.
[62] Katherine Gracki, "Writing Violence and the Violence of Writing in Assia Djebar's Algerian Quartet", *World Literature Today*, 70:4 (1996), pp. 835-43, p. 840. Gracki assumes that Part 1 of *Vaste est la Prison* is autobiographical.

about her own wounds at the hands of her husband" and inscribes herself "in the age-old story of sororal bonds by becoming not only Isma's double but Hajila's as well."[63]

The focus on female solidarity expressed in *Ombre sultane* is displaced in *Vaste est la prison* by the exposure of the *failure* of relationships *between the sexes*, in a novel that throws up a violent marriage and an ultimately unsatisfactory affair. The love story that opens the novel nevertheless stands out from the rest of Djebar's writing as the site of the most raw self-exposure. Although Djebar is itself a pseudonym, and although the narrator oscillates between first person and third person narration (between *je* and *elle-Isma*), there is a directness and openness about the writing that suggests that Djebar, while hiding behind other names, is no longer hiding behind the multiple voices that have shielded her in the previous two semi-autobiographical novels.

Whereas in *L'Amour, la fantasia* the Arabic language becomes the site of veneration, in the second part of *Vaste est la prison* Djebar turns *against* her maternal tongue, exposing it as a patriarchal language which, like the society it owns, serves only to promote separation and antagonism between the sexes. Here Djebar swiftly turns her attention to another language, the ancient Berber language, which becomes the object not only of a historical quest (resuming the historical vein of *L'Amour, la fantasia*), but of Djebar's personal quest for "*une écriture des femmes*" (the Berber language is revealed to have been the privileged property of women: "Dans la société touareg, ce sont les femmes qui conservent l'écriture..."[64]).

Since the Berber language is also the language of Djebar's maternal grandmother, it is not surprising that this historical quest is followed by chapters which rewrite the stories of her female relatives and ancestors. This third part of the novel highlights the importance for Djebar of renewing matrilineal bonds, a feature shared with the third part of *L'Amour la fantasia*. And, while *matrilineal* bonds are rediscovered at the ends of *L'Amour, la fantasia* and *Vaste est la prison*, the final part of *Ombre sultane* privileges the *sororal* bond, staging a series of encounters between the two female protagonists, Isma and Hajila. Similarly, this feminine finale is repeated at the end of *Loin de Médine*, which builds up to a final crescendo of female voices.[65]

---

[63] Ibid., p. 840-41.
[64] Lise Gauvin, "Assia Djebar, territoires des langues: entretien", p. 76.
[65] So the "architect" in Djebar constructs a "female structure" onto the end of each of these novels. Djebar has often described her works in terms of architectural

For Clarisse Zimra, *Loin de Médine*, while signalling "une rupture de ton" from the two semi-autobiographical works that precede it, does not represent what certain critics have interpreted as a change of direction in Djebar's writing, but rather maintains "un dialogue profond avec tous les autres textes signés de sa main."[66] For her, Djebar's evocation of the powerful women of the Pre-Islamic and early Islamic era remains firmly grounded in "la question de l'espace"[67], women's entry into public space, a founding theme which she traces back from Djebar's first volley of novels through to *L'Amour, la fantasia*:

> A la fois figure et sens, il [le jeu de l'espace] remet en question la représentation et le dire du corps féminin: question autour de laquelle *Fantasia*, ce roman va repenser le discours historique. *Loin de Médine*, dont les temps forts sont organisés autour de la conquête de l'espace par le corps féminin, ne saurait se comprendre sans cela. [68]

Meanwhile Clerc also points to continuities, this time between *Loin de Médine* and the third semi-autobiographical work, *Vaste est la prison*, which Djebar returned to after *Médine*'s completion:

> A travers la redécouverte de cette histoire des femmes de sa famille [in *Vaste est la prison*], l'auteur se trouve face à des "femmes en mouvement", opérant constamment "des passages qui peuvent être des fractures d'un lieu à l'autre, ou d'une langue à l'autre" ... C'est pourquoi les figures de femmes convoquées dans *Vaste* se situent dans la continuité de celles de *Loin de Médine*: ce sont des figures de "fugitives" dont les corps en mouvement disent la capacité de résistance face à la Loi qui veut les soumettre au confinement.[69]

As Djebar evokes a host of women in movement, another female figure, "l'Algérie-femme" (as she is called in *L'Amour, la fantasia*), whose increasing fanatisation was the catalyst for the writing of *Loin de Médine*, reimposes herself almost "like a character in a play"[70] as

---

constructions (as well as musical ones): "Plusieurs fois, elle signale, au début de sa carrière d'écrivain, ce projet architectural, qui se mêle d'ailleurs, à une aspiration musicale" (see Jeanne-Marie Clerc, *Assia Djebar: écrire, transgresser, résister*, p. 125). According to Clarisse Zimra, Djebar has commented on her "architectural imagination" as " what is left of my youthful urge to become an architect" (unpub. Interview, 1992).
[66] Clarisse Zimra, "Comment peut-on être musulmane?", p. 58.
[67] Ibid., p. 58.
[68] Ibid., p. 58.
[69] Jeanne-Marie Clerc, *Assia Djebar: écrire, transgresser, résister*, p. 120-21.
[70] Evelyne Accad, "Assia Djebar's Contribution to Arab Women's Literature: Rebellion, Maturity, Vision", *World Literature Today*, 70:4 (1996), pp. 801-12. In this article, it is "North African society itself [rather than Algeria that] emerges as a

an increasingly important figure in *Ombre sultane* and *Vaste est la prison*, firmly anchoring these novels in political reality.

Matches Made in Heaven?

An examination of the areas of commonality and difference between the three French feminist theorists invoked, and then of the thematic preoccupations of the Arab theorists consulted, will clarify the matching of particular novels with specific theories.

The common project of the French feminists is to privilege the neglected underside of the dually coded psychoanalytical system (whether designated as pre-oedipal/oedipal, unconscious/conscious, imaginary/symbolic, or maternal/paternal), to seek *out the buried maternal pre-oedipal bedrock* that underlies paternal, or symbolic, law and to articulate the debt that the symbolic owes to the feminine and the maternal.[71] Kristeva's, Cixous's and Irigaray's understanding of language can thus be interpreted in the different ways that they each affirm *"the archaic force of the pre-oedipal."*[72]

Kristeva affirms the pre-oedipal relationship between mother and child with the idea of the *semiotic*. The semiotic phase is associated with the rhythmic, energetic series of forces that strive to multiply the pleasures, sounds, colours and movements experienced in a child's body during the intense maternal stage. She suggests that it is at this stage that the first traces of the signifying process are established, and that the chaotic pulsations of the semiotic represent the *pre-condition* for signification. But, like "the repressed", these semiotic articulations can return as irruptions within symbolic expression, and therefore function not only as the pre-condition of language, but also as its *excess*.[73] For Kristeva, language is constituted as a dialectic process, as the constant interaction between the chaotic, libidinal force of the semiotic and the logical, controlling force of the symbolic.

Although Kristeva sees this dialectic as operating on three parallel levels, as the constitutive element not only of the linguistic, but also of the psychical and social orders of life, in my study of *L'Amour, la fantasia,* I have focused mainly on its linguistic manifestation. On a

---

character in the play, a character complete with principles of choice and action, and with both trivial and tragic flaws" (see p. 811).
[71] Elizabeth Grosz, *Sexual Subversions: Three French Feminists* (Sydney: Allen and Unwin, 1989), p. 102.
[72] Elizabeth Grosz, *Jaques Lacan: A Feminist Introduction* (London: Routledge, 1990), p. 149.
[73] Ibid., p. 152.

linguistic level, her dialectic can be utilised as a theoretical model to evaluate the way all texts function (forms of language can be characterised according to which disposition predominates – the semiotic or the symbolic). In evaluating the way Djebar's text functions, a Kristevan framework seemed appropriate for two reasons. With regard to this particular novel, Kristeva's theory is useful both in terms of its capacity to straddle the book's generic multiplicity, offering the possibility of differentiating its consequent series of divergent stylistic registers (I explain later why a Cixousian or Irigarayan approach would be more limiting in this regard). Secondly, Kristeva's conception of language as the interaction of two modalities provides a useful entry into the central issue that is played out in the novel, namely the interaction of maternal and paternal worlds/languages. In *L'Amour, la fantasia*, as in Kristeva's world, there are "struggles between powers and resistances on the margins of the symbolic, on the border between the paternal order and a (potentially psychotic) maternal imaginary."[74]

Although the semiotic and symbolic modalities are associated with the semiotic and symbolic functions respectively, they are not associated with feminine and masculine identities, but rather "within each subject and each social and signifying practice, there is a play of masculine/feminine, a play not of sexual difference, but of differentiation."[75] Kristeva's conception of identity as interaction between two modalities leads her to reject any notions of a fixed identity or of any specifically gendered sexual identity. She also rejects any attempt to assign any specific linguistic (or political) identity to women, and is therefore opposed to any ideas of a specifically feminine language or *écriture féminine*, which in her view would only serve to essentialise "woman".

For Cixous, however, the pre-oedipal does have a special (but not exclusive) connection to women and to a feminine libidinal economy, and it is this connection that is at the basis of her idea of *écriture féminine* (Although Cixous believes that women are more likely to be closer to a feminine libidinal economy than men, men too can enter into that economy, and produce feminine texts). Although Kristeva foregrounds the effects of the force of the pre-oedipal on the symbolic as transgressive, that transgression is eventually absorbed into the symbolic, and as such, leaves its dominance unchallenged. Cixous, on the other hand, also foregrounds the archaic force of the pre-oedipal,

---

[74] Ibid., p. 154.
[75] Elizabeth Grosz, *Sexual Subversions: Three French Feminists*, p. 69.

but does so in such a way as to bring about the possibility of *transforming* the symbolic.

Cixous believes that language is central to the hierarchical, oppositional, and repressive structures of thinking which construct the patriarchal socio-symbolic system, and sees language as the key to reformulating that system. Since woman has figured within man's socio-symbolic system only as lack, absence or other, Cixous believes that the inclusion of the other, that the *inscription* of a positive feminine sexuality and history could transform the system itself.[76] She sees a writing practice, based on the inclusion of the other, as the site and means of this transformation: "In particular, Cixous stresses that the inscription of the rhythms and articulations of the mother's body which continue to influence the adult self provide a link to the pre-symbolic union between self and m/other, and so affects the subject's relationship to language, the other, himself and the world."[77]

Cixous's repayment of the debt to the *archaic force of the pre-oedipal* is thus achieved by means of materially recasting its rhythms in language, by expressing (rather than repressing) the m/*other* in language, putting into being a revolutionary writing practice, *une écriture féminine*, that brings about alternative modes of expression, perception and relation to those dictated by the oppositional, hierarchical and *self*-referential masculine or paternal order.

Although the style of the next novel, *Vaste est la prison*, demonstrates only occasional irruptions of *écriture féminine*, its thematics find many echoes in Cixous's thinking. The two main themes which the novel elaborates are segregation (both in Algerian society and in the Arabic language), and the search for *une écriture des femmes*. Djebar's strong reaction against the segregation at work in the Arabic language seemed to find its echo in Cixous's rejection of patriarchal language on the basis of the oppositionary violence which it creates. Secondly, Cixous's response to that oppositionary violence, which takes the form of a search for an alternative mode of expression, or language, provides a way of reading Djebar's historical quest for a mysterious and ancient script: is she too, like Cixous, looking for another language, a feminine language, as a reaction to the divisive violence of masculine discourse? And does the comparison between a twentieth century feminist writing practice, *une écriture*

---

[76] Hélène Cixous, Susan Sellers (ed.), *The Hélène Cixous Reader* (London: Routledge, 1994), p. xxix.
[77] Ibid., p. xxix.

féminine, and an ancient North African language, *une écriture des femmes*, end there?

Although Irigaray, like Cixous, questions the phallocentrism of masculine models of language and sexuality, unlike Cixous, she does not do so by exploring an alternative nonphallogocentric language. For Irigaray such a concept is not possible since she believes that a socio-symbolic system which refuses a female subjectivity contains no space which a woman may use in order to express her subjectivity, or, in other words, to speak as woman. So instead of creating a woman's language, Irigaray uses the existing language system to expose the underlying sexualisation of masculine discourses, demonstrating that these dominant discourses which pose as universal and neutral are in fact produced according to male interests: "She aims excessively to overburden existing forms of language and dominant discourses with their own ambiguities, the affirmations they unconsciously make, the materiality they refuse to acknowledge."[78] This "overburdening" is achieved by a technique of self-conscious mimicry, involving extended and selective quotations of the discourses she seeks to undermine, which have the effect of making explicit what lies dormant within them, making the repressed maternal-feminine "conspicuous by its absence."

In Irigaray's thinking the buried maternal-feminine resurfaces again as the underside, the unconscious of discourse. She too affirms *the archaic force of the pre-oedipal*, by teasing out of the text its buried femininity, by giving speech to the unspoken, examining the absences and repressions contained within masculine discourses. As such, her approach has been compared to that of a psychoanalyst, whose "parole" (or whose writing) acts as the catalyst to unbind that which has been repressed.

Although I have not drawn extensively on Irigaray's mimetic strategies in my analysis of Djebar, it is possible to read such a strategy in Djebar's cynical evocation of metropolitan texts in *L'Amour, la fantasia*, just as it would be possible to look at this particular novel's use of voice, and inscriptions of female corporeality, in terms of Cixous's call to "write the body" (both approaches, would however, given limited access to the text as a whole). However, the analogy of Irigaray as the psychoanalyst to the "stars" (the Fathers of psychology and philosophy), releasing their feminine-unconscious, provides an entry into the next novel studied,

---

[78] Elizabeth Grosz, *Sexual Subversions: Three French Feminists*, p. 127.

Ombre sultane, whose narrative I argue also operates on the principle of the release of the feminine-unconscious (as I will explain below).

In any case, when it comes to the main issue addressed in *Ombre sultane*, namely, relationships between women, it is Irigaray's views on inter-subjective relations (rather than Cixous's or Kristeva's) which have most resonance with Djebar's thinking. Both Cixous and Irigaray draw on the features of the unconscious in their elaboration of inter-subjective relationships. But whereas Cixous believes that women can access or be open to the other/unconscious (in the context of a feminine writing which goes beyond the borders of the self towards the other), Irigaray believes that woman cannot yet access her *own* other, since she herself functions as man's other, as *his* unconscious, and since her lack of subjectivity precludes her from achieving positive (subject-to-subject) relations with others.

She maintains that the dividing line between conscious and unconscious is drawn *between* the sexes (with man representing the conscious and woman his unconscious) rather than *within* them, and argues that each sex must have its own other in order for woman to come into being. What she is advocating then is a *double syntax,* a complete symbolic realignment leading to the coming into being of two separated or differentiated sexes, each with its own other, each acceding to subjectivity and relationality.

In *Ombre sultane*, Djebar presents a situation where a woman (Hajila) exists only as the shadow (*ombre*) of another woman's (Isma's) consciousness. This shadow-woman who has been trapped within the narrator-woman's consciousness (and has no consciousness of her own) is eventually *released* into the outside world. The shadow finally become form, as Hajila acquires a materiality and subjectivity of her own. Once this release or separation has occurred, the way is then left open for the two women, Isma and Hajila, to relate to each other as two differentiated or separate subjectivities.

The positive change in the relation between the two women is thus conditional on the release of the repressed shadow-woman. An Irigarayan approach to the novel enabled me to enter into the mechanics of that *narrative* change, which appears to "imitate" the conditions for *symbolic* change specified by Irigaray, namely the *release* of the repressed maternal-feminine. Since this release, in both Djebar's narrative, and in Irigaray's philosophy, satisfies the pre-condition for the coming into being of relationality, the interest for me was to relate Djebar's conception of that relationality, expressed as sisterhood and embodied in the final encounters between Isma and Hajila, with Irigaray's view of relationality, expressed as a woman's sociality (or *entre femmes*), and elaborated in her blueprint for a future symbolic order.

An examination of the relationship between the two women, based on Cixous's idea of Voice would have been possible, utilising the contrast between masculine voices which annihilate and destroy, and feminine voices which "watch over and save [the other]..."[79] This approach would have drawn on the way in which the narratorial voice shadows, or "covers" the other woman, and the way in which the narrator, like Cixous, embarks on the project of "writing you"[80] in such a way that propels her (beyond the self-interest of the ego) towards the other woman. However, Irigaray's specific focus on relationships between women, which she elaborates both negatively in relation to the current symbolic, and positively in relation to another symbolic (in which relations between women would be restructured), has particular resonances in Djebar's work. This is particularly striking when it comes to Irigaray's concept of this restructured relationship being constructed on the basis of a *reciprocal duality*, a theme which finds an echo both in the interaction between the main narrator-shadow couple and in that of the mythical counter-couple, Shéhérazade and Dinarzade.

In *Ombre sultane*, Djebar also goes beyond the life stories of Isma and Hajila to examine other female figures (from Isma's past), whose stories are bound by the common theme of sexual repression. In this context, I draw on the Arab conceptions of sexuality, as analysed by Fatima Mernissi, who draws clear distinctions between Western and Arab understandings of the origins of repression.

The specific historical period covered by the final novel, *Loin de Médine*, opens up a dialogue with areas of feminist scholarship other than those circumscribed by the French feminists, namely with the general principles of feminist historical scholarship, and more specifically, with that of Arab feminist historical scholarship. With regard to the latter, I have drawn on Mernissi's *Sexe, idéologie, Islam*[81] but also on Leila Ahmed's *Women and Gender in Islam: Historical Roots of Modern Debate*[82], which, like *Loin de Médine*, covers the history of pre-Islamic Arabia and the founding discourses

---

[79] Hélène Cixous, Susan Sellers (ed.), *The Hélène Cixous Reader*, p. 83.
[80] See Hélène Cixous, *(With) Ou l'art de l'innocence* (Paris: des femmes, 1981), pp. 256-71.
[81] Fatima Mernissi, *Sexe, idéologie, Islam* (Paris: Tièrce, 1983).
[82] Leila Ahmed, *Women and Gender in Islam: Historical Roots of a Modern Debate* (New Haven and London: Yale University Press, 1992).

of Islam, but does so from a perspective which problematises Djebar's approach.

In *Loin de Médine,* Djebar goes back to the roots of Islam and attempts to reclaim the religion for women, going so far as to say that the Islamic age heralded "une révolution féministe" [a feminist revolution].[83] Ahmed's exploration of the historical roots of Islam reveals a more ambiguous relation between women and Islam, raising the following questions: Can Islam really be reclaimed for women? And is it really possible for Djebar to invent a politically correct Islam?

Whereas I have chosen to create a dialogue between *Loin de Médine* and Arab feminisms, other critics have interpreted the novel in the light of French feminism. Winifred Woodhull believes that the residues of an "a-political 1970's French feminism" threatens to *subvert* the political goals of the novel, which she interprets as the "liberating transformation" of woman's status in Muslim societies. Woodhull interprets Djebar's injunction for women to revolt, to break free "loin de Médine", as a call for women to "run away" from the power-centres of Islam (rather than engaging with them politically), and proceeds to lay this political disengagement at the feet of what is described as an a-historical, a-political type of French feminist thinking.[84]

Geesey on the other hand happily situates *Loin de Médine* in relation to French feminism, citing Cixous's injunction to woman to "put herself into the text – as into the world and into history – by her own movement." Geesey's main interest in the novel is in Djebar's method of authenticating her texts by linking the chains of women's words portrayed in *Loin de Médine* to the chain of transmission (*Isnad*) that must be established to *authenticate a hadith.*[85] According to Geesey, the association between Djebar's "revision" project and the pattern followed by *Hadith* transmission and authentication is evidence that the novel not a subversive rereading of Islam but rather one that favours continuity with the past "posit[ing] a relationship

---

[83] Assia Djebar, *Loin de Médine* (Paris: Albin Michel, 1991), p. 86, trans. Dorothy S. Blair, *Far from Madina* (London/New York: Quartet: 1994), p.68.
[84] Winifred Woodhull, "Feminism and Islamic Tradition", p. 42. Note that Woodhull later qualifies this judgement, finding enough evidence of political will in the novel to quell her doubts as to its political soundness.
[85] Patricia Geesey, "Women's Worlds: Assia Djebar's *Loin de Médine*", p. 43. Here, Geesey also explains that "[t]he Hadith are sayings attributed to Muhammad and brief narratives about his life and those of his companions, transmitted orally and then written down after the death of the Prophet".

between her fictional narrative and an established body of texts whose interpretation has been controlled by men."[86]

I have now set the scene for another chain of words (my own) which aims to *authenticate* this introduction.

---

[86] Ibid., p. 46. [My emphasis]

In Dialogue with Kristeva: *L'Amour, la fantasia*

Ode to Beethoven

L'Amour, la fantasia, the first volume of the Algerian quartet, draws on Djebar's multiple talents to create a potent mixture of history and autobiography, as both her own past and her country's past are summoned up with a vivid cinematographic sweep. "Quasi una fantasia", Beethoven's instruction to his Piano Sonatas Op. 27 1 and 2 (the Moonlight Sonata), appears as the epigraph to the final part of the novel, suggesting the exhilarating freedom of the experimental fantasias, a musical arrangement that liberated form, rhythm and tempo. Mimicking the freedom of movement of this musical fantasia, *L'Amour, la fantasia* moves fluidly between the French conquest of Algeria, Djebar's own youth under French colonial rule in the mid-20th century, and the Algerian War of Liberation.

"Fantasia" also recalls the Maghreban *fantazia*, "a set of virtuoso movements on horseback executed at a gallop, accompanied by loud cries and culminating in rifle shots."[1] Djebar's *fantasia* stylistically reproduces the movements of this ceremonial *fantazia*, as the skilled manoeuvres of the riders find their echo in an extravaganza of expertly manipulated language, with the sudden climax of rifles resounding in the unexpected outbursts of poetic prose.

The fluid linguistic movements of the novel recall the constant alternation of modalities, which for Julia Kristeva constitutes the marker of an ideal text. For Kristeva, identity and language are in process, a process constituted in the incessant interaction between semiotic and symbolic modalities. Does *L'Amour, la fantasia* favour one modality over the other, or does it achieve what Kristeva terms as the impossible dialectic of the two terms – a permanent alternation?

"Who" asks Kristeva "is capable of this permanent alternation?":

> Une alternance constante entre le temps et sa 'vérité', l'identité et sa perte, l'histoire et ce qui la produit hors-temps, hors-phénomène. Dialectique impossible des deux termes, alternance permanente:

---

[1] Assia Djebar, *L'Amour, la fantasia* (Casablanca: EDDIF, 1992), trans. Dorothy S. Blair, *Fantasia: An Algerian Cavalcade* (London/New York: Quartet, 1988). This quotation is taken from Blair's introduction (effectively fourth page, no page numbers cited). Unless stated otherwise, all subsequent quotations in English of *L'Amour, la fantasia* are drawn from Blair's translation.

jamais l'un sans l'autre. Il n'est pas sûr que quelqu'un en soit capable ici, maintenant. Peut-être une femme?[2]

Perhaps a woman? Perhaps Djebar?

Identity and the Semiotic Continuum

Kristeva's concept of the development of feminist politics in three distinct phases will serve as a model against which *L'Amour, la fantasia* will be examined. Before looking at this model and proceeding to a Kristevan reading of the work, I will examine Kristeva's theory of identity, which informs both her concept of psycholinguistics and her politics.

Kristeva's theory of identity adapts Lacan's opposition of the Imaginary and the Symbolic, reformulating it as the alternation between the semiotic and the symbolic. Despite their differences[3], Kristeva accepts the existence of Lacan's Symbolic Order, the patriarchal order of language and culture that constructs the subject's sense of identity: "The Kristevan symbolic, like Lacan's own, is founded on repression, on the 'splitting' of the subject into conscious and unconscious, signifier and signified."[4] Kristeva, however, diverges from Lacan in her shift away from his emphasis on the oedipal father, and in her focus on the pre-oedipal mother-child relationship, which she describes in terms of the semiotic. The main concepts associated with Kristeva's concept of identity can be described as follows:

The semiotic

"The semiotic refers to the first, pre-verbal but already social ordering of reality during the earliest pre-oedipal stage of infancy."[5] At this stage the child has no separate identity from its mother, and experiences life as part of a continuum with the maternal body. This semiotic existence is characterised by "les pulsions orales et anales, dirigées et structurées toutes deux par rapport au corps de la mère."[6]

---

[2] Julia Kristeva, *Des Chinoises* (Paris: des femmes, 1974), p. 44.
[3] For an analysis of the relation between Kristevan and Lacanian thought, see Elizabeth Grosz, *Jacques Lacan: A Feminist Introduction* (London: Routledge, 1990), p. 147-69.
[4] Makiko Minow-Pinkney, *Virginia Woolf and the Problem of the Subject* (Brighton: The Harvester Press, 1987), p.17.
[5] Pam Morris, *Literature and Feminism* (Oxford: Blackwell, 1993), p. 198.
[6] Julia Kristeva, *La Révolution du langage poétique* (Paris: Seuil, 1974), p. 26.

These rhythms of heartbeat and pulse, dark and light, hot and cold, the regular intaking and outgiving of breath, food and faeces translate into a range of sensory experiences that literally and metaphorically start to *make* sense: "Oralité, audition, vision: modalités archaïques sur lesquelles se produira la discrétion la plus précoce. Le sein donné et retiré; la lumière de la lampe captant le regard; le son intermittent de la voix ou de la musique ... Alors, le sein, la lumière, le son deviennent un *là*: lieu, point, repère."[7] It is the gradual ordering and patterning of this endless flow of pulsations, which are gathered into the semiotic "chora", in which Kristeva sees the emergence of the basis of signification.

The chora

The "chora", by nature an almost indefinable entity, is the "home" of semiotic pulsations, and is characterised by its mobility and resistance to fixity:

> Nous empruntons le terme de *chora* à Platon dans le *Timée* pour désigner une articulation toute provisoire, essentiellement mobile, constituée de mouvements et de leurs stases éphémères ... Sans être encore une position qui représente quelque chose pour quelqu'un, c'est-à-dire sans être un signe, la *chora* n'est pas non plus une *position* qui représente quelqu'un pour une autre position, c'est-à-dire qu'elle n'est pas encore un signifiant; mais elle s'engendre en vue d'une telle position signifiante. Ni modèle, ni copie, elle est antérieure et sous-jacente à la figuration donc à la spécularisation, et ne tolère d'analogies qu'avec le rythme vocal ou kinésique.[8]

This rhythmic space "without thesis or position", without unity or identity, is nevertheless subject to a regulating process, characterised by constant but irregular irruptions "une réglementation, différente de celle de la loi symbolique, mais qui n'effectue pas moins des discontinuités en les articulant provisoirement, et en recommençant continuellement."[9] As the child grows and "progresses"[10] socially, the distinguishing features of the pulsations begin to be identifiable: "Freinée par les contraintes des structures biologiques et sociales, la charge pulsionnelle subit donc des stases: son frayage se fixe provisoirement et marque des *discontinuités* dans ce qu'on peut

---

[7] Julia Kristeva, *Polylogue* (Paris, Seuil, 1977), pp. 480, 481
[8] Julia Kristeva, *La Révolution du langage poétique*, p. 23, pp. 23-24.
[9] Ibid., p. 25.
[10] Note that Kristeva's phraseology implies that she equates social progress with semiotic regression.

appeler les différents matériaux sémiotisables – la voix, les gestes, les couleurs."[11]
We can imagine the semiotic chora in "the cry, the sounds, and the gestures of the baby. In the adult discourse the semiotic functions as rhythm, prosody, word-games, the no-sense of sense, laughter."[12] These cries, sounds and gestures, or semiotic rhythms, both provide and remain the foundation of all language and represent the basis of signification. The semiotic, characterised by flow, fluidity, rhythm and movement, although providing the basis of meaning, is distinguished from signification itself, which is characterised by definition, unity, and fixed positions. If signification and indeed identity are to be produced, then the semiotic continuum, the state of child/mother indifferentiation must be split – a split which Kristeva terms "le thétique."

The thetic phase

> Nous distinguerons le sémiotique (les pulsations et leurs articulations) du domaine de la signification, qui est toujours celui d'une proposition ou d'un jugement; c'est-à-dire un domaine de *positions*. Cette positionnalité, que la phénoménologie husserlienne orchestre à travers les concepts de *doxa*, de *position* et de *thèse*, se structure comme une coupure dans le procès de la signifiance, instaurant l'*identification* du sujet et de ses objets comme conditions de la propositionnalité. Nous appellerons cette coupure produisant la position de la signification, une phase *thétique*.[13]

The thetic phase enables the subject to attribute differences, and therefore signification, to what was previously the ceaseless heterogeneity of the chora. This phase therefore marks the threshold between the semiotic and the symbolic. In this threshold position, the "thetic" functions as a powerful controlling mechanism. Without the impetus of "thetic control", the semiotic has the potential to overwhelm the symbolic, and to dominate language with the force of its unconscious drives, transforming it into psychotic utterance. In other words, the subject who cannot or will not adapt to the symbolic, who consciously or unconsciously retreats into the semiotic, is in danger of suffering from insanity.

---

[11] Julia Kristeva, *La Révolution du langage poétique*, p. 28. [My emphasis]
[12] Julia Kristeva, "Sujet dans la langage [sic] et pratique politique", in Armando Verdiglione, *Psychanalyse et Politique* (Paris: Seuil, 1974), p. 62. Quoted in "Sherry Turkle, *Psychoanalytical Politics: Freud's French Revolution* (London: Burnett, 1979), p. 82.
[13] Julia Kristeva, *La Révolution du langage poétique*, p. 41.

The symbolic

> Le thétique permet la constitution de l'ordre symbolique avec toute la stratification verticale de celui-ci (référent, signifié, signifiant) et toutes les modalités de l'articulation logico-sémantique qui s'ensuivent. Commencé au "stade du miroir" et achevé, à travers la phase phallique, par la réactivation pubertaire de l'Œdipe, il ne peut rester ignoré d'aucune pratique signifiante. Mais sa nécessité absolue n'est pas exclusive: le sémiotique qui le précède, le déchire constamment, et cette trangression occasionne toutes les transformations de la pratique signifiante: c'est ce qu'on appelle la "création."[14]

Kristeva follows Lacan in positing the mirror phase as the first step in the detachment from the chora, and the oedipal phase as the moment at which the splitting or thetic rupture is achieved. Once thetic detachment has occurred, and the subject enters into the symbolic order, "the *chora* will be more or less successfully repressed and can be perceived only as pulsational *pressure* on symbolic language: as contradictions, meaninglessness, disruption, silences and absences in the symbolic language."[15] It is this pulsational semiotic pressure on language which Kristeva associates with the creative process, creative language and "le langage poétique' in particular.

Language as Signifying Process

Language in Kristevan terms is thus a dialectic between its two modalities – the semiotic and the symbolic. Discourse is produced as a process, dependent on the interrelation of the two modalities, rather than as a static order of meaning: "Ces deux modalités sont inséparables dans le *procès de la signifiance* qui constitue le langage, et la dialectique de l'une et de l'autre définit les types de discours (narration, métalangue, théorie, poésie, etc.): c'est dire que le langage dit 'naturel' tolère différents modes d'articulation du sémiotique et du symbolique."[16]

Morris characterises language that tends towards the symbolic as being "objective" or "extrovert", in the sense that it is being directed towards the object world of other people and things.[17] It aims at making itself understood, at enabling social interaction to take place,

---

[14] Ibid., pp. 61-62.
[15] Toril Moi, *Sexual/Textual Politics: Feminist Literary Theory* (London: Routledge, 1985), p. 162.
[16] Julia Kristeva, *La Révolution du langage poétique*, p. 22.
[17] Pam Morris, *Literature and Feminism*, p. 144.

and its disposition is therefore towards fixed and unitary definition. This need for definition can be understood as an urge to control what is other (the semiotic) and potentially threatening to the self.

The origins of the semiotic modality, on the other hand, "lie in the non-gendered libidinal drives of the pre-oedipal phase" so that its disposition is towards "meaning as a continuum." It tends towards identification (with the maternal body) rather than separation (via the thetic) from what is other. The symbolic disposition imposes the necessary uniformity of meaning and syntactical structure to allow for social communication, while the semiotic destabilises the urge for fixity, "producing a 'revolution' in the controlling force of the symbolic so as to ensure the generative potential for new meaning."[18] Language that allows more opening to the "revolutionary" force of the semiotic is termed "poetic language": "Mais ce fait est surtout évident dans le langage poétique, puisque, pour que la transgression du symbolique se réalise, l'irruption pulsionnelle se produit dans l'ordre signifiant universel, celui du langage "naturel" qui soude l'unité sociale."[19]

The "transgression" of the symbolic manifests itself as "semiotic irruptions", which are characterised by rhythmic qualities, a heightening of sound patterning and disruption of syntax. Communication is a threshold between the pressure of this semiotic disruption and the controlling force of the symbolic, which Kristeva describes as a dialogue between unconscious desire ("I say what I like") and the social ("I say for you").[20]

A Kristevan Model

Kristeva views the semiotic/symbolic dialectic as operating on three parallel levels, as the constitutive element not only of the linguistic and the psychical, but also of the social order of life. This concept is also used as a basis of her interpretation of the development of the women's movement. She views the feminist struggle historically and politically as developing in three distinct phases, summarised as follows by Toril Moi:

---

[18] Ibid., p. 145.
[19] Julia Kristeva, *La Révolution du langage poétique*, p. 62.
[20] Toril Moi, *The Kristeva Reader* (Blackwell, Oxford 1986), p. 316. This quotation is taken from "Psychoanalysis and the Polis." No references to the original French version are provided.

1. Women demand equal access to the symbolic order. Liberal feminism. Equality.
2. Women reject the male symbolic order in the name of difference. Retreat into the semiotic. Radical feminism. Femininity extolled.
3. (This is Kristeva's own position.) Women reject the dichotomy between masculine and feminine as metaphysical.[21]

Although Kristeva is not directly critical of the early liberal feminists (phase 1), she points out that their demand to be part of the symbolic order presupposes an unquestioning acceptance of that order and essentially leaves the existing system unchallenged. Furthermore, this demand can be interpreted as a desire for the recognition of the other, implying a sense of identity derived from that other. She reserves harsher criticism towards those radical feminists (phase 2) who reject the male symbolic order in search of a maternal or semiotic utopia. Their construction of an idealised counter-society is seen by Kristeva as a denial of historic reality. Just as the semiotic may overwhelm language producing psychosis, so a return to an imagined semiotic order represents not only a potential threat to individual women, but a danger to the feminist movement as a whole for "to opt out of the symbolic altogether is, for her [Kristeva], to opt out of history."[22] What Kristeva advocates therefore is a threshold position – *a balance between the two modalities*, "a permanent alternation" between the semiotic and the symbolic, between control and disruption and between the unconscious and the social, a balance that she advocates not only in political life, but also in literary production.

Kristeva's model can be summarised as follows:

1. The symbolic mode
2. The semiotic mode
3. A balance between the two.

Using this model as a framework, I would like to suggest that the text of *L'Amour, la fantasia* displays all three tendencies. I propose to compare the impact of the semiotic on all three parts of the novel and to establish whether Djebar manages to achieve "a permanent alternation of the two modalities" in the final part of the work. I will start by looking at the subject and form of the work, as a background to my analysis of its tripartite structure, using Kristeva's notion of "écriture."

---

[21] Toril Moi, *Sexual/Textual Politics*, p. 12.
[22] Pam Morris, *Literature and Feminism*, p. 146.

The Incredible Mobility of Being

> Je ne suis pas prisonnier de l'Histoire. Je ne dois pas y chercher le sens de ma destinée.
> Je dois me rappeler à tout instant que le véritable *saut* consiste à introduire l'invention dans l'existence.
> Dans le monde où je m'achemine, je me crée interminablement. [23]

In *L'Amour, la fantasia,* Djebar, like Franz Fanon, refuses to be a prisoner of history – history is hers for the making – but she does look into the past, her own past and Algeria's past to seek the meaning of her destiny: "… l'histoire est utilisée dans ce roman comme quête de l'identité. Identité non seulement des femmes mais de tout le pays."[24] In the many worlds through which *L'Amour, la fantasia* travels, and travels fast, Djebar recreates herself, her people and her nation in a perpetual and multiple search for an identity:

> L'écriture instaure une légalité autre. Soutenue non pas par le sujet de l'entendement, mais par un sujet dédoublé voire pluralisé qui occupe non pas un lieu d'énonciation, mais des places *permutables, multiples* et *mobiles*…[25] [My emphasis]

The *multiple* subjects of *L'Amour, la fantasia* are "Djebar-enfant, Djebar-femme, L'Algérie-femme" and "Femmes d'Algérie." The novel tells the story of these subjects in the process of re-establishing a sense of self in the face of colonial/patriarchal subjugation.

These subjects occupy "*des places permutables*": in Parts 1 and 2, the chapters alternate between historical and autobiographical sections, between incidents from the first historical sequence, the French conquest of Algeria, on the one hand, and autobiographical fragments drawn from Djebar's childhood, adolescence and early adulthood on the other. In these first two parts of the work, the constant displacement of subjects, between "L'Algérie-femme" and "Djebar-femme/enfant", is balanced by moments of condensation, nodal points where clusters of associated feelings, memories and desires come together, simultaneously evoking history and her story, past and present.

Djebar uses Beethoven's instruction to his Piano Sonatas Op. 27 1 and 2, "quasi une fantasia", as the epigraph for Part 3, with reference to a composition in which style and form take second place to flights

---

[23] Franz Fanon, *Peau noire, masques blancs* (Paris: Seuil, 1965), p. 206.
[24] Quotation of Djebar's taken from Mildred Mortimer, "Entretien avec Assia Djebar, écrivain algérien", *Research in African Literatures*, 19:2 (1988), pp. 197-205, p. 201.
[25] Julia Kristeva, *Polylogue,* pp. 43-44. [My emphasis]

of the imagination.[26] This final part is divided into 5 movements, highlighting its musical associations. Here the displacement of subjects continues at a dizzying pace as the text moves faster, more fluidly, back and forth, from autobiographical incidents from the life of "Djebar-enfant" and "Djebar-femme" to the voices of "les femmes d'Algérie", "Mères de la Révolution" – the women who took part in the struggle for independence.

Djebar's interviews with these revolutionaries resulted in their oral testimonies being reproduced within the text, providing the basis for the second historical sequence covered, the War of Independence.[27] The simplicity and terseness of these transliterated oral testimonies provide a sharp and deliberate contrast not only to the written testimonies of the colonisers, incorporated in Parts 1 and 2, but also to the richness of Djebar's own virtuoso use of the French language.

The subject of *L'Amour, la fantasia* occupies "*des places mobiles.*" Although Djebar moves backwards and forwards through time and place in alternating chapters of Parts 1 and 2, the historical and autobiographical sections are themselves loosely chronological. The historical sections progress from the events building up to the conquest of Algiers (13 June to 4 July 1830) in Part 1, to selected incidents from the lengthy period of consolidation in Part 2 (1840 to 1845). Similarly, the autobiographical sections progress from stories from Djebar's childhood to incidents from her adolescence and early adulthood (moving from the Algerian village of her youth to "La France" which she encounters as an adult).

In Part 3, however, chronological linearity is completely abandoned, as Djebar draws in strands from both childhood and adult life, and revisits historical incidents from Algeria's close and distant past (1830-1950). The distinction between autobiography and biography is blurred as Djebar takes on the voice of her compatriots, and tells not only her story but their stories. Finally, history and

---

[26] "In the 18th century, the exhilarating freedom of the fantasy extended beyond form and concept to rhythm and tempo. Beethoven undertook some significant experiments under the guise of the fantasia. His two piano sonatas, Op. 27 1 and 2, the second of which is the familiar Moonlight Sonata, are marked 'quasi una fantasia', and find him wrestling with irregular movement and form. These two sonatas are possibly the first large-scale fantasia to be cast in separate movements. The Moonlight Sonata is relayed without a break – it comprises an opening triplet-dominated adagio, a central musical-like dance that is neither minuet nor scherzo, and a closing sonata-form presto" (*The Ultimate Encyclopaedia of Classical Music*, p. 92).

[27] The *Front de Libération Nationale* (FLN), which led the armed insurrection against the French, was founded in 1954. Independence was declared on July 5, 1962.

fiction also merge as Djebar incorporates fictional characters into her reconstruction of historical events.

In this chapter, I will use Kristeva's three phases as a model for my study of the three parts of Djebar's novel, which I have divided into four sections:

Symbolic mode: 1. Parts 1 and 2 – historical
                       2. Parts 1 and 2 – autobiographical
Semiotic mode: 3. Parts 1 and 2 – poetical
Balance between the two modes? 4. Part 3

The Symbolic Mode: Historical Orders and Disorders

To opt out of the symbolic is, according to Kristeva, to opt out of time: "L'ordre symbolique – ordre de la communication verbale, ordre paternel de la généalogie filiale – est un ordre temporel. Pour l'animal parlant, il est l'horloge du temps objectif; c'est lui qui donne le repère et, en conséquence, toute capacité de mesurer en découpant un avant, un présent et un après."[28] The historical sections of *L'Amour, la fantasia* (Parts 1 and 2) are placed within strict temporal and spatial boundaries, within the limits of the *symbolic order*. But to what extent do semiotic irruptions disrupt the uniformity of meaning and syntactical structure dictated by that order?

Part 1: The dawn of colonial power

Chapter 1[29] of Part 1 describes the dramatic "dawn" of colonial power, as the French navy first approaches the shores of Algiers. As "La France" comes face to face with "l'Algérie-femme", the "Empire" does not "write back" but rather looks back. The returning gaze of "L'Algérie-femme" asks her assailant to recognise her identity and humanity, in the face of the threat of subjugation represented as rape.

"Whereas the play is created before us at every performance, the film is more like a record of something that happened, or is happening, only once."[30] The opening paragraphs bring the on-coming ships into view with a strikingly visual, cinematic impact. A series of

---

[28] Julia Kristeva, *Des Chinoises*, p. 39.
[29] This is in fact the second chapter of the novel. In Part 1, the autobiographical chapters (one of which opens the book), are titled, while the historical chapters (of which this is the first) are numbered. This feature is reversed in Part 2.
[30] David Lodge, *The Modes of Modern Writing* (London: Edward Arnold, 1977), p. 83.

panoramic long shots suffused by muted colours and sounds create a sense of presence, an illusion of history happening before our very eyes. This illusion of history in the making is reinforced by the use of the present tense.

The tension perceptible in the silence and near immobility of the scene is a tension pervaded by desire. Although this historical reconstruction is placed within the symbolic boundaries of space and time, "Aube de ce 13 juin 1830" [Dawn on this thirteenth day of June 1830] (pp. 18; 6), Djebar subverts the symbolic overtones by pushing back the boundaries of thetic control and allowing desire to flood in. By transposing a historical relationship onto the plane of desire, the text demonstrates an anti-symbolic stand, reinforced on a linguistic level by sudden irruptions of the semiotic. The semiotic is present in the occasional heightening of sound patterning, in the contrast of sound and silence, in the foregrounding of lighting and colour, and in the disruption of syntax reinforcing the emotive power of the scene, which opens as follows:

> Aube de ce 13 juin 1830, à l'instant précis et bref où le jour éclate au-dessus de la conque profonde. Il est cinq heures du matin. Devant l'imposante flotte qui déchire l'horizon, la Ville Imprenable se dévoile, blancheur fantomatique, à travers un poudroiement de bleus et de gris mêlés. Triangle incliné dans le lointain et qui, après le scintillement de la dernière brume nocturne, se fixe adouci, tel un corps à l'abandon, sur un tapis de verdure assombrie. La montagne paraît barrière esquissée dans un azur d'aquarelle. (pp. 18; 6)

> Dawn on this thirteenth day of June 1830, at the exact moment when the sun suddenly blazes forth above the fathomless bowl of the bay. It is five in the morning. As the majestic fleet rends the horizon the Impregnable City sheds her veils and emerges, a wraith-like apparition, through the blue-grey haze. A distant triangle aslant, glinting in the last shreds of nocturnal mist and then settling softly, like a figure sprawling on a carpet of muted greens. The mountain shuts out the background, dark against the blue wash of the sky.

The wide-angle opening shot reveals the oncoming armada, as Algiers, "la Ville Imprenable" [the Impregnable City], the ungraspable object of desire, comes into view. This first glimpse, viewed from the enemy angle, "triangle incliné dans le lointain" [A distant triangle aslant], highlights the sexual tension of the scene where "le corps à l'abandon" [a figure sprawling] awaits its fate. The blurred opaques and gentle pastels give the scene a sense of eerie calm, as the colours detach themselves from their objects, producing an impressionist haze. The "blancheur fantomatique" [the wraith-like apparition] of "la ville" [the city] carries with it a hint of the mystery (reinforced by the image of the town shedding its veils), but also associations of purity and innocence. Muted colours, "un tapis de verdure assombrie ... couleurs délicates" [a carpet of muted greens ... pastel hues], suggesting the vulnerability of "l'Alger/ie-femme", are contrasted with the startling natural beauty of the setting, "le scintillement de la dernière brume nocturne ... La montagne paraît barrière esquissée dans un azur d'aquarelle" [glinting in the last shreds of nocturnal mist ... The mountain shuts out the background, dark against the blue wash of the sky] (pp. 18; 6).

"Premier face à face" [The first confrontation] (pp. 18; 6). The camera pans slowly from a long shot of the object of desire to the desiring subject: "La ville, paysage tout dentelures et couleurs délicates, surgit dans un rôle d'Orientale immobilisée en son mystère. L'Armada française va lentement glisser devant elle en un ballet fastueux, de la première heure de l'aurore aux alentours d'un midi éclaboussé" [The city, a vista of crenelated roofs and pastel hues, makes her first appearance in the rôle of 'Oriental Woman', motionless, mysterious. At first light the French Armada starts its slow glide past, continuing its stately ballet until noon spills its spangled radiance over the scene] (pp. 18; 6). The stillness of the scene is reinforced by the characterisation of the object of desire as "l'Orientale immobilisée" ['Oriental Woman', motionless] and by the slow parading of the subject of desire, captivated by the myth of orientalism (pp. 18; 6).

Immobility and silence are further emphasised by the verbless sentence where activity, like the missing verb, is suspended in space: "Silence de l'affrontement, instant solennel, suspendu en une apnée d'attente, comme avant une ouverture d'opéra" [Silent confrontation – this solemn moment of anticipation, breathless with suspense, the moment before the overture strikes up[31]] (pp. 18; 6). After the silence and suspense – the illusion of reality is suddenly broken: "Qui dès lors constitue le spectacle, de quel côté se trouve vraiment le public?" [But who are to be the performers? On which side shall we find the audience?] (pp. 18; 6). This defamiliarising question shatters the illusion – this is not simply a visual reconstruction, a scene from a film, but a show, a performance in which the relationship between actors and audience is called into question. As Djebar prefigures the active, returning gaze of the native, the challenge is not just to look, to take in the scene, but to see who is looking and to follow that gaze.

The first human figure comes into view: "L'homme qui regarde s'appelle Amable Matterer. Il regarde et écrit, le jour même: 'J'ai été

---

[31] Translation adapted.

le premier à voir la ville d'Alger comme un petit triangle blanc couché sur le penchant d'une montagne'" [The name of the lookout man is Amable Matterer. He keeps watch and that same day will write, 'I was the first to catch sight of the city of Algiers, a tiny triangle on a mountain slope.'] (pp. 18; 6). In Djebar's world, where "l'amour s'écrit" [love that is committed to paper], the act of writing, in the absence of the act of love, becomes an act of possession (pp. 13; 3).

A sense of activity and sound is suddenly introduced: "Par milliers, les corps des matelots et des soldats se relèvent sur les ponts, remontent des soutes par grappes cliquetantes, s'agglutinent sur les gaillards" [Units of able seamen and soldiers clatter up in their thousands on to the decks and swarm on forecastle and poop] (pp. 19; 7). Then the scene is suddenly blanketed in ominous silence, like a deafening soundtrack that is abruptly cut, leaving only an image of striking light: "Silence étalé d'un coup en un drap immense réverbéré, comme si la soie de lumière déjà intense, prodiguée en flaques étincelantes, allait crisser" [The scene is suddenly blanketed in silence, as if the intense silken light, squandered so lavishly in dazzling pools, were about to be rent with a strident screech] (pp. 19; 7).

The camera moves in, then freezes on a still of the city: "La ville barbaresque ne bouge pas. Rien n'y frémit, ni ne vient altérer l'éclat laiteux de ses maisons étagées que l'on distingue peu à peu: pan oblique de la montagne dont la masse se détache nettement, en une suite de croupes molles, d'un vert éclairci" [Nothing stirs in the Barbary city. Not a quiver disturbs the milky dazzle of the terraced houses than can gradually be distinguished on the slopes of the mountain whose mass is now clearly silhouetted in a series of gentle emerald-green undulations (pp. 19; 7). The city, "l'Alger/ie-femme" silently resists its assailant. While the negatives foreground her stubbornness, pride and impenetrability, the gentle, opaque colours highlight her innocence and desirability.

The scene is now set for "the look" and its "returning gaze": "Dans le désordre des hamacs suspendus en vrac, entre les pièces d'artillerie et les batteries sur le qui-vive, telles des bêtes de cirque prêtes à la cérémonie derrière un halo de projecteurs, la foule des futurs envahisseurs regarde" [Amidst the jumble of hammocks, in between pieces of artillery and big guns drawn up in their firing position, like circus animals waiting under the spotlights, ready to perform, the host of future conquerors waiting to invade, stand and watch[32]] (pp. 19; 7).

---

[32] Translation adapted.

The delay of the verb ascribes significance to the act of looking and prepares for the returning gaze:

> Amable Matterer, capitaine en second du *Ville de Marseille*, et ses compagnons demeurent immobiles. La Ville Imprenable leur fait *front de ses multiples yeux invisibles*. D'où cet excès même dans la blancheur de la cité, comme si le panorama aux formes pourtant attendues – ici une coupole de mosquée reflétée dans l'eau, là-haut quelque ciselure de donjon ou une pointe de minaret – se figeait dans une proximité troublante. (pp. 19; 7)
>
> Amable Matterer, first officer of the *Ville de Marseille*, does not stir, nor do his companions. The Impregnable City *confronts them with its many invisible eyes*. Although they had been prepared for its skyline – here a dome reflected in the water, there the silhouette of a fortress or the tip of a minaret – nevertheless the dazzling white panorama freezes before them in its disturbing proximity. [My emphasis]

A dynamic is reinscribed into the relationship between "la France" and l'Alger/ie-femme", a symbol of the woman who will not be possessed, who will not be penetrated and who silently resists the intruder with her stubborn gaze: "Des milliers de spectateurs, là-bas, dénombrent sans doute les vaisseaux" [Thousand of watchful eyes there are doubtless estimating the number of vessels] (pp. 19; 7). As the equation "les Français/spectateurs, les Algériens/spectacle" [Frenchmen/spectators, Algerians/spectacle] is now reversed, the eye of the beholder is now the Algerian eye that possesses the French army in its gaze. The tension implied in their "proximité troublante" captures the heightening of desire as the desiring subject approaches its object.

Here again Djebar defamiliarises by a series of questions interrupting the stillness and the sequence of events: "Qui le dira, qui l'écrira? Quel rescapé, et seulement après la conclusion de cette rencontre? Parmi la première escadre qui glisse insensiblement vers l'ouest, Amable Matterer regarde la ville qui regarde. Le jour même, il décrit cette confrontation, dans la plate sobriété du compte rendu" [Who will pass on the number? Who will write of it? Which of all these silent spectators will live to tell the tale when the encounter is over? Amable Matterer is at his post in the first squadron, which glides slowly westward; he gazes at the city which returns his gaze. The same day he writes of the confrontation, dispassionately, objectively] (pp. 19; 7).

The confrontation is not only between "la France" and "l'Algérie" but between Matterer's objective, dispassionate, detached prose and the subjective, impassioned, colourful writing by which Djebar inscribes herself into the telling of history:

A mon tour, j'écris dans sa langue, mais plus de cent cinquante ans après ... En cette aurore de la double découverte, que se disent les femmes de la ville, quels rêves d'amour s'allument en elles, où s'éteignent à jamais, tandis qu'elles contemplent la flotte royale qui dessine les figures d'une chorégraphie mystérieuse? ... Je rêve à cette brève trêve de tous les commencements; je m'insinue, visiteuse importune, dans le vestibule de ce proche passé, enlevant mes sandales selon le rite habituel, suspendant mon souffle pour tenter de tout réentendre... (pp. 20; 7-8)

I, in my turn, write, using his language, but more than one hundred and fifty years later ... As this day dawns when the two sides will come face to face, what are the women of the town saying to each other? What dreams of romance are lit in their hearts or are extinguished forever, as they gaze on the proud fleet tracing the figures of a mysterious ballet? ... I muse on this brief respite; I slip into the antechamber of this recent past, like an importunate visitor, removing my sandals according to the accustomed ritual, holding my breath in an attempt to overhear everything...

As "les femmes" look back at the French fleet and as Djebar writes back or over the plain prose of Matterer, the object of desire is transformed into the desiring subject. The outburst of poetic prose challenges Matterer's detached account. The highlighting of sound-patterning in the sustained use of alliteration and assonance (the repeated vowel sounds of "rêve", "brève", "trêve", giving way to the "v" in "visiteuse" and "vestibule", the "p" in "proche passé", the "s" in "sandales selon" etc.) represents an interference of semiotic language. This irruption of the semiotic points to Djebar's desire for unity with "l'Algérie-femme", with the lost motherland, a desire she hopes to fulfil by visiting Algeria's past and reinscribing herself into its history.

So although Djebar places her reconstruction of the dawn of colonisation within the boundaries of symbolic/historic time, her revision of the event manifests an *anti-symbolic* stance, culminating in Djebar's subjective invasion of the text. However, her reversal of the "gaze", allowing "l'Algérie-femme" to look back into the eyes of the oppressor, is reminiscent of the *symbolic* tendency of phase 1 of Kristeva's model, as it marks a desire to be acknowledged by "La France", betraying a sense of subjectivity gained not through the self, but via the other.

Part 2: Extermination

The historical reconstructions following the opening scene of invasion provide detailed accounts of various stages of France's territorial advances. One of the most dramatic of these "revisions" deals with the ruthless fumigations of the rebel tribes of Ouled Riah in the caves of Nacmaria, in 1845 (pp. 81-97; 64-80). Like the other historical reconstructions in *L'Amour, la fantasia*, this text is heavily dependent on information from and insertions of colonialist intertexts, raising a further question in relation to the Kristevan model. Does Djebar's dependence on these texts mimic the colonised/coloniser paradigm (in a variation of phase 1 of Kristeva's model, where the early feminist movement is seen as replicating female/male dependence), or does Djebar manage to manipulate these texts in such a way as to subvert the relationship of dependence?

Before turning to the passage in question, I will refer to the characteristics of different types of "colonialist" writings, using the distinctions drawn by JanMohamed in "The Economy of the Manichean Allegory."[33] JanMohamed divides colonialist literature into two broad categories, the 'imaginary', and the 'symbolic', drawing on Lacanian interpretation of the terms:

> The emotive as well as the cognitive intentionalities of the 'imaginary' text are structured by objectification and aggression. ... The 'imaginary' representation of indigenous people tends to coalesce the signifier with the signified. In describing the attributes or actions of the native, issues such as intention, causality, extenuating circumstances, and so forth, are completely ignored; in the 'imaginary' colonialist realm, to say 'native' is automatically to say 'evil', and to evoke immediately the economy of the Manichean allegory. The writer of such texts tends to fetishize a nondialectical, fixed opposition between the self and the native.[34]

Writers of 'symbolic' texts, "grounded more firmly and securely in the egalitarian imperatives of Western societies", tend to be more open to "a modifying dialectic of self and Other."[35] Symbolic texts are subdivided into two types. The first type, 'syncretic texts', attempt to find syncretic solutions to the Manichean opposition of coloniser and colonised, but ironically these texts are often "seduced by the specularity of 'imaginary' Otherness" and "better illustrate the economy and power of the Manichean allegory than the strictly 'imaginary' texts."[36] The second type of 'symbolic' text (no generic term given) realises that syncretism is impossible and, by examining

---

[33] Abdul R. JanMohamed, "The Economy of the Manichean Allegory" (1985), in Bill Ashcroft, Gareth Griffiths and Helen Tiffin (eds), *The Post-colonial Studies Reader*, (London: Routledge, 1994), pp. 18-28.
[34] Ibid., p. 19.
[35] Ibid., p. 19.
[36] Ibid., p. 20.

the 'imaginary' mechanism of colonialist mentality, manages to free itself from the Manichean allegory.

A close examination of this chapter (which is divided into two main sections with a short linking passage) reveals the way that Djebar manipulates the intertexts. In the first section, the events of the days and months leading up to the tragedy are recounted, as the French army subdues the local tribes and the Ouled Riah tribe takes refuge in the caves of Nacmaria. Negotiations with the tribe's emissaries eventually break down and the French take their revenge: the exits of the caves are blocked, the piles of brushwood prepared outside are set on fire, and the cave is lit up with flames which rise two hundred feet high. Djebar repeatedly builds up the story, but then stops short of disclosing its dramatic finale, a refusal that mimics the tension and frustration of the situation itself. This section ends with Djebar fast-forwarding to the morning after the tragedy, while maintaining a total silence over the full horror of the night before. It is not until the second half of the chapter that Djebar finally discloses the full truth.

Although the text starts off by adhering to strict chronological linearity, as the chapter proceeds, the reconstruction of the story becomes increasingly fragmented, taking on a cumulative structure, which subverts the progressive, linear style of traditional historical narrative. The chapter is constructed like a jigsaw puzzle, put together using a whole plethora of fragments taken from historical archives that are painstakingly pieced together. Djebar, however, carefully selects her fragments to present two alternative versions of the same story, and the division within the chapter is revealed to be the dividing line between the two alternative jigsaw images, each created to reveal a completely different picture of the past.

The first section presents the story of the caves strictly from the point of view of the coloniser, using excerpts and information from eyewitnesses with "imaginary" tendencies (Bugeaud who ordered the fumigation, and Pélissier who carried out his orders) and as a result constructs an "imaginary" puzzle. But this puzzle is never completed; every time Djebar comes close to setting down the last piece, she deliberately withdraws, unable to reveal "le secret violent des pierres" [the violent secret hidden in the rocks] (pp. 89; 71). It is as if an "imaginary" picture is by its very nature unable to reveal the whole truth.

Initially then, the various stages of the altercations are presented in strict chronological order: "En mai", "Le mois de juin commence", "Le 11 juin" etc. ["In May", "It is now the beginning of June", "On 11

June"] (pp. 82; 65). The content is factual, the tone detached, the sequence of events carefully reproduced:

> Les quatre premiers jours, Pélissier s'attaque aux tribus de Beni Zeroual et des Ouled Kelouf dont il obtient, après quelques combats, la soumission .... Le 16 juin, Pélissier place son camp au lieu-dit 'Ouled el Amria', sur le territoire d'un des adjoints du Chérif .... A l'aube du 18 juin Pélissier est décidé à trancher ... (pp. 83; 66)
>
> During the first four days Pélissier concentrates his action against the Beni-Zeroual and Ouled Kelouf tribes, and rapidly forces them to surrender ... On 16 June Pélissier pitches camp at the place known as Ouled el-Amria, where one of the Sharif's lieutenants holds sway ... At daybreak on 18 June, Pélissier decides to make a move ...

As the moment of climax approaches and negotiations drag on unsuccessfully, the text starts to fragment more and more, as various incidents related to the build-up of the tragedy are recounted, one after the other, but with no narrative links drawing them together. The impression of fragmentation is exacerbated by the distortion of the passage of time, at times stretching several hours over several pages, and at other times abruptly changing pace and racing through the days and months.

In a sense, both the fragmented nature of the text and its irregular rhythm could be seen as being dependent on the colonial father or master texts, which literally inform the story and whose rhythms impose themselves on the story. Each historical fragment drawn upon becomes a piece of the jigsaw puzzle, imprinting or leaving a trace of its particular style, emphasis and rhythm. Yet it is Djebar who creates the puzzle, manipulating the pieces at will in order to serve her own ends. If Djebar chooses to emphasise rather than disguise the fragmentation, it is to draw attention to the mechanics of recovering history, and to the possibility of putting together an alternative picture of the past.

The "imaginary" nature of this first puzzle is highlighted by direct insertions of Bugeaud's unashamedly narcissistic writings, best illustrated by his original instructions to Pélissier: "Si ces gredins se retirent dans leurs grottes, ordonne Bugeaud, imitez Cavaignac aux Sbéah, enfumez-les à outrance, comme des renards" ['If the scoundrels retreat into their caves,' Bugeaud orders, 'do what Cavaignac did to the Sbeah, smoke them out mercilessly, like foxes!'] (pp. 82; 65). This dehumanising reference to the tribes of Dahra demonstrates what JanMohamed describes as the "fetishization" of the native:

> The power of the 'imaginary' field binding the narcissistic colonialist text is nowhere better illustrated than in its fetishization of the Other.

This process operates by substituting natural or generic categories for those that are socially or ideologically determined. All the evil characteristics and habits with which the colonialist endows the native are thereby not presented as the products of social and cultural difference, but as characteristics inherent in the race – in the 'blood' – of the native.[37]

According to JanMohamed, this fetishizing strategy permits not only an exchange of denigrating images that can be used to maintain a sense of moral difference/superiority, but also allows the writer to transform social and historical dissimilarities into universal, metaphysical differences. If, as Pélissier has done, Algerian men, women, and children can be collapsed into beings from the animal world in an expression of metonymic displacement, then, in JanMohamed's words, "... clearly there can be no meeting ground, no identity, between the social, historical creatures of Europe and the metaphysical alterity of the Calibans and Ariels of Africa." [38]

In the second section, Djebar creates another and very different jigsaw picture – one that tells the same story, but that uses different pieces. This second picture again incorporates the words of *others*, but this time draws on the words of Europeans whose reports of events transcended the "imaginary" blindness of Bugeaud, and achieved a 'symbolic' dimension, revealing a frame of mind "more open to a modifying dialectic of self and Other."[39]

At this stage, Djebar also inserts herself directly into the narration: "Je reconstitue, à mon tour, cette nuit" [I, in turn, piece together a picture of that night] (pp. 88; 70) in order to retell the story, now her story, from the perspective of the colonialist's "Other". The jigsaw now becomes three-dimensional, as the people of Nacmaria appear graphically in the full horror of their asphyxiated bodies. The narrative becomes even more fragmented as not only the speed of the text but also its progression are distorted, as the text moves back and forward in time, engaging the reader's sympathy by following a cumulative rather than linear path. This technique of persuasion by "creating presence" through repetition rather than by logical, linear argumentation, can be seen as semiotic, not only because it mimics the endlessly repetitive pulsations of the chora, but also because it mimics the rhetorical style of the maternal language, Arabic.

As Djebar rewinds to the fateful night of the tragedy, she abandons the constraints of historical evidence and allows her imagination to

---

[37] Ibid., pp. 20-21.
[38] Ibid., p. 22.
[39] Ibid., p. 19.

take over: "J'imagine les détails du tableau nocturne" [I imagine the details of this nocturnal tableau] (pp. 88; 71), before finally bringing herself to spell out the extent of the horror: "la tribu des Ouled Riah – mille cinq cents hommes, femmes, enfants, vieillards, plus les troupeaux par centaines et les chevaux – a été tout entière anéantie par 'enfumade.'" [the fumigation has wiped out the entire Ouled Riah tribe – 1,500 men, some of them elderly, women, children, flocks by the hundred and all their horses...] (pp. 89; 72). We now relive the full horror of the tragedy with the help of two eyewitnesses, one French, the other Spanish, both of whom entered the caves on the day after the tragedy occurred, and recounted the tragedy in all its graphic symbolic reality:

> J'ai vu un homme mort, le genou à terre, la main crispée sur la corne d'un boeuf. Devant lui était une femme tenant son enfant dans ses bras. Cet homme, il était facile de le reconnaître, avait été asphyxié, ainsi que la femme, l'enfant et le boeuf, au moment où il cherchait à préserver sa famille de la rage de cet animal. (pp. 90-91: 73)

> I saw a dead man, with one knee on the ground, grasping the horn of an ox in one hand. In front of him lay a woman with her child in her arms. It was easy to see that this man had been asphyxiated, together with the woman, the child and the ox, while he was struggling to protect his family from the enraged animal.

But a crack in Pélissier's "imaginary" detachment enables Djebar to return, albeit reluctantly, to his words. For the consequences of his actions have filled him with feelings of remorse detectable in his official report of events, revealing an awareness of the Other to which Djebar gives grudging gratitude:

> J'oserais presque le remercier d'avoir fait face aux cadavres, d'avoir cédé au désir de les immortaliser, dans les figures de leurs corps raidis, de leurs étreintes paralysées, de leur ultime contorsion. D'avoir regardé l'ennemi autrement qu'en multitude fanatisée, en armée d'ombres omniprésentes. (pp. 96: 78)

> I venture to thank him for having faced the corpses, for having indulged a whim to immortalize them in a description of their rigid carcasses, their paralysed embraces, their final paroxysms. For having looked on the enemy otherwise than as a horde of zealots or a host of ubiquitous shadows.

This opening up of a dialectic of self and other permits a bridge to be built between Djebar's words and those of Pélissier: "Oui, une pulsion me secoue, telle une sourde otalgie: remercier Pélissier pour son rapport qui déclencha à Paris une tempête politique, mais aussi qui me renvoie nos morts vers lesquels j'élève aujourd'hui ma trame de mots français" [Yes, I am moved by an impulse that nags me like an earache: the impulse to thank Pélissier for his report, which unleashed a political storm in Paris, but which allows me to reach out today to our own dead and weave a pattern of French words around them] (pp. 96; 78).

In a final lyrical outburst, Djebar allows "la passion calcinée des ancêtres" [the charred passion of my ancestors] (pp. 97; 79) to invest her writing both literally, in the emotions it inspires, and metaphorically, as the charred bodies are inscribed onto the landscape: "Le paysage tout entier, les montagnes du Dahra, les falaises crayeuses, les vallonnements aux vergers brûlés s'inversent pour se recomposer dans les antres funèbres. Les victimes pétrifiées deviennent à leur tour montagnes et vallées. Les femmes couchées au milieu des bêtes, dans des étreintes lyriques, révèlent leur aspiration à être les soeurs-épouses de leurs hommes qui ne se rendent pas" [The whole countryside, the Dahra mountains, the chalk cliffs, the valleys with their charred orchards find their inverted mirror image in the funeral caves. The petrified victims are metamorphosed into mountains and valleys. The women, lying among the cattle in their lyrical embraces, reveal their aspirations to be the sister-spouses of their men who do not surrender] (pp. 97; 79).

As Djebar gradually abandons the objective tones of historical reporting and passionately relives the suffering of her people, her narrative increasingly demonstrates a strong sense of identification with the maternal, in this case the "motherland." Moreover, her manipulation of the colonialists' texts enables her to lay bare their "imaginary" perceptions, freeing not their texts, but her own from the "economy of Manichean dependence."

The Symbolic Mode: Autobiographical Ambiguities

In Parts 1 and 2 of *L'Amour, la fantasia*, the historical sections alternate with the autobiographical ones, as Djebar's double quest attempts to recreate a new sense of national and personal identity. The Algerian people's experience of colonial law, and their subsequent loss of *national identity* can be paralleled with their experience of another law, the law of *Oumma*, or "religious community/ nationhood", which dominates the personal, social and the political aspects of life in the Maghreb, and which causes the suppression of *personal identity*, which by extension has resulted in the suppression of "le moi autobiographique":

> La modernité, c'est d'abord l'individu et cette notion est totalement étrangère aux sociétés traditionnelles ... Dans la société traditionnelle

[du Maghreb], l'individu n'est perçu que comme 'partie intégrante du Tout, de cette Oumma, patrie qui l'englobe et le désire au point de viser à lui faire oublier sa dimension de sujet désirant' ... Celui qui se singularise paraît oublier le 'nous' et donner l'impression de se séparer du groupe, en [sic] encore de la *Oumma*, la mère islamique; il sort de la fusion maternelle; là où se trouve le salut collectif et individuel, dans une chaude singularité.[40]

Not only is the "je" considered to be a threat to the "nous", but it reverberates with associations of betrayal, of collaboration with the Other:

L'exil, la sortie, la séparation d'avec 'les frères' c'est le départ vers les ténèbres, la perdition ... vers l'Occident (la *ghurba*, la division et la séparation ne peuvent être que l'oeuvre de Satan le diviseur ou que l'oeuvre de l'étranger (avec son 'agression culturelle') cherchant toujours à diviser. L'émergence du 'je' est somme toute une *fitna*, une épreuve: dissension dans le tissu unitaire de l'identité nationale, surtout autrefois durant le temps de la colonisation et du combat contre celle-ci.[41]

The power of the law of *Oumma* over the individual consciousness is revealed in the traditional formulation: "Il est bien connu qu'au Maghreb on a une phobie tenace de la solitude, de la singularité. 'Que Dieu me protège du mot 'je'!' s'exclame l'individu que la teneur de sa conversation oblige à faire une entorse au pluriel de rigueur pour parler de lui-même à la première personne du singulier."[42] Djebar recognises in herself this resistance to "le moi autobiographique": "J'essaie de comprendre pourquoi je résiste à cette poussée de l'autobiographie. Je résiste peut-être parce que mon éducation de femme arabe est de ne jamais parler de soi, en même temps aussi parce que je parlais en langue française" [I try to understand why I resist the autobiographical impulse. Perhaps I resist because as an Arab woman I was taught never to speak about myself, and perhaps also because I spoke in French].[43]

The notion of "entry into language" as representing the key to the identity of the social being is complicated by the fact that Djebar "parlait en langue française" [spoke in French]. Djebar's entry into the French language causes a split, a rupture, a thetic crisis creating in her

---

[40] Jean Déjeux, *La Littérature féminine de langue française au Maghreb* (Paris: Karthala, 1994), pp. 65, 66.
[41] Ibid., p. 66.
[42] Ibid., p. 64. Déjeux here quotes Slimane Zeghidour, *Le Voile et la bannière* (Paris: Hachette, 1990), p. 15.
[43] Quotation of Djebar's taken from Mildred Mortimer, "Entretien avec Assia Djebar, écrivain algérien", p. 203. My translation.

a second and conflicting sense of self. It launches her into a new social order, which is also founded on rupture and repression, on the splitting of the subject into Algerian and French selves, leading to the repression of her Arab identity and language.

Djebar's split sense of identity brought about by her entry into the French language is, in Lacanian terms, also based on lack, on the loss of the maternal, in this case the maternal language. Her subsequent loss of Arab identity is displaced not into a chain of social meanings, but into a chain of social/historical memories in an impossible attempt to recover maternal plenitude.

Murdoch sees Djebar's constant alternation between the presentation of the events of the 1830 invasion and the presence of writing as autobiography as structurally reflecting the ambiguity with which colonisation is inscribed upon the colonial subject, "as it alternates between the erasure of its own culture, and the desire to assume that of the Other..."[44] Djebar's autobiographical sections are interpreted in terms of "the female subject awakening to desire [as she] seeks to chronicle the constitution of her own subjectivity in the face of patriarchal domination", and the main issues to which the text addresses itself as "desire and the subversion of patriarchy."[45]

However, what Djebar describes as her "*own* kind of feminism" appears to express a more ambiguous relation to the rule of the "patriarch", for some fathers, if not all fathers, are upholders of women:

> Donc le féminisme, chez nous, enfin l'émancipation des femmes, est passé par l'intercession des pères. Rappelez-vous simplement qu'en 52, le roi du Maroc, Mohamed V, qui était extraordinairement populaire et qui était considéré comme le descendant du Prophète, avait demandé à sa fille aînée, Lalla Aïcha, de se dévoiler publiquement. Cette 'libération', si on peut dire, du corps pour les filles se faisait avec l'assentiment du père. J'ai voulu évoquer cela. C'est ce qui m'amène à commencer ma propre histoire 'main dans la main' avec le père.

> For us then, feminism or the liberation of woman was associated with the intercession of fathers. Just remember that in 1953, the King of Morocco, Mohamed V, who was extremely popular and who was considered to be a descendant of the Prophet, asked his eldest daughter Lalla Aïcha to publicly unveil herself. This emancipation of the body, if one can call it that, took place with the father's consent. I

---

[44] H. Adlai Murdoch, "Rewriting Writing: Identity, Exile and Renewal in Djebar's *L'Amour, la fantasia*", *Yale French Studies*, 2: 83 (1993), pp. 71-92, p. 76.
[45] Ibid., pp. 76, 78.

wanted to evoke this. That is what drove me to start my own story 'hand in hand' with my father. [46]

This openness to dual maternal/paternal identification can be interpreted in the light of Virginia Woolf's embracing of androgyny. Woolf sees woman as privileged, or forced, to attain an androgynous position because she is situated at once outside and inside the dominant order: "Woolf, too, talks of the split in the woman's consciousness, which can 'think back through its fathers or through its mothers.'"[47] In *L'Amour, la fantasia* as a whole, Djebar can be seen to be *thinking back through her fathers and her mothers*. However, in the autobiographical sections of Parts 1 and 2, Djebar appears to be principally thinking back through her *father*, tracing her establishment in the paternal/social order into which she is propelled via her entry into the paternal language (French is the paternal language not only because it is associated with the colonial fathers, or her biological father, who initiated her into the French language, but also because it places her in a privileged position with relation to the world of men).

Kristeva, like Woolf, addresses the question of the identificatory choices of girls in relation to their parents[48]: "La fille, aussi, se trouve devant un choix: soit elle s'identifie à la *mère*, soit elle s'élève à la hauteur symbolique du *père*."[49] While it is the psychosexual consequences of these choices that are elaborated by Kristeva, she believes that paternal identification on the part of girls results in the obliteration of maternal traces, on both emotional and physical levels. Djebar's entry into the French language by the intervention of the father implies an inevitable path of *paternal* identification, which comes at the price Kristeva cites – her loss of identification with the maternal order.

The autobiographical sections that focus on Djebar's entry into the paternal order of language run in parallel with the historical sections

---

[46] Lise Gauvin, "Assia Djebar, territoires des langues: entretien", *Littérature – L'Écrivain et ses langues*, 101 (February 1996), pp. 73-87, p. 81. My translation.
[47] Virginia Woolf, *A Room of One's Own* (London: Hogarth, 1967), p.146. Quoted in Makiko Minow-Pinkney, *Virginia Woolf and the Problem of the Subject*, p. 22.
[48] Kristeva's theory is put forward in relation to monotheistic societies, albeit Western ones.
[49] Julia Kristeva, *Des Chinoises*, p. 33. [My emphasis]. In the first case (identification with the father), she achieves fulfilment, "les phases pré-oedipiennes (l'érotisme oral at anal) s'en trouvent intensifiées" and, as a heterosexual woman, attains "la jouissance vaginale." In the second case (identification with the father), the daughter gains access to the symbolic at the expense of the pre-oedipal phase and the vagina, "effaç[ant] les traces de la dépendance vis-à-vis du corps de la mère", obliterating the traces of the maternal.

that describe the entry of "'L'Algérie femme" into the paternalistic, colonial order. In both cases, Djebar is "thinking back through her fathers" – her biological father, the fatherland (France), and expressing her thought in the paternal language (French). But just as Djebar's look back into the history of Algeria via the paternalistic intertexts reveals semiotic desire – in her passionate identification with the motherland, so Djebar's look back into her own history via the paternal language reveals semiotic presence-as-absence, in the underlying story of a lost bond with the mother. This "thinking back through her fathers" therefore exposes a maternal or semiotic void, which Djebar will consciously try to fill in Part 3.

Looking back through the father figure

The opening chapter of *L'Amour, la fantasia* weaves together the conflicts of a young girl at the boundaries of two worlds, maternal and paternal, of two languages, French and Arabic, and of two eras, past and present, held together precariously by the act of writing in the language of the oppressor.

"Fillette arabe allant pour la première fois à l'école un matin d'automne, main dans la main du père" [A little Arab girl going to school for the first time, one autumn morning, walking hand in hand with her father] (pp. 15; 3). This simple, vivid and touching image opens the book on a note of closeness and identification with the father figure: "Celui-ci, un fez sur la tête, la silhouette haute et droite dans son costume européen, porte un cartable, il est instituteur à l'école française. Fillette arabe dans un village du Sahel algérien" [A tall erect figure in a fez and a European suit, carrying a bag of school books. He is a teacher at the French primary school. A little Arab girl in a village in the Algerian Sahel] (pp. 15; 3).

The note of simplicity is maintained in the description of the father from a child's perspective, "la silhouette haute et droite" [a tall erect figure], distinguished by the features a child might point out, "un fez", "un cartable." [school bag] But the simplicity is deceptive: there is already a note of ambiguity, the markers of a life lived between two worlds. Despite the fez, the dress is Western – "son costume européen" [a European suit], despite being "une fillette arabe" [a little Arab girl], her father is a teacher at "l'école française" [the French primary school].

For Djebar, the entry into the French language brings about a thetic crisis by which she is transposed into a man's world – the paternal order. According to Pinkney, the difficulties women face within that order are related to the necessary and yet problematic nature of paternal identification, which induces a state of simultaneous inclusion and exclusion:

> Even if she identifies herself with the mother, in the position of the repressed and marginal, she must have a certain identification with the father in order to sustain a place in the symbolic order and avoid psychosis. On the other hand, if she identifies herself with the father, denying the woman in herself, she is none the less biologically female: the father-identification remains precarious, stands always in need of defence.[50]

Djebar's paternal identification places her both inside and outside the dominant male order, but also, and more poignantly, places her both inside and outside the maternal order, which perceives her "annexation" of the outside world, the male/public world, as a threat:

> Dès le premier jour où une fillette sort pour apprendre l'alphabet, les voisins prennent le regard matois de ceux qui s'apitoient, dix, quinze ans à l'avance: sur le père audacieux, sur le frère inconséquent. Le malheur fondra immanquablement sur eux. Toute vierge savante saura écrire, écrira à coup sûr "la lettre". Viendra l'heure où l'amour qui s'écrit est plus dangereux que l'amour séquestré. (pp. 15; 3)

> From the very first day that a little girl leaves her home to learn the ABCs, the neighbours adopt that knowing look of those who in ten or fifteen years' time will be able to say 'I told you so!' while commiserating with the foolhardy father, the irresponsible brother. For misfortune will inevitable befall them. Any girl who has had some schooling will have learned to write and will without a doubt write that fatal letter. For her the time will come when there will be more danger in love that is committed to paper than love that languishes behind enclosing walls.

The threat to the *paternal* order is represented by desire: "The eruption of desire threatens the 'forging of links and chains' of the symbolic, and must be checked."[51] "L'amour qui s'écrit" [love that is committed to paper] is a love that is all the more threatening in that it can literally and metaphorically escape the control of the paternal order. Desire must be more than kept in check; it must be imprisoned: "Le geôlier d'un corps sans mots – et les mots écrits sont mobiles – peut finir, lui, par dormir tranquille: il lui suffira de supprimer les fenêtres, de cadenasser l'unique portail, d'élever jusqu'au ciel un mur orbe" [The jailer who guards a body that has no words – and written words can travel – may sleep in peace: it will suffice to brick up the windows, padlock the sole entrance door, and erect a blank wall rising up to heaven] (pp. 15; 3). Only the written word can fly through the

---

[50] Makiko Minow-Pinkney, *Virginia Woolf and the Problem of the Subject*, p. 22.
[51] Ibid., p.141.

bars and escape paternal censure, as desire relentlessly pursues its object: "Si la jouvencelle écrit? Sa voix, en dépit du silence, circule. Un papier. Un chiffon froissé. Une main de servante, dans le noir. Un enfant au secret. Le gardien devra veiller jour et nuit. L'écrit s'envolera par le patio, sera lancé d'une terrasse. Azur soudain trop vaste. Tout est à recommencer" [And what if the maiden does write? Her voice, albeit silenced, will circulate. A scrap of paper. A crumpled cloth. A servant-girl's hand in the dark. A child, let into the secret. The jailer must keep watch day and night. The written word will take flight from the patio, will be tossed from a terrace. The blue of heaven is suddenly limitless. The precautions have all been in vain] (pp. 16-17).

Djebar's third-person references to herself give way to the first person in an assertion of subjectivity that marks the first direct challenge to patriarchy: "A dix-sept ans, j'entre dans l'histoire d'amour à cause d'une lettre. Un inconnu m'a écrit; par inconscience ou par audace il l'a fait ouvertement. Le père, secoué d'une rage sans éclats, à déchiré devant moi la missive. Il ne me la donne pas à lire; il la jette au panier" [At seventeen, I am introduced to my first experience of love through a letter written by a boy, a stranger. Whether acting thoughtlessly or out of bravado, he writes quite openly. The father, in a fit of silent fury, tears up the letter before my eyes and throws it into the waste-paper basket without letting me read it][52] (pp. 16; 3-4). This surge of desire comes at the cost of alienation from the father, a distance underlined by the omission of the possessive pronoun ("le père"). Ironically, by initiating her into the French language, the patriarch has given her the key to her own liberation, and made possible the escape from paternal law into the uncharted waters of desire. Defiance of this paternal law brings liberation, then love: "A l'instar d'une héroïne d'un roman occidental, le défi juvénile m'a libérée du cercle que des chuchotements d'aïeules invisibles ont tracé autour de moi et en moi .... Puis l'amour conjugal s'est transmué dans le tunnel du plaisir, argile conjugale" [As with the heroine of a Western romance, youthful defiance helped me break out of the circle that whispering elders traced around me and within me ... Then love came to be transformed in the tunnel of pleasure, soft clay to be moulded by matrimony] (pp. 16; 4).

There is a sudden semiotic irruption in the narrative, as if the efflorescence of pleasure overcomes symbolic restraint:

---

[52] Translation adapted.

Lustration des sons d'enfance dans le souvenir; elle nous enveloppe jusqu'à la découverte de la sensualité dont la submersion peu à peu nous éblouit ... Silencieuse, coupée des mots de ma mère par une mutilation de la mémoire, j'ai parcouru les eaux sombres du corridor en miraculée, sans en deviner les murailles. Choc des premiers mots révélés: la vérité a surgi d'une fracture de ma parole balbutiante. De quelle roche nocturne du plaisir suis-je parvenue à l'arracher? (pp. 16-17; 4)

Memory purges and purifies the sounds of childhood; we are cocooned by childhood until the discovery of sensuality, which washes over us and gradually bedazzles us ... Voiceless, cut off from my mother's words by some trick of memory, I managed to pass through the dark waters of the corridor, miraculously inviolate, not even guessing at the enclosing walls. The shock of the first words blurted out: the truth emerging from a break in my stammering voice. From what nocturnal reef of pleasure did I manage to wrest this truth?

"Lustration des sons ... elle nous enveloppe": the repeated subject, in the form of a referencing pronoun, marks the entry into lyrical language. The materiality of sounds, the soft "s" sounds, of "sons", "sensualité", "submersion", "silencieuse", the alliteration in the phrase "coupée des mots de ma mère par une mutilation de la mémoire" subdues what Pinkney terms the "ideality of meaning" in a sensuous play of signifiers. But Pinkney also points to the dangers for women of such semiotic escapism: "...the rush of these nonsensical, periphrastic, maternal rhythms in her speech, far from soothing her, far from making her laugh, destroy the symbolic armour: makes her ecstatic, nostalgic or mad..."[53]

Here there is nostalgia for "les sons de l'enfance" [the sounds of childhood], for the infant's intimacy with the maternal, as Djebar finds herself split in half, cut off from her mother tongue: "coupée des mots de ma mere" [cut of from my mother's words]. Here too is a kind of madness – the imprisonment of consciousness in the dark recesses of "les eaux sombres" [the dark waters] but from which pleasure – the long lost words of the body, "le parler-corps", and the long-lost sensuousness of the mother-child bond, is finally recovered.

"J'ai fait éclater l'espace en moi, un espace éperdu de cris sans voix, figés depuis longtemps dans une préhistoire de l'amour" [I blew the space within me to pieces, a space filled with desperate voiceless cries, frozen long ago in a prehistory of love] (pp. 17: 4). As Djebar re-enters into the semiotic recesses of her mind, she accesses the repressed sounds of the maternal order, not only the lost voice of the

---

[53] Minow-Pinkney, *Virginia Woolf and the Problem of the Subject*, pp. 49, 22.

Mother, but also the repressed voices of other women whose cries have been stifled for generations.

This semiotic outburst is cut short by a thetic "rappel à l'ordre" [call to order]: "Les mots une fois éclairés – ceux-là mêmes, que le corps dévoilé découvre –, j'ai coupé les amarres. Ma fillette me tenant la main, je suis partie à l'aube" [Once I had discovered the meaning of the words – those same words that are revealed to the unveiled body – I cut myself adrift. I set off at dawn, with my little girl's hand in mine] (pp. 17; 4-5). In a final sentence which both echoes and subverts the opening sentence, Djebar lets go of her father's hand, and metaphorically takes hold of the hand of her childhood self, in a gesture which marks both a distancing from the father, and a clear sense of direction in her writing, as she marches back into "les eaux sombres" [the dark waters] of Algerian history: "je suis partie à l'aube" [I set off at dawn] (pp. 17; 5). For the dawn of her story becomes the dawn of Algeria's downfall – "Aube de ce 13 juin 1830" [Dawn on this thirteenth day of June 1830] (pp. 18; 6), as she inextricably links her history with that of "L'Algérie-femme."

Looking back at the paternal language

The site of language is the battleground between Djebar's maternal/paternal identification. While initiating her into the paternal order, the paternal language cuts her off from the language of the maternal. This linguistic rupture instigates a sense of emotional loss, a lack-in-language that is identified with a specific moment in Djebar's life as recalled in "La Fille du Gendarme Français" [The French Policeman's Daughter] (pp. 34-42; 20-27). Here again there is a "thetic" crisis in reverse, not a rupture of semiotic harmony, but a sudden consciousness of maternal lack, a recognition of the cost of her entry into the language and world of men.

In this chapter Djebar describes the passionate relationship between Marie-Louise, "la fille du gendarme français" [the French policeman's daughter], and her new fiancé, Paul, played out before the young Djebar and her companions. The amorous behaviour of "la fille du gendarme", who unselfconsciously boasts of her love for Paul, referring to him as "Pilou chéri" [Darling Pilou], causes a mixture of shocked disapproval and childish hilarity in her audience of "filles déjà puritaines" [girls ... who were already so straight-laced] (pp. 42; 27):

> "Pilou", c'était Paul et le "chéri" qu'elle ajoutait devait être un vocable réservé, pensions-nous, aux alcôves et aux secrets des couples... "Pilou chéri", mots suivis de touffes de rires sarcastiques;

que dire de la destruction que cette appellation opéra en moi par la suite? Je crus ressentir d'emblée, très tôt, trop tôt, que l'amourette, que l'amour ne doivent pas, par des mots de clinquant, par une tendresse voyante de ferblanterie, donner prise au spectacle, susciter l'envie de celles qui en seront frustrées.... Je décidai que l'amour résidait nécessairement ailleurs, au-delà des mots et des gestes publics. (pp. 41-42; 27)

'Pilou' was her nickname for Paul and in our minds the 'darling' that she added was a word that should be reserved for the bedchamber and secrets between married couples... 'Darling Pilou'; words followed by bursts of sarcastic laughter; what can I say of the damage done to me in the course of time by this expression? I seemed to feel, as soon as I heard it – all too soon – that a love affair, that love itself ought not to give rise to meretricious words, ostentatious demonstrations of affection, so making a spectacle of oneself and arousing envy in frustrated women... I decided that love must necessarily reside elsewhere and not in public words and gestures.

This love expressed in the paternal language is exposed as a sham, as show, "une tendresse voyante de ferblanterie, un spectacle." The object of its desire is not "Pilou chéri" [Darling Pilou] but the recognition of its audience ("susciter l'envie" [arousing envy]). Reverberating into Djebar's adult consciousness, the words "Pilou chéri" [Darling Pilou] mark the emotional sterility of the French language. And, because the order of language constructs identity, the emotional sterility at the level of language is projected onto a damaged sense of self:

Anodine scène d'enfance: une aridité de l'expression s'installe et la sensibilité dans sa période romantique se retrouve *aphasique*. Malgré le bouillonnement de mes rêves d'adolescence plus tard, un noeud, à cause de ce 'Pilou chéri', résista: la langue française pouvait tout m'offrir de ses trésors inépuisables, mais pas un, pas le moindre de ses mots d'amour ne me serait réservé.... Un jour ou l'autre, parce que cet état *autistique* ferait chape à mes élans de femme, surviendrait à rebours quelque soudaine explosion. (pp. 42; 27)

An innocuous scene from my childhood: but later, when I reach the time for romance, I can find no words, I cannot express my emotions. Despite the turmoil of my adolescent dreams, this 'darling Pilou' left me with one deep-rooted complex: the French language could offer me all its inexhaustible treasures, but not a single one of its terms of endearment would be destined for my use... One day, because all of my spontaneous impulses as a woman would be stifled by this *autistic* state, one day the pressure would suddenly give and a reaction would set in. [My emphasis]

According to Kristeva, the price of father-identification is high and results in emotional/sexual ambiguity: "... la fille refoule le stade oral-sadique, en même temps qu'elle refoule le vagin et la possibilité de trouver un partenaire allogène..."[54] Similarly, the price of Djebar's entry into the paternal language is high. The terms that describe it, "aphasia" and "autism", also speak of deep-seated psychological trauma. Her aphasia (loss of speech caused here by emotional rather than cerebral damage) creates "une aridité de l'expression" [an emotional desert]; her autism (withdrawal, not from the world of reality, but from the world of affective relationships) stifles her spontaneous impulses and creates a pressure-hose of repressed emotions.

The rejection of the image of love associated with "Pilou chéri" [Darling Pilou] is projected onto a repression of romantic love in adolescence. The words mark a process of condensation, whereby the image of the flirtatious Marie-Louise and the sound of the words imprinted on the unconscious of her mind create "un noeud", a nodal point, an intersection for a whole cluster of associated feelings, repressed memories and desires, which threaten to surface explosively.

The latent explosion of her inner being is linked to another explosion, "Explosion du Fort l'Empereur" [Explosion of Fort Emperor] (pp. 43; 28), marking the French army's entry into Algiers. There are parallels between Marie-Louise's joy, "son éclat de bonheur" [her radiating happiness], and the joy of the triumphant French army as it takes possession of the significant stronghold (pp. 41; 26). Both explosions are associated with tragedy for the Arab side – tragedy for the Arab camp, now headed for defeat, and tragedy for a young Arab girl, now scarred by emotional lack.

Challenging paternal authority

The heightening of violence and desire in the relationship between "la France" and "l'Algérie-femme" in Part 2 (historical) of *L'Amour, la fantasia* is paralleled in the autobiographical sections by the heightening of subjective desire. Djebar no longer merely observes the desire of others (her parent's love, the romance of "la fille du gendarme" [the French policeman's daughter]) but is the receiver of "lettres d'amour" [love letters]. She becomes the object of desire, but also the desiring subject, and as such comes to represent a challenge to patriarchal order, and to her father in particular:

> Chaque mot d'amour, qui me serait destiné, ne pourrait que rencontrer le diktat paternel. Chaque lettre, même la plus innocente, supposerait

---

[54] Julia Kristeva, *Des Chinoises*, p. 33.

l'oeil constant du père, avant de me parvenir. Mon écriture, en entretenant ce dialogue sous influence, devenait en moi tentative – ou tentation – de délimiter mon propre silence. Mais le souvenir des exécuteurs du harem ressuscite; rappelle que tout papier écrit dans la pénombre rameute la plus ordinaire des inquisitions! (pp. 79: 61)

Every expression of love that would ever be addressed to me would have to meet my father's approval. I could assume that he had had his watchful eye on every letter, even the most innocent, before it reached me. By keeping up a dialogue with this presence that haunted me, my writing became an attempt – or a temptation – to set the limits on my own silence ... But the memory surfaces of the harem executioners; I am reminded that every page written in the dim light will stir up a hue and cry, leading to the usual cross-examination!

As a desiring subject in her own right/write, she 'uncensors', unmasks love, exposing desire in language: "Ecrire *devant* l'amour. Eclairer le corps, pour aider à lever l'interdit, pour dévoiler .... Décrire le visage de l'autre, pour maintenir son image; persister à croire en sa présence, en son miracle. Refuser la photographie, ou toute autre trace visuelle. Le mot seul, une fois écrit, nous arme d'une attention grave" [To write *confronting* love. Shedding light on one's body to help lift the taboo, to lift the veil ... To lift the veil and at the same time keep secret that which must remain secret, until the lightning flash of revelation] (pp. 79; 62). But the desire to challenge paternal "diktat", to expose desire *in* language, only displaces a deeper primeval desire *for* language: "En fait, je recherche, *comme un lait* dont on m'aurait autrefois écartée, la pléthore amoureuse de la langue de ma mère. Contre la ségrégation de mon héritage, le mot plein de l'amour-au-présent me devient une parade hirondelle" [And now, I too seek out the rich vocabulary of love of my mother tongue – *milk* of which I had been previously deprived. In contrast to the segregation I inherited, words expressing love-in-the-present become for me like one token swallow heralding summer] (pp. 80; 62) [My emphasis]. The mother/mother tongue from which she is cut off is the original source and object of her semiotic yearnings, expressed in language reminiscent of Hélène Cixous's:

> Même si la mystification phallique a contaminé généralement les bons rapports, la femme n'est jamais loin de la "mère" (que j'entends hors-rôle, la "mère" comme non-nom, et comme source des biens). Toujours en elle subsiste au moins un peu du bon lait-de-mère. *Elle écrit à l'encre blanche.*[55]

---

[55] Hélène Cixous, "Le Rire de la méduse", *L'Arc*, 61, p. 44. [My emphasis]

Djebar can no longer draw the white ink of her maternal language. Instead she writes in blood-red ink, as she suffuses her writing with the flesh and blood of "mes aïeules, mes semblables" [my ancestors, women like myself] (pp. 80; 62), revealing a longing for the mother tongue, and the mother figures of the past, and an identity constructed not only by her entry into the paternal language, but also by her "exit" from the maternal language.

The Semiotic Mode: Desire in "Sistre"

The passages examined so far, from Parts 1 and 2 of the work, demonstrate a certain resistance to the symbolic but are nevertheless situated in symbolic time and place. On two occasions, however, at the ends of Parts 1 and 2 respectively, Djebar abandons symbolic restraint and "retreats" into semiotic language, as we encounter two prose poems, the first, "Biffure" [Deletion] (pp. 62; 46), a poem about the conquest of Algeria, and the second "Sistre" [Sistrum] (pp. 129; 109), a poem about desire, which will now be examined:

> Sistre [Sistrum][56]
> Long silence, nuits chevauchées, spirales dans la gorge. Râles, ruisseaux de sons précipices, sources d'échos entrecroisés, cataractes de murmures, chuchotements en taillis tressés, surgeons susurrant sous la langue, chuintements, et souque la voix courbe qui, dans la soute de sa mémoire, retrouve souffles souillés de soûlerie ancienne.
> Râles de cymbale qui renâcle, cirse ou ciseaux de cette tessiture, tessons de soupirs naufragés, clapotis qui glissent contre les courtines du lit, rires épars striant l'ombre claustrale, plaintes tiédies puis diffractées sous les paupières clauses dont le rêve s'égare dans quelque cyprière, et le navire des désirs cule, avant que craille l'oiseau de volupté.
> Mots coulis, tisons délités, diorites expulsés des lèvres béantes, brandons de caresses quand s'éboule le plomb d'une mutité brutale, et le corps recherche sa voix, comme une plie remontant l'estuaire.
> De nouveau râles, escaliers d'eau jusqu'au larynx, éclaboussures, aspersion lustrale, sourd la plainte puis le chant long, le chant lent de la voix femelle luxuriante enveloppe l'accouplement, en suit le rythme et les figures, s'exhale en oxygène, dans la chambre et dans le noir, torsade tumescente de "forte" restés suspendus.
> Soufflerie souffreteuse ou solennelle du temps d'amour, soufrière de chaque attente, fièvre des staccato.
> Silence rempart autour de la fortification du plaisir, et de sa digraphie.
> Création chaque nuit. Or broché du silence. (pp. 129; 109)

---

[56] This poem appears in italics in the original version.

Long silence, night rides, coils curling in the throat. Rhonchial râles, streams of abyssal sounds, springs from which issue interlacing echoes, cataracts of murmurs, susurrus in braided brushwood, tendrils soughing under the tongue, hushed hisses, and the flexured voice hauls up sullied sighs of past satiety from memory's subterranean store-house.

Cacophony of recalcitrant cymbal, thistle or scissors rending this tessitura, shards of shipwrecked sighs, water lapping against the valanced bed, scattered laughter striating claustral darkness, plaints pacified then diffused behind closed eyelids whose dream strays through some cypress grove, and the ship of desire drops astern, before the raven of sexual ecstasy croaks its contentment.

Molten words, splintered firestones, diorites expelled from gaping lips, fire-brand caresses when the harsh leaden silence crumbles, and the body seeks for its voice, like a fish swimming upstream.

Renewed râles, watery stairways to the larynx, splashes, lustral sprinkling, the plaintive moan escapes then the prolonged song, the drawn-out song of the rich female voice closes round the copulation, follows its tempos and its figures, is exhaled as oxygen, in the bedchamber and the darkness, a tumescent twisted coil of forte notes hanging in the air.

Suffering or solemn gasps of act of love, sulphur-mine of anticipation, fever of staccato notes.

Silence, pleasure's defensive rampart, protecting the final reckoning – in what language written, Arabic or French?

Creation every night. Brocaded gold of silence.

"Sistre"[57] is a poem about dual desire, sexual desire, and desire for the maternal language, Arabic. The emotional "autism" associated with the paternal language can be "sensed" in Djebar's writing-in-French. As Gauvin remarks, "… dans votre rapport à la langue française, dans cette écriture en français, on sent comme une nostalgie, une limite" [… in your relationship to the French language, in the writing itself, one can sense a feeling of nostalgia, of restraint].[58] And, as Djebar herself acknowledges, this autism or "disorder of communication" interfered with her adolescent/adult relationships with disastrous results: "Je ne pouvais dire le moindre mot de tendresse ou d'amour dans cette langue, à tel point que c'était un vrai questionnement de femme. Ainsi avec certains hommes avec qui pouvait se dérouler un jeu de séduction, comme il n'y avait pas de passage à la langue maternelle, subsistait en moi une sorte de barrière invisible" [I could not speak any words of love or tenderness in that language, to the extent that it made me question my identity as a

---

[57] "Sistre" refers to a jingling instrument used by ancient Egyptians, especially in the rites of Isis (Oxford English Dictionary).
[58] Lise Gauvin, "Assia Djebar, territoires des langues: entretien", p. 79. My translation.

woman. And when it came to relationships with certain men, where games of seduction were played out, since I could not draw on my maternal language, a kind of invisible barrier still remained inside me].[59]

The nostalgia that Gauvin senses is a yearning for the Arabic language, which Djebar herself explicitly associates with "Sistre." In "Sistre" we find echoes of the maternal language, in an outpouring of desire expressed in the paternal language:

> Ce n'est pas par hasard si dans *L'Amour, la fantasia* il y a un poème qui s'intitule "Sistre"... C'est un poème sur le désir et sur le plaisir. Je suis contrainte de passer à la poésie parce que ce texte-là tente d'investir par les mots français, tous mes dits de femme ... Et si je dis 'tessons de soupirs', si je dis 'cirse ou ciseaux de cette tessiture', ce n'est pas pour écrire de la poésie savante. C'est parce que je tente de retrouver de possibles vers de la poésie arabe, où la langue fonctionne par allitérations.

> It is no coincidence that there is a poem in *L'Amour, la fantasia* with the title "Sistrum"... It is a poem about desire and pleasure. I was compelled to express myself through poetry because this text with its French words attempts to give voice to myself as a woman ... And when I say 'shards of sighs' or 'thistle or scissors rending this tessitura', it is not because I want to write learned poetry. It is because I am trying to recall possible lines of Arabic poetry, where the language works by alliteration.[60]

Here Djebar confronts her emotional autism with a dual appeal to the maternal; firstly, by exploring the semiotic possibilities of the French language, and secondly, by suffusing it with the rhythms of the maternal language.

The poem is literally framed by silence, "Long silence...", "Or broché du silence" ["Long silence, Brocaded gold of silence"], and between the silences desire arises, captured in the rolling waves of rhythmic language:

> La langue rythmée porte donc une représentation, mais c'est une représentation, une vision striée: pas d'exclusion de l'oeil par l'oreille; la représentation retentit, le son se fait image, la pulsion invocante rencontre l'objet signifiable, vraisemblablement poly-logique.... La langue est là pour faire éclater la musique dans le vu..."[61]

In "Sistre", "le son fait image"; sounds proliferate and multiply, both phonetically, by the sustained use of alliteration, and semantically, by the repeated references to a whole spectrum of

---

[59] Ibid., p. 79. My translation.
[60] Ibid., p. 79. My translation.
[61] Julia Kristeva, *Polylogue*, p. 194.

sounds from "murmures", "chuchotements", to "soupirs", "rires", "plaintes", "chants" [murmurs, susurrus, sighs, laughter, plaints, song] as well as to musical tone, "forte" and style "staccato." "La pulsion invocante" of this "langue rythmée" recalls its "objet signifiable", the sexual coalescence of man and woman.

The elongated vowels of "long silence" (l. 1) reinforce an initial sense of stillness, the soft consonants suggesting sensuousness and the increased number of syllables in the next two phrases, building up a slow sense of anticipation (l. 1-5), a linguistic foreplay preceding the onset of bodily rhythms: "Most primitive and profound of instincts, rhythm is central to Kristeva's semiotic."[62] A rhythmical wave effect, mimicking bodily rhythms, is achieved by the sudden stream of short phrases, piling up one after the other, lashing against the shore of desire, reinforced by the seductive semiotic pleasures of alliteration. The irregular, but continuous rhythms of the phrases mimic the oscillating pulsations of the chora. The intensity of desire is reinforced by the incessant use of alliteration and assonance, urgently and intimately linking each word to the next in a dizzy and sensual interlacing of sounds and signifiers, of "échos entrecroisés" (the "r " sound of "râles", "ruisseaux", interlacing with "s" of "ruisseaux" and "précipices", the repetition of "t", "r" and "c" sounds in "entrecroisés" echoed in "cataractes", the "t" interlacing with "s" in "taillis tressés, surgeons susurrant" etc.), as the coalescence of man and woman is echoed by the coalescence of signifier and signified in the onomatopoeia of "cataractes", "chuchotements", "chuintements" and "souffles."

In the second half of the second sentence the pace suddenly changes. The climax is achieved as the pile-up of nominal and prepositional phrases is abruptly halted by the conjunction "et." The pace is then slowed down by a cumbersome embedded phrase within a relative clause, finally giving way to the delayed verb. This, combined with the use of assonance, the barrage of "ou", and "sou" sounds, slows down the tempo to a final stop: "... et souque la voix courbe qui, dans la soute de sa mémoire, retrouve souffles souillés de soûlerie ancienne" (l. 4-5).

In the second paragraph, the accumulation of sounds "tessons de soupirs naufragés, clapotis qui glissent contre les courtines du lit, rires épars striant l'ombre claustrale, plaintes tiédies puis diffractées sous

---

[62] Makiko Minow-Pinkney, *Virginia Woolf and the Problem of the Subject*, p. 175.

In Dialogue with Kristeva: *L'Amour, la fantasia* 71

les paupières closes" [thistle or scissors rending this tessitura, shards of shipwrecked sighs, water lapping against the valanced bed, scattered laughter striating claustral darkness, plaints pacified then diffused behind closed eyelids] appear to reverberate from the impact of resounding clashes "Râles de cymbale qui renâcle, cirse ou ciseaux de cette tessiture" [Cacophony of recalcitrant cymbal, thistle or scissors rending this tessitura] and ripple out in decreasing waves, as the momentum subsides, as "le navire des désirs cule" [the ship of desire drops astern], while the "embedded" reference to the bodily "cul" acts as a reminder that this is the calm before the storm "avant que craille l'oiseau de volupté" [before the raven of sexual ecstasy croaks its contentment] (l. 10).

The cry of release comes in the fourth paragraph, with the song ("le chant long, le chant lent de la voix femelle luxuriante enveloppe l'accouplement" [the prolonged song, the drawn-out song of the rich female voice]) reaching a crescendo "torsade tumescente de 'forte'" [a tumescent twisted coil of forte notes], as the body relives the corporeal harmony which Cixous associates with the pre-oedipal: "La Voix, chant d'avant la loi, avant que le souffle soit coupé par le symbolique, réapproprié dans le langage sous l'autorité séparante. La plus profonde, la plus ancienne et adorable visitation. Et chaque femme chante le premier amour sans nom."[63] In "Sistre" the very expression of "the song" attests to the fact that the body has not only searched for ("le corps recherche sa voix" [the body seeks for its voice]) but also found its voice – "La voix femelle luxuriante" [the rich female voice], in a triumphant victory over "[la] mutité brutale" – the violent silencing it had endured.

But whereas "Sistre" clearly reveals feminine desire, how far does it succeed in fulfilling Djebar's other project, that of recapturing the rhythms of the Arabic language? I will now look at Djebar's claim that the poem recalls the versification of Arabic *poetry*. A brief history of Arabic poetry will demonstrate that Djebar's poem is in fact closer in style to the writings of Arabic mystics than that of classical Arabic poetry.

A brief history of Arabic poetry.

The form of the prose poem is not common in Arabic poetry. Traditionally, the Arabic poem, or *quasida*, was confined to a rigid two-hemistich, monorhymed, monometred form, with each hemistich

---

[63] Hélène Cixous (in collaboration with Catherine Clément), *La Jeune née* (Paris: UGE, 10/18, 1975) p. 172.

ending in a caesura. In *Modern Arabic Poetry*, Jayyusi asserts that the use of the caesura gives the "old" Arabic poem its permanent qualities of symmetry and equilibrium.[64] Because audiences were so used to the seasoned, well-measured, age-old rhythms, any departure from the traditional form was unacceptable. The ideals of symmetry and balance also determined the internal structure of the poem and its syntactic and semantic arrangements, making the form even more resistant to change.[65]

Most of the poets who rose to fame in the twentieth century had access to foreign literature. Experiments took place concentrating on developing new rhyme schemes, abandoning rhyme altogether, or creating poems with mixed metres with various stanzaic arrangements. These experiments were unsuccessful, as long as the poets still regarded the verse as the sole unit of poetic composition, and kept the caesuras, which determined symmetry and balance. When in the mid-1940s poets succeeded in creating an acceptable form of free verse, it was because they finally abandoned the age-old adherence to a fixed number of feet and to two caesuras in each line. In this new free verse, a poet made the single foot his or her basic unit, repeating it as many times as the artistic instinct dictated, in a single line. The form of the Arabic poem was liberated at last. Continued experiments led to the blossoming of prose poetry introduced by Khalil Gibran at the turn of the century.[66]

The whole idea of prose being another medium for writing poetry was very difficult to impose on poetic audiences accustomed to the strong balanced rhythms of the old two-hemistich form. This resistance was further complicated by the revelation of the Koran (which, although written in a highly rhetorical, rhythmical and

---

[64] The caesura ensured that the verses were self-contained in terms of meaning and imagery. The self-contained quality made the single verse, with its balanced measures and symmetrical divisions, the unit in the poem. The self-contained single verse in this form became a closed unit "sealed" by the rhyme. However, the repetition of this unit, which could continue "as far as intention and rhyme allow", made the poem as a whole "open and expansive." The presence of these two opposing factors, closeness and openness, represented "the two opposing primary trends in art, which satisfy at once the need for limitation and freedom, containment and continuity, restraint and release". Salma Khadra Jayyusi (ed.), *Modern Arabic Poetry: An Anthology* (New York: Columbia University Press, 1987), p. 8.
[65] Ibid., pp. 8-11.
[66] Ibid., pp. 10-12.

rhyming prose which slips from time to time into metrical rhythm), contains within it a denial that it is poetry.[67]

Only in the 1950s and 1960s was prose accepted as an element of form in poetry. This happened with the rise of avant-garde poets who wrote only in prose, whose movement was strengthened by prominent modernists such as Adunis and Yusuf al-Khal, who wrote poems in verse and who also used prose as a poetic medium. Adunis is the poet whose influence is paramount on younger poets of the 1960s and later. His writing rises up from the heart of the classical tradition and demonstrates a great affinity with the diction of the Islamic mystics:[68]

> Writing in a diction as far removed from common speech as possible, he shunned direct statement and invested his language with mystery, obliquity, connotativeness, always creating new combinations of words that contravened conventional, logical sentence order ... Influenced by such great French poets as Rimbaud and particularly St. John Perse, he broke "the neck of logic" and produced highly original words and phrases derived from all aspects of poetic experience, as well as from philosophy, religion, and politics. There are times when he is too difficult, and resorts to exaggerated ambiguity, often sounding esoteric and pretentious. [69]

The accusations of pretentiousness are echoed in Djebar's "defence" of the deliberately obscure language of her own poem: "Et si je dis "tesson de soupirs", si je dis "circe ou ciseaux de cette tessiture', ce n'est pas pour écrire de la poésie savante" [And when I say "shards of sighs" or *"thistle or scissors rending this tessitura"*, it is not because I want to write learned poetry. It is because I am trying to recall the versification of Arabic poetry, where the language works by alliteration].[70]

Djebar's use of prose poetry, like that of Adunis, borrows its form from Western poetry and aspects of its style not from traditional Arabic poetry but from the discourse of the Islamic mystics:

> Islamic poetic prose is intellectual and clear, rhythmical and rhymed, highly polished, garnished with archaic expressions and rare and literary words ... It employs complicated techniques of alliteration, assonance, stereotype adjectives balanced with their synonyms and similes, with extensive use of nouns of pre-eminence, intensive and extensive verbs. The diction is noble and allows only the highly

---

[67] In Surah 36:69, the Prophet affirms that the Koran in not to be interpreted as poetry, but as a spiritual message.
[68] Salma Khadra Jayyusi (ed.), *Modern Arabic Poetry: An Anthology*, p. 27.
[69] Ibid., p. 27.
[70] Lise Gauvin, "Assia Djebar, territoires des langues: entretien", p. 79. My translation.

polished, rare and poetic words to be used in vague and imprecise expressions.[71]

Djebar's use of rhythm, assonance, and alliteration in "Sistre" mimics the style of Islamic mystical discourse, as does her predilection for embellished language, rare words, paradigmatic constructions and her resistance to fixed meaning and to the "developmental urgency" of the syntagmatic chain. Her prose poetry nevertheless avoids what Moreh calls the "monotonous elegance" of the Islamic mystics.

In *Repetition in Arabic Discourse*, Barbara Johnstone argues the Arabic language naturally tends towards the paradigmatic chain of language. She demonstrates that by means of the juxtaposition of paradigmatic structure in syntagmatic discourse, repetition, parallelism and paraphrase function as the main persuasive devices in Arabic discourse: "Repetition creates linguistic cohesion by *evoking* classes of items; it creates persuasive force by *creating* classes; and in doing each of these things it creates language."[72] Arabic argumentation is structured by the notion that it is in the presentation of an idea, "the linguistic forms and the very words that are used to describe it", that is persuasive, rather than the logical structure of proof characteristic of Western rhetoric. Texts are characterised by repetition at all levels: phonological, morphological, lexical, syntactical and semantic.

One form of syntactical parallelism that is analysed, "cumulative parallelism", is similar to the technique Djebar uses in "Sistre." Johnstone quotes examples from Arabic discourse and concludes as follows:

> The parallelism in these examples is very tight at the beginnings of sentences ... but it becomes loose or non-existent at the ends. While in these examples as well, the parallelism is clearly cohesive, it is also what I have called cumulative, in that it reflects and signals a rhetorical rise in momentum. The ideas seem to come in increasingly larger waves, and the parallel or repeated terms at the beginning of each idea signal a new surge. While listing parallelism [exact syntactical parallelism and lexical echoing producing the effect of a list] indicates that the new item is textually and rhetorically the same as the preceding one, cumulative parallelism indicates that a new, more intense item is about to begin.[73]

---

[71] Shmuel, Moreh, *Modern Arabic Poetry 1800-1970* (Leiden: E.J.Brill, 1976), p. 291.
[72] Barbara Johnstone, *Repetition in Arabic Discourse: Paradigms, Syntagms, and the Ecology of Language* (Amsterdam/Philadelphia: John Benjamins, 1991), p. 119.
[73] Ibid., p. 106.

Johnstone claims that cumulative parallelism is a rhetorical device as well as a text-building one and that these two functions are in fact inseparable. As the paradigmatic class of items that share the repeated parallel "refrain" gets larger, the rhetorical effect of alluding to the class gets more forceful: "Each return to the parallelistic beginning resonates with more echo than the one before."[74]

In "Sistre", the rhythm of the first paragraph and of the following three paragraphs mimics the waves of desire, as each reaches a climax and then subsides in a long, slow ebbing. "Sistre" exemplifies a loose form of cumulative parallelism. The first three paragraphs are characterised by a pile-up of nominal and prepositional phrases (7 in the first, 6 in the second, 4 in the last), in each case suddenly interrupted by a break (comma), followed by a conjunction "et", and completed by a verbal phrase "et souque la voix courbe" [and the flexured voice tightens] (l.5; 4), "et le navire des désirs cule" [and the ship of desire drops astern] (l.11; 9-10), "et le corps recherche sa voix" [and the body seeks for its voice] (l.15; 13-14).

Whereas the parallelism at the beginning of each paragraph suggests increasing tension, the parallelism at the end of the paragraph serves to gradually slow down the pace and release the tension. The climaxing conjunction does not, as might be expected, occur sooner each time but follows an irregular pattern. The effect of repeated but irregular waves of language mimics the constant but erratic pulsations of the chora.

Johnstone comes to the conclusion that the Arabic language itself is inherently paradigmatic – it naturally works by pulsations, repetitions and waves rather than by rational persuasion along the logical syntagmatic chain: "... there are ways in which Arabic itself, and not just discourse in Arabic is parallelistic and paratactic."[75] According to her, most of the Arabic discourse features which she examines (such as lexical couplets or conjoined, parallel verb phrases) were the result of a relatively conscious choice on the part of the writers. She observes, however, that there are many cases in which the choice is not so free, cases in which a parallelistic or paratactic structure is chosen because it is *preferred* by the grammar of Arabic, or even because it is the *only choice* that the grammar allows.[76]

If this is the case, then in Kristeva's terms Arabic is an inherently more "maternal" language than French, a language more open to the

---

[74] Ibid., p. 106.
[75] Ibid., p. 109. [My emphasis]
[76] Ibid., p. 110.

semiotic, since it naturally resists the logical syntagmatic chain of language. Therefore, in terms of Djebar's writing, the Arabic language is doubly maternal – not only is it literally her mother tongue but it is by nature more maternal than the French language. However, because the syntagmatic resistance demonstrated by the Arabic language is "inbuilt" in the language, creating a sort of "compulsory repetitive/rhythmic tendency", it simultaneously implies a rigidity, which in turn perversely subverts Kristeva's notion of the semiotic's resistance to fixity.

So in Arabic we have a built-in or constructed rhythmic tendency. This apparently contradictory quality of pre-constructed poeticism also seems to find an echo in "Sistre", which comes across as a highly constructed poem. Although "Sistre" inscribes the desire of the female subject into language, and incorporates the female body or "writes the body", as Cixous would have it, the poem comes across as a highly crafted work of art rather than as one of the unconscious outpourings of Cixous's *écriture féminine*. But ironically it is this very conscious crafting, its carefully constructed rhythms, and its recourse to a deliberately grandiloquent lexis which, while distancing it from the unconscious flow of *écriture féminine* and its primeval Mother, nevertheless brings it closer to its other Mother – the mother tongue. So despite being doubly silenced by "la sensibilité aphasique de la langue française" [the emotional aridity of the French language] and by "les interdits de [l']éducation musulmane" [the taboos of Islamic education], in "Sistre" the female body finds its voice not only in French but also in Arabic.[77]

Semiotic and Symbolic: A Permanent Alternation?

In Parts 1 and 2 of *L'Amour, la fantasia*, Djebar's desire to identify with the motherland surfaces in the occasional irruptions of semiotic language. This yearning resurfaces as the desire for the mother tongue, in the semiotic waves of language of her prose-poems. In Part 3, however, the semiotic is neither an occasional nor an overwhelming presence but exists in a relationship of permanent alternation with the symbolic.

---

[77] See pp. 42 (27) and also pp. 35 (35) of Assia Djebar, *Vaste est la prison* (Paris: Albin Michel, 1995), trans. Betsy Wing, *So Vast the Prison* (New York, Seven Stories Press, 2001).

In Dialogue with Kristeva: *L'Amour, la fantasia* 77

Part 3 is divided into five "movements" or "variations on a theme", each of which is divided into six parallel chapters that can be distinguished as follows:
1. Cris[78] [Cries]
2. Voix [Voice]
3. Sons [Sounds[
4. Corps-langue [Body-language]
5. Voix [Voice]
6. Corps enlaces [Embraces]

Although Part 3 is not limited to a single historical period, it deals mainly with the War of Independence, relying on the oral testimonies of women who took part in the struggle, recorded by Djebar, and incorporated into the text. While in Parts 1 and 2, the semiotic is evident in occasional or overwhelming presence, in this final Part of the novel, semiotic harmony with the motherland is achieved in experiences rooted in symbolic/historic time and place – in Djebar's communion with the "Mothers of the Revolution." Relying on the oral testimonies of these women, Djebar now frees her historical narrative completely from dependence on paternalistic colonialist texts.

Here too is evidence of a creative tension between the maternal and the paternal orders, between the semiotic and the symbolic, as the simple language of these ordinary women's stories is shot through by semiotic pulsations or rhythms, not by the oscillations of pre-oedipal life but by the rhythms and pulsations of the *mother tongue* captured within the signifiers of the *paternal language*.

As we have seen, although in Parts 1 and 2 Djebar "thinks back through her fathers", these sections also reveal a maternal void – the motherland stripped of her identity and the adolescent alienated from the mother figures of her childhood. In Part 3 Djebar frees herself from the paternal filter and attempts to fill this maternal void by consciously "thinking back through her mothers", by revisiting the world of women, mother figures of past and present, and by reinvesting her language with the rhythms of the mother tongue.

Les Cris

In "Les transes" [The Trance] (pp. 167-69), the semiotic is present within the boundaries of symbolic society, in the socially or "symbolically" acceptable ritual cries of "les femmes d'Algérie"

---

[78] I have used the titles "Cris", "Sons", and "Corps-langue" as my own categories in these three instances where Djebar does not provide a generic name.

[women of Algeria]. The "cry" is the language of the body – female bodies, repressed by patriarchal law, who find temporary release in the frenzied hysteria of primeval sounds and movements. This ritualised form of temporary madness, while permitted by the laws of symbolic society, nevertheless allows the boundaries of the symbolic to recede, as "les femmes d'Algérie' luxuriate in the semiotic indifferentiation of pre-oedipal sounds and rhythms, liberating mind and body from the pain of the present of history.

In "Les Transes", Djebar describes how her maternal grandmother convenes her peers for a ritual dance, which holds no promise of celebration "malgré les apparences, ce n'était pas la fête qui commençait" [in spite of appearances, this was not the beginning of a festivity] (pp. 168; 144). This is no party but a parting, a release of repressed emotions and an escape into the realm of the senses. As the grandmother and her entourage work themselves up into a state of frenzy, there is a build-up of sound – "Les doigts bagués des 'chikhats' se mettaient à frapper les tambours" [The *chikhats*, ladymusicians, began to strike the drums with their ringed fingers], of voice – "l'insidieuse litanie du choeur montait dans la chambre enveloppée de fumées" [the insidious invocation rose up in the smokefilled room], of colour and movement – "Droite, la tête enturbannée de foulards bariolés, le corps allégé dans une tunique étroite, elle se mettait à danser lentement" [Upright, clad only in a tight-fitting tunic, her head turbaned in multi-coloured scarves, she began a slow dance], and of rhythmic incantations, all building up to create a hothouse of emotions: "'Laisse sortir le malheur! Que les dents de l'envie et de la convoitise t'épargnent, ô ma dame! ... Mets au jour ta force et tes armes, ô ma reine' ... La mélopée des autres reprenait son antienne, dans la torpeur chaude" ['Flush out the ill fortune! May the teeth of envy and covetousness not harm you, O my lady! ... Bring out your strength and all your armoury into the light of day, O my queen! ... The others resumed their monotonous hypnotic singsong as torpor descended on the overheated room] (pp. 168; 144).

The escape into the rhythmic sensations brings the grandmother dangerously close to the madness present at the boundaries of thetic rupture: "Enfin la crise intervenait: ma grand-mère, inconsciente, secouée par les tressaillements de son corps qui se balançait, entrait en transes. Le rythme s'était précipité jusqu'à la frénésie" [Finally came the crisis: my grandmother, oblivious to everything, jerked spasmodically to and fro till she went into a trance] (pp. 168; 144). The reins of thetic control are in the hands of the blind woman: "L'aveugle entonnait son chant en solo continu et lyrique; à elle seule,

In Dialogue with Kristeva: *L'Amour, la fantasia* 79

elle tenait ferme les rênes de l'émotion collective" [The blind woman went on chanting her solo; she alone orchestrated the collective hysteria] (pp. 168; 144). But, as the reins are gradually pulled back, raw emotion is let loose: "L'aveugle adoucissait le thrène, le rendait murmure, râle imperceptible; s'approchant de la danseuse, elle chuchotait pour finir, des bribes du Coran" [The blind woman's threnody grew softer, reduced to a murmur, an imperceptible guttural groan; she finally drew near to the prancing woman and whispered scraps of the Quran in her ear] (pp. 168; 144). Finally, thetic control is relinquished, as the grandmother's cries, posture and attire mimic those of a madwoman:

> Un tambour scandant la crise, les cris arrivaient: du fond du ventre, peut-être même des jambes, ils montaient, ils déchiraient la poitrine creuse, sortaient enfin en gerbes d'arêtes hors de la gorge de la vieille. On la portait presque, tandis que, transformant en rythmique ses plaintes quasi animales, elle ne dansait plus que de la tête, la chevelure dénouée, les foulards de couleurs violentes, éparpillés sur l'épaule. (pp. 168-69; 144)
>
> A drum beat out the tempo for the crisis; the cries began: drawn up from the depths of her belly, perhaps even from her legs, rending her hollow chest, emerging at last in rasping squawks from the old lady's throat. Now she could hardly stand, her loosened hair, her gaudy headscarves were tossed about her shoulders, only her head swayed from side to side as she grunted rhythmically.

Surrendering to the beckoning rhythms of the semiotic, the old woman finally expels the pain of symbolic exclusion: "Les cris se bousculaient d'abord, se chevauchaient, à demi étouffés, puis ils s'exhalaient, gonflés en volutes enchevêtrées, en courbes tressées, en aiguilles. Obéissant au martèlement du tambour de l'aveugle, la vieille ne luttait plus: toutes les voix du passé bondissaient loin d'elle, expulsées hors de la prison de ses jours" [At first the choking cries came thick and fast, jostling each other, then they swelled and swirled in spreading spirals, intersecting arches, tapering to needle points. The old lady gave up the struggle, surrendering herself completely to the insistent beat of the blind woman's drum: all the voices of the past, imprisoned in her present existence, were now set free and leapt far away from her] (pp. 169; 144-45). But release is short-lived, and as the climax to the final exorcism ends, she is cruelly returned to the grim reality of symbolic life: "Une demi-heure ou une heure après, elle gisait au fond de son lit, en une masse qu'on apercevait à peine, tandis que, parmi les odeurs d'encens, les musiciennes mangeaient et devisaient. Leur magie de prêtresses païennes avait disparu pour laisser place, dans le jour, qui, à midi, semblait seulement commencer, à la laideur des visages exagérément fardés" [Half an hour or one hour later she lay bunched up in her bed, an almost invisible heap, while the musicians ate and gossiped amid the smell of incense. Their magic as pagan priestesses had vanished, and now in the tardy noonday light they were simply ugly old women with faces extravagantly painted] (pp. 169; 145).

In this section, the semiotic surfaces in the ritual reactivation of sensory experience. However, both the socially acceptable and temporary nature of this "escape" means that although it represents a departure from the symbolic, it also exists in relation to it. As such, it represents a balance between the two modalities, a desire for the semiotic that respects the laws of the symbolic.

Voix

In the "Voix" [Voice] chapters, "les femmes d'Algérie" who took part in the War of Independence tell their stories in the first person. Here the semiotic is present on a *linguistic* level, in the traces of the maternal language perceptible in the signs of the paternal language. The opening paragraphs of these sections provide no referential markers – the reader is not told who the voices belong to, nor who they are addressed to, neither are the voices situated precisely in time or place[79], giving the impression that the texts rise up as if from nowhere: "Le moment vient où l'effet immédiatement bouleversant de ces voix fait place à la perception d'un étrange silence qui les entoure, et dans lequel elles font un écho d'autant plus poignant qu'il semble déjà lointain."[80] Despite the vacuum from which they emerge, the voices succeed in creating their own presence, as, in their strikingly simple language, they assert defiance in the face of unspeakable adversity.

In these "Voix" [Voice] sections, Djebar "thinks back through the Mothers of the Revolution" and writes back through her mother tongue, incorporating the oral testimonies of these women into the text "par une traduction voulue au premier degré" [deliberately direct translation].[81] Before examining one of the "Voix" [Voice] sections, I will look at the problems of reproducing Arab speech within a French

---

[79] When Djebar proceeds to describe her meetings with the women behind the voices in the "Corps enlacés" sections, it becomes clear that the voices are addressed to her.
[80] Denise Brahimi, Post-face to Assia Djebar, *L'Amour, la fantasia* (Casablanca: EDDIF, 1992). p. 265.
[81] Quotation of Djebar's in Mildred Mortimer, "Entretien avec Assia Djebar, écrivain algérien", p. 201. My translation.

text. In her examination of the processes at work when simulating the character of African speech in a European text, Zabus considers the terms "translation", "transference" and "transmutation" to be unsatisfactory, and settles for the linguistic term *"relexification"*, referring to what she calls "Loretto Todd's felicitous formulation – 'the relexification on one's mother tongue using English vocabulary but indigenous structures and rhythms.'"[82]

The emphasis here is both on "the lexis in the original sense of speech, word or phrase and on *lexicon* in reference to the vocabulary and morphemes of a language and, by extension, to word formation."[83] Zabus expands the term to include semantics and syntax as well, redefining relexification as "the making of a new register of communication out of an alien lexicon."[84] This new register of communication, which is "neither the European target language nor the indigenous source language" functions as an "interlanguage" or as a "third register."[85] Zabus also draws a distinction between interpretative translation and relexification:

> Unlike interpretative translation or the 'lesser' activity of *transcodage* which both take place between two texts – the original and the translated version – relexification is characterised by the absence of an original. It therefore does not operate from the language of one text to the other but from one language to the other within the same text. Such texts are ... palimpsests for, behind the scriptural authority of the target European language, the earlier, imperfectly erased remnants of the source language are still visible.[86]

Djebar's "Voix" [Voice sections] are a combination of transcodage[87] and relexification – transcodage does take place between two "message events" (her original recorded interviews conducted in Arabic with the "Mothers of the Revolution", and her "scriptural" French version of these interviews) but they are nevertheless also palimpsests, as Djebar consciously "operates from

---

[82] Loretto Todd, "The English Language in West Africa", in R. W. Bailey and M. Görlach (eds), *English as a World Language* (Ann Arbor: University of Michigan Press, 1982), p. 303. Quoted in Chantal Zabus, "Relexification", in Bill Ashcroft, Gareth Griffiths and Helen Tiffin (eds), *The Post-colonial Studies Reader* (London: Routledge, 1995), pp. 314-18, p. 314.
[83] Ibid., p. 314.
[84] Ibid., p. 314.
[85] Ibid., p. 315.
[86] Ibid., p. 317.
[87] In the process of transcodage, Djebar occasionally slips into "un faux style oral", using literary inversions (s'exclama-t-il) and inappropriate tenses, such as "le subjonctif imparfait" ("J'eus peur qu'il me surprît").

one language to the other within the same text", using the techniques of relexification to "render visible the source language." In the "Voix" [Voice] sections, this technique allows not only the recovery of a repressed identity but also, as Zabus suggests, the recovery of a repressed language: "... the linguistic remnants inhabiting the relexified text may lead to the discovery of the repressed source language."[88]

On a strategic level, the aim of relexification is "... to subvert the linguistically codified, to decolonize the language of early, colonial literature and to affirm a revised, non-atavistic orality via the imposed medium."[89] On a strategic level Djebar also aims to decolonise, or deterritorialise the intertexts of "Les Pères de la Colonisation" in Parts 1 and 2 of the work, by placing them in direct but conflictual dialogue with the voices of "Les Mères de la Révolution."

The section entitled "Voix" [Voice] (pp. 137-42; 117-121) tells the story of Chérifa and begins when she is only thirteen years old. She tells of her experience at the hands of the French soldiers who burnt down her home three times. Her resistance to them precipitates her removal to "the plains." She escapes, is reunited with her brother Ahmed, only to be expelled yet again. She then witnesses her brother's death as he falls to the ground, shot. She escapes only to return to the scene later, where she finds her other brother, Abdelkader.

The story is introduced with very vague time and place markers: "Mon frère aîné, Abdelkader, était monté au maquis, cela faisait quelque temps déjà. La France arriva jusqu'à nous, nous habitions à la zaouia sidi M'Hamed Aberkane ... La France est venue et elle nous a brûlés" [My elder brother Abdelkader had taken to the hills to join the maquis, some time ago. 'France' came right up to out doorsteps; we were living at the Sidi M'hamed Aberkane *zaouia* ... 'France' came and burnt us out] (pp. 137; 117). The simplicity and slowness of Chérifa's expression, combined with the terseness of her language, conveys an effect of dignified suffering. The first sentence, with its broken syntax (proper name "Abdelkader" juxtaposed and placed between commas), sets the slow, deliberate pace. Here, and throughout the text, the adverbial clauses of time are relegated to the end of the sentence and placed after a comma, as Djebar rejects syntactical convention to mimic the pregnant pauses of speech.

---

[88] Ibid., p. 317.
[89] Ibid., p. 318.

In order to suffuse her "voices" with the sounds and signs of the maternal language, Djebar makes considerable use of transliteration (a technique not restricted to the voice sections, but which predominates here), as well as the direct translation of Arabic expressions: "La France arriva jusqu'à nous, nous habitions à la zaouia Sidi M'hammed Aberkane" ['France' came right up to out doorsteps; we were living at the Sidi M'hamed Aberkane *zaouia*] (pp. 137; 117).[90] Here Chérifa says "France", meaning the French army. Other phrases such as "ceux de la montagne" echo the Arabic term, in this case "jabaliin", "jabal" meaning mountain with the suffix "in", denoting possession. Djebar also reproduces Arabic syntax, in sentences such as "Toi, avec l'une de tes soeurs, reviens ..." [You, with one of your sisters, come back ...] (pp. 139; 118).[91] In Arabic the pronoun can be used before or after the imperative verb and can be separated from it by an adverbial phrase.

The most significant way in which the text mimics the repressed source language is, however, by the use of repetition. Repetition not only slows down the text but also emphasises its lack of linearity. Its use as a persuasive device is characteristic of Arabic discourse, where "persuasion is as much the result of the sheer number of times an idea is stated than it is the consequence of 'logical' organization."[92]

The use of repetition reinforces the emotional impact of Chérifa's story. Repeated references to "La France" on the one hand, and "les Frères" [the Brothers] on the other, introduce the Manicheistic opposition between "them" and "us", coloniser and colonised. The reiteration of the verb "brûler" [to burn], which occurs seven times in the first seven paragraphs, and the use of syntactical parallelism – "La France est venue et elle nous a brûlés ... De nouveau les soldats revinrent; de nouveau ils nous brûlèrent ... La zaouia a brûlé; notre douar aussi va brûler!" ['France' came and burnt us out ... The soldiers came again; again they burnt our house down ... The *zaouia* has been burnt and our *douar* will be burnt down too] (pp. 137; 117) – mimic the rhythm of the mother tongue, and serve to foreground the persistent cruelty of the French army.

The death of Chérifa's brother is described in very simple yet moving language. Paraphrase is used to convey the force of Chérifa's pain on witnessing the shooting: "Il courait devant moi quand il est tombé: une balle l'atteignit à l'oreille. Il est tombé devant moi .... Il est

---

[90] "La zaouia" refers to the headquarters of the Moslem brotherhood.
[91] Translation adapted.
[92] Barbara Johnstone, *Repetition in Arabic Discourse: Paradigms, Syntagms, and the Ecology of Language*, p. 108.

tombé sur la face et, dans sa chute, il a même renversé un garçon qui s'est blessé sur la pierre. Mais le garçon s'est relevé" [He was running in front of me when he fell: a bullet hit him behind the ear. He fell right in front of me ... He fell forward on his face and as he fell he even knocked down a boy who cut himself on a rock. But the boy picked himself up] (pp. 140; 120). The first sentence provides the basic fact of the incident. In sentences two and three, this fact is restated more concisely, and then more graphically.

Johnstone uses the notion of "presence" to illustrate the rhetorical force of paraphrase. She argues that the very fact of making something present in discourse makes it valuable and important. The implication is that the more often it is made present, the more valuable and important it appears. "Presence" can be created in a number of ways – by "the extensions of spatial and temporal deixis to the realm of the rhetorical" (with the use of expressions such as "Look here" or "Now the first point is"), by "the use of the present tense in historical accounts to create a sense of temporal proximity" (as Chérifa does) or by "giving details and piling up conditions for, or the consequences of, an act."[93] A slow style invokes "presence" by creating emotional closeness: "While a rapid style is effective in reasoning, a slow style creates emotion."[94] Presence can also be created by accumulation or insistence. According to Johnstone, one of the most important ways that presence is created in Arabic is through repetition, and paraphrastic repetition in particular."[95]

Djebar's use of a slow style and repetitive rhythms allow the traces of the maternal language to affect the signifiers of the paternal language, which in turn resist the syntagmatic chain of language. Because of this resistance to logical or syntagmatic succession, this voice section appears to have no construction, just as the pulsating oscillations of the chora appear to have no controlling force, no unity or identity. But just as the rhythmic space of the chora is nevertheless subjected to a "regulating process", so the rhythmic space of the text, which appears "unconstructed", is nevertheless subject to a regulating process, which creates presence through the effect of accumulated repetition. The result is not a well-constructed argument against

---

[93] Ibid., p. 92.
[94] Vico, cited in Chaim Perelman and Lucie Olbrechts-Tyteca, *The New Rhetoric: A Treatise on Argumentation*, trans. John Wilkenson and Purcell Weaver (Notre Dame, IN: The University of Notre Dame Press, 1969), p. 144. Quoted in Barbara Johnstone, *Repetition in Arabic Discourse: Paradigms, Syntagms, and the Ecology of Language*, pp. 92-93.
[95] Ibid., p. 94.

colonisation but the eloquent rhetoric of "la voix qui chavire", quietly but convincingly condemning her oppressors.

Sons

The "Sons" [Sounds] sections represent lyrical rewritings of the "Voix" [Voice] sections that immediately precede them. Whereas the "Voix" [Voice] sections represent Djebar's attempts to stay as close to the language of the transcribed testimonies of "Les Mères de la Révolution", in the "Sons" [Sounds] sections, Djebar resumes her own style again. Here the semiotic modality is displaced from the maternal to the paternal language. The simple tone of Djebar's young compatriots, pervaded by the slow rhythms of the maternal language, now contrast dramatically with Djebar's own virtuoso exploitation of the poetic possibilities of the French language, as she begins to retell these women's stories in her own words.

Having met "Les Mères de la Révolution" [Mothers of the Revolution], and listened to their stories, it is as if Djebar has a vivid, dream-like vision of their experiences, which she then inscribes into the text, leaving traces of sounds, colours and movements. Here again we have semiotic resonances, not so much in the refusal of linearity, but in the privileging of the senses. The retelling of Chérifa's story in "Clameur" [Clamour] (pp. 143-45; 122-24)[96], is a subjective, sensuous echo of her suffering rather than a rational analysis of it. Djebar is "feeling" Chérifa's suffering not "colonising" her story, as all the emotions held back in Chérifa's slow lamento burst forth and are poured into her clamour.

In this passage Djebar bypasses the facts of the story already provided in the preceding "Voix" [Voice section], and instead focuses on the moment of highest emotion – the moment at the end of Chérifa's story when she returns to find the dead body of her brother. She takes hold of Chérifa's cry and sets it to music, replaying the haunting tune of suffering again and again, endlessly revisiting that ultimate moment of discovery.

Reinforcing the initial impressionist haze, Chérifa emerges in a blur of yellow, red, green and gold: "Les longs cheveux jaunâtres de la fillette ont dû virer d'un coup au rouge flamboyant, autrefois. Les commères soupçonneuses avaient qualifié ses yeux verts de 'yeux de chatte rôdeuse.' Larges yeux verts aux prunelles tachetées d'or" [The girl's long yellowish hair must at one time have suddenly turned

---

[96] This chapter appears in italics in the original.

flaming red. The suspicious-minded old busybodies had said her green eyes were like those of a 'prowling cat.' Wide green eyes whose irises were flecked with gold] (pp. 143; 122). The blood red of her henna-stained hands gives way to her brother's bloodied corpse: "La voici orpheline du frère tombé, dans cette aube de l'été immobile; nouvelle Antigone pour l'adolescent étendu sur l'herbe, elle palpe, de ses doigts rougis au henné, le cadavre à demi dénudé" [And now she grieves for her dead brother, in this dawn of a still summer day; a new Antigone, mourning for the adolescent lying on the grass, stroking the half-naked corpse with henna-stained hands] (pp. 143; 122).

The story proceeds as if in slow motion, as Djebar foregrounds the odours, sounds and gestures of a moment suspended in time, as if trying to hold back the inevitable cry of suffering: "L'oued, pas tout à fait sec, circule dans un creux de ronces et de mousses parfumées. En contrebas, la source fait entendre son bruissement. A quelques pas, en un cercle irrégulier, quatre hommes circonspects sont tournés vers un cinquième, plus trapu, raidi dans son uniforme: c'est le second frère Amroune. Il halète, il esquisse un geste vers la fille" [The wadi is not quite dry; the rustle of water can be heard flowing far down between steep banks covered with brambles and sweet-scented moss. A few feet away, four men stand watching in an irregular circle; they turn towards a fourth man, stockier, seeming awkward in his uniform: the second Amroune brother. He's out of breath from running; he points vaguely in the girl's direction] (pp. 143; 122).

Time and the elements stand still in a moment of uneasy expectation as Djebar's screen is filled with the image of Chérifa alone before the corpse, the background slowly receding: "Tout alors a fait silence: la nature, les arbres, les oiseaux (scansion d'un merle proche qui s'envole). Le vent, dont on devinait la brise à ras du sol, s'asphyxie; les cinq hommes se voient devenir témoins inutiles, dans le gel de l'attente. Elle seule ..." [Then all is stilled: nature, trees, birds (a blackbird flying past silences its song). The faint soughing of the breeze dies away as it sweeps the ground; the five men look on helplessly, waiting, motionless. She alone ...] (pp. 144; 123).

The silence is suddenly broken by a prolonged cry, its pathos reinforced by the reminder of Chérifa's youthfulness: "Elle a entonné un long premier cri, la fillette" [One prolonged, preliminary cry has escaped her] (pp. 144; 123). Taking on a life of its own, the voice becomes a song of suffering: "... la voix jaillit, hésitante aux premières notes, une voile à peine dépliée qui frémirait, au bas d'un mât de misaine. Puis le vol démarre précautionneusement, la voix prend du corps dans l'espace" [... her voice shrills out, stumbling over the first notes, like the shudder of a sail before it is hoisted on the foremast] (pp. 144; 123). The song, slowly soaring to a full-throated clamour, merges with the voices of "les femmes d'Algérie": "... quelle voix? Celle de la mère que les soldats ont torturée sans qu'elle gémisse, des soeurs trop jeunes, parquées mais porteuses de l'angoisse aux yeux fous, la voix des vieilles du douar qui, bouches béantes, mains décharnées, paumes en avant, font face à l'horreur du glas qui approche" [... what voice? That of the mother who bore the soldier's torture with never a whimper? That of the little cooped-up sisters, too young to understand, but bearing the message of wild-eyed anguish? The voice of the old women of the *douar* who face the horror of the approaching death-knell, open-mouthed, with palms of fleshless hands turned upwards?] (pp. 144; 123).

Rising to join those of her sisters, Chérifa's cry then returns to the scene of death, where it is still darkly suspended in mid-air: "Au-dessus de l'abîme, les hommes rivés la regardent: faire face à la durée du cri qui tangue, tel le balancement d'un drap de sang s'égouttant au soleil" [The men stare down at her from the edge of the ravine: standing there throughout that cry that lurches like a pall dripping with blood and flapping in the sun] (pp. 144-45. 123). The cry's final resting place is the body, and, as signifier and signified coalesce, their movement mimics the rhythm of its cadences: "Le cadavre, lui, s'en enveloppe, semble retrouver sa mémoire: miasmes, odeurs, gargouillis. Il s'inonde de touffeur sonore. La vibration de la stridulation, le rythme de la déclamation langent ses chairs pour parer à leur décomposition" [The dead man swathes himself in it, using it to retrieve his memory: noxious emanations, foetid gases, borborygmic rumblings. Suffusing him in the reverberating, stifling heat. The plangent chirring, the rhythm of the cadences swaddle his flesh to protect it from decay] (pp. 145; 123).

Although the rhythmic tribute that is "Clameur" [Clamour] is Djebar's, the cry, the story and the last word belong to Chérifa: "Elle s'appelle Chérifa. Quand elle entame le récit, vingt ans après, elle n'évoque ni l'inhumation, ni un autre ensevelissement pour le frère gisant dans la rivière" [Her name is Cherifa. When she tells her story, twenty years later, she mentions no internment nor any other form or burial for the brother lying in the river bed] (pp. 145,; 124).

Corps-langue.

"L'Ecole Coranique" [The Quranic School] (pp. 206-13; 179-185) explores the relationship between language and body. Although the French language is associated with physical freedom, it is Arabic that is dubbed the language of the soul. Djebar describes how her initiation into the French language brings her freedom of movement: "A l'âge où le corps aurait dû se voiler, grâce à l'école française, je peux davantage circuler" [At the age when I should be veiled already, I can still move about freely thanks to the French school] (pp. 206; 179). In contrast, the act of writing in Arabic is compared to an act of physical love:

> Quand la main écrit, lente posture du bras, précautionneuse pliure du flanc en avant ou sur le côté, le corps accroupi se balance comme dans un acte d'amour. Pour lire, le regard prend son temps, aime caresser les courbes, au moment où l'inscription lève en nous le rythme de la scansion: comme si l'écriture marquait le début et le terme d'une possession. (pp. 208; 180)

> When the hand writes, slow positioning of the arm, carefully bending forward or leaning to one side, crouching, swaying to and fro, as in an act of love. When reading, the eyes take their time, delight in caressing the curves, while the calligraphy suggests the rhythm of the scansion: as if the writing marked the beginning and the end of possession.

The slow, comforting, rhythmic pace of Arabic is contrasted with the heady, speedy release that the French language brings: "Comme si soudain la langue française avait des yeux, et qu'elle me les ait donnés pour voir dans la liberté, comme si la langue française aveuglait les mâles voyeurs de mon clan et qu'à ce prix, je puisse circuler, dégringoler toutes les rues, annexer le dehors pour mes compagnes cloîtrées, pour mes aïeules mortes bien avant le tombeau" [As if the French language suddenly had eyes, and lent them to me to see into liberty; as if the French language blinded the peeping Toms of my clan and, at this price, I could move freely, run headlong down every street, annex the outdoors for my cloistered companions, for the matriarchs of my family who endured a living death] (pp. 208; 181). But "la chance", the stroke of luck that enables her to acquire the French language, brings only a superficial freedom – it frees the body but not the soul. Propelling her into a "symbolic world" which is literally hundreds of miles away, the French language creates in her a sense of geographical dislocation:

> J'écris et je parle français au-dehors: mes mots ne se chargent pas de réalité charnelle. J'apprends des noms d'oiseaux que je n'ai jamais vus, des noms d'arbres que je mettrai dix ans ou davantage à identifier ensuite, des glossaires de fleurs et de plantes que je ne humerai jamais avant de voyager au nord de la Méditerranée. En ce sens, tout vocabulaire me devient absence, exotisme sans mystère, avec comme une mortification de l'oeil qu'il sied pas d'avouer ... Les scènes des livres d'enfant, leurs situations me sont purs scénarios; dans la famille

In Dialogue with Kristeva: *L'Amour, la fantasia* 89

> française, la mère vient chercher sa fille ou son fils à l'école; dans la rue française, les parents marchent tout naturellement côte à côte ... Ainsi, le monde de l'école est expurgé du quotidien de ma ville natale tout comme de celui de ma famille. A ce dernier est dénié tout rôle référentiel. (pp. 212; 185)

> I write and speak French outside: the words I use convey no flesh-and-blood reality. I learn the names of birds I've never seen, trees I shall take ten years or more to identity, lists of flowers and plants that I shall never smell until I travel north of the Mediterranean. In this respect, all vocabulary expresses what is missing in my life, exoticism without mystery, causing a kind of visual humiliation that it is not seemly to admit to ... Settings and episodes in children's books are nothing but theoretical concepts; in the French family the mother comes to fetch her daughter or son from school; in the French street, the parents walk quite naturally side by side ... So, the world of the school is expunged from the daily life of my native city, as it is from the life of my family. The latter is refused any referential rôle.

The virtual reality that the French language compels her to inhabit engenders intellectual and emotional disconnection. Yet, in the first "Corps-langue" [Body-language] section, Djebar suggests that emotional absence/distance can be and was overcome, as if by miracle, by a return to the mother tongue:

> Si je désirais soudain, par caprice, diminuer la distance entre l'homme et moi, il ne m'était pas nécessaire de montrer, par quelque mimique, mon affabilité. Il suffisait d'opérer le passage à la langue maternelle: revenir, pour un détail, au son de l'enfance, c'était envisager que sûrement la camaraderie complice, peut-être l'amitié, et pourquoi pas, par miracle, l'amour pouvait surgir entre nous comme risque mutuel de connaissance. (pp. 150; 128-29)

> If the whim took me to react to the man's advances, I did not need to put on some show of graciousness. All I had to do was to revert to the mother tongue: by returning to the sounds of childhood to express some detail, I was ensuring that we would agree to a spirit of good fellowship, that we might become friends and perhaps – why not? – by some miracle, we might take the mutual risk of our acquaintanceship developing into love.

And, just as emotional distance is bridged here, on a personal level, by a return to the mother tongue, so emotional distance, recalled on a thematic level in the "Corps-langue" [Body-language] sections, is structurally bridged by the construction of the text. For these sections are surrounded by the presence of the semiotic – a presence perceptible in the lyrical resonance of the preceding "Sons" [Sounds sections], and in the maternal rhythms of the succeeding "Voix" [Voice sections].

Corps enlacés

In "Corps enlacés" [Embraces], Djebar uncovers the faces behind the "Voix" [Voice] sections, as she recounts her actual meetings with Chérifa and Lla Zohra, whom she visited in their mountain homes. Lla Zohra, the cousin of Djebar's grandmother, is now in her eighties; Chérifa is married to "un veuf taciturne." As Djebar thinks back through the "Mothers of the Revolution", the pressure of the semiotic on the symbolic of language (in the "Voix/Sons" [Voice/Sounds sections]) becomes the presence of the mother figures in the symbolic present of history.

Standing in counterpoint to Djebar's "aphasie amoureuse", the mutual embrace of "Corps enlacés" reveals women united by the bonds of sisterly love. The encounter with these women is energised by a sense of Djebar's own presence and charged by a sense of emotional openness. The anguish and confusion generated by this "préparation à l'autobiographie" is temporarily subdued, as she expresses unbridled affection for her "petite soeur" [little sister] and "petite mère" [little mother]: "Nous nous embrassons, nous nous touchons, nous nous admirons" [We embrace, we touch, we tell each other how well we look] (pp. 190; 164). It is the intimacy of this maternal embrace that finally enables her to recapture "le mot plein de l'amour-au-présent" [words expressing love-in-the-present] (pp. 80; 62).

But the "Corps enlacés" [Embraces] sections reveal not only the comforts but also the limits of the semiotic. For, just as the state of semiotic indifferentiation must eventually be ruptured by the thetic phase, so the state of harmony with the maternal figures cannot be preserved. Djebar's ultimate separation from "les femmes d'Algérie" is the inevitable result of her writing in the paternal/symbolic language: "Mots torches qui éclairent mes compagnes, mes complices; d'elles définitivement, ils me séparent. Et sous leur poids, je m'expatrie" [Torch words which light up my women-companions, my accomplices; these words divide me from them once and for all. And weigh me down as I leave my native land] (pp. 165, 142).

And just as the semiotic exerts pressure on language but cannot dominate it without causing psychosis, so the maternal rhythms of Arabic, although exerting pressure on Djebar's French, cannot be fully realised in it, without causing unintelligibility. The realisation of the limits of the paternal language cause Djebar to cry out in frustration as she realises the impossibility of capturing the voice and image of Chérifa within the signs of the oppressor's language: "A peine si je frôle l'ombre de ton pas!" [I barely brush the shadow of your footsteps!] (pp. 165; 142). Language, identity and society must all submit to the rule of symbolic detachment that separates not only the mother-child continuum, but also the maternal and paternal languages, and ultimately separates Djebar from her compatriots.

However, in the "Corps enlacés" [Embraces] sections, the comfort of pre-oedipal indifferentiation is recovered, if only fleetingly. Djebar's meeting with Lla Zohra offers the most striking example of this, their physical closeness allowing Djebar to relive the maternal security of childhood. In her article "Acting Bits/Identity Talk", Gayatri Spivak also cites this incident as a key passage, but pays less attention to the emotional intimacy between the two women than to the act of storytelling that takes place.[97] Djebar tells Lla Zohra the story of a fateful incident in the lives of two nineteenth century Algerian prostitutes. The story originates in the writings of Eugène Fromentin, who heard it from the mouth of the French officer involved in the tragedy (pp. 191-93; 164-67).

For Spivak, the significance of this moment lies in the way Fromentin's narrative is wrested from the artist's text and translated into Arabic for a new addressee, "the gendered subaltern": "I think one of the major motifs of *Fantasia* is a meditation on the possibility that to achieve autobiography in the double bind of the practice of the conqueror's writing is to learn to be taken seriously by the gendered subaltern who has not mastered that practice."[98] The words that preface this act of storytelling: "I [Djebar], your cousin, tell you [Lla Zohra in Arabic]" announce both the displacing of the French language and that of the implied francophone reader in favour of the subaltern. For Spivak, this act of narration is therefore predicated on a play of presence and absence: "... forever present (in every act of reading) and forever absent for it is in the mother tongue."[99]

But if autobiography in French is likened by Djebar to the opening of the wound[100], the passage here to Arabic appears to effect a temporary healing: "Ces nuits de Ménacer, j'ai dormi dans ton lit, comme autrefois je me blottissais, enfant, contre la mère de mon père"

---

[97] Gayatri Spivak, "Acting Bits/Identity Talk", in Kwame Anthony Appiah and Henry Louis Gates, Jr (eds), *Identities* (Chicago: University of Chicago Press, 1995) pp. 147-81. p. 147-48.
[98] Ibid., p. 147-48.
[99] Ibid., p. 148.
[100] "Tenter l'autobiographie par les seuls mots français, c'est, sous le lent scalpel de l'autopsie à vif montrer plus que sa peau. Sa chair se desquame, semble-t-il, en lambeaux du parler d'enfance qui ne s'écrit plus. Les blessures s'ouvrent, les veines pleurent, coule le sang de soi et des autres, qui n'a jamais séché." Assia Djebar, *L'Amour, la fantasia*, p. 182.

[The nights I spent in Ménacer, I slept in your bed, just as long ago I slept as a child curled up against my father's mother] (pp. 193; 167). Representing a salutary moment of presence and harmony, this rare moment of belonging is offered to Djebar by the accepting presence of the mother figure, to whom she addresses her words:

> Là, ta voix a poursuivi le récit. Le soleil demeurait haut. Tu t'es assise, le voile rabaissé à la taille, parmi les ajoncs et les herbes de printemps. Ton visage finement ridé mais austère – une rêverie fermant légèrement ses traits – je le photographiai parmi les coquelicots... Le soleil baissa peu à peu. Nous sommes revenues dans le silence du soir. (pp. 191; 165)
>
> There, your voice took up your tale. The sun was still high. You let your veil fall around your waist and sat down among the gorse bushes and spring flowers. Your face, a network of fine wrinkles, was austere; you were lost for a moment in your own memories – I took a photograph of you among the poppies ... The sun gradually sank low in the sky. We returned in the evening silence.

This moment of harmony has a dream-like quality about it. Djebar captures the moment in a photograph, its image the ultimate evidence that she was, if only fleetingly, at one with herself, her land and her people.

Conclusion

An analysis of the impact of the semiotic on the four identified divisions of *L'Amour, la fantasia* reveals only a superficial conformity to the Kristevan model. Djebar's historical sections at first appear to conform to the symbolic/historic tendencies of phase 1 of that model. They reconstruct events framed in historic time and place, they display Algeria's desire for French recognition, and they depend on paternalistic colonialist texts. However the text manages to subvert this superficial parallelism. Djebar's increasingly subjective writing, her transposition of the relationship between France and Algeria onto the plane of desire, her fragmented style and her manipulation of symbolic time conspire to undermine any analogy with traditional "objective" historical discourse. Moreover, her manipulation of colonialist discourse reinforces rather than undermines her increasingly passionate identification with the motherland, with its overtones of subjectivity and semiotic desire.

The autobiographical sections appear to conform to the symbolic/paternal tendency as Djebar "thinks back through her fathers" and retraces her entry into the paternal language/order. However, despite the paternal filter, these sections also reveal the presence of the semiotic/maternal as absence. For although Djebar's identity is reconstructed by her entry into the paternal language, it is nevertheless marked by the absence of the mother tongue. Subjectivity is constructed in opposition to the objectifying tendency of the paternal order but also in relation to the lost maternal order – a lost order which Djebar consciously attempts to recover in the final part of the work.

Part 3 goes a long way towards achieving the Kristevan ideal of the permanent alternation of the semiotic and symbolic modalities. The original loss of maternal identification revealed in the historical/autobiographical sections is consciously redressed as Djebar "thinks back through her mothers." The semiotic becomes a constant presence existing in an alternating relationship to the symbolic. Her desire for the motherland is transposed into symbolic/social experiences rooted in historical time and place – her re/union with the "Mothers of the Revolution." The voices of these women are trapped in the signs of the paternal language but are nevertheless shot through by the maternal or semiotic, not by the rhythms and pulsations of the mother-child continuum, but by the rhythms and pulsations of the mother tongue, Arabic.

The dynamic interplay between the semiotic and the symbolic in *L'Amour, la fantasia*, especially in the final part, marks Djebar out as a writer of Kristevan credentials.

> Une alternance constante entre le temps et sa "vérité", l'identité et sa perte, l'histoire et ce qui la produit hors-temps, hors-phénomène. Dialectique impossible des deux termes, alternance permanente: jamais l'un sans l'autre. Il n'est pas sûr que quelqu'un en soit capable ici, maintenant. Peut-être une femme?[101]

Perhaps a woman? Surely Djebar.

---

[101] Julia Kristeva, *Des Chinoises*, p. 44.

In Dialogue with Cixous:
Vaste est la prison

Patriarchal Prison-Houses

Djebar and Cixous, who share the common experience of an Algerian childhood[1], come to the same conclusions about the way patriarchy constructs both language and the dynamics of human relationships. Both authors identify patriarchal society as a "prison-house", "une vaste prison", where both sexual identity and language are imprisoned within rigid oppositional structures. Their response to these linguistic and sexual structures influences their relationship to writing and their portrayal of male-female dynamics.

The form of their response is very different. Whereas Cixous presents her *sorties* both in her novels and in her "more theoretical" texts (which I will draw from), *La Jeune née* and *La Venue à l'écriture*, Djebar's response takes the form of a novel which contains three distinct stories, a love story, a historical quest and a family history.

Cixous discovers many *sorties*, or ways out from the hegemony of patriarchy. She achieves this by exploring new ideas of *écriture* and sexuality. The question I would like to explore is the following: Does Djebar find ways out of the prison-house of patriarchy and if she does, how do her *sorties* compare to those of Cixous?

I will start by looking at Cixous's analysis of the oppositionary patriarchal value system and then touch on other aspects of Cixous's thinking, which will be expanded on in the study of *Vaste est la prison*.

---

[1] Hélène Cixous, who was born in Oran on June 5, 1937, details her complex family origins as follows: "Mon père, sépharade – Espagne-Maroc-Algérie – ma mère askhenaze – Autriche-Hongrie-Tchécoslovaquie (son père) + Allemagne (sa Mère)." See Hélène Cixous (in collaboration with Catherine Clément), *La Jeune née* (Paris: UGE, 10/18, 1975), p. 244. See also Christa Stevens, "Hélène Cixous, auteur en 'algériance'", *Expressions maghrébines*, Vol. 1, No. 1 (Summer 2002), pp. 77-97, for an evaluation of the importance of Cixous' Judeo-Algerian roots to the construction of her identity and the trajectory of her writing.

Cixous and the patriarchal value-system

Cixous analyses the phenomenon of opposition at the heart of the patriarchal value system and then proceeds to challenge this opposition (which can be reduced in relational terms to the opposition of the self to the other) with an embracing of otherness or "le procès du même et de l'autre."[2]

"Sorties" begins with Cixous's well-known analysis of patriarchal binary thought. Although her analysis is derivative, not to say 'derridative', its originality lies in her identification of the process of death at work within this kind of thought. Cixous introduces it simply with the words "Où est-elle?", inviting the reader to locate woman, or rather to find the place where she has been located by the patriarchal value system:

> Où est elle?
> Activité/passivité
> Soleil/Lune
> Culture/Nature
> Jour/Nuit
> Père/Mère
> Tête/sentiment
> Intelligible/sensible
> Logos/Pathos...
> Homme
> Femme[3]

"Où est elle?" Within each of these binary oppositions woman is located as the "weaker sex" or the weaker term, "the negative, powerless instance."[4] Each opposition (active/passive, father/mother) operates as a hierarchy, replicating the underlying male/female paradigm, with its inescapable positive/negative association: "Homme/Femme ... Supérieur/Inférieur ... La pensée a toujours travaillé par opposition ... Par oppositions duelles, *hiérarchisées*."[5] According to Cixous, these opposite or binary terms are not on "equal terms", but exist within a hierarchical relationship in which death is at work, and where one term must destroy the other in order to assert its own identity, its own signification: the battle for "signifying

---

[2] Hélène Cixous, "Le Rire de la méduse", *L'Arc*, 61, pp. 39-54, p. 46.
[3] Hélène Cixous (in collaboration with Catherine Clément), *La Jeune née* (Paris: UGE 1975), p.115.
[4] Toril Moi, *Sexual/Textual Politics: Feminist Literary Theory* (London and New York: Routledge, 1985), p. 104.
[5] Hélène Cixous, *La Jeune née*, p. 115.

supremacy" is on[6]: "Champ de bataille général. Chaque fois une guerre est livrée. La mort est toujours à l'oeuvre."[7]

As well as determining the relationship between these dialectical couples, opposition is also at work within the fundamental male/female couple:

> Et tous les couples d'oppositions sont des *couples*. Est-ce que cela veut dire quelque chose? Que le logocentrisme soumette la pensée, – tous les concepts, les codes, les valeurs à un système à deux termes est-ce que c'est en rapport avec "le" couple homme/femme?[8]

So men and women are also locked together in the battle for signifying supremacy, where man's inevitable victory deprives woman, the vanquished party, of any positive identity. She exists only as an object, a receptacle for male desire, a blank page onto which he can inscribe himself: "Elle n'existe pas, elle peut ne pas être; mais il faut qu'il y en ait. De la femme, dont il ne dépend plus, il ne garde alors que cet espace, toujours vierge, matière soumise au désir qu'il veut imprimer."[9] It is this annihilation of positive identity that Cixous equates with death. And, as woman is annihilated, erased, man is constructed as the norm, "éternel-naturel"[10]:

> La mise en question de cette solidarité du logocentrisme et du phallocentrisme est aujourd'hui devenue assez pressante – la mise au jour du sort fait à la femme, de son enfouissement – pour menacer la stabilité de l'édifice masculin qui se fait passer pour éternel naturel; en faisant surgir du côté de la féminité des réflexions, des hypothèses nécessairement ruineuses pour le bastion qui détient encore l'autorité.[11]

For Cixous the challenge is to resist this logocentrism by defying the logic of binary oppositions that underpins both patriarchal ideology and the rigid concepts of identity and language that it creates. And the enemy she resists is everywhere. For patriarchy operates like an unstoppable sorting machine, sifting through all discourses and compulsively creating oppositions within them: "Partout (où) intervient une mise en ordre, une loi organise le pensable

---

[6] Ibid., p. 105.
[7] Ibid., pp. 116-17.
[8] Ibid., p. 116.
[9] Ibid., p. 118.
[10] Feminist critique usually points to patriarchy's association of *woman* to "nature". In this context, however, where Cixous refers to the *masculine* using the terms "éternel-naturel", it is in the sense of masculinity being perceived as "the eternal *norm*".
[11] Hélène Cixous, *La Jeune née*, p. 119.

par oppositions (duelles, irréconciliables; ou relevables, dialectiques)."[12]

Countering opposition with otherness

Cixous "opposes", or rather challenges this law of opposition with the concept of *différance*, where signification is achieved in relation to *the absent other*.[13] Appropriating Derrida's anti-structuralist stance, Cixous believes that meaning is not produced through a system of opposites (opposite terms by which the "higher" term is dependant on the "lower" term for its meaning) but rather through the potentially endless process of referring to other, absent signifiers: "The function or meaning of an element is never fully present because it depends on its association with other elements to which it harks back and refers forward."[14]

For Cixous *une écriture* that works by deferral rather than opposition defies the hierarchical male economy. Working on the difference, this *écriture féminine* "revel[s] in the pleasures of open-ended textuality"[15], where meaning can never be pinned down to the fixed positions of the binary strait jacket, where it is always elusive, always deferred, constantly propelled forward by the endless free play of the signifier: "dynamisés à l'infini par un incessant échangement de l'un entre l'autre sujet différent ... parcours multiple et inépuisable à milliers de rencontres et transformations du même dans l'autre et dans l'entre..."[16]

Cixous not only proposes a release from unitary meaning through the free play of the signifier; she also proposes a release from a unitary sexual identity, through her idea of bisexuality. Her answer to opposition in sexual identity is found in a new definition of bisexuality that replaces the exclusive, hierarchical relationship between "les deux sexes" with an inclusive notion of masculinity and femininity, which allows for the coexistence of the same and the other:

---

[12] Ibid., p. 116.
[13] "The word is of Derrida's own coinage and is deliberately ambiguous ... being derived from the French *différer*, which means both to 'defer, postpone, delay' and to 'differ, be different from." Ann Jefferson and David Robey (eds), *Modern Literary Theory: A Comparative Introduction* (London: Batsford, 1982), p. 115.
[14] Jefferson and David Robey (eds), *Modern Literary Theory: A Comparative Introduction*, p. 114.
[15] Ibid., p. 108.
[16] Hélène Cixous, "Le Rire de la méduse", p. 46.

> Bisexualité, c'est-à-dire repérage en soi, individuellement, de la présence, diversement manifeste et insistante selon chaque un ou une, des deux sexes, non-exclusion de la différence ni d'un sexe, et à partir de cette "permission" que l'on se donne, multiplication des effets d'inscription du désir, sur toutes les parties de mon corps et de l'autre corps.[17]

This process of the same and the other also forms the basis of Cixous's writing practice, of her *écriture féminine*. Here the positive relation to the other is associated with motherhood and childbirth as a metaphor for the writer's potential to develop beyond the self towards a creative rather than destructive relationship to the other. This openness to the other, which challenges the self-referential limits of the male economy of relations, is achieved by engaging with the unconscious (or the *other* within the self).

By submitting to the unconscious, the writer travels beyond the self-referential boundaries of the symbolic, to join with the collective unconscious (the others outside the self) to produce *une écriture de l'autre*. Because this *écriture* is located in what Cixous describes as an in-between zone, on the boundary between the symbolic and the imaginary, the writer can tune into the primeval Voice of the Mother: "La Voix, chant d'avant la loi, avant que le souffle soit coupé par le symbolique, réapproprié dans le langage sous l'autorité séparante. La plus profonde, la plus ancienne et adorable visitation"[18], thus transgressing the order of patriarchy and its Law of the Father.

Before relating Djebar's "vaste prison" to Cixous's binary prison-house, I will look at the form and content of the novel, using Cixous's conception of the subject.

A Subject is at Least a Thousand People

> ... A subject is at least a thousand people.
>
> This is why I never ask myself "who am I" (*qui suis-je?*) I ask myself "who are I?" (*qui sont-je?*) an untranslatable phrase. Who can say who I are, how many I are, which I is the most of my Is? Of course we each have a solid social identity, all the more solid and stable as all our other phases of identity are unstable, surprising. At the same time *we are all the ages, those we have been, those we will be, those we will not be*, we journey through ourselves (Joyce, Shakespeare remind us) as the child who goes snivelling to school and as the broken old man ... We: are (untranslatable). Without counting all the

---

[17] Hélène Cixous, *La Jeune née*, pp. 155-56.
[18] Ibid., p. 172.

combinations with others, *our exchanges between languages, between sexes* – our exchanges which change us, tint us with others.[19]

Vaste est la prison is divided into four parts, as follows:

Part 1: "L'effacement dans le coeur" [What is Erased in the Heart] tells the story of "*an exchange between sexes*." It is the chronicle of the thirty-something Isma's[20] infatuation with a younger man (both are Algerian – she is married at the time).

Part 2: "L'effacement sur la pierre" [Erased in Stone] is the site of "*an exchange between languages*." This second story takes the form of a historical quest dating back to the 17th century, following the journeys made by explorers to a stele on the Algerian-Tunisian border, where a mysterious script is inscribed. The script is eventually revealed to be an ancient Libyan script, from which evolved the *tifinagh* script, the written form of the Berber dialect used by the Tuareg tribe. As a language "owned" by a matriarchal society, it is dubbed *une écriture des femmes*.

Part 3: "Un silencieux désir" [A Silent Desire] is a family history where, like Cixous, Djebar identifies with those members of her family "*of all the ages*", journeying through the lives of relative past and present, concentrating on the principal female figures down the matriarchal line.

Part 4: "Le sang de l'écriture" [The blood of writing] is Djebar's response to the horror of modern-day Algeria.

The four parts of *Vaste est la prison* (introduced by a preface), corresponding to the four sections of this chapter, will be examined in relation to Cixous's ideas. I will examine the way both Djebar and Cixous address the problem of *écriture* and the way they relate oppositions in language to *oppositions between the sexes*, the main

---

[19] Hélène Cixous, Susan Sellers (ed.), *The Hélène Cixous Reader* (London: Routledge, 1994), with English preface by Hélène Cixous, pp. xvii-xxii, pp. xvii-xviii. [My emphasis]

[20] Lise Gauvin, "Assia Djebar, territoires des langues: entretien", *Littérature – L'Écrivain et ses langues*, 101 (February 1996), pp. 73-87. Although Djebar uses first-person narration in both Parts 1 and 3, in Part 3 she also occasionally refers to the narrator in the third person, as Isma. I have used the name Isma in Part 1, to avoid the clumsier term "Narrator", and the unambiguously autobiographical, Djebar. In the interview with Gauvin, Djebar refers to incidents in the Preface and Part 3 of *Vaste est la prison*, in such a way as to suggest that they are definitely autobiographical. This is not the case with Part 1, which she refers to as "l'histoire d'amour chez une femme..." Nevertheless, most critics assume that Part 1 is either autobiographical or semi-autobiographical.

theme explored in the love story. I will demonstrate how in both cases the response to the oppositionary and exclusive logic of patriarchal language and society becomes a catalyst for a search for "another" mode of relations between men and women and for "another" language which would elude that binary economy.

Writing's Silent Voice

Like Cixous, Djebar's starting-point is the association of *language* with death, although her reasons for making the association are very different. In Djebar's case, this association is not made because of the relationship between patriarchal thought and the construction of language, where "la mort est toujours à l'oeuvre", but, as we will see, because of the relationship between what Lejeune calls "le présent de l'écriture" [the present time of the act of writing] and "le passé raconté par l'écriture" [the past recounted by the writing].[21]

Cixous, like Djebar, uses the image of death in two ways in her "coming to writing." She uses *écriture* as a means of resisting death, and evokes the death of the author as the prerequisite for the coming into being of *écriture*. Cixous first comes to writing as a means of resisting not only her own death, but also the death of the other: "Ma voix repousse la mort; ma mort; ta mort; ma voix est mon autre. J'écris et tu n'es pas mort. Si j'écris, l'autre est sauf."[22] In order to prevent the death of the other, in order to write the other, the writer must die to the self: " Et je dis: il faut avoir été aimée par la mort, pour naître et passer à l'écriture."[23]

Cixous, like Djebar, refers to silence, not as in Djebar's case "le silence de l'écriture" [the silence of writing] but as the silence that precedes "l'écriture", the silence that precedes voice, or the death that precedes life: "Quand la chair se taille, se tord, se déchire, se décompose, se relève, se fait femme nouvelle-née, il y a une souffrance qu'aucun texte n'est assez doux et puissant pour accompagner d'un chant. C'est pourquoi, pendant qu'elle se meurt, – puis se naît, silence."[24] This silence that accompanies death is shattered by voice, by "le cri": "Sans elle – ma mort – je n'aurais pas

---

[21] Philippe Lejeune, *Le Pacte autobiographique* (Paris: Seuil, 1975), p. 199.
[22] Hélène Cixous (in collaboration with Annie Leclerc and Madeleine Gagnon), *La Venue à l'écriture* (Paris: UGE, 10/18, 1977), p. 12.
[23] Ibid., p. 44.
[24] Ibid., p. 42.

écrit. Pas déchiré le voile de ma gorge. Pas poussé le cri qui déchire les oreilles, qui fend les murs."[25]

In Djebar's preface, writing remains in the deadening grip of the past, it does not undo the work of death but rather replicates it. The act of writing slowly saps away the lifeblood of existence: "Longtemps j'ai cru qu'écrire c'était mourir, mourir lentement" [For a long time I believed that writing meant dying, slowly dying], the echoing effect of "longtemps" and "lentement", the assonance in "écrire", with the repeated "mourir", mimicking the effect of a slow painful death" (pp. 11; 11).[26]

"Déplier à tâtons un linceul de sable ou de soie sur ce que l'on a connu piaffant, palpitant. L'éclat de rire – gelé. Le début de sanglot – pétrifié" [... groping to unfold a shroud of sand or silk over things that one had felt trembling and pawing the ground. A burst of laughter – frozen. The beginnings of a sob – turned into stone] (pp. 11; 11). The *différance* that marks Cixous's writing relates to the continuous displacement of the signifier. The "difference" for Djebar relates to the displacement, between "le présent de l'écriture" [the present time of the act of writing] and "le passé raconté par l'écriture" [the past recounted by the writing].[27] Here again there is a hierarchical opposition between terms, for the act of writing in the present, "le présent de l'écriture", inevitably destroys "le passé raconté par l'écriture" [the past recounted by the writing]. So unlike Cixous's writing, which rejoices in an unfettered relationship with the present, Djebar's writing exists within a rigid relationship to the past, a relationship that implies the subjugation of "le passé raconté par l'écriture" [the present time of the act of writing] to "le présent de l'écriture" [the past recounted by the writing].

Writing for Djebar occupies a site of uncertainty, conveyed by images of the blind groping for the past. Writing is the site of death – images of a shroud envelop the past, distorting its text/ure with its grainy film. The binding but destructive relationship between the present site of writing and the past recounted by the writing is intensified in the syntactical and phonetic parallelism. "L'éclat de rire – gelé. Le début d'un sanglot – pétrifié" [A burst of laughter – frozen. The beginnings of a sob – turned into stone] (pp. 11; 11). The

---

[25] Ibid., p. 42.
[26] Assia Djebar, *Vaste est la prison* (Paris: Albin Michel, 1995), trans. Betsy Wing, *So Vast the Prison* (New York/Toronto/London: Seven Stories, 1988). Unless stated otherwise, all subsequent quotations in English of *Vaste est la prison* are drawn from Wing's translation.
[27] Philippe Lejeune, *Le Pacte autobiographique*, p. 199.

exuberance, vitality and movement of "piaffant, palpitant" contrasts with the coldness and inertia of "gelé, pétrifié". Laughter and tears, life in all its fullness, emptied of life as the past, already dead to the present dies a second death, becomes dead to writing.

For Djebar, the act of writing represents not only the conflict between past and present, but also the conflict between her reluctance to write, on the one hand, and the compulsion to write on the other. The site waiting to be occupied by writing is an uncertain desert, a large empty space waiting to be enveloped in darkness, in death:

> ... au pied d'une dune friable, sous le ciel immense d'un soleil couchant. Silence de l'écriture, vent du désert qui tourne sa meule inexorable, alors que ma main court, que la langue du père (langue ailleurs muée en langue paternelle) dénoue peu à peu, sûrement, les langes de l'amour mort... (pp. 11; 11)

> ... at the foot of a crumbling dune under the immense sky at sunset. The silence of writing, the desert wind turning its inexorable millstone, while my hand races and the father's language (the language now, moreover, transformed into a father tongue) slowly but surely undoes the wrapping cloths from a dead love...

The active/passive oppositional relationship is transferred onto the relationship between the active movement of writing and the literal pass/ivity of the past. The past in the mind's eye is darkened, its soundtrack silenced. Cixous also explores the relation between activity and passivity (in a productive rather than a destructive sense), as the writer consciously (actively) entreats herself to submit (passively) to the unconscious: "... c'est que la 'venue' au langage, est une fusion, une coulée en fusion, s'il y a 'intervention' de ma part c'est dans une sorte de 'position', d'acitivité-passive [sic] comme si je m'incitais: "laisse-toi faire, laisse passer l'écriture..."[28]

In the preface Djebar touches on Cixous's "inclusive" view of writing, on the opening up of self to the other, in her capacity to propel her *écriture* beyond the repressive, self-referential viewpoint of the masculine. For Djebar, however, the experience of identification with others through writing, of the multiple subject, is painful rather than liberating. "... et le murmure affaibli des aïeules loin derrière, la plainte hululante des ombres voilées flottant à l'horizon, tant de voix s'éclaboussent dans un lent vertige de deuil – alors que ma main court..." [the faint murmur of ancestors, the ululations of lament from veiled shadows floating along the horizon – while my hand races on...] (pp. 11; 12).

---

[28] Hélène Cixous, *La Venue à l'écriture*, p. 61.

Emerging on the boundaries of the desert wasteland, the voices of others, of "les aïeules" [the ancestors], impose themselves with greater insistence onto the silence, "le murmure affaibli" [the faint murmur] becoming "la plainte hululante" [the ululations of lament] and a chorus of voices "tant de voix s'éclaboussent dans un lent vertige de deuil" [so many voices spatter into a lingering vertiginous mourning], their slow, circular dance of death, "un lent vertige de deuil" [a lingering vertiginous mourning], mimicking the swirling movement of the *khamsin*, in a surreal vision of a procession of veils haunting the horizon. Writing as death is displaced by writing as escape from life: "Longtemps j'ai cru qu'écrire c'était s'enfuir, ou tout au moins se précipiter sous ce ciel immense, dans la poussière du chemin, au pied de la dune friable .... Longtemps" [For a long time I believed that writing meant getting away, or at the very least, leaping out under this immense sky, into the dust of the road along the foot of the crumbling dunes... For a long time] (pp. 11-12. 12). The text has gone full circle as the writer is propelled into the wide open site of language, where each step forward is a step back into a past progressively shrouded in darkness, situating the writer in a position of uncertainty at the boundaries of past and present.

The Problem of Segregation: All in a Word

From the problematics of writing, Djebar turns to the cutting edge of words. Djebar's relationship to one word in particular propels her closer to Cixous. For both of them recognise in this word the same process at work, the work of death. To her surprise and shock, Djebar discovers the association of the Arabic word *e'dou* (which in normal usage means enemy) with the signified *husband*, and, as a result comes to acknowledge, like Cixous, that patriarchal language is a sexual battlefield. Whereas in Cixous' work "l'ami est aussi l'ennemi"[29], in *Vaste est la prison*, "le mari devient l'ennemi." For the process of death that Cixous associates with the hierarchical relationship between man and woman finds its echo in the process of destruction that Djebar associates with the segregating force at work within her society.

Djebar finds the process of segregation at work not only in society but also in language itself. Her association between social segregation and the construction of language occurs at a particular time and place and by a process of condensation "whereby one idea or image in the

---

[29] Hélène Cixous, *La Jeune née*, p. 137.

unconscious becomes a nodal point or intersection for a whole cluster of associated feelings, primal memories and desire."[30] This process of condensation is usually associated with dreams: "In this way, especially in dreams, a single image, word or sound can evoke through its compression a whole range of repressed wishes, emotion and thoughts."[31]

The catalyst for the moment of condensation is not a dream but an everyday encounter that takes place during a visit which Djebar makes to the local *hammam*, with her mother-in-law. The atmosphere of the baths is dreamlike – the luxuriant, fragrant surroundings representing an escape from the harsh realities of the outside world:

> Le plaisir pour moi, comme beaucoup d'autres femmes, s'avivait à la sortie du bain. L'antichambre, tapissée de matelas, de nattes, où l'on vous servait à satiété oranges épluchées, grenades ouvertes et du sirop d'orgeat, devenait havre des délices. Les parfums se mêlaient au-dessus des corps des dormeuses, ou autour de celles qui, frémissantes, s'habillaient lentement tout en dévidant de menus commérages. (pp. 12; 12)
>
> Like many of the women, I felt the pleasure of the baths upon leaving them. Carpeted with mats and mattresses, the antechamber became a haven of delights where you were served peeled oranges, open pomegranates, and barley water to your heart's content. Perfume mingled above the bodies of sleeping women and engulfed the shivering ones, who slowly dressed as they spun their colourful threads of gossip.

The moment of condensation takes place at the end of the visit, as her mother-in-law tries unsuccessfully to retain one of her friends:

> Un jour, une dame opulente, la cinquantaine épanouie, les pommettes rosies de chaleur et le front auréolé d'une coiffe de taffetas blanc aux franges violacées, débita les longues formules des adieux. Ma belle-mère, qui aimait sa compagnie, voulut la retenir. – "Encore un quart d'heure, ô lumière de mon coeur!" insista-t-elle. (pp. 13; 13)
>
> One day an amply endowed lady in the splendour of her fifties, cheeks pink with heat and her forehead crowned with a white taffeta headdress fringed in shades of purple, began the lengthy formulas of farewell.
> My mother-in-law, who enjoyed her company, wanted her to stay longer.
> "Another fifteen minutes, O light of my heart," she insisted.

The friend's excuse puzzles Djebar:

---

[30] Pam Morris, *Literature and Feminism* (Oxford: Blackwell, 1993), p. 98.
[31] Ibid., p. 98.

– Certes, rétorqua la dame enveloppée de son voile immaculé et qui, pour finir, masqua tout à fait son visage dans un geste non dénué de hauteur, impossible de m'attarder aujourd'hui. L'ennemi est à la maison!
Elle sortit.
– "L'ennemi?" demandai-je, et je me tournai lentement vers ma belle-mère. (pp. 13; 13)

"Yes I am," retorted the lady through her immaculate veil. She then closed the matter by concealing her face entirely with a haughty gesture. "I cannot possibly stay later today. The enemy is at home!"
She left.
"The enemy?" I asked, slowly turning toward my mother-in-law.

The cosy atmosphere of the *hammam* is abruptly shattered by the word *e'dou* [enemy] as this signifier starts to resonate and move towards a new and threatening signified:

Ce mot, dans sa sonorité arabe, *l'e'dou*, avait écorché l'atmosphère environnante.
Ma compagne contempla, désemparée, le total étonnement qui emplissait mes yeux. Elle esquissa un sourire contraint; peut-être aussi ressentit-elle seulement en cet instant une sorte de honte.
– Oui "l'ennemi", murmura-t-elle. Ne sais-tu pas comment, dans notre ville, les femmes parlent entre elles? ... (Mon silence durait, chargé d'interrogation.) L'ennemi, eh bien, ne comprends-tu pas: elle a ainsi évoqué son mari! (pp. 13-14; 13-14)

The word *l'e'dou*, resonant in Arabic, had sounded a dissonate note.
My companion helplessly contemplated the complete astonishment that filled my eyes. She forced a half smile; perhaps she felt also at that moment a sort of shame.
"Yes, 'the enemy,'" she whispered. "Don't you know how women in our town talk among themselves?" (My silence continued thick with questions). "Don't you understand? By enemy, she meant her husband."

The moment of bewilderment is prolonged as the signifier *e'dou* hovers in space before acquiring its new signification:

– Son mari l'ennemi? Elle ne semble pas si malheureuse!
Mon interlocutrice, sur le coup, parut agacée par ma candeur.
– Son mari, mais il est comme un autre mari!... "L'ennemi", c'est une façon de dire! Je le répète: les femmes parlent ainsi entre elles depuis bien longtemps... Sans qu'ils le sachent eux!... (pp. 14; 14)

"Her husband, the enemy? She doesn't seem so unhappy!"
My naïveté suddenly seemed to irritate my mother-in-law.
"Her husband is no different from any other husband! 'Enemy' is just a manner of speaking. Women, as I said before, have called them that for ages... without the men knowing it."

Not only does the signifier *e'dou* acquire a new signified, but it acquires physical presence, becoming "torpille étrange", "flèche de silence":

> Ce mot, *l'e'dou*, que je reçus ainsi dans la moiteur de ce vestibule d'où, y débouchant presque nues, les femmes sortaient enveloppées de pied en cap, ce mot d'"ennemi" proféré dans cette chaleur émolliente, entra en moi, torpille étrange; telle une flèche de silence qui transperça le fond de mon coeur trop tendre alors. En vérité, ce simple vocable, acerbe dans sa chair arabe, vrilla indéfiniment le fond de mon âme, et donc la source de mon écriture... (pp. 14; 14)

> This word, *l'e'dou*, I first hear it this way, in the damp of the vestibule from which women arrived almost naked and left enveloped head to toe. The word *enemy*, uttered in that moist warmth, entered me, strange missile, like an arrow of silence piercing the depths of my too tender heart. In truth the simple term, bitter in its Arab flesh, bored endlessly into the depths of my soul, and thus into the source of my writing...

The warm stultifying cocoon of the surroundings is contrasted with the sudden, unexpected, propulsion and metallic hardness of "la torpille" [missile]. Here Djebar does not enter into language, but language enters into her, and ironically, the silent arrow of language mutes the source of writing. The word literally becomes flesh "dans sa chair arabe" [in its Arab flesh], its signified changing course with dizzying speed, its poisoned tip piercing her flesh. As the signified is displaced from husband to enemy, Djebar realises that language itself is a battlefield and that the destructive force of segregation is at work in the structure of language itself:

> Comme si, parce qu'une langue soudain en moi cognait l'autre, parce que la voix d'une femme, qui aurait pu être ma tante maternelle, venait secouer l'arbre de mon espérance obscure, ma quête muette de lumière et d'ombre basculait, exilée du rivage nourricier, orpheline. (pp. 14; 14)

> Suddenly one language, one tongue, struck the other inside me. The voice of a woman who could have been my maternal aunt came to shake the tree of my hidden hope. My silent quest for light and shade was thrown off balance, as if I had been exiled from the nurturing shore, orphaned.

Ironically it is the voice of a woman that drowns out the other voice, the primeval Mother/tongue voice, cutting her off from the nurturing mother-source, leaving her adrift. Not only is Isma separated from her paternal language, French, she is now also exiled from her mother tongue and has become an orphan of language. Adrift on foreign shores, bereft of hope, she is surrounded by people speaking a "foreign" language, a language from which she suddenly feels alienated and which is itself paralysed by "la désespérance depuis longtemps gelée entre les sexes" [despair long frozen in place between the sexes] (pp. 15; 15).

The maternal language, source of maternal riches, turns against her: "... la langue maternelle m'exhibait ses crocs" [the mother tongue had shown me her teeth] (pp. 15; 15). Betraying her trust, revealing its true nature, becoming threatening, violent, its bite, its divisive power killing her hope "espoir obscur", inscribing in her "une fatale amertume" [a deadly bitterness] (pp. 15; 15). Djebar's yearning for the maternal tongue is now displaced by a new yearning, the desire to find another language, which, unlike Arabic or French, does not expel her from its shores.

Looking for a Way out

Before embarking on this quest for a language that would defy the oppositional logic of patriarchal thinking, Djebar tells a love story, in which she, like Cixous, looks for a mode of relations between men and women that would defy this same logic. But is it *possible* to find a way of escaping the full force of segregation, which, with gravitational force, wrenches man and woman apart? Djebar's heroine, Isma, in any case attempts to find her own ways out or *sorties* when she embarks on her relationship with "l'Aimé." But despite Isma's attempts to defy the dynamics of segregation, the relationship ends up imprisoning her within the same oppositional dynamics from which she sought to escape. I suggest, however, that although the main body of the love story charts the failure of Isma's attempt to escape the dynamics of segregation, the structure of the text releases her from those dynamics. For although Djebar describes Isma's imprisonment within a male economy of relationships[32], both the beginning and the end of the narrative foreground her escape from that economy. But first I will examine Isma's relation with her husband whose violent ending places it comfortably within the patriarchal mould.

---

[32] Cixous makes a distinction between a male libidinal economy, which is based on a return to the self or the selfsame, with a female libidinal economy, which is traversed by the other.

Friend or foe?

At first not much seems to separate "l'Aimé" [the Beloved] from "le mari" [the husband] – for he too is "l'ami" [the friend]: "Je regardais l'époux ... Nous n'étions plus un couple, seulement deux anciens amis qui ne savent plus se parler" [I watched my husband ... We were no longer a couple, just two old friends who no longer know how to talk to each other] (pp. 51; 50). The relationship does not appear to be characterised by the battle for signifying supremacy, but more prosaically, by mutual indifference. But Isma's husband eventually crosses the enemy line, moving from a position of "ami" to "ennemi", when Isma spontaneously reveals to him her infatuation with the Beloved. "L'ami" becomes her enemy not only because she has refused his advances ("Tout en moi disait non" [Everything about me said no], pp. 83; 83) but because she is no longer as Cixous puts it in "his parenthesis", her words are no longer an echo of his needs but an affirmation of her own desire:

> ... l'ami est aussi l'ennemi. Toutes les femmes ont vécu ça, le vivent, comme je continue à le vivre. "On" lutte ensemble, oui, mais qui: un homme, et à côté de lui, chose, quelqu'un – (une femme: toujours dans sa parenthèse, toujours refoulée ou annulée en tant que femme, tolérée en tant que non-femme, "acceptée"! – et vous n'en êtes pas conscients – à condition qu'elle s'efface, qu'elle fasse l'homme, qu'elle parle l'homme et pense de même...).[33]

By threatening "l'édifice masculin", by choosing to walk out of the parenthesis, she becomes intolerable to him:

> Il finit tout le whisky. Il se dressa. Il frappa. La large baie béante derrière nous (était-ce lui auparavant, je ne sais, qui l'ouvrit?) introduisait comme l'imminence d'un dangereux courant d'air qui, pensais-je, allait risquer de me précipiter, pour un rien, dans le puits de ces dix étages... Il frappa et je ne pouvais me réfugier vers le fond, comme si la baie ouverte faisait immédiatement appel; de ses bras d'homme grand et athlétique, il me saisirait aveuglément, il me lancerait pour que j'explose au-dehors. Il frappa et je glissai au sol, une prudence extraordinairement affûtée veillant en moi pour mesurer le risque moindre ... Il insulta auparavant. Il frappa ensuite. Protéger mes yeux. Car sa folie se révélait étrange: il prétendait m'aveugler. (pp. 84-85; 85)
>
> He finished all the whiskey. He stood up. He struck. The large, wide-open French doors behind us (was he the one who opened them earlier? I don't know who did) let in something like the impending danger of a breeze that, I thought, was likely to hurl me at the drop of a hat into a ten-storey pit... He struck and I could not take refuge in

---

[33] Hélène Cixous, *La Jeune née*, p. 137.

the back of the room, as if the opening called me straight to it; this man who was large and athletic, with his man's arms would blindly seize me, would fling me so I exploded outside. He struck and I slipped to the floor, an unusually sharp sense of caution on the lookout within me to figure out what was least dangerous.
First he insulted. Then he struck. Protect my eyes. Because his frenzy was proving to be strange: He intended to blind me.

The relationship enters into the binary mode; the battle for signifying supremacy begins. As the enemy tries to ensure his victory by an act of violence, his words literally voice the work of death: "'–Femme adultère', répéta-t-il, ailleurs que dans cette ville de perdition, tu mériterais d'être lapidée!" ["Adulteress!" he repeated, "Anywhere, except this city of iniquity you would deserve to be stoned!] (pp. 85; 85). The end of "l'amitié" with her husband is signalled by this act of violence. The end of her infatuation with "l'Aimé", which opens the love story, is signalled by an act of awakening.

The Big Sleep

In Cixous's revision of Charles Perrault's archetypal fairy story, "la Belle au bois dormant", the love story is stripped bare to reveal a death story:

> Il était une fois ... et encore une fois
> Les belles dorment dans leurs bois, en attendant que les princes viennent les réveiller. Dans leurs lits, dans leurs cercueils de verre, dans leurs forêts d'enfance comme des mortes. Belles, mais passives; donc désirables: d'elles émane tout mystère. Ce sont les hommes qui aiment jouer à la poupée. Comme on le sait depuis Pygmalion. Leur vieux rêve: être dieu la mère. La meilleure mère, la deuxième, celle qui donne la deuxième naissance.
> Elle dort, elle est intacte, éternelle, absolument impuissante.[34]

Cixous's "belles" exist only as objects of desire; they are petrified into a permanent state of waiting that Cixous equates not with sleep but with death. Perrault's handsome prince is transformed by Cixous first into a divine Pygmalion, saviour and father-figure rolled into one, and then into a female deity – "dieu la mère." The female saviour gives birth to her child, Pygmalion brings his statue to life, man gives birth to woman as patriarchal relationships are revealed to mimic the ultimate power relationship: that of creator and creation.

Cixous, however, begins the story with its ending, presuming an eventual awakening from the sleep of death, transforming the fairy story into an ideological diatribe, a tale of feminist conversion:

---

[34] Ibid., p. 120.

Il était une fois...
De l'histoire qui suit on ne peut encore dire: "ce n'est qu'une histoire". Ce conte reste vrai aujourd'hui. La plupart des femmes qui sont réveillées se souviennent d'avoir dormi, d'avoir été endormies.[35]

Djebar, like Cixous, begins the love story with its ending, with the moment of awakening, implying a *sortie* from the sleep of death, a release from prison, a conversion experience. Isma emerges from a "sleep" of thirteen months, cured of her infatuation with "L'Aimé", "le coeur effacé", liberated from the grip of an all-consuming passion. The liberation functions on both literary and literal levels, since the act of writing her release itself represents a form of empowerment. Her life/story was in his hands: now his life story is in hers.

Si la femme a toujours fonctionné *"dans"* le discours de l'homme, signifiant toujours renvoyé à l'adverse signifiant qui en annihile l'énergie spécifique ... *il est temps qu'elle disloque ce "dans", qu'elle l'explose, le retourne et s'en saisisse, qu'elle le fasse sien*, le comprenant, le prenant dans sa bouche à elles, que de ses dents à elles elle lui morde la langue, qu'elle s'invente une langue pour lui rentrer dedans.[36]

Dislocation, in the case of Isma, is affirmed by the language of liberation used to describe the awakening that catapults her "dehors", outside his "emprise." She moves from a level of consciousness "dans" to another level of consciousness "dehors": "...depuis ce réveil de l'après-midi, je ne suis plus sous l'influence, je suis moi-même, pleine de vide, disponible et tranquille, affamée du dehors et sereine..." [I can see that, ever since this afternoon's awakening, I am free of influence, I am myself, full of emptiness, available and tranquil, starving for the outside and serene...] (pp. 22; 22-23). She has come out of "la prison", escaped from "inside", the spell has been broken, the image of "l'Aimé" then inscribed on her heart now blotted out. The sleepy daze of the newly awakened woman is accompanied by the indefinable awareness of a new beginning:

Que se passe-t-il? Une seconde d'incertitude; la lumière qui traverse la fenêtre est différente: non pas affaiblie, autre. Je fais effort pour comprendre peu à peu, malaisément, puis avec certitude, que quelque chose de neuf et de vulnérable à la fois, un commencement de je ne sais quoi d'étrange – en couleur, en son, en parfum, comment isoler la sensation? – que "cela" est en moi et cependant m'enveloppe. Je porte en moi un changement et j'en suis inondée. (pp. 20; 20-21)

---

[35] Ibid., pp. 119-20.
[36] Ibid., pp. 176-77. [My emphasis]

What's going on? A moment of uncertainty: the light coming through the window is different, not weaker, different. I make an effort to try to understand, then very gradually, uneasily, I sense finally with certainty, something both new and vulnerable, a beginning of something, I don't know what, something strange. It is color, sound, odour? How can I isolate the sensation? And this "something" is inside me and at the same time it envelops me. I am carrying some change inside me, and it floods through me.

Like a shining vision of truth, the revelation of new life comes in a flash of blinding light, bathing her surroundings in its glow: "Tout, autour de moi, les meubles, la bibliothèque rustique, la chambre blanche, tout apparaît irisé d'un éclairage vierge. Justement parce que en [sic] cet instant, je me sens nouvelle. Je découvre en moi une surprenante, une brusque reviviscence" [Everything around me, the furniture, the rustic library, the white room, everything seems lit by some pure iridescence. All because in that instant I feel new. I discover an amazing and abrupt revitalization within] (pp. 21; 21). As her inner turmoil recedes, the material world (re)emerges and she basks in its physical presence: "Je ne fais pas de projet, je vais et je viens pour le plaisir de me mouvoir; je m'habille pour sentir, sous l'étoffe froide, mes jambes, mes bras, mes épaules, ma peau" [I make no plans, I move about for the sheer pleasure of it. I dress in order to feel my legs, my arms, my shoulders, my skin beneath the cool cloth] (pp. 21; 21).

This *sortie* into the world is lived with all the joy of a rebirth, the joy of a newly born woman. Like a newborn baby, she has to adjust to the new world that she suddenly discovers around her: "...j'écarquille les yeux. Une béance de l'atmosphère se creuse autour de moi; je suis toujours assise, encore étourdie. La strie d'une poussière dorée scintille en biais devant les volets baissés. S'installe un gel concerté des choses" [I stare wide-eyed. Space gapes open around me; I sit, still dazed. In front of the shutters a diagonal strip of golden dust sparkles. Everything fits] (pp. 21; 21). Like a newborn baby, she slowly starts to recognise sound, touch, movement and colour:

> Tout ce temps, je ne peux oublier l'étrangeté, le miracle de mon réveil, dans la bibliothèque. J'apprends peu à peu à m'habiter, dans un début de stabilité paisible: l'épaisseur rassurante des autres réaffluent, ainsi que le poids des choses que je vérifie lentement, comme si leur volume jusque-là faisait obstacle ... Entendre et se laisser porter par les écharpes de couleurs, les sursauts de voix proches, l'impétuosité dans le désordre et son jaillissement! (pp. 22, 23; 22, 23)

All this time I cannot forget the strangeness, the miracle of my awakening in the library. I gradually learn how to inhabit myself, in the first stages of calm stability: the reassuring density of others floods back as well as the weight of things. I slowly confirm this for myself as if, before, their physical shape and substance had been their mere obstructions ... To hear and let oneself be carried along by nearby voices, colors, surging impetuously in disorder, gushing, springing!

Unlike Cixous's passive sleeping beauties who resist the present, Isma is no longer a prisoner of the past. She has been propelled into active time and has recovered a sense of self. *Born again*, she has arisen from the sleep of death to a new awareness of self and of the world around her. In the light of this life-changing experience, the love story in *Vaste est la prison*, in the words of Philippe Lejeune, can be viewed as belonging to "les autobiographies religieuses de la conversion." So from *La Jeune née* to Lejeune...

> Conversion à rebours, ici, cela va sans dire. Mais peu importe. Le nouveau converti examine ses erreurs passées à la lumière des vérités qu'il a conquises. ... le livre est un règlement de comptes. Mais en même temps, c'est un plaidoyer invoquant les "circonstances atténuantes..."[37]

As in Lejeune's interpretation of Sartre's *Les Mots*, the main body of Djebar's love story, following the retrospective "awakening", is cast in the light of a conversion experience, allowing the new "convert" to examine her "past mistakes" in the light of her subsequent enlightenment. Like Sartre, Djebar also invokes "attenuating circumstances" with regard to Isma's involvement with "l'Aimé." She does this not by appealing to outward circumstances, but by foregrounding the *inner compulsion* that motivated Isma's connection with "L'Aimé", namely the desire to find a relationship which would defy the oppositional logistics of the segregated society she inhabited – a desire we find echoed in the words of Cixous:

> Il doit y avoir des modes de relation hétérogènes à la tradition ordonnée par l'économie masculine. Je cherche donc, de façon pressante et plus angoissée, une scène où produirait un type d'échange qui serait différent, un désir tel qu'il ne serait pas complice de la vieille histoire de la mort.[38]

New man, new mode?

Isma presents us with a man who seems like an ideal candidate for a partner with whom to embark on her quest for a new mode of relations with the opposite sex. "L'Aimé" does not conform to the

---

[37] Philippe Lejeune, *Le Pacte autobiographique*, p. 206.
[38] Hélène Cixous, *La Jeune née*, p. 143.

pattern of masculinity prescribed by patriarchy, and so appears to represent Isma's best hope of finding a relationship that subverts the male economy of relationships. Djebar's description of Isma's first "close encounter" with him confirms this:

> ... cette face recelait une paix étrange, ce physique de jeune homme *frêle*, ce regard clair avec des lueurs d'acier le traversant quand il parlait de sa voix hachée de drogué (drogué de musique, ou de nostalgie, ou de haschisch), cet homme – pas encore la trentaine, l'ombre de son adolescence fêlée, de sa jeunesse froissée l'enrobant encore – portait au-devant moi son *secret*. ... *le saccage de cet homme, et l'absence et le rêve de l'absence* ... *Habitait en cette face la poésie*, la jeunesse aussi qui trop souvent est étrangère à la poésie. (pp. 27, 28; 27, 28)

> ... I felt this face harbored a strange peace. In his frail young man's build, in the bright gaze with steely glints flickering across it when he spoke in the broken voice of a drug user (whether music, nostalgia, or hashish was the drug), this man – not yet in this thirties, still wearing hints of his slightly crazy adolescence and the offended air of youth – lay his secret before me ... *the devastation within this man, the sense of absence, and the dream of that absence ... There was poetry dwelling in this face* (too often youth has no connection with poetry). [My emphasis]

Djebar foregrounds those aspects of "l'Aimé", which subvert the traditional code. Physically, he is slight and slim, with delicate features, and a sunken look; emotionally, he is a complex and poetic being. A far cry from the macho fairy tale prince of Perrault's tale, "L'Aimé" can rather be identified with Cixous's "exceptions", a rare group of men and women who have defied the laws of patriarchy by accepting "la composante de l'autre sexe."[39]

> Il y a des *exceptions*. Il y en a toujours eu, ce sont ces êtres incertains, *poétiques*, qui ne se sont pas laissés réduire à l'état de mannequins codés par le refoulement impitoyable de la composante homosexuelle. Hommes ou femmes, êtres complexes, mobiles, ouverts. D'admettre la composante de l'autre sexe les rend à la fois beaucoup plus riches, plusieurs, forts et dans la mesure de cette mobilité, très fragiles.[40]

Isma's relationship with "L'Aimé" becomes an experimental field in which she will attempt to find a mode of relation that defies the oppositionary logistics of segregation. In Cixous's case, the answer to the opposition between the male/female couple is found in her redefinition of the term bisexuality, which allows for masculinity and

---

[39] Ibid., p. 153.
[40] Ibid., p. 153. [My emphasis]

femininity to exist in an inclusive rather than an exclusive or oppositionary relation to each other:

> Bisexualité, c'est-à-dire repérage en soi, individuellement, de la présence, diversement manifeste et insistante selon chaque un ou une, des deux sexes, non-exclusion de la différence ni d'un sexe, et à partir de cette "permission" que l'on se donne, multiplication des effets d'inscription du désir, sur toutes les parties de mon corps et de l'autre corps.[41]

But can Isma find her own solution to the dividing wall erected by Islam between the sexes? Is it possible to find a way of escaping the full force of segregation, which, with gravitational force, wrenches man and woman apart? At the beginning of her relationship with "l'Aimé", Isma in any case attempts to find her own ways out or *sorties*. But how? She does so by *projecting a succession of new roles* onto her Beloved, each of which places him outside the magnetic field of segregation. As the male acquaintance of a married woman, he falls squarely within this field, but in the new roles Isma assigns to him, he is propelled outside its pull.

In the first instance, Isma imagines "L'Aimé" to be a childhood friend. In what begins as a sexually charged scene, set in the Beloved's garden, Isma imagines him first as lover ("s'il y a jouissance, y aura-t-il jouissance .... Tout à l'heure, un peu plus tard dans la chambre", [if I come, will I come?... Soon, a bit later, in the bedroom], pp. 34; 34), but then suddenly refigures him as childhood companion: "Comme c'est bon l'enfance à deux!', me suis-je soudain avoué, interloquée de ma découverte (du coup j'oublie de parer, je perds, fais semblant de le regretter, je suis si loin en arrière!). Ma surprise grandit: Vais-je revivre un passé englouti? Me trouver dans l'enfance avec toi? Est-ce cela tout le mystère?" ["How much fun it is, being children together!" I suddenly confess, taken aback by my discovery (with the result that I forget to parry, I lose, pretend to be sorry, I'm so far behind!) My surprise increases: *Am I going to relive a past I never knew? Find myself in childhood with you? Is that the whole mystery?*] (pp. 34 35; 34).

The build up of sexual tension is suddenly displaced by a yearning for the freedoms of past innocence, for the golden age when the wall of segregation was not yet erected: "Vais-je revivre un passé englouti? Me trouver dans l'enfance avec toi? Est-ce cela tout le mystère? ... je me crois âgée de six ans, de dix, tu es mon compagnon de jeu, ce jardin devient celui du village où j'ai vécu fillette..." [*Am I going to*

---

[41] Ibid., pp. 155-56.

relive a past I never knew? Find myself in childhood with you? Is that the whole mystery? ... I think I am six or ten years old, you are my playmate, this yard becomes the one in the village where I lived as a little girl...] (pp. 34, 35; 34, 35). The Beloved's Garden is transformed into a latter-day garden of Eden as the sexual divide imposed by the Law of Islam is defied by a return to an imaginary past, and to a time and space *before* segregation: "...tout amour n'est-il pas retour au royaume premier, cet éden, puisque je n'avais pu autrefois le connaître (les interdits de mon éducation musulmane ayant fonctionné doublement)" [Is every love not a return to the first realm, that Eden? Since I could not have known him before (the prohibitions of my Muslim education having operated in two ways)] (pp. 35; 35).

This first attempt to defy the strictures of segregation is thus achieved by a return to a time of *imaginary* harmony. Isma, however, soon changes tack, substituting the image of a *paternal cousin* to that of childhood friend. For, as Isma comes to realise, even young children of the opposite sex would be subject to the law of segregation. Only a young cousin could escape its dualistic force, celebrated by Islam as a miracle:

> Everything is double and that is the sign of the divine miracle. Bivalence is the will of God, and sexuality, which is the relating of male and female, is merely a particular case of an absolutely universal divine wish ... A view of the world based on bivalence and dual relations emerges from the Quran: opposition of contraries, alternation of the various, the coming into being of all things, love, causality, surrection and resurrection, order and call and, in the last analysis, prayer (*qanut*) ... It is no accident that the quranic text is placed under the sign of the Sign and that the word *aya* should recur in it so frequently. This is because all signs (*aya*) taken together sing the praise of the Lord by describing the miracle of opposition and relation, order and call. It may even be said that sexuality, by virtue of the central, universal position it occupies in the process of renewal of creation, is a sign of signs, an '*ayat al-ayat*'.[42]

In this second projection, that of paternal cousin, it is the *closeness* of the bonds of kinship, rather than the abolishment of symbolic time, which now works against the separation between the sexes. The context is now their shared workplace, where the couple makes contact by telephone. Characterised by the exaggerated intimacy of the telephone medium and the thrill of shared secrets, their conversations recall the innocent banter of youth. This illusory

---

[42] Abdelwahab Bouhdiba, *Sexuality in Islam*, trans. Alan Sheridan (London: Routledge and Kegan Paul, 1985), p. 7.

intimacy prompts Isma to reveal to "l'Aimé" her visualisation of him as "le cousin paternel":

> Il me semblait tout à l'heure que, dans mon coin de la pièce assombrie, je chuchotais à l'adresse de mon cousin germain, à l'autre bout!
> Il murmura, amusé:
> – Ainsi, je suis votre cousin germain! Bien content de cette alliance! (pp. 41; 40)
>
> "... It seemed to me just now that I was whispering from my corner of the darkened room to my first cousin at the other end!"
> He murmured, amused: "So I'm your first cousin! Pleased to discover the bond!

But this projection is soon discarded in favour of that of *maternal cousin*, displacing the notion of marriage of convenience, "les mariages d'intérêts", associated with the marriage of paternal cousins, with that of disinterested love, associated with the relationship of maternal cousins:

> – Vous seriez le fils de mon oncle paternel? ... Non ce n'est pas possible, je viens de rappeler que mon père est le seul fils, qu'il a perdu son frère adolescent, dans un accident d'autocar, il y a longtemps de cela! Vous seriez plutôt le fils de mon oncle maternel! Vous savez bien, la branche paternelle compte pour l'héritage, et donc pour les mariages d'intérêts, tandis que la ligne maternelle, par contre, est celle de la tendresse, des sentiments, de...
> J'allais ajouter "de l'amour"... (pp. 41; 40)
>
> "Could you be my paternal uncle's son? (that is what I had just said in Arabic). No, it's not possible. I've just remembered that my father is the only son, because he lost his adolescent brother in a bus accident a long time ago. You might be the son of my maternal uncle, though! You know that the paternal branch is what counts for inheritance, and consequently, in a marriage for money, whereas the maternal line is, on the other hand, the line of tender emotions, affection, and..."
> I was going to add "love"...

Djebar moves from a conception of the relationship based on inheritance, interest and property (paternal cousin), to one based on loving and giving (maternal cousin), symbolising a transition from Cixous's Realm of the *Proper* to her Realm of the *Gift*. The notion of the paternal cousin is no longer acceptable because of its association with what Cixous terms "L'Empire du Propre", the masculine value system, based on a practice of returns: "'Revenir': l'économie est fondée sur quelque chose qui s'appelle le revenu. Si un homme dépense, c'est à condition que ça revienne."[43]

The masculine law of return orders the Islamic marriage system[44], assuring the return of property to (or the preserving of property within) the paternal family. In this sense it can be regarded as a form of self-preservation, whose root-cause is identified by Cixous as fear: "L'Empire du Propre, la culture fonctionne à l'appropriation qui est articulée, agie par la crainte de l'homme classique, de se voir exproprié..."[45] By contrast, the relationship of maternal cousins, like the Realm of the *Gift*, is free from self-interest:

Elle aussi donne pour. Elle aussi donnant se donne – plaisir, bonheur, valeur augmentée, image rehaussée d'elle-même. Mais ne cherche pas "à rentrer dans ses frais." Elle peut ne pas revenir à elle, ne se posant jamais, se répandant, allant partout à l'autre. Elle ne fuit pas l'extrême; n'est pas l'être-de-la-fin (du but); mais de la portée ... S'il y a un "propre" de la femme, c'est paradoxalement sa capacité de se dé-proprier sans calcul...[46]

By associating Isma's relationship with disinterested love, with the Realm of the *Gift*, Djebar is visualising it in terms that defy the implacable masculine law of return. The image of the maternal cousin thus represents yet another attempt to defy the male economy of relations and the logic of segregation.

However, all Isma's reformulations of her relationship with "L'Aimé" remain in the realm of imaginary harmony, because they represent an appeal to an *imagined* past or to an *imagined* relationship, and because they do not transform the symbolic – they leave the realities of the social dynamics in which the relationship is played out, unchanged. And, unlike *Cixous's* bisexuality, which is proffered as a means of increasing desire ("multiplication des effets d'inscription du désir"[47]), Djebar's imaginary harmony between the sexes is achieved *at the expense* of desire: the imagined asexual bonds of early friendship and kinship artificially circumvent, but do not *transform* the sexualised oppositions imposed by patriarchy. What remains is a triangulated "virtual" relationship, mediated by an artificially imposed imagined third party, whether young friend or maternal cousin.

---

[43] Hélène Cixous, "Le Sexe ou la tête?", *Les Cahiers du GRIF*, 13 (1976), pp. 5-15, p.11.
[44] Marriages between cousins are still relatively common in the Arab world, and have not acquired the connotations of Western taboos on the subject.
[45] Hélène Cixous, "Le Sexe ou la tête?", p. 11.
[46] Hélène Cixous, *La Jeune née*, pp. 161-62.
[47] Ibid., pp. 155-56.

Reversing the roles; retaining the power-dynamics

As "l'Aimé" continues to undergo various transformations in Isma's imagination, the relationship takes on a life of its own. Not only does Isma project labels onto him, but she projects thoughts into his mind, and puts words into his mouth. One reason for this is "l'Aimé's" inherent passivity. He takes little initiative either in speech or in conversation. His lack of agency and natural reticence in speech creates a zone of ambiguity, silence and inertia, which Isma interprets at will:

> Je sais qu'il s'étonne, en ce moment, que, au cours de toute la soirée, ainsi que durant notre station devant le crépuscule sur la plage, "rien, finalement, ne se soit passé entre nous!"
> Se dit-il vraiment ces mots ordinaires? Ou simplement en a-t-il la pensée abstraite, je le sens confusément à son regard quelque peu amusé posé sur moi avec indulgence, et une tendresse diffuse – celle-ci n'ayant rien à voir avec la moire de mon trouble que je parviens à dissimuler. (pp. 91; 92)

> I know that he is amazed now that, during the entire evening, as well as during the time we sat there before the twilight on the beach, *nothing in the end happened between us!*
> Does he really say these ordinary words? Or did he just think it in the abstract? I feel it vaguely in the somewhat amused, indulgent look he gives me and a diffuse tenderness – which has nothing to do with the changeable fabric of the turmoil I am managing to hide.

Increasingly, Isma becomes the active half of the relationship. In speech this manifests itself in the repeated use of the imperative, reinforcing the fact that not only their meetings, but also the thrust of their conversations take place at her initiative.

> – Vous êtes seul? aurais-je demandé.
> – Oui!
> – Bavardons! (pp. 38; 37-38)

> "Are you alone?" I would have asked.
> "Yes!"
> "Let's talk!"

Despite this reversal of active/passive roles, the power dynamics remain the same as in Cixous's revised story.[48] For it is Isma who succumbs to "l'Aimé's" spell, and "l'Aimé" who has power over her. And, as Isma senses the beginnings of "l'Aimé's" retreat from the

---

[48] In the context of the binary oppositions, Cixous encourages woman to resist the passive stereotype. In the context of *écriture*, however, passivity, in the sense of the passive submission to the unconscious, is encouraged (see *La Venue à l'écriture*, p. 61).

relationship, she falls further under his spell. No longer attempting to break down the barriers between them, she now elevates him to a role which Cixous identifies as "l'homme-Dieu": "Il faut dire qu'il y a toujours eu un dieu ou un autre, embusqué au bon endroit, avec son allure rassurante d'énigme personnifiée."[49] Like Cixous's man-God, "L'Aimé" retains an aura of mystery, remains an enigma: "cet homme ... portait au-devant de moi son secret" [this man ... lay his secret before me] (pp. 27; 27).

While pointing out the mortal danger of this type of wish fulfilment, Cixous demonstrates the lengths to which woman will go to keep believing in the dream, the dream of salvation through man:

> Oui, pendant la moitié du chemin de ta vie, tu as prouvé tous les jours qu'il y avait du vrai dans cette conception. Non sans mal. Que de difficultés tu as eues à rendre vraie au moins personnellement cette "vérité"! Les paniques, les affres, chaque fois qu'une source a séché; chaque fois qu'un dieu t'a confié que, fatigué de nourrir, il se voyait obligé de t'avouer à quel point il était capable de mortalité.[50]

Before the revelation of "l'Aimé's" own mortality, Isma endures "the anguish, the panics" of the source drying up, of the Beloved's absence from her life. She becomes the languishing "female", whose reflection we find in James Joyce's "Molly":

> "Bridebed, childbed, bed of death": lit de noces, lit d'accouchée, lit de mort c'est le trajet de la femme qui s'inscrit ainsi de lit en lit dans *l'Ulysse* de Joyce... lit de Molly épouse, adultère, cadre d'une infinie rêverie érotique, périple des réminiscences. Elle erre, mais couchée. En rêve. Rumine. Se parle à elle-même. Voyage de la femme: en tant que *corps*. Comme si, séparée de l'extérieur où se font les échanges culturels, à l'écart de la scène sociale où il s'agit de l'Histoire, elle était destinée à être, dans le partage que les hommes instituent, la moitié non-sociale, non-politique, non-humaine dans la structure vivante, côté nature bien sûr, à l'écoute inlassable de ce qui se passe à l'intérieur, de son ventre, de sa "maison". En rapport immédiat avec ses appétits, ses affects.[51]

Like her literary sister, Isma lies on the bed of death, sapped of her energies, separated from the outside world and locked in the world of inner torment:

> Dans ma demeure le lendemain, allongée et inactive, tant la souffrance de l'absence me rongeait – comme j'aurais souhaité, à la place, subir un mal de dents sournois ou me paralysant la face de son intensité, au moins bénéficierais-je d'une anesthésie–, je ne me sentais

---

[49] Hélène Cixous, *La* (Paris: Gallimard, 1976), p. 255.
[50] Ibid., p. 253.
[51] Hélène Cixous, *La Jeune née*, p. 121.

plus assez forte pour me tenir simplement debout. Pourrais-je aller le lendemain à mes cours? ... Je finissais par me traîner dans l'appartement vide: le temps se suspendait comme au théâtre, au nom d'une fatalité a priori décrétée. (pp. 75; 75)

The next day at home, stretched out, inactive, I was so devoured by the pain of absence that I did not feel strong enough to stand up – how much I would have preferred having a toothache, a sneaky, low-level one or the kind that paralyses your face with its intensity, at least there would be some anaesthetic that would do some good! Would I be able to go to my classes tomorrow? ... I ended up hanging around in the empty apartment: like in the theatre, where time is suspended while you await a fated decided in advance.

However the spell is broken when "l'Aimé", like all men-God, eventually reveals his mortality. This development comes about not so much as a result of the revelation of his physical weakness (in the face of her husband's defiance), but as a consequence of the exposure of his moral weakness. It is the sight of his back, turning away from him, turning away from her, that constitutes the moment of elucidation: "Ensuite j'ai fixé son dos. Je veux dire: le dos de celui qui m'occupait l'âme, qui me griffait le coeur depuis des mois et des mois. Le dos fuyant" [Then I looked straight at his back. I mean the back of the man who occupied my soul, who for months and months had been clawing at my heart. A fleeing back] (pp. 102-103; 104). This act of cowardice strikes at her inner being, where an inner voice takes over, shattering her illusions: "Une voix en moi, blanche: 'J'ai aimé un enfant, un adolescent, un jeune frère, un cousin, pas un homme. Je ne le savais pas encore'" [Inside me a colorless voice. *I loved a child, an adolescent, a young brother, a cousin, not a man. I did not know it yet*] (pp. 103; 104-105). The God has revealed his mortality: not even a man, he is nothing but a child.

Rather than curing her completely of her illusory faith, the experience returns her to the bed of death: "Une heure après, je m'écroulais dans la chambre de ma fille; seule. Sur le matelas, à même le sol. Je ne quittais plus cette place. Une journée; peut-être deux. Je gisais. Je fixais devant moi le dos de l'Aimé – et je me disais 'autrefois l'Aimé', puisque j'avais vu son dos" [An hour later I collapsed in my daughter's room. Onto the mattress on the floor. Alone. I was not leaving this place anymore. One day, maybe two, I lay there. I was starting at my Beloved's back before me – and because I had seen his back, I said to myself he was "my formerly Beloved"] (pp. 104; 105).

Unable to find a relationship that would escape the laws of patriarchal relations, Isma is imprisoned first within her marriage and then by her affair. She has been doubly overpowered, first by violence and then by infatuation. Her attempts to defy the binary modes of relation have ended in failure. But although Djebar chronicles Isma's eventual release from the prison-house of relationships (at the beginning of her narrative), there Isma is released from the infatuation – the relationship itself was never liberated from the patriarchal mode of relations. It is only at the end of her narrative, where Isma recounts a final meeting with "L'Aimé" several years after the end of the affair, that Isma finds a way of reconceptualising it outside the male economy of relations. But before entering this "bisexual" mode, Isma first reverses the paradigm, and establishes a position of dominance over him.

Towards the final *sortie*

Isma's final meeting with "l'Aimé" at the railway station, on the day of his return from a year of "co-opération" abroad, is presented as magical encounter, orchestrated by fate: "Avec l'Aimé – enfin, 'l'autrefois aimé' – , une autre rencontre eut lieu. Sur une scène vaste: comme si notre face-à-face avait été l'objet de préparations secrètes ordonnancées par un magicien" [The Beloved – really, "the formerly beloved" – and I had yet another encounter. On a vast stage, as if our coming face-to-face were something arranged secretly in advance by a magician] (pp. 114; 116).

In this finale of the relationship, a dizzying sequence of relations is presented to us. First, it appears that "l'Aimé" is reinstated in her emotions: "A mi-chemin de ce trajet, je le reconnus: lui, l'Aimé avec passion, 'l'Aimé' pensai-je, et non 'l'autrefois aimé'" [Halfway to where I was going, I recognized him: It was he, the passionately Beloved, *the Beloved*, I thought, *not "the formerly beloved"*] (pp. 115; 117). But the balance of power has changed, the meeting is marked by a dramatic shift in her conceptualisation of the relationship: Images of Pygmalion bringing Galatea to life, of Perrault's prince kissing life into the princess, of man, "dieu la mère", giving birth to his creation, woman, all dissolve – as Galatea, the princess and the newly born child take power into their own hands. It is Isma who is now taking on the role of "dieu la mère", looking on benevolently at the child-man she helped to "create."[52]

> Mais je le sentis soudain – à moins que je ne le comprisse plutôt en le quittant – , mon coeur s'emplissait d'un attendrissement véritablement

---

[52] Ibid., p. 120.

maternel: il était devenu un homme vigoureux et séduisant! ... "Je l'aime, me dis-je, comme une jeune mère! Comme si, bien qu'il fût loin de moi, j'avais contribué à le transformer, à l'amener à cet état de maturité! (pp. 116; 118)

Suddenly, then I was aware – unless rather, it was only after I left him that I understood this – that seeing him thus grown into a vigorous and seductive man my heart was filling with love that was really maternal! ... *I love him*, I said to myself, *like a young mother! As if, even though he was far away, I had contributed to transforming him, to bringing him to this mature state!*

But the child Isma has begotten suddenly becomes an adult, in images displacing the intensity of labour with the intimacy of sexuality:

Et cet homme, ni étranger ni en moi, comme soudain enfanté, quoique adulte, de moi, soudain moi tremblant contre sa poitrine, moi pelotonnée entre sa chemise et sa peau, moi tout entière contre le profil de son visage tanné par le soleil, moi sa voix vibrante dans mon cou, moi ses doigts contre ma joue, moi regardée par lui et aussitôt après, allant me contempler pour me voir par ses yeux dans le miroir, tenter de surprendre le visage qu'il venait de voir, comment il le voyait, ce "moi" étranger et autre, devenant pour la première fois à cet instant même, précisément grâce à cette translation de la vision de l'autre. (pp. 116; 118-19)

And that man, who was neither foreign to me nor someone inside me, as if I had suddenly given birth to him, almost an adult; me suddenly trembling against his chest, me curled up between his shirt and his skin, me all of close against the profile of his face tanned by the sun, me his voice vibrant within my neck, me his fingers on my face, me gazed upon my him and immediately afterward going to look at myself to see me through his eyes in the mirror, trying to catch sight of the face he had just seen, as he saw it, this "me", a stranger and another, becoming me for the first time in that very instant, precisely because of this translation through the vision of the other.

It is as if this fantastic coalescence finally achieves the bisexuality of Cixous, the coexistence of same and other, "ce 'moi' étranger et autre, devenant pour la première fois moi à cet instant même, précisément grâce à cette translation de la vision de l'autre." As Isma and "l'Aimé" come together in a dynamised finale, Cixous's vision of *écriture* harmonises with Djebar's vision of desire:

Admettre qu'écrire [que le désir] c'est justement travailler (dans) l'entre, interroger le procès du même *et* de l'autre sans lequel rien ne vit, défaire le travail de la mort, c'est d'abord vouloir le deux, et les deux, l'ensemble de l'un et de l'autre non pas figés dans des

séquences de lutte et d'expulsion ou autre mise à mort, mais
dynamisés à l'infini par un incessant échangement...[53]

This magical harmonised relation of self and other is displaced onto the ultimate image of proximity, self next to other:

> Lui ni étranger ni en moi, mais si près, le plus près possible de moi, sans me frôler, voulant pourtant m'atteindre et risquant de me toucher, l'homme me devenait le plus proche parent, il s'installait dans la vacance originelle, celle que les femmes de la tribu avaient saccagée autour de moi, dès mon enfance et avant ma nubilité, tandis que s'esquissait le premier pas de ma vacillante liberté.
> Lui, mon plus proche; l'Aimé. (pp. 116-17; 119)
>
> He, neither foreign to me nor inside me, but so close, as close as possible to me, without touching me, but still wanting to reach me and taking the risk of touching me, the man became my closest relative, he moved into the primary vacancy laid waste around me by the women of the tribe, from the days of my childhood and before I reached nubility, while I took the first shaky step of my freedom.
> Him, the one closest to me; my Beloved.

In these sexualised images of proximity, the reference to familial ties now foregrounds the *physicality* of blood relations, rather than the asexuality of family bonds. Finally healing the empty inner spaces of the ravages of segregation, this new-found intimacy creates a site beyond patriarchy, a place where Isma can start to walk toward freedom and where man and woman may finally be released from *la vaste prison*.

Ecriture des Femmes/Ecriture Féminine

The love story of Part 1 is displaced in Part 2 by a historical narrative centred on the Berber script, which has also been referred to as "une écriture des femmes."[54] Having rejected patriarchal language because of its oppositionary/segregating properties, both Cixous and Djebar turn to another language – Cixous explores *une écriture féminine* whereas Djebar reappropriates *une écriture des femmes*.

In this section I will compare two very different forms of *écriture*, one a writing practice, the other the written form of a "specific" language, Berber, and assess whether Djebar's *écriture des femmes*, like Cixous's *écriture féminine*, represents *une sortie* from the patriarchal prison-house of language.

---

[53] Hélène Cixous, 'Le Rire de la méduse', p. 46. [My addition]
[54] Lise Gauvin, "Assia Djebar, territoires des langues: entretien", p. 76. While it is Gauvin who coins the phrase, Djebar's reply confirms her interpretation.

In comparing the two *écritures*, I suggest that despite their fundamental differences, there are also distant echoes to be heard between them.

Proliferation of languages

Both *écritures* can be located at the locus of the repressed. In Djebar's case, the repression of the Berber language is represented by absence or erasure, by "l'effacement sur la pierre."[55] This script has been erased not only from the stone but also from historical memory. The stone refers to a historical monument, a stele located at Dougga, on the Algerian-Tunisian border, which was discovered and rediscovered at various points during the 17th and 18th centuries, by Western travellers and archaeologists. These explorers (all male) either fail to identify the script at all or identify it incorrectly. The script is eventually revealed to be an ancient Libyan script, from which evolved the *tifinagh* script, the written form of the Berber dialect used by the Tuareg tribe. But why the Berber language? Djebar explains:

> Parce qu'il y a trois langues dans la culture algérienne. Il y a l'arabe depuis quatorze siècles avec sa diglossie, avec son aspect populaire et son aspect littéraire ... Une nation, c'est tout un faisceau de langues et cela est vrai plus particulièrement pour l'Algérie. En dehors de ce territoire de l'arabe, il y a donc la langue berbère qui était la langue de ma grand-mère mais dans mon adolescence j'étais persuadée que c'était une langue orale, qu'elle n'avait pas d'alphabet.

> Because there are three languages in Algerian culture. For fourteen centuries, there has been Arabic with its dualism, its everyday and literary versions. A nation is a whole kaleidoscope of languages and this is especially true of Algeria. Beyond the territory claimed by Arabic, there is the Berber language, which was my grandmother's tongue although as a teenager I thought it was an oral language, that it did not have an alphabet.[56]

Strangely enough, Cixous and Djebar share the same experience with their mother and grandmother tongues respectively, namely the belief that these languages did not exist in written form: "Effroi le jour tardif où j'ai découvert que l'allemand, ça s'écrit ... Tenter de faire de la langue primitive, de la chair du souffle, une langue-objet. Ma lalemande!"[57]

---

[55] "L'effacement sur la pierre" is the title of Part 2.
[56] Lise Gauvin, "Assia Djebar, territoires des langues: entretien", p. 74. My translation.
[57] Hélène Cixous, *La Venue à l'écriture*, p. 29.

Cixous also writes about being caught not *between* but *with* three languages [langues], the subject in this case being herself (as opposed to the nation!), as she puts in an appearance at the doctor's complaining of a sore throat, which is preventing her from writing:

> – Alors, me dit le docteur, on veut écrire?
> – Un peu mal à la gorge, dis-je, angineuse d'épouvante...
> – Ouvrez la bouche, montrez ça.
> J'ouvre la bouche, je fais Ach, je tire la langue. J'en ai trois. Trois langues?[58]

Why three "langues"? Cixous is also caught between three languages, French, German and English[59], but here she is also making a humorous point about a serious issue, that of woman's mutism. Woman has been forced to hold her tongue (in): "Ne lui dis pas, ne lui dis pas. Il te coupera les langues..."[60] But inside her mouth the tongues (languages) proliferate, and we return to the theme of repression. The more these "langues" are repressed, the more they abound or multiply: "Et encore il ne sait pas que j'en ai une ou deux qui ne sont pas accrochées là, mais peut-être une seule mais changeante et multipliante."[61]

In her journey towards writing, Cixous dares to open her mouth, to stick out her multiple tongue(s), and to write the world with the contours of her now cosmic organ: "Les eaux du monde s'écoulent de mes yeux, je lave mes peuples dans mon désespoir, je les baigne, je les lèche avec mon amour..."[62] The writing practice which Cixous develops counters woman's learned instinct to hold (the tongue) in: "Car, à une 'femme', toute empreinte par l'héritage socio-culturel, on a inculqué l'esprit de 'retenue.'"[63] Cixous encourages if not implores the writer not to hold back but to let go: "Lâche-toi! Lâche tout! Perds tout! ... La condition à laquelle commencer à écrire devient nécessaire – (et) – possible: *tout perdre*, avoir une fois tout perdu."[64]

Cixous's *écriture féminine* also engages with the locus of the repressed, in the sense that it obeys the call to let go, to abandon the illusion of conscious intellectual control, and to open itself up to the unconscious as the site of "that which has been repressed by the brutal

---

[58] Ibid., p. 38-39.
[59] Hélène Cixous wrote her doctoral thesis on James Joyce and has been a Professor of English Literature since 1968.
[60] Hélène Cixous, *La Venue à l'écriture*, p. 39.
[61] Ibid., p. 39.
[62] Ibid., p. 53.
[63] Ibid., p. 45.
[64] Ibid., pp. 46, 44.

severing of the corporeal and the linguistic, and by the processes of sexual differentiation."[65] By letting go of her conscious self, and delving into her other, her unconscious, the writer is free to travel into the realms of the Imaginary. Unfettered by the self-referential boundaries of the symbolic world, she can roam into the limitless world of (the) other(s): "...c'est pourquoi je suis partout, mon ventre cosmique, je travaille mon inconscient mondial..."[66], before returning to inscribe her experiences into symbolic language. She has no permanent abode either in the Symbolic or in the Imaginary but rather occupies a space in-between the two realms, a boundary line which liberates a third perspective, a third body: "... il nous vient un *Troisième Corps*, une troisième vue, et nos autres oreilles, – entre nos deux corps notre troisième corps surgit, vole et va voir plus haut le sommet des choses ... mais pour que s'écrive le troisième corps il faut que l'extérieur entre et que l'intérieur s'ouvre."[67]

Looking forwards, looking back

One of the most fundamental ways in which *une écriture féminine* and *l'écriture des femmes* differ is in their relation to time. Djebar looks back in time to locate her écriture des femmes whereas Cixous looks both to the future ("Je parlerai de l'écriture féminine: de ce qu'elle fera."[68]) and to the past:

> Je dis qu'*il faut*: puisqu'il n'y a pas eu encore, à quelques rares exceptions près, d'écriture qui inscrive de la féminité. Si rares, qu'on ne peut en sillonnant les littératures à travers temps, langues et cultures, revenir qu'effrayé de cette presque vaine battue; on sait que le nombre de femmes écrivains, (tout en ayant augmenté très peu à partir du XIXe siècle), a toujours été dérisoire. Savoir inutile et leurrant si de cette espèce d'écrivantes on ne déduit pas d'abord l'immense majorité dont la facture ne se distingue en rien de l'écriture masculine.[69]

In a footnote to this paragraph, Cixous clarifies that she is referring here exclusively to western culture: "Je ne parle ici que de la place 'réservée' à la femme par le monde occidental." Back in the oriental

---

[65] Morag Shiach, *Hélène Cixous: A Politics of Writing* (London and New York: Routledge 1991), p. 70.
[66] Hélène Cixous, *La Venue à l'écriture*, p. 53.
[67] Ibid., pp. 58-59.
[68] Hélène Cixous, "Le Rire de la méduse", p. 39.
[69] Ibid., pp. 41-42. In a footnote to this paragraph Cixous lists Colette, Marguerite Duras and Jean Genet as the only twentieth century writers whose writing she regards as inscribed by femininity.

world, Djebar is looking to the ancient past to locate her *écriture des femmes*:

A.D. – ...L'alphabet berbère, l'alphabet libyque est un des plus anciens de la terre. Il est aussi ancien au moins que l'alphabet étrusque; or c'est comme si on se mettait à entendre l'alphabet étrusque. Pourquoi et à quel moment cet alphabet s'est retrouvé être le patrimoine des Touaregs et de leurs femmes essentiellement? Il y a en moi un questionnement, mais par le rêve. Ce qui m'amène à...
L.G. – ...une littérature de femmes, une écriture des femmes?
A.D. – Dans la société touareg, ce sont les femmes qui conservent l'écriture...

A.D.: ...The Berber alphabet, the Libyan alphabet is one of the most ancient in the world. It is at least as ancient as the Etruscan alphabet; it's as if you could hear the Etruscan alphabet. Why did this alphabet at some stage become the Tuaregs' language and especially that of their women? This is the question I examine by means of a dream. Which leads me to...
L.G.: ... a woman's literature, *une écriture des femmes?*
A.D.: In Tuareg society, it is the women who are keepers of the written word.[70]

On a psychoanalytical level, these two *écritures* also occupy very different loci. Cixous's *écriture* is located on the boundaries of the conscious and the unconscious, in between the Symbolic and the Imaginary, whereas Djebar's *écriture* appears to be located firmly in historic/symbolic time. Despite these differences I would like to suggest that the starting-point of both authors' journeys, of both their "venues à l'écriture" is the same, that they both come to writing from the same point of departure, because of a feeling of *exclusion*.

Starting-point exclusion

This feeling of exclusion in language is what drives both authors to look for an/other *écriture*. Cixous uses religious imagery to express her feelings of exclusion or alienation in language. Language is the realm of the divine and *écriture* is God, a male God at whose altar only a male élite can worship. Afraid to approach the throne of grace, woman accepts her relegation to obscurity with all the fatalism of the impoverished masses: "Ecrire? Je n'y pensai pas. J'y songeai sans cesse, mais avec le chagrin et l'humilité, la résignation, l'innocence des pauvres. L'Ecriture est Dieu. Mais ce n'est pas le tien."[71]

---

[70] Lise Gauvin, "Assia Djebar, territoires des langues: entretien", p. 76. My translation.
[71] Hélène Cixous, *La Venue à l'écriture*, p. 19.

Woman is allowed to look but not to touch, to read but not to write. Writing is God and whereas the woman who reads is already transgressing His Law, the woman who writes commits the ultimate sacrilege:

> Mais écrire? De quel droit? Après tout, je les lisais sans droit, sans permission, à leur insu.
> Comme j'aurais pu prier dans une cathédrale, et envoyer à leur Dieu un message imposteur.[72]

If writing is God, the great I am, the one and only Truth, Cixous wonders who is woman ("J'étais personne") to presume to make herself equal with God? ("Je suis"...: qui oserait parler comme dieu? Pas je...").[73] Cixous is outside the sacred law, prevented from writing for multiple reasons – historical, personal, racial, sexual – as well as linguistic:

> Tout de moi se liguait pour m'interdire l'écriture: L'Histoire, mon histoire, mon origine, mon genre. Tout ce qui constituait mon moi social, culturel. A commencer par le nécessaire, qui me faisait défaut, la matière dans laquelle l'écriture se taille, d'où elle s'arrache: la langue.[74]

Language, and the French language in particular, erects its barriers against her, refusing to let her enter the holy of holies, its site of *écriture*: "J'ai dit 'écrire français'. On écrit *en*. Pénétration. Porte. Frappez avant d'entrer. Formellement interdit."[75]

Cixous contrasts this prohibitive relationship to the French language with her positive relationship to German, her maternal language. This language, which she experiences as *voix* and not *écriture*, holds no such barriers, but rather opens its floodgates, letting in *la mère*: "J'ai eu cette chance, d'être la fille de la voix .... Dans la langue que je parle, vibre la langue maternelle, langue de ma mère, moins langue que musique, moins syntaxe que chant de mots, beau Hochdeutsch..."[76]

---

[72] Ibid., p. 19.
[73] Ibid., pp. 23, 24.
[74] Ibid., p. 20. The reference to "History" refers to Cixous' Jewish roots, which marked her out as a "foreigner", as far as the French were concerned, even though she had French citizenship at birth. Between 1940 and 1943, however, French Jews were stripped of their citizenship but the "spirit of Vichy" continued to "flourish" long after, as Cixous experienced at first hand as a child in Algeria. See Christa Stevens, "Hélène Cixous, auteur en 'algériance'", pp. 82-83.
[75] Hélène Cixous, *La Venue à l'écriture*, p. 20.
[76] Ibid., pp. 28-29.

But there are two sides to Cixous's relation to the French language. As we have seen, she has been exiled from it because of her status as a woman, but she is also a stranger to it because of her status as a "foreigner" (since German is her mother tongue). But rather than reacting negatively to this "strangeness" in language, Cixous embraces the distance between her and the French language as opening up creative possibilities:

> C'est elle [l'allemand] qui me rend la langue française toujours étrangère. A elle, mon indomptée, je dois de n'avoir jamais eu avec aucune langue un rapport de maîtrise, de propriété... d'avoir toujours voulu m'approcher délicatement de toute langue, jamais mienne, pour la lécher, la humer, adorer ses différences, respecter ses dons, ses talents, ses mouvements. Surtout la garder en l'ailleurs qui la porte, laisser intacte son étrangeté ... Si tu ne possèdes pas une langue tu peux être possédée par elle: Fais que la langue te reste étrangère. Aime-la comme ta prochaine. [77]

Much later, staying with the concept of "strangeness", Cixous would come to describe both the French and German languages as "venues à moi charmantes comme la fiancée étrangère."[78] Djebar, on the other hand, is ambiguous about her position as "étrangère" to the French language, which for her is both physically liberating and emotionally destructive. The experience or growing as the only Arab female child in the area to be educated in French exiles her from her compatriots. She is rejected by them because she has entered into forbidden and dangerous territory. She has dared to push open "The Door", leading to the site of learning reserved for man. And because she has transgressed this unwritten law, she is exiled by those around her: "Dès le premier jour où une fillette "sort" pour apprendre l'alphabet, les voisins prennent le regard matois de ceux qui s'apitoient, dix, quinze ans à l'avance: sur le père audacieux, sur le frère inconséquent. Le malheur fondra immanquablement sur eux" [From the very first day that a little girl leaves her home to learn the ABCs, the neighbours adopt that knowing look of those who in ten or fifteen years' time will be able to say 'I told you so!' while commiserating with the foolhardy father, the irresponsible brother. For misfortune will inevitably befall them].[79]

---

[77] Ibid., p. 29.
[78] Hélène Cixous, "Mon algériance", *Les Inrockuptibles* 115 (20 August 1997), p. 70.
[79] Assia Djebar, *L'Amour, la fantasia* (Casablanca: Editions EDDIF 1992), p. 15, trans. Dorothy S. Blair, *Fantasia: An Algerian Cavalcade* (London/New York: Quartet, 1988), p. 3.

Like Djebar, Cixous' Algerian childhood leads to social exclusions, but in her case its multiple causes are more complex, originating in endemic French racism, in a generalised anti-Semitism and in her family's particular circumstances:

> En plus du racisme fondateur français du racisme racine raison socle piliers société culture coutume en plus de cette inoculation congénitale triomphale de cette greffe tout ce qu'il y a de plus réussie et commune dans le monde en plus du classicisme français, en plus de cette morbidité considérée comme une belle santé, bon appétit, il faut ajouter les anti-sémitismes, lesquels naturellement s'additionnent entre eux: l'antisémitisme de chaque composante de l'ensemble à l'égard des Juifs (Français français d'Algérie espagnols arabes corses médecins fonctionnaires avocats) … et par-dessus il faut ajouter l'antiveuvisme, dont nous vîmes surgir les manifestations, une fois mon père disparu, parmi les proches, les amis de mon père qui voulaient tous maintenant être les amants de ma mère sinon, et leurs épouses qui toutes sans aucune exception mirent ma mère à la porte préventivement.[80]

To all these generalised and particular exclusions is added the rejection the young Hélène and her brother experienced at the hands of local Algerian children: "The Cixous children those not really Jewish false French odd inadequate people who loved the Algerians who spurned us as enemy Francaouis, Roumis and Jews."[81] The hand of friendship was extended in vain:

> A la fin du lycée, dans les années 51-53, il y eut dans ma classe à *numerus clausus* où j'étais la seule juive, trois musulmanes. Leur façon d'être au dernier rang et de sourire en coin. Ma façon d'être en colère et au premier rang. Cette fois je voulus être avec. Je sus immédiatement qu'elles étaient l'Algérie qui se préparait. Je leur tendais la main, je voulais faire alliance avec elles contre les Françaises. En vain. Pour elles j'étais la France. Elles n'ouvrirent jamais. Je comprenais leur prudence.[82]

But, as Cixous explains, feelings of loss and exclusion represent the springboard to the creative process: "A l'origine le geste d'écrire est lié à l'expérience de la disparition, au sentiment d'avoir perdu la clé du monde, d'avoir été jeté dehors."[83] Language provides the

---

[80] Hélène Cixous, *Les Rêveries de la femme sauvage* (Paris: Galilée, 2000), p. 43.
[81] Hélène Cixous, "My Algeriance: in other words to depart not to arrive from Algeria", trans. Eric Prenowitz, in Hélène Cixous *Stigmata: Escaping Texts* (London/New York, Routledge, 1989), p. 161.
[82] Hélène Cixous "Mon algériance", p. 70.
[83] Hélène Cixous, "De la scène de l'inconscient à la scène de l'Histoire: Chemin d'une écriture", in Françoise van Rossum-Guyon, Myriam Díaz-Diocaretz (dir.),

antidote to exile, it becomes "another country", a home for those without a home (*"Je ne me suis trouvée bien nulle part"*)[84] and opens up other worlds: "Tout est perdu sauf les mots. C'est une expérience d'enfant: les mots sont nos portes vers tous les autres mondes. A un certain moment pour qui a tout perdu, que ce soit d'ailleurs un être ou un pays, c'est la langue qui devient pays. On entre au pays des langues."[85]

While founded upon a sense of loss and exile, language in both Djebar and Cixous's case bring a sense of freedom and possibility. But in *L'Amour, la fantasia* this sense of exhilarating freedom brought to her by the French language is associated with physical release (rather than creative liberty), with a door opening onto the outside world, conveyed by the association of language and the power of sight, both given and withdrawn:

> Comme si soudain la langue française avait des yeux, et qu'elle me les ait donnés pour voir dans la liberté, comme si la langue française aveuglait les mâles voyeurs de mon clan et qu'à ce prix, je puisse circuler, dégringoler toutes les rues, annexer le dehors pour mes compagnes cloîtrées, pour mes aïeules mortes bien avant le tombeau.
>
> As if the French language suddenly had eyes, and lent them to me to see into liberty; as if the French language blinded the peeping Toms of my clan, and at this price, I could move freely, run headlong down every street, annex the outdoors for my cloistered companions, for the matriarchs of my family who endured a living death.[86]

Cixous uses her idea of *écriture féminine* to challenge the dichotomy of mind and body. By engaging with the unconscious, she unsettles the illusion of conscious control that upholds intellectual mastery at the expense of erasing the body. In contrast, in *L'Amour, la fantasia* Djebar *asserts* the dichotomy of body and *soul* when describing her relationship to the French language. French frees the body but imprisons the soul. Ironically, here it is the paternal language, French, rather than the maternal language, Arabic, which is associated with bodily freedom. This bodily freedom is nevertheless contrasted with a sense of emotional detachment and alienation that the French language also brings.

Hélène Cixous, chemins d'une écriture (St.-Denis: Presses Universitaires de Vincennes and Amsterdam/Atlanta: Rodopi, 1990), pp. 15-34, p. 19.
[84] Hélène Cixous, "Mon Algériance", p. 70.
[85] Hélène Cixous, "De la scène de l'inconscient à la scène de l'Histoire: Chemin d'une écriture", p. 19.
[86] Assia Djebar, *L'Amour, la fantasia*, p. 208, trans. Dorothy S. Blair, *Fantasia: An Algerian Cavalcade*, p. 181.

So whereas, for Cixous, the "strangeness" of the French language liberates creative possibilities, for Djebar its "strangeness" merely creates emotional blockage. In *L'Amour, la fantasia*, this was described as emotional aphasia, as an inability to express love: "Je ne pouvais dire le moindre mot de tendresse ou d'amour dans cette langue..."[87] In this novel, the counterpoint to French, the "alien" paternal language, is the maternal language, Arabic, which at this stage is still regarded as the language of love. Here Djebar's yearning for Arabic is expressed in terms of a longing for the Voice of the Mother, in language reminiscent of Cixous's "bon lait de mère":

> En fait, je cherche, comme un lait dont on m'aurait autrefois écartée, la pléthore amoureuse de la langue de ma mère. Contre la ségrégation de mon héritage, le mot plein de l'amour-au-présent me devient une parade d'hirondelle.

> And now I too seek out the rich vocabulary of love of my mother tongue – milk of which I had been previously deprived. In contrast to the segregation I inherited, words expressing love-in-the-present become for me like one token swallow heralding summer.[88]

In *Vaste est la prison*, the opposition between French (as the language of absence – in the sense of *geographical* absence – and of alienation) and Arabic (as the language of presence and pleasure) abruptly breaks down, as the Arabic language reveals its true colours: "La langue maternelle m'exhibait ses crocs" [the mother tongue had shown me her teeth] (pp. 15; 15). The Arabic language no longer represents *protection* from the segregation at work in her society but is now associated with the very process of segregation. The image of the swallow's flight in *L'Amour, la fantasia* is displaced in *Vaste est la prison* by the winging arrow of segregation piercing her flesh, as the opposition between French and Arabic is displaced by a new opposition, that of Arabic and Berber.

Matriarchal languages

In the preface of *Vaste est la prison*, Djebar rejects Arabic as a patriarchal language, and in Part 2 of the novel she turns instead to a "matriarchal language", an *écriture* which belongs to a matriarchal society:

---

[87] Lise Gauvin, "Assia Djebar, territoires des langues: entretien", p. 79.
[88] Assia Djebar, *L'Amour, la fantasia*, p. 80, trans. Dorothy S. Blair, *Fantasia: An Algerian Cavalcade*, p. 62.

Dans la société touareg, ce sont les femmes qui conservent l'écriture. C'est une société matriarcale, c'est-à-dire que les femmes étant au centre, l'ascendance noble passe par les femmes. On y devient "amenokal" par la lignée des femmes.

In Tuareg society, it the women who are the keepers of the written word. It is a matriarchal society, that is to say that the women were central to it, given that nobility was passed down through the women of the tribe. One became "amenokal" through the female line.[89]

This language not only belongs to a matriarchal society, but in a sense also belongs to her: "...il y a donc la langue berbère qui était la langue de ma grand-mère" [... and then there is the Berber language which was my grandmother's tongue].[90] Cixous, like Djebar, also wants to find a language that belongs to her, a writing practice in which she feels at home and that escapes the traps of patriarchal language. She comes up with the idea of an *écriture féminine*, a writing practice which undermines patriarchal language by *exceeding* it, rather than setting itself up in opposition to it. Djebar thus rejects patriarchal language in favour of a *matriarchal language*, whereas Cixous exceeds patriarchal language with "*une écriture matricielle*":

> *Femmes pour femmes*: en la femme toujours se maintient la force productive de l'autre, en particulier de l'autre femme. *En* elle, matricielle, berceuse-donneuse, elle-même sa mère et son enfant, elle-même sa fille-soeur. [91]

Cixous's *matricial* writing is also centred on the status of the mother, not in her position as the head of the family but in her childbearing role. She explores a writing practice linked to what she calls the female libidinal economy or "cette 'libido de l'autre'"[92] related to woman's capacity to *give* birth: "Il y a un lien entre l'économie libidinale de la femme – sa jouissance, l'imaginaire féminin – et sa façon de se constituer une subjectivité se divisant sans regret..."[93]

The feminine libidinal economy offers the possibility of an alternative relation to the other, based on woman's experience of childbirth. The process of *giving* birth is associated with the concept of giving in the sense of a gift, and of giving up in the sense of relinquishing without regret. The bonding between mother and child

---

[89] Djebar, quoted in Lise Gauvin, "Assia Djebar, territoires des langues: entretien", p. 76. My translation.
[90] Ibid., p. 74. My translation.
[91] Hélène Cixous, "Le Rire de la méduse", p. 44.
[92] Hélène Cixous, *La Jeune née*, p. 169.
[93] Ibid., p. 167.

represents a relation to the other which is not oppressive or repressive but literally and metaphorically life-giving:

> Il ne s'agit pas seulement de cette ressource supplémentaire du corps féminin, de ce pouvoir spécifique de la production du vivant dont sa chair est le lieu, pas seulement d'une transformation de rythmes, des échanges, du rapport à l'espace, de tout système de perception ... Mais aussi de l'expérience du "lien" à l'autre, tout ce qui passe par la métaphore de la mise au monde.[94]

Whereas the female libidinal economy favours a positive bond with the other, the masculine libidinal economy is incapable of a relationship with the other, occupying as it does a self-referential position that tends towards the obliteration of the other. Because a feminine subject position has this privileged position toward the other, Cixous believes that feminine writing will bring alternative positions of relation and therefore of expression. Like the female libidinal economy, feminine writing offers a passageway to a new relation between self and other in which both coexist: "L'écriture, c'est en moi le passage, entrée, sortie, séjour, de l'autre que je suis et ne suis pas, que je ne sais pas être, mais que je sens passer, qui me fais vivre..."[95]

Cixous links the feminine capacity for a positive relation to the other first of all to childbirth, with woman's capacity to *give* birth, and secondly to woman's generosity, with her ability to *give*. She then relates this capacity to give "endlessly", to woman's sexuality, to her endless body. Woman's ability to give is contrasted with man's fear of letting go of himself, with his compulsion to return to the "selfsame". In the context of desire, of exchange, man cannot *give* of himself without thought of return (to the selfsame), but only gives what he can be assured of getting back. Women, on the other hand, give without thought of return: "S'il ya un "propre" de la femme, c'est paradoxalement sa capacité de se déproprier sans calcul..."[96]

This capacity to give endlessly is linked to woman's "endless body, without end." Sexual difference is no longer reduced to the visual (absence or presence of the male "attribute') but identified with the indefinable capacity for sexual pleasure or *jouissance*. By redirecting the definition of sexual difference to the level of the unseen, to the libido, Cixous reaffirms a positive female sexuality, as the opposition between male presence and female absence is displaced by the difference between female plurality and male limitation. For

---

[94] Ibid., pp. 166-67.
[95] Ibid., p. 158.
[96] Ibid., pp. 162-63.

Cixous contrasts woman's endless "cosmic" libido to man's "regionalised" masculine sexuality, and then links this "endlessness" to writing: "Sa libido est cosmique, comme son inconscient est mondial: son écriture ne peut aussi que se poursuivre..."[97] Her writing goes on and on into the inside place: "Elle seule ose et veut connaître du dedans, dont elle, l'exclue n'a pas cessé d'entendre résonner l'avant-langage", a place beyond the Symbolic, where she can draw on the rhythms and articulations of the mother's body.[98]

Ecriture as resistance

Apart from the role of the mother, which is central to both *écritures*, there are other distant echoes between *une écriture féminine* and *l'écriture des femmes*. Both *écritures* occupy a site of resistance, one challenging the colonial order, the other challenging the symbolic order.

From the beginning, Djebar foregrounds her *écriture* as mysterious and strange: "une inscription bilingue dont le mystère dormira encore deux siècles" [a bilingual inscription whose mystery will lie dormant for two more centuries] (pp. 128; 130), "l'alphabet étrange garde son mystère" [The strange alphabet keeps its mystery] (pp. 132; 134). This mysterious writing will not submit to the desire of the male European enquirers to grasp its significance, despite their persistent curiosity: "Devant la stèle de Dougga, à la frontière algéro-tunisienne, j'ai essayé de ressusciter tous les voyageurs qui sont passés devant et se sont demandé: "Qu'est-ce que cette écriture mystérieuse?" [Standing in front of the stele at Dougga, on the Algerian-Tunisian border, I tried to bring to life all the travellers who had passed by and wondered, "What is this mysterious script?"].[99] This male quest echoes Cixous's phrase "masculine interrogation": "Dès qu'on *pose* une question, dès qu'on *demande* une réponse, eh bien *on est déjà pris dans l'interrogation masculine.*"[100]

The masculine interrogation in Djebar's historical narrative is both persistent and misguided, as each of the travellers, and the academics whom they consult, come to their erroneous conclusions about the nature of this mysterious script. Their task is made more difficult by the initial false assumption that they make, namely that they are

---

[97] Ibid., p. 162.
[98] Ibid., p. 162.
[99] Lise Gauvin, "Assia Djebar, territoires des langues: entretien", p. 76. My translation.
[100] Hélène Cixous, "Le Sexe ou la tête?", p. 7.

dealing with a "dead language": "Et les savants, dans leurs cabinets, de chercher, d'étudier, d'ausculter, de supposer... croyant toujours aller à la quête d'un sens perdu, d'échos souterrains" [And leaving scholars in their studies to seek and study and listen and suppose... always with the thought that they are on a quest for some lost meaning – underground echoes] (pp. 145; 148). In this male assumption that this *écriture des femmes* (which is alive in myriad voices around them) is dead, there is a distant echo of Cixous's observations on men being deaf to the female voice: "... sa parole choit presque toujours dans la sourde oreille masculine, qui n'entend dans la langue que ce qui parle au masculin."[101]

Each of the Western sojourners in turn fails to recognise the nature of "les signes mystérieux" [these mysterious signs] (pp. 127; 129) that they come across, as one false interpretation is displaced by the next – "antique égyptien" [ancient Egyptian] (pp. 127; 130), "punico-ispanico" [*punico-ispanico*] (pp. 131; 133), "un vieil africain" [some form of old African] (pp. 135; 137). The mysterious signs are elusive, the signifiers stubbornly refuse to yield their meanings to the Western gaze. This *écriture des femmes* refuses to be known, to be possessed, refuses to submit to the coloniser's desire. There is a certain irony in the fact that this *écriture des femmes* cannot be grasped by men. It exceeds their understanding because they cannot make the connection between *écriture* and *voix*, whereas, as we will see, Cixous's *écriture féminine* exceeds the thought processes of patriarchy *because* of its connection of *écriture* and *voix*.

Cixous's *écriture* also demonstrates resistance, in this case against the symbolic order. First and foremost, it resists the symbolic at its most fundamental level of meaning, that of separation. Cixous first comes to writing as a means of confronting separation in the form of death (the death of her father): "Ecrire: pour ne pas laisser la place au mort, pour faire reculer l'oubli, pour ne jamais se laisser surprendre par l'abîme. Pour ne jamais se résigner, se consoler, se retourner dans son lit vers le mur et se rendormir comme si rien n'était arrivé; rien ne pouvait arriver."[102]

Writing resists death because it takes on the infiniteness and the immortality of the divine. It "steals" the attributes of God, becoming the ultimate source of goodness and of love, as the image of "la Parole de Dieu" shedding His blood for the world is displaced by "la parole du sang" which shares itself with all others "dans le sang-rapport":

---

[101] Hélène Cixous, *La Jeune née*, p. 171.
[102] Hélène Cixous, *La Venue à l'écriture*, p. 11.

> J'ai peut-être écrit pour voir; pour avoir ce que je n'aurais jamais eu... Avoir? Un avoir sans limites, sans restriction; mais sans aucun "dépôt", un avoir qui ne détient pas, qui ne possède pas, l'avoir-amour, celui que se soutient d'aimer, dans le sang-rapport. Ainsi, donne-toi ce que tu voudrais que dieu-s'il-existait te donne... L'écriture est bonne: elle est ce qui n'en finit pas. En moi circule le plus simple, le plus sûr autre. Comme le sang: on n'en manque pas. Il peut s'appauvrir. Mais tu le fabriques et tu le renouvelles. En moi la parole du sang, qui ne cessera pas avant ma fin.[103]

This new form of shared identity "dans le sang-rapport" allows the writer to journey beyond herself to a limitless space of shared unconsciousness, a space of "shared unconscious patterns and forms, which are the product of shared histories worked out across shared bodies."[104]

Language as a weapon of war

By engaging with the unconscious, woman liberates not only her writing, but also her self, and as such, writing becomes an agent for social change: "... l'écriture *est la possibilité même du changement, l'espace d'où peut s'élancer une pensée subversive, le mouvement avant-coureur d'une transformation des structures sociales et culturelles.*[105] *L'écriture féminine* does not express itself as the voice of political opposition but as the mouthpiece of a resistance movement. In her mind's eye, Cixous stages the return of the repressed as the newly empowered agents of "la Résistance" rise up : "'Le Refoulé' de leur culture et de leur société, quand il revient c'est d'un retour explosif, *absolument* ruinant, renversant, d'une force encore jamais libérée, à la mesure de la plus formidable des répressions..."[106]

This active resistance to the Symbolic contrasts with the writer's passive submission to the Imaginary: "... je ne barre pas, je ne ferme pas mes terres, mes sens, l'espace charnel qui s'étend derrière mes yeux: je me laisse traverser, imprégner, affecter..."[107] And it is because *l'écriture féminine* draws its inspiration from beyond the Symbolic (although it is materially inscribed in symbolic language) that it is resistant to symbolic thought processes:

---

[103] Ibid., p. 12.
[104] Morag Shiach, *Hélène Cixous: A Politics of Writing*, p. 26.
[105] Hélène Cixous, "Le Rire de la méduse", p. 42.
[106] Ibid., p. 48.
[107] Hélène Cixous, *La Venue à lécriture*, p. 56.

> Impossible de *définir* une pratique féminine de l'écriture, d'une impossibilité qui se maintiendra car on ne pourra jamais *théoriser* cette pratique, l'enfermer, la coder, ce qui ne signifie pas qu'elle n'existe pas. Mais elle excédera toujours le discours que régit le système phallocentrique...[108]

The subversiveness of Cixous's *écriture* used as a revolutionary weapon finds its echo in Djebar's story of the way the Berber language was used as a secret weapon in the context of war, not against the patriarchal order, but against the colonial system. Before the fall of Constantine at the hands of the French army in 1837, Hamdane Khodja, a prominent Algerian official, tries unsuccessfully to get the Turks to come to the aid of its ruler, the bey Ahmed. After the fall of Constantine, Khodja's son turns up in Paris and meets up with a French orientalist, De Saulcy, to whom he hands over some letters he has in his possession. These letters, items of correspondence between the bey and Hamdane Khodja, are mostly in Arabic, but also contain a mysterious script, which De Saulcy eventually discovers to be the Berber language:

> Soudain le Français comprend: et si le bey Ahmed, parlant évidemment le berbère chaoui, ayant appris à Constantine, grâce à des nomades sahariens de passage, cette écriture du secret, l'utilisait comme code: considérant que cet alphabet, devenu si rare, peut seul parer au danger de l'interception. (pp. 148; 150)
>
> Suddenly the Frenchman understands: and what if the bey Ahmed, who could obviously speak Chaoui Berber, has learned – thanks to Saharan nomads passing through Constantine – this mysterious writing and used it as a code, thinking that this alphabet, now so rare, is the only thing that can ward off the danger of interception?

The subversive script is thus used as a secret code, as a way of avoiding the detection of the enemy. Although Cixous makes it clear that her *écriture* cannot be coded, it too is resistant, and, like Djebar's *écriture des femmes*, is used to destabilise the prevailing order.

Ecriture and voice

Although Cixous makes it clear that *une écriture feminine* cannot be defined, she does nevertheless ascribe to it a "proximity to voice." The central irony of Djebar's narrative also lies in the proximity of *écriture* and voice – in this case the Berber voices are literally present in the areas surrounding the *écriture* on the stone. For the whole parade of academics, researchers, archaeologists who survey this

---

[108] Hélène Cixous, "Le Rire de la méduse", p. 45.

écriture are blind to the fact that *écriture* is alive, that this *écriture* that they cannot grasp is being spoken all around them. Djebar visualises it coming to life before their very eyes, becoming voice, presence, cry and song: "Si cette écriture étrange s'animait, se chargeait d'une voix au présent, s'épelait à voix haute, se chantait?" [Then suppose this strange writing came alive, was a voice in the present, was spoken out loud, was sung] (pp. 145; 147).

This writing on the stone comes alive, swirling around the sojourners, circling around in space and after finding its way into the desert land, stretches out geographically, and stretches back prehistorically to find form in dancing signs:

> Or l'écriture vivait; or ses sonorités, sa musique, son rythme se dévidaient autour d'eux, autour des voyageurs, leurs émules, circulant entre Dougga et Cirta, et jusque dans Constantine prise, et sur les montagnes kabyles insoumises quinze ans après Constantine puis, au-delà des dunes et des sables sahariens, jusqu'au coeur du désert même! Car là, depuis le Fezzan jusqu'en Mauritanie, parmi les nomades ayant cru oublier les Numides, les lettres libyques d'antan se sont glissées subrepticement dès l'époque peut-être des Garamantes – qui perdaient leurs chevaux pour des chameaux nouvellement introduits, qui laissaient disparaître de leur terre les troupes d'autruches dont ne resteraient, en foule dansante et mobile, que les silhouettes gravées sur les parois des cavernes millénaires. (pp. 146; 148)

> And yet the writing was alive. Its sonority, its music, its rhythms still reeled on around them, around the travellers and their followers going back and forth between Dougga and Cirta. It travelled into conquered Constantine and onto the Kabylian mountains, still rebellious fifteen years after the fall of Constantine, and then, beyond the dunes and sands of the Sahara, it went all the way to the heart of the desert itself! For there, from the Fezzan to Mauritania, among the nomads who thought they had forgotten the Numidians, Libyan letters from earlier times have stealthily slipped in ever since. Perhaps they came in the days of the Garamantes – who gave up their horses for the newly introduced camels, who let the herds of ostriches disappear from their lands until only their silhouettes, in a dancing, animated crowd, remained, engraved on the walls of caves a thousand years old.

It is as if Djebar wants to trace this writing as far back into the past as possible – it is its anteriority, its ancient origins which give it its specificity. Djebar wants to restore the Berber script to historical memory, and in particular to foreground its "qualities", its capacity to survive, its affinity with women and its mobility, not in terms of "migrations de mots" but in terms of *migration de langues*[109], creating

---

[109] Hélène Cixous, *La Venue à l'écriture*, p. 28.

not *une* écriture plurielle but "une écriture polygame" [polygamous writing] (pp. 158; 162):

> Si ce supposé "dialecte" d'hommes qui parlèrent tour à tour punique avec Carthage, latin avec les Romains et les romanisés jusqu'à Augustin, et grec puis arabe treize siècles durant, et qu'ils continuèrent, génération après génération, à garder vivace pour un usage endogamique (avec leurs mères, leurs épouses et leurs filles essentiellement), si ce parler remontait jusqu'à plus loin encore? Cette langue, celle de Jugurtha exprimant son énergie indomptable à combattre et à mourir, celle-là même de Masinissa tout au long de ses soixante ans de règne! Si, plus arrière encore, les Barbares/Berbères, hôtes et quelquefois amis ou rivaux des grands Pharaons... (pp. 145; 147)

> Suppose this so-called dialect of men who spoke by turn Punic with Carthage, Latin with the Romans and the romanized until Augustine's time, and Greek, then Arab for thirteen centuries, continued, generation after generation, kept alive for endogamic use (mainly with their mothers, their wives, and their daughters). Suppose this speech, this language – the one in which Jugurtha expressed his insurmountable energy as he fought and died, the very one Masinissa spoke throughout his sixty-year reign – went back even farther! Suppose, even longer ago, the Barbarians/Berbers, the great pharaohs' guests and sometimes their friends and rivals...

Djebar wants to trace her *écriture* back as far as possible to its most ancient of *origins*, as if wishing to confer onto it a sense of historical authority. Although Cixous relates her *écriture féminine* to voice and to the Voice of the Mother in particular, she on the other hand refuses the concept of origin, of the Voice-as-origin, and opts instead for the idea of writing as a journey into the unknown, towards a second innocence, which resonates with, rather than originates from, the primeval Mother-song: "Pas l'origine: elle n'y revient pas. Trajet du garçon: retour au pays natal, *Heimweh* dont parle Freud, nostalgie que fait de l'homme un être qui a tendance à revenir au point de départ, afin de se l'approprier et d'y mourir. Trajet de la fille: plus loin, à l'inconnu, à inventer."[110]

As in Djebar's narrative, Cixous makes an association between writing and voice: "La féminité dans l'écriture je la sens passer d'abord par: un privilège de la *voix*..."[111] Cixous gives "voice" to her *écriture* because of the proximity of voice to the unconscious and to song.

---

[110] Hélène Cixous, *La Jeune née*, p. 173.
[111] Ibid., p. 170.

According to Cixous, a woman's voice or speech is closer to the *unconscious* than is her writing. In speech a woman involuntarily reveals what patriarchal culture has taught her to repress – her body (Cixous gives the example of a woman's *body* language when she is engaged in public speaking: "Ecoute parler une femme dans une assemblée...: elle ne 'parle' pas, elle lance dans l'air son corps tremblant..."[112]). A woman's thoughts are literally revealed in body/language: "elle matérialise charnellement ce qu'elle pense."[113] Thus, although a woman represses her body in writing, she cannot do so in her speech. By privileging the voice in her *écriture*, Cixous thus reappropriates the body into writing.

The privileging of voice allows proximity not only to the unconscious but also to song, to the "associative logic of music over the linear logic of philosophical and literary discourse."[114] The logical progression of "la syntaxe ... ce fameux fil"[115] is subverted by the associative powers of "le chant", the echo of the primeval song: "La Voix, chant d'avant la loi, avant que le souffle soit coupé par le symbolique, réapproprié dans le langage sous l'autorité séparante. La plus profonde, la plus ancienne et adorable visitation. Et chaque femme chante le premier amour sans nom."[116] And, as the rhythms of The Song are inscribed into symbolic language, the Law of the Father is transgressed by the Voice of the Mother:

> ... c'est, te touchant, l'équivoix qui t'affecte, te pousse depuis ton sein à venir au langage, qui lance *ta* force; c'est le rythme qui te rit; l'intime destinataire qui rend possible et désirable toutes les métaphores, corps (le? les?), pas plus descriptible que dieu, l'âme ou l'Autre; la partie de toi qui entre toi t'espace et te pousse à inscrire dans la langue ton style de femme. Voix: le lait intarissable. Elle est retrouvée. La mère perdue. L'éternité: c'est la voix mêlée avec le lait.[117]

---

[112] Ibid., p. 170. Cixous proceeds to point out why this is more likely to apply to women than to men: "Comment ce rapport privilégié à la voix? Parce que aucune femme n'empile autant de défenses anti-pulsionnelles qu'un homme" (p. 173).
[113] Ibid., p. 170.
[114] Morag Shiach, *Hélène Cixous: A Politics of Writing*, p. 22.
[115] Hélène Cixous, *La Jeune née*, p. 177.
[116] Ibid., p. 172.
[117] Ibid., pp. 172-73. "L'équivoix" plays on the multiple resonances of the Voice of the Mother: "voix, équilibre, équivoque."

Writing as preservation: Historiography and mythography

In writing, Cixous sees the possibility of change, and this is especially true of her staging of history, where she focuses on moments of crisis that carry within them the possibility of change.[118] Her interest in writing and staging history is also linked to "a more general project of protecting that which is threatened with effacement, and of restoring historical memory."[119] Djebar, like Cixous, uses writing as a site of preservation, and, again like Cixous, is caught between historiography and mythography, as the story of Tin Hinan will illustrate.

By the act of writing "L'effacement sur la pierre" [Erased in Stone], Djebar protects the Berber script and Berber heroes, such as Jugurtha and Tin Hinan, from effacement. The main section of Part 2 is built around the reconstruction of historical facts. Although Djebar takes some liberty with chronological linearity, she retains clear historical markers and references, and as such her writing remains within a symbolic temporal framework. However, in the final chapter of Part 2, which deals with the Princess Tin Hinan, Djebar goes beyond the historical world, as if obeying Cixous's call not to be limited by the constraints of symbolic time and space, but to tune her ears to an inner voice: "... il faut que l'extérieur entre et que l'intérieur s'ouvre."[120]

So with the story of Tin Hinan, the internal world opens up as Djebar goes to Cixous's School of Dreams: "J'ai rêvé là-dessus. J'ai rêvé sur une princesse, la princesse Tin-Hinan, dont on a retrouvé le sanctuaire en 1925 et dont le corps a été transporté à Alger dans un musée." [I dreamt about it. I dreamt about a princess, the princess Tin-Hinan, whose shrine was found in 1925 and whose body was transported to a museum in Algiers].[121] Tin Hinan is a fourth-century Tuareg princess who flees her native northern territory to settle in Abalessa, where she is eventually buried with two female companions. In the course of the twentieth century her mausoleum is discovered in Alabessa and her remains taken to the museum in Cairo.

---

[118] Morag Shiach, *Hélène Cixous: A Politics of Writing*, p. 107.
[119] Ibid., p. 130. Quotation taken from Véronique Hotte, "Entretien avec Hélène Cixous", *Théâtre/Public*, 68 (1986), pp. 22-29.
[120] Hélène Cixous, *La Venue à l'écriture*, p. 59.
[121] Lise Gauvin, "Assia Djebar, territoires des langues: entretien", p. 76. My translation.

Cixous tells us that "[i]n order to go to the School of Dreams something must be displaced, starting with the bed."[122] In Djebar's case, what is displaced? Not the bed, although that is where the dream starts:

> "*Je rêve, décidément, à ce jour où Tin Hinan fut couchée à Abalessa: on l'étendit sur un lit en bois sculpté. Son corps mince, recouvert d'étoffes et de larges ornements de cuir, fut allongé sur le dos, orienté vers l'est, bras et jambes légèrement repliés*"
>
> *I find that I am always dreaming about the day that Tin Hinan was laid to rest at Abalessa. They stretched her out on a bed of sculptured wood. Her thin body, pointed east and covered with cloth and large leather ornaments, lay on its back with its arms and legs slightly bent under.* (pp. 163; 166)

In her dream, Djebar displaces historiography with mythography, returning us to a question raised by Cixous's historical novels: "... if it is a fiction, to what extent does its factual accuracy matter? If is a history, can it also, productively, be a myth?"[123]

In Djebar's case, it is a history that is also productively a myth. The essentials of the story depend on historical fact, which validate the anteriority of the Berber language, while the mythological element diverges from historical records to *produce* an eternal home for her *écriture des femmes*, ensuring that it remains forever in the hands of woman and in the heart of Africa.

The result of this combination of history and myth comes close to becoming what Cixous refers to as "[c]et être d'air et de chair qui s'est composé en moi avec des milliers d'éléments de significations arrachés aux divers domaines du réel et liés ensemble par mes émotions, ma rage ma joie mon désir..."[124] For in this final chapter Djebar links together "des éléments de significations arrachés aux divers domaines du réel" in the sense that she brings together the various strands of her historical narrative, and links them together in a dream: "*mon rêve tenace qui tente de rassembler les cendres du*

---

[122] Hélène Cixous, *Three Steps on the Ladder of Writing* (New York: Columbia University Press, 1993), trans. Sarah Cornell and Susan Sellers, p. 65. *Three Steps on the Ladder of Writing* is the translation of the script of the Wellek Library Lectures, given by Cixous in May 1990. Cixous refers here to her rewriting of a Grimm fairy tale. It is the story of a king who kept his daughters imprisoned and who could not understand why the princesses kept wearing out their shoes. Unknown to him, his daughters were escaping into the forest night after night by opening a trap door under their *bed*.
[123] Morag Shiach, *Hélène Cixous: A Politics of Writing*, p. 105.
[124] Hélène Cixous, *La Venue à l'écriture*, p. 57.

temps..." [*my stubborn dream in its attempts to reassemble the ashes of time...*] (pp. 163; 166).

The dream centres on the writing found on the walls of the sepulchres of the princess's companions. This writing on the wall, another example of the Berber script, predates even that of the Dougga; in other words, it is more than four centuries older than Tin Hinan. In a scene reminiscent of Daniel and King Belshazzar, Djebar's interpretation of the writing on the wall comes to her in a dream. In her dream, it is the princess who conserves this ancient writing, and gives it to her companions before taking her last breath. Djebar then takes hold of this *écriture* and visualises it stretching back into time, going back four centuries to Jugurtha's reign, and then forward four centuries to that of Tin Hinan, effectuating a neat closure to her historical narrative.

> *J'imagine donc la princesse du Hoggar qui, autrefois dans sa fuite, emporta l'alphabet archaïque, puis en confia les caractères à ses amies, juste avant de mourir.*
>
> *Ainsi, plus de quatre siècles après la résistance et le dramatique échec de Yougourtha au Nord, quatre siècles également avant celui, grandiose, de la Kahina – la reine berbère qui résistera à la conquête arabe –, Tin Hinan des sables, presque effacée, nous laisse héritage – et cela, malgré ses os hélas aujourd'hui dérangés – : notre écriture la plus secrète, aussi ancienne que l'étrusque ou que celle des "runes" mais, contrairement à celles-ci, toute bruissante encore de sons et de souffles d'aujourd'hui, est bien legs de femme, au plus profond du désert.*
>
> *Tin Hinan ensevelie dans le ventre de l'Afrique!* (pp. 164; 167)
>
> *And so I imagine the princess of the Hoggar who, when she fled in the past, carried with the archaic alphabet, then confided the characters to her friends just before she died.*
>
> *Thus more that four centuries after the resistance and dramatic defeat of Yougourtha in the north, also four centuries before the grandiose defeat of la Kahina – the Berber queen who will resist the Arab conquest – Tin Hinan of the sands, almost obliterated, leaves us an inheritance – and does so despite her bones that, alas, have now been disturbed. Our most secret writing, as ancient as Etruscan or the writing of the runes, but unlike these a writing still noisy with the sounds and breath of today, is indeed the legacy of a woman in the deepest desert.*
>
> *Tin Hinan buried in the belly of Africa!*

The image of Tin Hinan becomes mythologically charged as she is reinstated as the female guardian of *une écriture*, which at the end of the narrative belongs not to the Occident or to the Orient but to "le continent noir" – Africa. This *écriture* is buried in the heart of Africa, yet alive in the form of "souffle."

Souffles and sorties?

Cixous also refers to writing as "souffle" when she describes the compulsion to write as being swept up by a powerful wind emanating from an unfathomable inner source: "Le souffle 'veut' une forme. 'Ecris-moi!'"[125] In Djebar's narrative, it is *l'écriture* rather than *le souffle* that is the starting point: "L'écriture est souffle. Ecoute-la!"[126] Cixous obeys the command to write, and eventually finds her home in *une écriture féminine*, a site of writing where she is no longer excluded. Djebar's explorers eventually open their ears to the voices around them. Yet even as the Europeans discover the truth about the Berber language, even as they discover its true usage, the Berber people themselves are ironically losing its usage. Djebar, who sets off on her journey from the starting-point of exclusion, finds herself back where she started – excluded from *écriture*.

> Tandis que le secret se dévoile, femmes et hommes, depuis l'oasis de Siwa en Egypte jusqu'à l'Atlantique, et même au-delà jusqu'aux îles Canaries, combien sont-ils encore – combien sommes-nous encore – toutes et tous à chanter, à pleurer, à hululer, mais aussi à aimer, installés plutôt dans l'impossibilité d'aimer – ,oui, combien sommes-nous, bien qu'héritiers du bey Ahmed, des Touaregs du siècle dernier et des édiles bilingues de Dougga, à nous sentir exilés de leur première écriture? (pp. 150; 152)

> While the secret is revealed, how many women and men are there still, from the oasis of Siwa in Egypt to the Atlantic and even beyond – to the Canary Islands, how many of them – how many of us still – all singing, weeping, ululating, but also loving or rather being in a position where it is impossible to love – yes, how many of us are there who, although the heirs of the bey Ahmed, the Tuaregs and the last century and the *aediles*, bilingual Roman magistrates in charge of the monument of Dougga, feel exiled from their first writing?

Djebar's *écriture des femmes* leaves her in a position of exclusion. She is still an orphan of language, whereas Cixous has found not a "hommicile fixe"[127] but a "mobile" home, in her in-between spaces. So unlike Cixous, Djebar's return to *l'écriture des femmes* does not provide a *sortie* from the prison-house of language but returns to her original starting-point of exile.

Nevertheless, Djebar's historical narrative, and in particular her reappropriation of a matriarchal language, can be interpreted as a means of challenging the dominance of patriarchal language. Cixous

---

[125] Ibid., p. 18.
[126] My phraseology.
[127] Hélène Cixous, *La Venue à l'écriture*, p. 42.

recognises the merits of this kind of historical approach, but at the same time points out its limitations. For although *l'histoire de l'écriture des femmes* does challenge the pre-eminence of patriarchal society and language, and is "une façon de penser autrement l'histoire de la domination masculine", this challenge relates only to the past and not to the future – it does not provide a mechanism for change. Change, claims Cixous, can only be achieved by inventing the other story, not by reinventing history:

> On peut divaguer longtemps sur une hypothétique préhistoire et sur une époque matriarcale. Ou on peut, comme le fit Bachofen, tenter de refigurer une société gynécocratique, d'en tirer des effets poétiques et mythiques à portée puissamment subversive quant à l'histoire de la famille et du pouvoir mâle. Toutes les façons de penser autrement l'histoire du pouvoir, de la propriété, la domination masculine ... ont une efficacité. Mais le changement en cours n'a que faire de la question de "l'origine". Il y a du phallocentrisme. ... Le phallocentrisme est l'ennemi. De *tous* ... Et il est temps de transformer. D'inventer l'autre histoire.[128]

Whether or not *l'écriture féminine* has such revolutionary potential is itself another story.

A Sisterhood of Suffering

In Part 3, Djebar moves on from a writing that is matriarchal in the sense that it is "owned" by a matriarchal society, to one that is matriarchal in the sense that it tells the family history on her maternal side. Here Djebar's *écriture* rejoins Cixous's "écriture matricielle" in its strong identification with other women, blurring the boundaries of autobiography, as the self is traversed by the other:

> *Femmes pour femmes:* en la femme toujours se maintient la force productive de l'autre, en particulier de l'autre femme. *En* elle matricielle, berceuse-donneuse, elle-même sa mère et son enfant, elle-même sa fille-soeur.[129]

Eyes – open and shut

In a succession of moving short stories, Djebar foregrounds the sisterhood and suffering of her relatives and ancestors, who are trapped within the prison walls of patriarchy and colonialism. By allowing these women to hold centre stage, she aims to dislocate the

---

[128] Hélène Cixous, *La Jeune née*, pp. 151-52.
[129] Hélène Cixous, "Le Rire de la méduse", p. 44.

traditional male viewpoint that denies woman her subjectivity. Djebar's women are no longer reduced to being the object of the ubiquitous male gaze ("Car ils épient, ils observent, ils scrutent, ils espionnent! ... la rue est à eux, le monde est à eux..." ["Because they spy, they watch, they search, they snoop! ... the street is theirs, the world is theirs..."] pp. 175; 180), as Cixous's appeal to women to "disloque[r] ce 'dans', qu'elle l'explose, le retourne..." is answered in Djebar's collective mission statement:

> Nous toutes, du monde des femmes de l'ombre, renversant la démarche: nous enfin qui regardons, nous qui commençons. (pp. 175; 180)
>
> All of us from the world of the shadow women, reversing the process: We are the ones finally who are looking, who are beginning.

The writer resists the male gaze with the female eye, but also with the eye of the camera. Interlaced with the short stories in Part 3 are Djebar's memories of the experience of directing her film *La Nouba des femmes du Mont Chenoua*. The camera and her text both become eyes with which she can resist the male gaze, but Djebar takes the image further as the filmmaker passes the camera to a veiled silhouette, a gesture Mortimer foregrounds as "the giving of a gift ... to a veiled silhouette, the cloistered sister who, by peeking through the lens, may reclaim her subjectivity":[130]

> Cette image – réalité de mon enfance, de celle de ma mère et de mes tantes, de mes cousines parfois du même âge que moi, ce scandale qu'enfant j'ai vécu norme –, voici qu'elle surgit au départ de cette quête: silhouette unique de femme, rassemblant dans les pans de son linge-linceul les quelque cinq cents millions de ségréguées du monde islamique, c'est elle soudain qui regarde, mais derrière la caméra, elle qui, par un trou libre dans une face masquée, dévore le monde. (pp. 174; 179-80)
>
> This image is the reality of my childhood, and the childhood of my mother and my aunts, and my girl cousins who were sometimes the same age as me. Suddenly this scandal that I experienced as normal looms at the beginning of this quest: a single silhouette of a woman gathering in the folds of this shroud, her linen veil, the five hundred million or so segregated women in the Muslim world. Suddenly she is the one looking, but from behind the camera, she is the one devouring the world through a hole left in the concealment of a face.

With this gift Djebar enters into Cixous's Realm of the *Gift*, by symbolically stepping aside to allow the cloistered woman to look out.

---

[130] Mildred Mortimer, "Assia Djebar's Algerian Quartet: A Study in Fragmented Autobiography", *Research in African Literatures*, 28: 2 (1997), pp. 102-17, p. 113.

The veiled woman is on both sides of the camera, looking out through the camera lens, giving her access to the world, and looking out from the text-screen, giving the world access to her.

The image of the eye is double. Djebar *resists* with her eyes, by reappropriating the female gaze but like Cixous ("... j'entre à l'intérieur de moi les yeux fermés, et ça se lit." [131]) also *submits* to the unconscious by shutting her eyes, in an image where she, like Cixous, evokes "le lit", in her case "le lit d'enfant" as she observes a sleeping child, a young shepherdess turned film prop who has succumbed to tiredness on set:

> Telle fut aussi ma manière d'aborder l'image-son: les yeux fermés, pour saisir d'abord le rythme, le bruit des gouffres qu'on croit noyés, remonter ensuite à la surface et enfin, regard lavé, tout percevoir dans une lumière d'aurore. (pp. 273; 279)
>
> And it was also how I approached the work of images and sound. First with my eyes shut, to grasp the rhythm, the noises from submerged depths believed lost, then rising back to the surface again where finally, eyes washed clean, I see everything lit by dawn.

With her eyes shut, her ears, like those of Cixous, are attuned to "les silencieux désirs", the silent cries of her people:

> M'ai taillé de nouvelles oreilles pour l'avenir et j'ai entendu les cris du monde, les rages et les appels des peuples, les chants des corps, la musique des supplices et la musique des extases. J'écoute.[132]

In the succession of stories that comprise Part 3, what emerges above is a litany of silent suffering and a celebration of silent courage from the quiet dignity of her great grandmother following her marriage, at the age of fourteen, to an octogenarian, to a young child's self-imposed mutism in the aftermath of her sister's death, to the mother's silent tears at the imprisonment of her son at the hands of the colonial authorities. In Part 3 Djebar is "à l'écoute", her ears attuned to the sounds of silence, the silent tears, the silent screams of her people, echoing Cixous's universal embrace: "Que de larmes je verse la nuit! Les eaux du monde s'écoulent de mes yeux, je lave mes peuples dans mon désespoir, je les baigne, je les lèche avec mon amour, je vais aux rives des Nils, pour recueillir les peuples abandonnés dans des berceaux d'osier."[133]

---

[131] Hélène Cixous, *La Venue à l'écriture*, p. 57.
[132] Ibid., p. 47.
[133] Ibid., p. 53.

The dream

At the end of Part 3, Djebar describes a dream whose violent images evoke, through their compression, the depth of suppressed emotions contained within the main body of the text. In this dream Isma is aware of an obstruction in her vocal chords, removes an offending muscle at the back of her throat with a knife, and then releases not her own voice, but a piercing cry, the continuous lament of her people, "la souffrance des autres."

In the dream the narrator physically *materialises* the suffering of her people: her body literally becomes the conduit of her people's suffering as she physically disgorges their silent screams. Then by a tortuous process of identification, the writer and the silent scream become one: "Je ne crie pas, je suis le cri" [I do not cry, I am the cry] (pp. 339; 350). And, just as her body physically materialises their pain, the dream-text itself materialises, exposes in material signs, the underlying currents of repressed suffering contained in the main body of the text.

In the dream, the writer embodies what Cixous calls "the process of the same and the other", as Djebar interiorises within her self the sufferings of the other. This process of identification, when taken to the extreme, can entail a loss of self which Cixous identifies and which Isma then experiences, as self recedes and she becomes other:

> Or écrire c'est travailler; être travaillé; (dans) l'entre, interroger, (se laisser interroger) le procès du même *et de* l'autre ... en voulant ensemble de l'un-avec-l'autre, dynamisé à l'infini par un incessant échange de l'un entre l'autre ... Et cela ne se fait pas sans risque, sans douleur, sans perte, de moments de soi, de conscience, de personnes que l'on a été, que l'on dépasse, que l'on quitte.[134]

In the liberating locus of the unconscious, both Djebar and Cixous focus on the mouth as the site of release: "Le jour se cache? La nuit *les langues* sont déliées, les livres s'ouvrent et se révèlent, ce à quoi je n'arrive pas, mes rêves y arrivent pour moi."[135] The mouth is the orifice from which repressed language (in the case of Cixous) and repressed suffering (in the case of Djebar) are released.

In the beginning of Isma's dream, however, the mouth is obstructed by a mysterious substance, preventing this release: "Et ce rêve récurrent qui hante mes nuits! Au fond de ma bouche ouverte, une pâte molle et visqueuse, une glaire stagne, coule peu à peu et je m'enfonce dans le malaise irrémédiablement" [And this recurrent

---

[134] Hélène Cious, *La Jeune née*, p. 159.
[135] Hélène Cixous, *La Venue à l'écriture*, p. 50. [My emphasis]

dream that haunts my nights! In the bottom of my open mouth a soft, viscous paste, phlegm, stagnates, then gradually flows and I sink irremediably into the feeling of sickness] (pp. 338-39; 349). The focus shifts from a feeling of discomfort in her throat to an awareness of a specific obstruction of her vocal chords. This obstruction is preventing her from *expressing* the repressed suffering of her people, impeding the disgorging of this suffering through the passage of the throat, preventing *la sortie de l'autre*:

> L'écriture, c'est en moi le passage, entrée, sortie, séjour, de l'autre que je suis et ne suis pas, que je ne sais pas être, mais que je sens passer, qui me fait vivre, – qui me déchire, m'inquiète, m'altère, qui? – une, un, des?, plusieurs, de l'inconnu qui me donne justement l'envie de connaître à partir de laquelle s'élance toute vie...[136]

In Isma's dream the passage through which the other must pass is physically materialised as the pharynx and the obstruction of this passage is literally life threatening, as the desire to give voice to the suffering of others becomes an urgent physical necessity:

> Il me faut arracher cette pâte de mon palais, elle m'étouffe; je tente de vomir, je vomis quoi, sinon une puanteur blanchâtre, enracinée au plus profond de mon gosier. Ces dernières nuits, l'encombrement pharyngien a été pis: il m'a fallu couper au couteau une sorte de muscle inutile qui m'écorche, crachat enserré à mes cordes vocales. (pp. 339; 349)

> I have to get this paste off my palate; it is smothering me; I try to vomit. What do I vomit other than whitish stench stuck deep down in my throat? These last few nights the blockage in my pharynx has been worse: I have had to take a knife and cut some kind of useless muscle that hurts me, spit covering my vocal cords.

Djebar, like Cixous, describes the relationship to writing in terms of giving birth to the other ("Chaque nuit, l'effort musculaire de cet enfantement par la bouche, de cette mise au silence me lancine" [Every night I am tormented by the muscular effort of giving birth through the mouth this way, this silencing], pp. 339; 350), and in both cases the process of labour is preceded by an experience of a giving up of the self, in Cixous's case death to the self, and in Djebar's case a detachment from the self. For in Isma's urgent need to express the suffering of others, her own physical pain is sublimated to the sufferings of the other:

> Ma bouche demeure béante; mes doigts tenaces s'activent entre mes dents, un spasme me tord l'abdomen, rancoeur ou embarras

---

[136] Hélène Cixous, *La Jeune née*, p. 158.

irrépressible. Je ne ressens pas l'horreur de cet état: j'ai pris la lame, je tâche de trancher tout au fond, lentement, soigneusement, cette glu suspendue sous ma glotte. Le sang étalé sur mes doigts, ce sang qui ne m'emplit pas la bouche, semble soudain léger, neutre, un liquide prêt non à s'écouler, plutôt à s'évaporer au-dedans de mon corps.

J'exerce cet effort d'amputation avec précision: je ne me demande pas si je souffre, si je me blesse, surtout si je vais demeurer sans voix. (pp. 339; 349-350)

My mouth still hangs open; my persistent fingers are busy among my teeth, a spasm wrenches my abdomen – rancor or irresistible nausea. I do not experience the horror of this state: I have picked up the blade, I try to cut all the way down, slowly, carefully, to the bottom of the gluey stuff hanging under my glottis. Blood is all over my fingers, this blood not filling my mouth suddenly seems light, neutral, a liquid prepared not to flow out but to evaporate inside my body instead.

I perform this attempted amputation very carefully: I do not ask myself if I am suffering, or if I am wounding myself, and especially not whether or not I will remain voiceless.

This "perte de soi", expressed physically in terms of amputation, echoes Cixous's conviction that in order to give birth to the other the writer must first die to the self: "Et je dis: il faut avoir été aimée par la mort, pour naître et passer à l'écriture":[137]

D'abord elle meurt. Ensuite elle aime ... Je n'ai rien à dire sur ma mort. Elle a été trop grande pour moi jusqu'ici. D'une certaine manière tous mes textes en sont "nés". L'ont fuie. En sont issus ... Sans elle – ma mort je n'aurais pas écrit. Pas déchiré le voile de ma gorge. Pas poussé le cri qui déchire les oreilles, qui fend les murs.[138]

Cixous's own image of an obstructed pharynx (interestingly it is Cixous but not Djebar who incorporates the torn *veil*) could almost be superimposed on that of Djebar's. Both are travailed by the process of the same and the other, a physical process that involves suffering/death, giving birth, a rending of the pharynx, and the disgorging of a powerful cry:

Chaque nuit l'effort musculaire de cet enfantement par la bouche, de cette mise au silence me lancine. Je vomis quoi, peut-être un long cri ancestral. Ma bouche ouverte expulse indéfiniment la souffrance des autres, des ensevelies avant moi, moi qui croyais apparaître à peine au premier rai de la première lumière. (pp. 339; 350)

Every night I am tormented by the muscular effort of giving birth through the mouth this way, this silencing. I vomit something, what? Maybe a long ancestral cry. My open mouth expels, continuously, the suffering of others, the suffering of the shrouded women who came

---

[137] Hélène Cixous, *La Venue à l'écriture*, p. 44.
[138] Ibid., p. 42.

before me, I who believed I was only just appearing at the first ray of the first light.

Both Cixous and Djebar are "writing the body" and the physicality of this act is reinforced in both cases by the muscular effort of giving birth to the other/text:

> Ecrire: comme si j'avais encore envie de jouir, de me sentir pleine, de pousser, de sentir la force de mes muscles, et mon harmonie, d'être enceinte et au même moment de me donner les joies de la parturition, celles de la mère et celles de l'enfant.[139]

Both writers are travailed by the process of the same and the other. For Cixous, the writer can be both mother and child, the one who gives birth and the one who is begotten. For Djebar, she is first of all the voice of the other, but then becomes the embodiment of that voice: "Je ne crie pas. Je suis le cri" [I do not cry; I am the cry] (pp. 339; 350). But whereas in the scriptural delivery room, Cixous's child-text is dripping with mother's milk ("Je déborde! Mes seins débordent! Du lait. De l'encre. L'heure de la tétée.")[140], Djebar's text-cry is covered in rapidly evaporating blood ("Le sang étalé sur mes doigts, ce sang qui ne m'emplit pas la bouche, semble soudain léger, neutre, un liquide prêt non à s'écouler, plutôt à s'évaporer au-dedans de mon corps" [Blood is all over my fingers, this blood not filling my mouth suddenly seems light, neutral, a liquid prepared not to flow out but to evaporate inside my body instead], pp. 339; 349).

The cosmic mouth

As both writers rejoin the other, their images of writing coalesce in the cosmic scale of their vision of themselves in their relation to that other. In the place of the cosmic mother strutting her pregnant belly, we have a cosmic mouth, incessantly expelling the sufferings of others ("Ma bouche ouverte expulse indéfiniment la souffrance des autres"). This cosmic perspective is perpetuated in the final image of the dream:

> Je ne crie pas, je suis le cri tendu dans un vol vibrant et aveugle; la procession blanche des aïeules-fantômes derrière moi devient armée qui me propulse, se lèvent les mots de la langue perdue qui vacille, tandis que les mâles au-devant gesticulent dans le champ de la mort, ou de ses masques. (pp. 339; 350)
>
> I do not cry, I am the cry, stretched out into resonant blind flight; the white procession of ghost-grandmothers behind me becomes an army

---

[139] Hélène Cixous, *La Venue à l'écriture*, pp. 37-38.
[140] Ibid., p. 37.

propelling me on; words of the quavering, lost language rise up while the males out in front gesticulate in the field of death or of its masks.

"Le cri" becomes *a weapon* wielded by an army of veiled women in a scene reminiscent of Cixous's *"champ de bataille."* Here we have a battle between man and woman in which *language is a powerful weapon*, resonating with the echo of *the lost Voice,* "les mots de la langue perdue", and which carries within it the possibility of transformation, as the *passive* floating shadow-like figures of the preface are transformed into *an active army* of veiled women driving her writing forward, as its cry cuts through *"le silence de l'écriture"* [the silence of writing]. It is as if she goes back to the preface, takes hold of the piercing arrow of patriarchal language aimed *inwards* at her soul, and then aims it *back* into *"le champ de la mort"* [the field of death] in the form of her winged cry-self.

As the text goes full circle, Djebar, like Cixous, discovers the power of language as a weapon against the prevailing powers of patriarchy, and the power of the voice to recapture the repressed. Writing is no longer paralysed by its relationship to the past but dynamised by the presence of the voice: "Ce regard réflexif sur le passé pouvait susciter une dynamique pour une quête sur le présent, sur un avenir à la porte" [This introspective, backward-looking gaze could make it possible to search the present, a future on the doorstep] (pp. 298; 306). Ironically, however, the neat closure of the dream-text (with its counter-relation to the preface) suggests that the dream itself is not merely the product of the other (unconscious), but rather a very conscious construction.

The Blood-Streams of Writing

In this final part, Djebar's writing rejoins the present, no longer in the sense of the *presence* of voice, but in the sense of "l'actualité." And, as Algeria's "champ de la mort" [field of death] fills the horizon, "l'Algérie mère" mutates into "Algérie amère" [bitter Algeria] (pp. 347; 358), the motherland suddenly transformed into a macabre monstrosity: "... le monstre Algérie – et ne l'appelez plus femme, peut-être goule, ou vorace centauresse surgie de quels abysses, non, même pas 'femme sauvage'" [... the monster Algeria – and do not call it a woman anymore, unless it is a ghoul (which is feminine), or a voracious female centaur risen from some abyss, no, not even madwoman] (pp. 345; 356). And as *l'écriture* struggles to express "le massacre des autres" [the massacre of others], the writer's body materialises the thoughts of the dead:

> Car les morts qu'on croit enterrer aujourd'hui désormais s'envolent. Eux, les allègres, les allégés ... Les morts qu'on croit absents se muent en témoins qui, à travers nous, désirent écrire! ... Ecrire, les morts d'aujourd'hui désirent écrire: or, avec le sang, comment écrire? (pp. 346; 357)
>
> Because from now on the dead we think we bury today will fly off. They are the lighthearted ones now, relieved, lightened ... We think the dead are absent but, transformed into witnesses, they want to write through us ... Write, the dead of today want to write: now, how can one write with blood?

In a variation on Cixous writing in mother's milk, in white ink, Djebar writes in the freshly shed blood, in red ink: "Comment inscrire traces avec un sang qui coule, ou qui vient juste de couler? ... Mais avec le sang même: avec son flux, sa pâte, son jet, sa croûte pas tout à fait séchée?" [How can one inscribe with blood that flows or has just finished flowing? ... But with blood itself: with its flow, its paste, its spurt, its scab that is not yet dry?] (pp. 346-47; 357-58). And, as the lifeblood is sucked out of her people, the fire red blood of writing turns to embers, not milky white, but deathly white: "Le sang, pour moi, reste blanc cendre ... Le sang ne sèche pas, simplement il s'éteint" [Blood for me remains ash white ... Blood does not dry, it simply evaporates] (pp. 347; 358).

Writing is forever displaced not by the endless movement of the signifier but by the continuous stream of blood. In a final spiralling movement, *l'écriture* endlessly pursues the cycle of death perpetuated by an "Algérie-monstre" hounding the antelope of death. And, as the bloodthirsty nation and the writing existing in the *sang-rapport* themselves become caught up in a final battle of mythic proportions, the writer ingests "l'Algérie-monstre" in a dramatic finale:

> Ecrire pour cerner la poursuite inlassable
> Le cercle ouvert à chaque pas se referme
> La mort devant, antilope cernée
> L'Algérie chasseresse, en moi, est avalée. (pp. 348; 359)
>
> Writing to encircle the relentless pursuit,
> The circle that each step opens closes up again,
> Death ahead, antelope encircled,
> Algeria the huntress, is swallowed up in me.

Conclusion

In *Vaste est la prison*, Djebar, like Cixous, is trying to find ways out of the oppositionary prison-house of patriarchy, both on the level of human relationships, and on the level of language. The preface identifies the phenomenon of opposition in language and society in the form of segregation, whereas Part 1 materialises the phenomenon, as "le mari" and "l'Aimé" conform to oppositional roles pinpointed by Cixous, "l'homme-ennemi" and "l'homme-Dieu."

In the final images of Part 1, Djebar does manage to effectuate *une sortie* from the oppositionary mode of relations, and following on from Cixous, this *sortie* is achieved at the level of *écriture*, in an in-between zone, beyond the symbolic, where Isma and "l'Aimé" enter into a mobile space of same and otherness, resonant of Cixous's process of the same and the other.

On the level of language, Djebar and Cixous use different strategies to combat what is essentially the same problem, namely their feeling of alienation with regard to patriarchal language. But whereas Cixous finally finds ways out of the linguistic prison-house, by exploring *une écriture féminine*, Djebar's return to a matriarchal language does not provide a *sortie*. At the end of her historical quest (Part 2), she is still an exile of language: she has no language to call her own.

In the final part of the work, however, Djebar embraces another kind of matriarchal writing, not one that belongs to a matriarchal society but rather one that gives voice to the women down the maternal line of her family. As it gives voice to the other, Djebar's writing rejoins Cixous's "écriture matricielle." And, as *écriture* is travailed by "le procès du même et de l'autre", Djebar finally finds another way of accessing the lost Mother-Voice, so longed for in *L'Amour, la fantasia*:

> En fait, je recherche, comme un lait dont on m'aurait autrefois écartée, la pléthore amoureuse de la langue de ma mère. Contre la ségrégation de mon héritage, le mot plein de l'amour-au-présent me devient une parade hirondelle.
>
> And now I too seek out the rich vocabulary of love of my mother tongue – milk of which I had been previously deprived. In contrast to the segregation I inherited, words expressing love-in-the-present become for me like one token swallow heralding summer.[141]

As Djebar's eyes are opened to the law of opposition at work in the Arabic language (in *Vaste est la prison*), she may no longer yearn for her mother tongue, but she does discover another m/other from which her texts can be born. In Part 3, Djebar, like Cixous, writes in white ink, creating "une écriture presque invisible", "une écriture de

---

[141] Assia Djebar, *L'Amour, la fantasia*, p. 80, trans. Dorothy S. Blair, *Fantasia: An Algerian Cavalcade*, p. 62.

l'autre", which can be materialised but not appropriated into the self-referential order of patriarchy.

But, as the writing of the past catches up with the present, Djebar finds herself exiled not only from the mother tongue, but from the motherland. The metamorphosis of the motherland produces a transmutation in the substance of *écriture*, as the writing of the m/other, "l'écriture du lait" encounters rivers of blood and her text becomes stained with the indelible mark of "le sang des autres."

In Dialogue with Irigaray:
Ombre sultane

The Repressed Maternal-Feminine

"Elle s'est voulue marieuse de son propre mari" [She had decided to act as matchmaker to her own husband].[1] In *Ombre sultane*, by a twist of fate, a woman becomes her ex-husband's matchmaker. Isma, an educated, emancipated Algerian divorcée, arranges for her ex-husband to marry Hajila, an illiterate traditional woman from "le bidonville." In the course of the novel, a fundamental change takes place in the relationship between these two women. In this chapter I propose to focus on this change, which I will analyse in the light of Luce Irigaray's ideas.

Both Irigaray and Djebar are concerned with the problematic of relations between women, which they view as characterised by a fundamental rivalry in relation to men and to each other. Irigaray attributes the negative relations between women to their lack of subjectivity. Having been denied subjectivity they are incapable of subject-to-subject relations.

For Irigaray the problem of women's subjectivity is not a social or biological one but a symbolic one. It originates in the "original sin" committed by the symbolic order, what Margaret Whitford refers to as "a buried act of matricide."[2] According to Irigaray, the paternal symbolic order is founded on the "murder", the non-symbolisation, *non-recognition*, or repression of the maternal-feminine. Irigaray's objective is to bring about symbolic change. If the symbolic order is founded on this act of non-recognition, then any change in the symbolic can only be achieved *as a result of the recognition of that other, the repressed or unconscious maternal-feminine*. It is only when that "other" is recognised, when woman can take her place in the symbolic order as subject, that she will be capable of positive subject-to-subject relations.

---

[1] Assia Djebar, *Ombre sultane* (Paris: Editions Jean-Claude Lattès, 1987), p. 9. trans. Dorothy S. Blair, *A Sister to Scheherazade* (London/New York: Quartet, 1988), p. 1. Unless stated otherwise, all subsequent quotations in English of *Ombre Sultane* are drawn from Blair's translation.
[2] Margaret Whitford, *Luce Irigaray: Philosophy in the Feminine* (London and New York: Routledge 1991), p. 33.

In *Ombre sultane*, the problem of rivalry between women resurfaces on a narrative rather than on a philosophical level. The problem of rivalry and the possibility of change, of another, positive mode of relations between women is embodied in the relationship between the two principal characters, Hajila and Isma. In this chapter, using a psychological model, I demonstrate that the condition for symbolic change specified by Irigaray, *namely the recognition of the repressed maternal-feminine*, operates on a narrative level in *Ombre sultane*. In the novel, change in the relationship between Hajila and Isma also takes place as a result of the acknowledgement of the repressed or unconscious maternal-feminine.[3]

Taking as my starting-point Irigaray's proposition that such a shift in consciousness is necessary before female subjectivity and sociality can come into being, I will examine the novel with the aim of demonstrating how the unconscious maternal-feminine is acknowledged in *Ombre sultane*. I will then compare the change in the relationship between Hajila and Isma (as a result of this shift of consciousness) to the transformation of subject-to-subject relations that Irigaray envisions for women.

The Absent Sex: Irigaray and Symbolic Exclusion

> In all forms of feminism there is a tension between the critique of an unsatisfactory present and the requirement, experienced as psychological or political, for some blueprint, however sketchy, of the future.[4]

In my introduction to Irigaray I will mainly concentrate on her "critique of an unsatisfactory present." This critique, which is single-

---

[3] Although the unconscious is commonly associated with what cannot be expressed, Irigaray refers to the possibility of the unconscious or unconscious thoughts being acknowledged or "released" through psychoanalysis. It is in the sense that I refer to the "acknowledgement or release of the feminine-unconscious." Moreover, as the term "feminine-unconscious" suggests, Irigaray posits a relation between the unconscious and feminine imaginary. In the first instance, she uses Freud's notion of the unconscious as a metaphor for the *cultural* position of femininity. Taking this idea further, Irigaray posits: "a close resemblance between the unconscious in its relation to consciousness and women in relation to patriarchal social relations". Using Freud's identification of the repressed with femininity, she goes a step further still: "if what is repressed is feminine, she claims, it is possible to regard women, not as *having* an unconscious, but as *being* it (for men, for the phallic, for patriarchy)." See Elizabeth Grosz, *Sexual Subversions* (Sydney: Allen and Unwin, 1989), pp. 106-07.
[4] Margaret Whitford, *Luce Irigaray: Philosophy in the Feminine*, p. 18.

minded in its focus, but wide-ranging in its application, has been deftly summarised as follows:

> Irigaray is dealing with a single problem, in its multiple aspects: the absence of and exclusion of woman/women from the symbolic/social order, and their representation as nature. This problem is reworked and restated repeatedly, in a variety of discursive formulations, in terms borrowed from a variety of philosophers, and in relation to a wide variety of different conceptual systems.[5]

In this theoretical résumé, I will examine both the *basis* of Irigaray's critique of the symbolic (its *"exclusion of women"*) and her critical *strategy* (mimicry), as well as alluding to the analogy between her critical method and the workings of psychoanalysis. As far as Irigaray's "blueprint for the future" is concerned, I here refer to her idea of a maternal genealogy. Finally, I would suggest that the reference (in the first citation above) to the tension between an unsatisfactory present and a utopian future is reductive in terms of Irigaray's *later* thinking, which acknowledges the influence of *past* genealogies and hazards the possibility of achieving sexual difference in the *present* (I will return to these last two ideas in the sections on *Ombre sultane*).

Masculinity and mimicry

Irigaray's analysis of an "unsatisfactory present" takes the form of a sweeping critique of the symbolic order and all its conceptual systems: "... lois au sens strict et aussi langues, religions, arts, sciences, techniques."[6] According to her, the founding gesture of the symbolic order is "a buried act of matricide"[7], a proposition that is reformulated as the repression of the feminine, and in particular of the mother-figure.

Irigaray believes that the very construction of the patriarchal symbolic order hinges on this "murder" of the maternal-feminine. The maternal-feminine represents the foundation upon which the symbolic order is constructed: as the Law of the Father is erected, the Body of the Mother is removed from view (forgotten, disavowed). Irigaray's project can be compared to that of a criminal pathologist, as she exhumes the Body of the Mother, revealing the underlying maternal-feminine, exposes the perpetrators of the crime (masculine systems of

---

[5] Ibid., p. 170. [My emphasis]
[6] Luce Irigaray, *Le Temps de la différence* (Livre de Poche, 1989). Insert from back cover.
[7] Margaret Whitford, *Luce Irigaray: Philosophy in the Feminine*, p. 33.

thought), denounces their repressive methods, and attempts to perform a miracle in bringing the maternal-feminine back to the symbolic.

According to Irigaray, "Toute théorie du 'sujet' aura toujours été appropriée au 'masculin.'"[8] The masculine has not only monopolised all sense of personal subjectivity but also all areas of conceptual subjectivity. On the level of personal subjectivity, any sense of self that woman achieves is necessarily in relation to the masculine and therefore not her own: "S'y réobjectivant elle-même quand elle prétend s'identifier 'comme' un sujet masculin."[9] Irigaray makes a direct connection between the objectivisation of the female subject and the repression of the feminine on a conceptual level: "La subjectivité déniée à la femme telle est, sans doute, l'hypothèque garante de toute constitution irréductible d'objet: de représentation, de discours, de désir."[10]

For Irigaray, women inevitably figure as the object of masculine discourse. This objectification of women on a personal level is reformulated on a conceptual level as the repression of the maternal-feminine. Thus all conceptual systems are masculine systems that have repressed the maternal-feminine. All subjects (*subjects* of philosophy, psychology, religion, law and language) are dominated by an all-embracing masculine imaginary.

Of particular interest to Irigaray is the masculine dominance of the linguistic code. Irigaray argues that woman has no language of her own and that she can therefore never speak as herself – her language is always caught up in the discourse of the dominant linguistic code. Women are therefore compelled to imitate masculine discourse in order for their language to be "symbolically received." Aware of the difficulty of entering into masculine discourse in order to criticise it, and the impossibility of expressing herself outside its boundaries, Irigaray comes up with another strategy, that of mimicking the female position of mimicry: "Hers is a theatrical staging of the mime: miming the miming imposed on woman, Irigaray's subtle specular move (her mimicry *mirrors* that of all women) intends to *undo* the effects of phallocentric discourse simply by *overdoing* them."[11]

Irigaray's mimetic strategy hinges on her selective, extensive quoting from the discourses that she wants to undermine, quotations interwoven with her own writing in such a way as to make it difficult

---

[8] Luce Irigaray, *Spéculum de l'autre femme* (Paris: Minuit, 1974), p. 165.
[9] Ibid., p. 165.
[10] Ibid., p. 165.
[11] Toril Moi, *Sexual/Textual Politics: Feminist Literary Theory* (London and New York: Routledge, 1985), p. 140.

to work out where one ends and the other begins. The effect of this selective quotation is to highlight the points where the maternal-feminine is "conspicuous by its absence": "Le féminin étant dès lors à déchiffrer comme inter-dit: dans les signes ou entre eux, entre des significations réalisées, entre les lignes..."[12] Imitation in the Irigarayan sense is no longer a form of flattery but a sophisticated form of ridicule, a way of destabilising masculine discourse from within, of turning masculine discourse against itself.

The aim of Irigaray's mimetic strategy is to show that all its masculine theories not only repress the feminine other but also conform to a specular logic, a logic of the same: "'Specularization' ... hints at a basic assumption underlying all Western philosophical discourse: the necessity of postulating a subject that is capable of *reflecting* on its own being."[13] Irigaray posits the masculine subject in front of the mirror, gazing at his own reflection. In this scenario, the woman becomes the material basis (the tain of the mirror), which permits the specularisation to take place, and which at the same time denies her any possibility of representation.

Woman comes to be equated with the absent image, with that which is beyond representation, but also with the forbidden image, with that which is censored or repressed. Irigaray not only identifies the feminine with the repressed, but proceeds to identify the feminine imaginary with the process of the unconscious, both being characterised by fluidity, mobility, and a resistance to the laws of logic, and finally to equate the two as one:

> Ainsi pourrait-on se demander si certaines propriétés attribuées à l'inconscient ne sont pas, pour une part, référables au sexe féminin censuré de la logique de la conscience. Si le féminin *a* un inconscient ou s'il *est* l'inconscient.[14]

In *Luce Irigaray: Philosophy in the Feminine*, Whitford relates Irigaray's own position to a psychoanalytical model in relation to the philosophers she criticises. She visualises Irigaray attempting to "unbind or unloosen" the feminine-unconscious of the masculine discourses with which she engages. In this model Irigaray functions as analyst, and her masculine subjects (such as the subjects or fathers of philosophy and psychology) function as analysands. With Freud and then Plato on the couch, Irigaray takes on the role of psychoanalyst,

---

[12] Luce Irigaray, *Spéculum de l'autre femme*, p. 20.
[13] Toril Moi, *Sexual/Textual Politics*, p. 132.
[14] Luce Irigaray, *Ce sexe qui n'en est pas un* (Paris: Minuit, 1977), p. 71.

releasing their unconscious thoughts, liberating the feminine-unconscious of philosophical and psychoanalytical discourse:

Freud on the couch

In *Spéculum de l'autre femme*, Irigaray comes face to face with her first patient, Freud, and finds this particular analysand in profound denial, refusing to acknowledge the specificity of a feminine sexuality.

Irigaray contends that underlying Freud's theory of sexuality is the assumption of "sexual indifference" (the presupposition that there is only one *masculine* sex rather than two differentiated sexes), and the imposition of a male model of sexuality. Stripping Freud down to basics, Irigaray reduces his theory of sexual "difference" to the presence or absence of the male attribute. And, with this scopophilic interpretation of sexuality, *female* sexuality is reduced to a negation:

> En effet, cette sexualité n'est jamais définie par rapport à un autre sexe que le masculin. Il n'y a pas, pour Freud, *deux sexes* dont les différences s'articuleraient dans l'acte sexuel, et plus généralement dans les processus imaginaires et symboliques qui règlent un fonctionnement social et culturel. Le "féminin" est toujours décrit comme défaut, atrophie, revers du seul sexe qui monopolise la valeur: le sexe masculin.[15]

Freud proceeds from his theory of want (lack) of the male attribute to his theory of want (desire for or envy of) the male attribute, "la trop célèbre 'envie du pénis.'"[16] This is a transition that Irigaray refuses to make : "Comment accepter que tout le devenir sexuel de la femme soit commandé par le manque, et donc l'envie, la jalousie, la revendication, du sexe masculin?"[17] She prefers to dismiss Freud's "penis envy" as a projection of his own unconscious fears: "'l'envie du pénis' telle qu'elle est attribuée à la femme pallie l'angoisse de l'homme, de Freud, concernant la cohérence de son édifice narcissique, le rassure contre ce qu'il appelle la peur de la castration."[18]

According to Irigaray, the theory of penis envy serves to validate the masculine sex, to affirm the primacy of masculinity (reflecting man's sexuality back to himself), and to reduce both masculine and feminine sexuality to the economy of the same, (defining the

---

[15] Ibid., pp. 67-68.
[16] Ibid., pp. 67-68.
[17] Ibid., p. 68.
[18] Luce Irigaray, *Spéculum de l'autre femme,* p. 58.

other/feminine in terms of the same/masculine sexuality): "Mais, prisonnier lui-même d'une certaine économie du logos, il définit la différence sexuelle en fonction de l'a priori du Même, recourant pour étayer sa démonstration, aux procédés de toujours: l'analogie..."[19]

Redirecting death drives

Irigaray rejects Freud's theory of sexuality based on the economy of the same and looks to another economy, the economy of the other (unconscious), to explain both the absence of, and the possibility of recovering sexual difference. According to Irigaray, sexual difference, or the presence of two separate sexual subjectivities (male and female) is not realised in the symbolic because of the different way in which men and women relate to the economy of the unconscious. Men externalise their (unconscious) death drives, projecting them onto women, whereas women cannot sublimate their death drives (at some other's expense) and are forced to internalise them (making them more vulnerable to self-destructive impulses). The result of this is that woman is deprived of her subjectivity, she is reduced to becoming the object or "receptacle" of man's repressed drives. She occupies the locus of his unconscious or, as Irigaray would have it, she functions *as* his unconscious.

So, according to Irigaray, the dividing line between the conscious and the unconscious is currently drawn *between* the sexes, (with man representing the conscious, and woman *his* unconscious). What Irigaray then advocates is a realignment of this split, arguing that the divisions between conscious and unconscious should not be drawn *between* the sexes but *within* them – "[the divisions] should be internal to each sex."[20] Each sex should be able to sublimate its own death drives, each should have its *own* unconscious or other. Openly challenging Lacan's statement that "there is no Other of the Other",[21] Irigaray proclaims female otherness to be the very condition for woman's coming into being, for her accession to subjectivity and for the realisation of sexual difference.

Irigaray suggests that the symbolisation (validation, representation) of the mother-daughter relationship is one of the keys to the coming into being of a symbolic order in which both men and women exist as subjects, each sublimating their own death drives. This is because she

---

[19] Luce Irigaray, *Ce sexe qui n'en est pas un*, p. 70.
[20] Margaret Whitford, *Luce Irigaray: Philosophy in the Feminine*, p. 93.
[21] Jacques Lacan, *Ecrits: A Selection*, trans. Alan Sheridan (London: Tavistock, 1977), p. 311.

believes that the objectification of women is perpetuated by the mother-daughter relationship, and that the transformation of that relationship could signal a way forward towards female subjectivity. As evidence of this objectivisation, she points to the way female identity is formed, claiming that the daughter objectifies herself in the very process of identifying herself with her mother (who is already posited as object): "Elle ne peut réduire sa mère en objet sans s'y réduire elle-même parce qu'elles ont le même sexe."[22]

Within the masculine economy of the same, both mother and daughter exist not only as objects of man's death drives but also as objects of desire. Irigaray points to the paralysis of relations between mother and daughter caused by the fact that they are both in constant competition for what Irigaray describes as *the same space*, in other words that of the desire (or attention) of the father. According to Irigaray, the static positionality or paralysis created by the competition of the two for the one space needs to be transformed into a dynamic relationality where mother and daughter relate not to men as objects but to each other as separate subjects. For there to be separation or difference between mother and daughter, the daughter must relate to her mother not just as a mother but as a "separate" subject in her own right.

For Irigaray the restoration of the mother-daughter relationship is the key to the restoration of other relationships between women. Having acceded to subjectivity, they would then be able to enter into subject-to-subject relations with other women, and to be part of what Irigaray calls an "entre-femmes."

Material Girl

Irigaray's encounter with her next analysand, Plato, focuses on her analysis of his cave myth. Her critique of Plato's thinking reveals that he too excludes women, not from the domain of sexuality, but from the realm of the transcendental. For in Plato's universe, women are relegated to the material world, existing merely as "corps-matière."

In *Spéculum*, Plato's three scenes of the cave, the world and the Idea, become the staging ground for a reformulation of Irigaray's recurrent themes – the underlying sexual bias of masculine discourse, its perpetuation of the economy of the same, and the exclusion of woman from philosophical discourse.

---

[22] Luce Irigaray, *Sexes et parentés* (Paris: Minuit, 1987), p. 210.

Irigaray sees in the myth a re-enactment of the sexual act, with the cavern featuring as the womb of the mother, and the realm of the Idea starring as the seed of the Father. Although the prisoner starts his journey from the cavern (origin, mother), he moves progressively away from the cave towards the Realm of Ideas (or Origin, Father). The allegory is structured as a hierarchical progression from cave to Idea, from mother to father via the world. In the last scene of the allegory, only the Realm of the Idea remains, suggesting for Irigaray the elision of the mother from the scene of representation – woman is now "off-stage": "Éclipse de la mère, du lieu (du) devenir, qui soutient de sa non-représentation, voire sa (dé)négation, l'être absolu attribué au père."[23]

The three elements of the allegory, the Idea, the world and the cavern are also reformulated as the same, the 'other of the same', and 'the other of the other', and, as Whitford explains: "this schema later becomes expanded in subsequent texts..."[24], as follows:

'The Realm of the Idea', which is equated with the economy of the same, is reached by a complex system of mirrors, copies and echoes, and as such comes to represent the self-referential, "homosexual" world of men.

'The world' functions as man's other, his "home base", or "base camp", that other space from which he can "take off", and which he leaves behind when he ascends towards the transcendental. Irigaray makes a connection between that "home-base" and the "home", the private, domestic world of women, and so the 'other of the same' comes to represent the position of women in patriarchy.

'The cavern' is equated with the 'other of the other', a space-time that woman can call her own, and that is not identified or defined in relation to the same or to the economy of the same: "[It is] an as yet non-existent female homosexual economy, women-amongst-themselves, love of self on the side of women."[25]

What Irigaray also draws from the myth is the same's *unacknowledged dependence on the other* or man's unacknowledged dependence on woman. Man needs his "home base", he cannot progress toward the Realm of the Transcendental, without a starting-point, a place where he can make his journey from and return to for material sustenance. His identity, his capacity for transcendence, are conditional on the support of the same. Thus, underlying the

---

[23] Luce Irigaray, *Spéculum de l'autre femme*, p. 383.
[24] Margaret Whitford, *Luce Irigaray: Philosophy in the Feminine*, p. 104.
[25] Ibid., p. 104.

disappearance of the mother from the final scene of the allegory is the disavowal of the material support required by man to ascend to the transcendental.

Finally, Irigaray wishes to challenge the fundamental separation that underlies this scene of representation, the separation of the spiritual and material worlds, with its underlying positive/negative, male/female connotation, a separation that she reformulates as existing between the "sensible" and the "transcendental."

What Irigaray is looking for is a way for women to be able to access the transcendental while not denying their corporeality, a state of being that she refers to as the "sensible transcendental." In the next section we will see how Irigaray's idea of a female divinity represents one of the ways in which she believes this could be achieved.

A female genealogy

> Il nous manque, nous sexuées selon notre genre, un Dieu à partager, un verbe à partager et à devenir. Définies comme substance-mère, souvent obscure, voire occulte, du verbe des hommes, il nous manque notre *sujet*, notre *substantif*, notre *verbe*, nos *prédicats*: notre phrase élémentaire, notre rythme de base, notre identité morphologique, notre incarnation générique, notre généalogie.[26]

Both Irigaray's critique of the symbolic, and her blueprint for the future or "symbolic solutions", are voiced in a variety of discursive formulations. Her various projections, whether expressed in relation to the philosophical, the sexual, the social or the religious, can be assembled under the umbrella of her idea of a maternal genealogy.[27]

Irigaray does not believe that a maternal genealogy should replace the paternal one, but rather that there should be two genealogies coexisting in relation to each other ("Mais, si leur projet visait simplement à renverser l'ordre des choses ... l'histoire reviendrait finalement au même. Au phallocentrisme."[28]). The paternal genealogy, based on *sacrifice* (on the child's renunciation of the mother in favour of the father) sacrifices women's relations to their mothers, to their daughters and to each other. This founding notion of *sacrifice* is countered in Irigaray's thinking by a maternal genealogy, which is

---

[26] Luce Irigaray, *Sexes et parentés*, p. 83.
[27] In this section I refer to Irigaray's blueprint for a new symbolic. Later, in the main body of the text, I will refer to her work on the "forgotten mystery of *forgotten genealogies*" published in *Le Temps de la différence*.
[28] Luce Irigaray, *Ce sexe qui n'en est pas un*, p. 32.

based on the notion of *fertility* (where the mother agrees to be fertile *with* her daughter[29]):

> Comment affirmer ensemble ces valeurs élémentaires, ces fécondités naturelles, les célébrer, les garder, les conserver, les monnayer en devenant ou restant femmes?[30]

This idea of fertility provides a way of restoring for women the *specificity of their gender*, providing them with a marker of difference. So what may appear at first reading to represent nothing but an exhortation to motherhood, is in fact, as Whitford explains, the very opposite:

> On the contrary it is a picture which allows women an identity *distinct* from motherhood ... So *fertility* should be read ... as a counter term to *sacrifice*, to indicate the possibility of a different mode of social organisation in which woman's difference is represented, symbolized, and codified.[31]

Irigaray also provides a way of restoring for women the *specificity of their sexuality*, countering Freud's specular theory (and the singularity of the male organ) by a tactile notion of sexuality celebrating the plurality of the two lips:

> La femme "*se touche*" tout le temps, sans que l'on puisse d'ailleurs le lui interdire, car son sexe est fait de deux lèvres qui s'embrassent continûment. Ainsi, en elle, elle est déjà deux – mais non divisibles en un(e)s – qui s'affectent ... Le *un* de la forme, de l'individu, du sexe, du nom propre, du sens propre ... supplante, en écartant et divisant, ce toucher *d'au moins deux* (lèvres) qui maintient la femme en contact avec elle-même, mais sans discrimination possible de ce qui se touche.[32]

The two lips stand as a figure not only for plurality but also for contiguity, for that which touches, associates or combines. The idea of contiguity is integrated into Irigaray's vision of a woman's sociality, which is based on *contiguous* relations between women. In this social context, the figure of the two lips operates as a symbol of what Whitford calls "vertical and horizontal relationships between women" (vertical relationships being those between mothers and daughters, and horizontal relationships being those between women), which could be achieved by women within their own genealogy: "Contiguity, then, is a figure for the vertical and horizontal relationships between women,

---

[29] Luce Irigaray, *Sexes et parentés*, p. 9.
[30] Ibid., p. 95.
[31] Margaret Whitford, *Luce Irigaray: Philosophy in the Feminine*, p. 183.
[32] Luce Irigaray, *Ce sexe qui n'en est pas un*, pp. 24, 26.

the maternal genealogy and the relation of sisterhood (since there are two pairs of two lips, of which one pair – the mouth – can be seen as horizontal, and the other pair – the labia – as vertical, each representing each other). It stands for women's sociality, love of self on the woman's side, the basis of a different form of social organization and a different economy."[33]

No female genealogy would be complete without its own female divinity. The possibility of a female divinity would provide a horizon of "otherness" or becoming for women. Women would therefore be able both to assume their reinstated bodies as well as accessing the divine or transcendental. As a result, the split between the corporeal and the transcendental would be broken down, enabling accession to the "sensible transcendental."

The maternal genealogy not only allows for the restoration of female subjectivity and relations between women, it also permits the restoration of relations between women and men: "Passage oblitéré entre le dehors et le dedans, le haut et le bas, l'intelligible et le sensible, le "père" et la "mère."[34] The passage between the two is now reopened as Irigaray leaves us with a vision of two separate, different genealogies in relation with each other. The differences between these two genealogies have been reformulated in various ways (see columns below):

Similarity	Contiguity
Metaphor	Metonymy
Condensation	Displacement
Paradigm	Syntagm
System	Discourse
Code	Context
Finite	Infinite
Lacan	Irigaray
Male	Female
Sacrifice	Fertility
Substitution	Contiguity
Identification	Identification
Paternal genealogy	Maternal genealogy[35]

In the main part of the text I will refer in particular to the opposition between sacrifice and fertility, substitution and contiguity, and show how this opposition can be applied to the narrative development of *Ombre sultane*. In the next section I will review the

---

[33] Margaret Whitford, *Luce Irigaray: Philosophy in the Feminine*, p. 180-81.
[34] Luce Irigaray, *Spéculum de l'autre femme*, p. 431.
[35] Margaret Whitford, *Luce Irigaray: Philosophy in the Feminine*, p. 179.

content of *Ombre sultane* before applying Irigaray's theories to the novel.

A Double Take on the Novel

"Difference", the slogan of Irigaray's philosophical campaign, is often expressed in terms of duality. For Irigaray, duality is the key to establishing difference and relation between subjectivities. The danger of indifferentiation (of the two becoming one), which often threatens relationships between two women, is countered by the notion of duality (of the two engaging in *mutual* giving *and* receiving), expressed as "rejouer ou redoubler deux fois amoureusement ce qu'elles sont."[36]

The idea of duality also pervades the content, the thematics and, to some extent, the form of *Ombre sultane*:

Preface: The most obvious example of duality is presented to us in the preface. Here we have two women – an ex-wife (Isma) who *was* married to, and a newlywed (Hajila) who *is* married to, the same man "l'homme" (as he is referred to). Isma, the ex-wife, has arranged for Hajila to marry her ex-husband and to take over the running of house and family. In the preface, these two women also double as "l'ombre" and "la sultane", anticipating Djebar's mirroring of the story of Isma and Hajila with that of the two sisters, Schéhérazade and Dinarzade of *Les Mille et Une Nuits*.

Part 1: Isma, the narrator, alternates between first- and second-person narration, between describing her own experiences (saying "je"), and addressing Hajila, (saying "tu" to Hajila). While the first person narrative (Isma sections) describes Isma's own past marriage to "l'homme", the second person narrative (Hajila sections) follows Hajila's present experiences as her ex-husband's new bride as seen through Isma's eyes. Towards the end of Part 1, Isma starts to combine first and second person narration.

Hajila sections: In these sections, Isma's narration operates like the eyes and ears of a secret camera, following and recording Hajila's every movement, filling the text-screen with the images and sounds of Hajila's daily life. Hajila emerges as a "Cinderella" figure, poor, submissive and illiterate, whose days are spent looking after the needs

---

[36] Luce Irigaray, *Éthique de la différence sexuelle* (Paris, Minuit 1984), p. 103.

of the new French-speaking[37] family she has inherited (Isma's ex-husband and two children, only one of whom, Mériem, turns out to be Isma's) and who largely ignore her. The two key developments in this section are Hajila's decision to make clandestine outings outside her new home, and the rape she later suffers at the hands of "l'homme."

Isma sections: Whereas Hajila is taking forays into the outside world, journeying through space, Isma journeys through the past, delving into the history of a marriage, recounting both its construction (here the celebration of physical intimacy contrasts with the physical abuse described in the Hajila sections) and, to a lesser extent, its disintegration. The relationship between Isma and her mother-in-law is also given prominence in this section.

Combined first and second person narratives: In Chapter XI, "Le Retour" [The Return], there is unity of time and space as Isma's story is fast-forwarded to the present of Hajila's narrative. Isma has now returned to the city where Hajila and "l'homme" reside. The duality here finds its expression in the revelation of shared experience of male violence, as Isma reveals that she too has suffered at the hands of "l'homme."

Part 2: In Part 2 Djebar suspends the story of Hajila, and delves into Isma's past. Isma's memories of childhood are alternated with snapshots of the lives of other women from her past. The relationships between these women, characterised by bitter rivalry, are contrasted with the relationship between Schéhérazade and Dinarzade, who represent the ideal of sisterhood.

Part 3: In Part 3 the story of Hajila is taken up again as the two protagonists finally meet face to face. Isma gives Hajila the key to her apartment (and to her escape from "l'homme") before the two women take their separate paths, Hajila into the outside world, Isma resolving to return to the traditional village of her childhood.

I suggest that the narrative development of *Ombre sultane* can be viewed as a series of shifts of consciousness in which the relationship between Isma and Hajila moves from what Irigaray describes as a *sacrificial* male economy of relations towards a female economy of relations. I will examine these shifts of consciousness, in relation to Irigaray's theories, with two aims in mind:

---

[37] Presumably, "l'homme" and Mériem are Algerian, but Nazim, the product of "his" liaison with a French woman, is therefore only half Algerian. All three communicate with each other in French.

To show that the shift towards a female economy of relations takes place as a result of the *acknowledgement of the feminine-unconscious*, and;

To evaluate to what extent Djebar's vision of a female economy of relations (or sisterhood) compares to *Irigaray's ideal of subject-to-subject relations*.

Moving away from a Masculine Economy of Relations

Hajila sections: A psychoanalytical model

In *Spéculum,* Irigaray articulates the unthinkable question "What if the other had an other?" In *Ombre sultane,* it seems at first that the other (woman) does have an other (woman). The story gives narrative form to the quip sometimes voiced by women: "I wish I had a wife." Isma wants "a wife", and then acquires a "wife" to look after her children and their home.

However, by examining Isma's relation to Hajila, it becomes clear that Hajila does not represent 'the other of the other' (a position which Irigaray equates with "an as yet non-existent female homosexual economy, women-amongst-themselves, love of self on the side of women"[38]), but rather represents *'the other of the same'* (a position that Irigaray equates with the role of women within patriarchy). Within this second configuration, Isma represents 'the same', taking on the male role, as she oppresses her female 'other', casting onto Hajila the material responsibilities of a domestic situation she herself (Isma) has rejected.

> What Irigaray finds in the [Plato's] myth is an imaginary primal scene ... which has attempted to remove the mother ... The effect is that the male function takes over and incorporates the female function, *leaving woman outside the scene, but supporting it, a condition of representation.*"[39]

The dynamics between the same and the other as put forward in Irigaray's reading of Plato's myth are also at work in the relation between Isma and Hajila. Here it is Hajila who is in the supporting role, and it is *her* subjugation which is the condition for Isma's new-found freedom. Here too we find that the same's (Isma's) sense of self, her subjectivity, her freedom, *is conditional on* the repression of the other (Hajila): "Elle s'est voulue marieuse de son propre mari; elle

---

[38] Margaret Whitford, *Luce Irigaray: Philosophy in the Feminine*, p. 104.
[39] Ibid., p. 106. [My emphasis]

a cru, par naïveté, se libérer ainsi à la fois du passé d'amour et du présent arrêté" [She had decided to act as matchmaker to her own husband; thinking naïvely to free herself by this means from her own past – enslaved to passionate love – and from the stalemate of the present] (p. 9; 1).

What Irigaray returns to again and again in her interpretation of the myth is the obliteration of the relationship between the two (same and other): "Passage oblitéré entre le dehors et le dedans, le haut et le bas, l'intelligible et le sensible, le "père" et la "mère."[40] In order for there to be a relationship between the same and its other, the maternal-feminine must be reinstated into the scene of representation – the other must be acknowledged.

For this to happen in *Ombre sultane*, for a relationship to be possible between the same (Isma) and the other (Hajila), Isma must first acknowledge her other, Hajila. This process of recognition is set in motion the moment that Isma starts to say "tu" to Hajila. For as soon as Isma (literally) *addresses* Hajila, as soon as she addresses her *other*, that unconscious other (Hajila) begins to be released.

According to Irigaray's studies of the enunciative structures of men and women in psychoanalytical sessions, women tend towards the mimetic "you" pole (which is indicative of a desire for validation) whereas men tend towards the self-referential "I" pole.[41] For sexual difference to be realised, women would have to assume an "I" in their own right (as a mark of their separate subjectivity) and men would have to venture out of the closed world of the "I" towards the "you."[42] This polarisation reflects the respective subject/object positions of men and women in the symbolic.

Returning to Djebar's narrative, we note that Isma starts off in the "I" or masculine pole of enunciation. She is concerned about herself and her own liberation. For her to move out of the masculine economy of relations, she needs to (and does) venture towards the "you" pole of enunciation. Although Isma is saying "tu" to Hajila as early as Chapter I, it is not until Chapter XII that Isma recalls the precise moment when this enunciative shift occurs, a moment that coincides with her decision to return to Algeria to reclaim her daughter:

> Insomnies de minuit, siestes le jour suivant: ma mémoire retrouve un halètement ancien. "C'est là que j'ai fini par dire 'tu' à l'étrangère; toi, Hajila, que d'autres imaginent ma rivale." (pp. 89; 80)

---

[40] Luce Irigaray, *Spéculum de l'autre femme*, p. 431.
[41] Luce Irigaray, *Sexes et parentés*, p. 188.
[42] Margaret Whitford, *Luce Irigaray: Philosophy in the Feminine*, p. 35.

> At midnight, when sleep eludes me, the next day during the siesta, memory revives my former aspirations. And it was there that I eventually began to speak to you, Hajila, the stranger, who others imagine to be my rival, but who is my intimate.

Given that the transformation of the relationship between Hajila and Isma operates on the basis of (Isma) addressing the unconscious (other, Hajila), it is possible to draw a parallel between the mechanics of Djebar's narrative and the mechanics of psychoanalysis as applied to Irigaray's work, both of which operate on the principle of *the release of the feminine-unconscious*, and both of which can be assimilated into a psychoanalytical model.

"Et si l'inconscient était à la fois le résultat de censures, de refoulements, imposés dans et par une certaine histoire, *mais aussi* un encore à advenir, la *réserve d'un à venir.*"[43] For Irigaray, the unconscious is a site where change can take place, psychoanalysis is the medium in which shifts of consciousness can be effected, and the word, or "la parole", is the catalyst that sets the whole procedure in motion: "A la parole de l'autre revient de débrider ce qui ainsi se sclérose."[44] Applying this principle to Irigaray's work, we find Irigaray in the role of the psychoanalyst whose "words" operates as the mechanism that unbinds the feminine-unconscious of her analysands, the Fathers of Western philosophy.

Adapting this psychoanalytical model to *Ombre sultane,* I suggest that Isma functions as analysand, that Hajila functions as her unconscious (as the unacknowledged maternal-feminine), and that the writing functions as "la parole", which unbinds the repressed maternal-feminine. I will now address the text to show how this process of unbinding begins.

The empty gestures of an enforced everydayness...

> Dépourvue d'idéalité autonome, la femme-mère ne risque-t-elle pas d'être réduite à une fiction? Puis gestes *d'une quotidienneté imposée*, image unique ou plurielle, mécanique ou rêve, *ombre,* voire fantôme...[45]

In Part 1 Isma observes a woman whose life is punctuated by the "empty gestures of an enforced everydayness." Like the eye of the camera, Isma's words rove over the sounds and sights of the mundane routines of Hajila's everyday life: "Tu débarrasses la table .... Tu plies

---

[43] Luce Irigaray, *Parler n'est jamais neutre* (Paris: Minuit, 1985), pp. 255-56.
[44] Ibid., p. 15.
[45] Ibid., p. 295. [My emphasis]

la nappe, tu essuies le bois clair de la table; tu poses le chiffon humide..." [You are clearing the table ... You fold the tablecloth, wipe the light wooden surface of the table; you put down the damp cloth] (pp. 15; 7). However, as Isma's words envelop Hajila, these gestures are no longer *empty* but are imbued with the projections of Isma's sympathy.

Isma's observant eye records not only Hajila's actions but hints at the emotions that accompany them: "Tes yeux sont embués. Tu renifles ... tu regardes tes mains vides ..." [Your eyes grow dim. You sniffle ... you look at your empty hands] (pp. 15; 7). The description of simple tasks reveals the sympathy and sensitivity of the observer to the other: "Une tasse, sous tes doigts soudain fébriles, se fêle contre la faïence de l'évier" [Your fingers, suddenly out of control, chip a cup against the porcelain sink] (pp. 15; 7). The insistent repetition of the "tu" and the total absence of the "I" in this first chapter mark a dramatic transition away from the "I" pole of enunciation and an intense concentration on the other, as Isma becomes more aware of how the "other half lives."

All Isma's observations point to Hajila's deep unhappiness, which is hinted at in the first sentence: "Hajila, une douleur sans raison t'a saisie, ce matin, dans la cuisine qui sera le lieu du mélodrame" [This morning, Hajila, as you stand in the kitchen, which is to be the setting of the drama, you are suddenly, for no reason, overcome by grief] (p. 15; 7). This is reinforced by the repeated references to Hajila crying, in the morning as her husband is getting ready to leave, when she is left alone in the house, and when the children return from school, suggesting that she is in a constant state of melancholy:

> Tes yeux sont inondés de larmes ... Tes larmes reprennent, s'égouttent sur l'évier... [Your eyes have filled with tears ... Your tears start up again...] (pp. 15, 16; 7, 8)
>
> De nouveau, ton visage s'inonde de larmes. [Once again your face is flooded with tears.] (pp. 17; 9)
>
> Tu pleures maman, ce n'est pas bien! ['You're crying, maman, that's not nice!'] (pp. 18; 10)

In this portrait of unhappiness, Hajila's alienation from her husband soon becomes apparent. His refusal to acknowledge either her tears or her words, casts her into a lonely silence:

> Qu'as-tu?
> Sa voix saccadée a traversé l'espace. "Il" se tient sur le seuil, non loin.
> – Je pleure!
> Tu réponds sans te retourner. Tu attends. Nul écho. (pp. 16; 8)
>
> 'What's the matter with you?'

His sharp voice is heard across the distance between you. 'He' is standing in the doorway close by.
— 'I'm crying!' you reply without turning round. You wait. No echo.

The sense of alienation from the new family she has acquired is later reinforced by the revelation of her fundamental ignorance about her new husband and stepchildren: "Ces enfants, de quelle mère, de quelle étrangère sont-ils?" [What unknown woman is the mother of these children?] (pp. 18; 10). "Veuf ou divorcé avec deux enfants, qu'il avait eus d'une épouse ou de deux, comment savoir, qui allait le lui demander?" [A widower or divorced, with two children, from one wife or two, how could they find out? who was going to enquire?] (pp. 22; 14).

The sustained focus of Isma's words on Hajila's movements has the effect of revealing the repetitiveness and emptiness of Hajila's life: "Tu plies la nappe, tu essuies le bois clair de la table; tu poses le chiffon humide, tu regardes tes mains vides, tes mains de ménagère active" [You fold the tablecloth, wipe the light wooden surface on the table; you put down the damp cloth, look at your empty hands, the hands of a busy housewife] (pp. 15; 7). Her estrangement from herself is reinforced not only by her detachment from the objects that surround her, but also by her alienation from her own body: "Ta main, inerte. Ne pas fermer le robinet. Écouter les gouttes d'eau ... Main sur le robinet de cuivre: 'ta' main. Front sur un bras nu tendu: 'ton' front, 'ton' bras" [Your hand lies motionless. Let the tap run. Listen to the sound of the water dripping ... A hand is poised on the brass tap: 'your' hand. A brow rests against a bare outstretched arm: 'your' brow, 'your' arm] (pp. 16; 8).

The text proceeds as if in slow motion, as if Hajila is going through the motions of living: "Tu as marché jusqu'au lit. Tu refais celui-ci sans en secouer les draps. Mouvement cassé de tes bras. Tu t'assois, lustrant de tes doigts à demi rougis d'un henné passé le couvre-lit rêche, une cotonnade écrue" [You walk to the bed. You make it without shaking out the sheets. It is an effort to move your arms. You sit down, stroking the counterpane of coarse, unbleached calico with fingers still bearing faint red stains of henna] (pp. 17; 9). The slow rhythm of her day comes to an almost complete halt as she becomes completely inert, lifeless: "Une heure plus tard, tu t'installes dans la plus petite des chambres. Dame assise: nature morte" [An hour later, you go and sit in the smallest of the bedrooms. Still life with seated woman] (pp. 17, 9).

Like Irigaray's "woman-mother", Hajila exists as a dream, or a shadow, or a ghost. Although it is Isma who is literally shadowing

Hajila, although it is she who is "[l']ombre derrière la sultane" [[the] shadow behind the sultan's bride] (pp. 9; 1), Hajila too is "l'ombre", in the sense that she is but a shadow of a person. Further on in the narrative the idea of "la femme-fantôme" is foregrounded from within the text, as Hajila recalls the first time her stepson Nazim talks to her: "Tu te rappelles la première fois où il t'a parlé – tu as tourné la tête pour chercher l'interlocuteur: tu n'existes pas plus qu'un fantôme!" [You recall the first time he addressed you – you turned round to look for the person he was speaking to: you were no more present than a ghost!] (pp. 37, 28). Hajila exists as a mechanism, not only a mechanism to ensure the accomplishment of domestic tasks, but also a mechanism to ensure that the children she has acquired learn Arabic: "Ainsi le sens de ta présence dans ces lieux est vérifiable: tu as été choisie, sans le savoir, comme institutrice à demeure, 'maîtresse Hajila'" [So the reason for your presence in this place is confirmed: without your realizing it, you were chosen as a governess, 'Miss Hajila'] (pp. 37; 28).

Isma's secret 'camera' not only follows Hajila's outward movements, but also has access to her thoughts. Some of these thoughts (like the one quoted above) are expressed in the simple language of an illiterate woman. Others, however, are articulated in Isma's voice:

> "Vous [les hommes] qui surgissez au soleil! Chaque matin, vous vous rincez à grande eau le visage, les avant-bras, la nuque. Ces ablutions ne préparent pas vos prosternations, non, elles précèdent l'acte de sortir, sortir! ... Vous vous présentez au monde vous les bienheureux! ..."
> Ces mots en toi rythment la mélopée du deuil. (pp. 17; 9)
>
> 'You who can all go forth into the sunshine! Every morning, you splash water over your face, neck and arms. These are not the ablutions preparatory to prostrating yourself in prayer; no, they are a preparation for the act of leaving the house ... You can present yourself to the world, you fortunate males!' ...
> These works throb in your head to the beat of a funeral dirge!

This superimposition of Isma's voice onto Hajila's thoughts reinforces the impression of Hajila's lack of subjectivity. She (Isma) is speaking for Hajila – Hajila cannot speak for herself. Her language is caught up in the linguistic code of the other. On the level of the story, Hajila is also rendered silent because she cannot understand French, the language in which her new family communicate: "'Face de la douleur', tu murmures ces mots en langue arabe, pour toi seule, pour toi muette" ['The face of sorrow,' you murmur to yourself in Arabic to your solitary, mute self] (pp. 17; 9).

Although Isma's observations reveal Hajila's general unhappiness, one phrase in particular points to recent circumstances as the specific cause of her misery, and, by implication, to Isma herself as the unspoken cause of Hajila's present unhappiness: "'Je n'ai pas pleuré depuis tant d'années!'" ['I have not wept for so many years!'] (pp. 16; 8). Isma has placed Hajila in her new circumstances in order to enable herself to escape from them. She has vacated a space that Hajila is now occupying. In other words, Isma has substituted Hajila for herself.

According to Irigaray, the masculine economy of relations is based on substitution or sacrifice, on the sacrifice of the mother: "In Lacan's economy, the founding sacrifice which underlies the social order is a relation of metaphor and substitution. It is the male position in the Oedipus complex, the instinctual renunciation made by the boy, and the identification with the father."[46] The status of Isma as a "free-agent" in society depends on Isma substituting or sacrificing the (step)mother Hajila for herself. Their relationship can therefore be viewed as conforming to the sacrificial masculine economy.

As Hajila wanders aimlessly around her new house, and looks into the mirror, Djebar foregrounds the idea of the substitution of one subjectivity for the other: "... ton visage serait-il celui d'une autre?" [... could your face be that of another woman?] (pp. 15; 7) "... une inconnue qui aurait été ton double" [an unknown woman, who could have been your double] (pp. 24; 15). It is not until the end of Part 1, however, that Isma herself consciously acknowledges the fact that she has sacrificed Hajila for her own ends.

Passing from interior to exterior...

> ... elle [la femme-mère] n'est jamais unifiée dans son insistance ou existence à défaut de paroles qui l'enveloppent, la couvrent, la situent dans une identité, l'assistent à passer de l'intérieur à l'extérieur d'elle, la revêtent d'elle-même, tel un abri qui l'accompagne et la protège sans adhérence ni allégeance au monde de l'autre....[47]

As Isma starts to acknowledge her unconscious, as she listens to her other, that other (Hajila) starts to be released into the outside world – that which has been repressed is liberated. And it is Isma's words that effect that movement, it is her words that literally *assist Hajila in passing from interior to exterior*, that literally propel her into

---

[46] Margaret Whitford, *Luce Irigaray: Philosophy in the Feminine*, p. 180.
[47] Luce Irigaray, *Parler n'est jamais neutre*, p. 295. [My emphasis]

the outside world and accompany her first hesitant steps into the streets. The connection between Isma's words and Hajila's movements is reinforced by Isma's emphatic statement: "Tu vas 'sortir' pour la première fois, Hajila ... dans ton visage entièrement masqué, un seul oeil est découvert ... Tu entres dans l'ascenseur, tu vas déboucher en pleine rue..." [You are 'going out' for the first time, Hajila ... your face completely hidden, leaving only one tiny gap exposed from which you peep to see where you are going ... You enter the lift, you are about to step out onto the street...] (pp. 27; 19).[48]

"The task of the other's word is to unbind/loosen what has been petrified."[49] So Isma's words act as a catalyst for Hajila's hesitant steps into the forbidden outside world. This journey into space is also a journey of self-discovery, the discovery of "an identity, like a shelter that would accompany her, clothe her in herself and protect her without need to cling or give allegiance to the world of the other." Significantly, the process of being *clothed in herself* requires her to remove her "clothes" (her veil) precisely because they are clothes imposed on her by her allegiance to the "world of the other." The process of "unclothing" happens gradually, over a period of time (she starts by pushing the veil away from her face, and ends up by removing the veil altogether) during which her forbidden visits into the outside world become more and more frequent.

Hajila's first steps into the outside world take place in a mixture of fear and exhilaration: "L'oeil en triangle noir regarde à droite, à gauche, encore à droite, puis ... le coeur se met à battre sous le tissu de laine ... Pouvoir lâcher le bord du drap, regarder, le visage à découvert, et même renverser la tête vers le ciel, comme à dix ans!" [The black triangle of your eye darts to right and left – to the right again then ... You can feel your heart thumping under the woollen cloth ... Oh, to be able to let go of the material altogether, to look about you with unveiled face, to be able to throw your head back and look up at the sky, as you did when a child!] (pp. 27; 19). She is both overcome with feelings of elation, and overwhelmed by space, by the vast expanses of sea and sky: "Je m'immobilise, puis j'avance, je glisse dans l'azur, je décolle de la terre, je ... ô veuves de Mohammed, secourez-moi! ... Est-ce, là-bas, la même mer que celle que tu aperçois du balcon de la cuisine? A présent la voici mare géante, proche et

---

[48] Translation adapted.
[49] Luce Irigaray, *Parler n'est jamais neutre*, p. 15. Quoted (in English) in Margaret Whitford, *Luce Irigaray: Philosophy in the Feminine*, p. 32.

lointaine à la fois" [I stand still, I take a step forward, I glide through the air, I no longer feel the ground beneath my feet, I ... O, widows of Mohammed, come to my aid! ... Is that the same sea, there, that you can glimpse from the kitchen balcony? At present it lies before you, at once near and extending far into the distance, like a gigantic lake] (pp. 28; 19).

Hajila proceeds in the outside world as if in a dream: "Tu marches, Hajila, baignée par la lumière qui te porte. Qui te sculpte" [On you walk, Hajila, borne along by the light that enfolds you, models you] (pp. 28; 19). It is as if Hajila, the ghost woman, is being given form by the outside world. But the dream becomes a nightmare as reality sets in and "Cinderella" hurries home: "Moins d'une heure plus tard, essoufflée, pour avoir presque couru, comme dans une poursuite de cauchemar, tu parviens devant l'immeuble où tu habites" [Nearly an hour later, breathless from running as if pursued by some nightmare, you reach the building where you live] (pp. 28; 20).

Hajila's second visit into the forbidden public spaces is prompted by a strong image that both haunts and inspires her. From inside the window of a moving car, she catches sight of a young woman who is laughing and holding a baby in a park – an image that she turns over and over again in her mind:

> Le bébé gigote, la femme rit, les bras tendus...
> Et tu rêves:
> "Sans voiles, dehors, en train d'aimer son enfant!" Tu reprends:
> "Sans voiles dehors, en train..."
> "Sans voile, dehors..." (pp. 36; 27)
>
> The baby wriggles, the woman laughs...
> And you muse, 'Without a veil, 'Without a veil, out of doors, playing lovingly with her child!'
> You repeat, 'Out of doors, without a veil, loving...'
> 'No veil, out of doors ...'

This image has a powerful effect on Hajila and inspires her second foray into the outside world. The power of the image on Hajila's psyche, acting as a catalyst for her propulsion into the outside world, recalls Irigaray's conviction about the importance of public images in helping women move from the private to the public realm:

> A qui se soucie aujourd'hui de justice sociale, je propose d'afficher dans tous les lieux publics de belles images figurant le couple mère-fille .... Ces représentations sont absentes de tous les lieux civils et religieux. Cela signifie une injustice culturelle facile à réparer ... Cette restauration culturelle commencera à soigner une perte d'identité

individuelle et collective pour les femmes ... *Elle les assistera à passer du privé au public*, de leur famille à la société où elles vivent.[50]

Hajila too is confronted with "une belle image" (not in the form of a poster but in the form of a picture filling the screen of the car window) of a woman freely inhabiting the outside world, and this image helps her to pass from the interior to the exterior:

> Dans le noir où tu plonges, tu vois encore l'inconnue aux cheveux rouges trôner au centre du square, le visage élargi de bonheur.
> Surgissant au dehors, tu sens peser sur ton dos le regard du concierge. Tu dévales la première pente de la première rue. (pp. 37-38; 28-29)
>
> You sink down into the darkness where the vision of the unknown redhead appears before your eyes, seated in the little garden, her face radiant with joy.
> As you emerge into the open, you can feel the concierge's eyes staring at your back. You hurry down the first incline of the first hill.

Buoyed by the image of the veil-less woman, Hajila decides to expose even more of her body this time: "Là tu te décides avec violence: 'enlever le voile!' Comme si tu voulais disparaître ... ou exploser! – La laine du voile glisse sur ta chevelure tandis que tu ralentis le pas; tu te représentes ta propre silhouette tête libre, cheveux noirs tirés" [There you make your sudden decision to take off that veil! As if you wished to disappear ... or explode!] (pp. 39; 30). Like the hands of a sculptor, the narrative slowly unveils Hajila's face, and then her entire head. Finally, as the whole cloth falls at her feet, it is as if she is reborn: "... toi la nouvelle, toi en train de te muer en une autre" [... you the new woman, you who have just been transformed into another woman] (pp. 40; 31).

Hajila's rebirth is short-lived. On the way home she slips into the corridor of a nearby building and transmutes back into Irigaray's "femme-mère-fantôme": "... mains tremblantes, visage crispé, fermant les yeux de désespoir, créant dans ce noir ton propre noir, tu te réenveloppes du *haïk*! Dehors te revoici fantôme et la colère grisâtre replie ses ailes sous la blancheur du drap" [... with trembling hands, your face contorted in despair, your eyes closed, creating the darkness that reflects your own dark misery, you wrap yourself once more in the *haïk*! You emerge into the street, a ghostly figure once more, and under the white veil anger folds up its wings] (pp. 42; 34).

For Djebar, and for Irigaray, the passage into the outside world is an important step towards the restoration of female corporeality and

---

[50] Luce Irigaray, *Le Temps de la différence*, pp. 27-28.

the accession to subjectivity. As Hajila's "passes from interior to exterior", Djebar foregrounds the connection between her exploration of public spaces and the discovery of her own body-space:

> Déshabillée, tu plonges dans la baignoire fumante. Tu contemples ton corps dans la glace, l'esprit inondé des images du dehors, de la lumière du dehors, du jardin-comme-à-la-télévision. Les autres continuent à défiler là-bas; tu les ressuscites dans l'eau du miroir pour qu'ils fassent cortège à la femme vraiment nue, à Hajila nouvelle qui froidement te dévisage. (pp. 43; 35)

> You undress and lie down in the steaming bath. You study your body in the mirror, your mind filled with images from outdoors, the light from outdoors, the garden-like-on-the-television. The others are still walking about there; you conjure them up in the water reflected in the mirror, so that they can accompany this woman who is truly naked, this new Hajila who stares back at you coldly.

Situate her in an identity, like a shelter...

> ...elle n'est jamais unifiée dans son insistance ou existence à défaut de paroles qui l'enveloppent, la couvrent, *la situent dans une identité*, l'assistent à passer de l'intérieur à l'extérieur d'elle, la revêtent d'elle-même, *tel un abri* qui l'accompagne et la protège sans adhérence ni allégeance au monde de l'autre.[51]

It is Hajila's secret knowledge of the outside world that gives her the strength to overcome the next difficult experience of her life, six months into her marriage: "Le viol, est-ce le viol?" [Rape! Is this rape?] wonders Isma (pp. 66; 57). Ironically, this traumatic experience acts as a catalyst to further self-discovery, allowing Hajila *"to situate herself in an identity ... like a shelter."* After the rape, as we will see, Djebar likens Hajila's newfound sense of identity to "une grotte", offering us images that echo Irigaray's association of identity with refuge, and that recall her insistence on the accession to otherness as a precondition for that identity.

During the rape, Hajila summons up the images of the outside world, of her new space-time to mentally resist the intrusion of her body space.

> Faut-il céder? Non, rappelle-toi les rues, elles s'allongent en toi dans un soleil qui a dissous les nuées; les murs s'ouvrent; arbres et haies glissent. Tu revois l'espace au-dehors où chaque jour tu navigues. Quand le phallus de l'homme te déchire, épée rapide, tu hurles dans le silence, dans ton silence: "non! ... non!" ... La déchirure s'étend, les

---

[51] Luce Irigaray, *Parler n'est jamais neutre*, p. 295. [My emphasis]

rues déroulées en toi défilent, les ombres des passants reviennent et te dévisagent, chaînes inconnues aux yeux globuleux. (pp. 67; 58)

Must you surrender? No! Think of the streets, they stretch out within you, bathed in the sunshine that has dissolved the storm clouds; the walls open; trees and hedges glide past. You can see the space out of doors through which you sail each day. When the man's penis ruptures you, with one rapid sword-thrust, you scream out in the silence, breaking your own silence, 'No! ... No!' ... You are being torn apart; the procession of streets unwinds within you, shadowy passers-by turn back and stare at you, steady streams of unknown people with bulging eyes.

Her ability to survive by drawing strength from her own separate world gives her a new self-confidence:

Ce lendemain du viol, tu ne le crains plus. Il te suffit de te rappeler tes déambulations, ton corps sans puanteur aux jambes, auréolé de la lumière solaire quand tu traversais les espaces de la ville.
La porte claque. Tu retournes à la salle de bains. Sûre de toi. (pp. 71; 62)

This morning, the day after the rape, you are no longer afraid of him. You only have to remember the times you stroll at liberty through the sunlit spaces of the town, with no stench between your legs.
The door slams, you return to the bathroom, full of confidence in yourself.

The following day Hajila becomes conscious of her body as a safe house for herself – it is no longer the territory of man. This discovery takes place in the *hammam*, a cavern-womb-like space, which can be likened to Irigaray's space for woman, her 'other of the other', where women can "become" and where Hajila now reclaims her body for herself. The image of the cave is then compounded as Hajila's own body becomes a cavern, a shelter in which she can find herself: "Cheveux dénoués et trempés, le dos étalé sur la dalle de marbre brûlant, ventre, sexe et jambes libérés, creuser *une grotte* et au fond, tout au fond, parler enfin à soi-même, l'inconnue" [To lie, resting one's back on the scorching marble slab, wet hair spread loosely, belly, genitals, legs liberated, hollowing out a *cave* where one can commune with oneself at last, that real self whom no one knows] (pp. 73, 64) [My emphasis].

As Isma's "unconscious" slowly gains consciousness, as her "paroles" slowly release Hajila into the outside world, it is as if Hajila's subjectivity is slowly coming into being. But as we will see in the "combined narrative sections", the process of release is not yet complete...

Isma sections: The dividing wall

> ... le corps de l'homme devient mur mitoyen de nos antres qu'un même secret habite. (pp. 91; 82)
>
> ... the body of the man becomes the party wall separating our lairs, which house a common secret.

Hajila's journey through space runs in parallel with Isma's journey through time, as she relives the days and nights of her past marriage to the very same "homme." Djebar, like Irigaray, posits man as the dividing wall between women, creating an interminable rivalry between them. So whereas in the 'Hajila sections', "l'homme" is the dividing-wall between Isma and Hajila, in the 'Isma sections' we discover that this same "homme" has created a dividing wall between Isma and her mother-in-law in the past.

Irigaray relates the fundamental rivalry between women to the mother and daughter's relation to the father. Because both mother and daughter are always in competition for the desire or attention of the father, the two are therefore competing for what she calls "one space." Always in competition for the one, they cannot be two (i.e. in relation to each other):

> La place de la mère étant unique, devenir mère supposerait d'occuper ce lieu, sans relation avec elle en ce lieu. L'économie, ici, serait *ou l'une ou l'autre*, ou elle ou je-moi. Pour se faire désirer, aimer de l'homme, il faut évincer la mère, se substituer à elle, l'anéantir pour devenir même. Ce qui détruit la possibilité d'un amour entre mère et fille. Elles sont à la fois complices et rivales pour advenir à l'unique position possible dans le désir de l'homme.[52]

In *Ombre sultane,* the mother-daughter rivalry can be transposed to the relationship between Isma and her mother-in-law, both of whom are in competition for the desire of one man, "l'homme." The struggle for supremacy is initially described as operating between Isma and her husband's family: "Longtemps je le cernais de cette manière, je tentais de l'extraire de sa familiarité avec ceux auxquels il est attaché par des liens du sang" [For long I used this means of possessing him, trying to extricate him from the hold his flesh and blood have on him] (pp. 57; 49). It soon becomes obvious, however, that Isma's chief rival is the mother-in-law, "le fantôme maternel" [the mother's ghost], whose image haunts their relationship: "La mère de l'homme, ennemie ou rivale, surgit dans les strates de nos caresses" [The man's mother, enemy or rival, appears between the strata of our love-making] (pp.

---

[52] Luce Irigaray, *Éthique de la différence sexuelle,* p. 101.

59, 61; 51, 53). In this battle for maternal supremacy, Isma struggles to disempower, to depose the mother-in-law, and to take her place in the affections of her son.

Isma traces this competition with her mother-in-law back to its origin, which she identifies as her mother-in-law's relation to her son, "l'homme", and more particularly to his desire for origin: "Hantise de l'origine, épée droite fichée en l'homme, qui le blesse et le redresse. Moi, je renie la matrone omniprésente" [The obsession with his origins is a sword thrust into the man, wounding him, startling him to his feet. For my part, I repudiate the ubiquitous matron] (pp. 59; 51). As Isma draws her mother-in-law into conversation, the latter's intense relation with the son is again brought into focus by Isma's surprised echo:

> D'un ton incrédule, je m'exclame:
> – Tu as allaité ton fils pendant... pendant trois ans? (pp. 61; 52-53)
>
> Incredulously, I exclaim, 'You mean to say you breast-fed your son ... for three years?'

Irigaray, like Djebar, makes a connection between the mother-son relationship, the desire for origin and breast-feeding. Irigaray takes as her starting-point Freud's comments on the way breast-feeding has been equated with love: "'Le plus ancien en date des méfaits reprochés à la mère, c'est d'avoir donné trop peu de lait à son enfant, et montré ainsi qu'elle ne l'aimait pas assez.'"[53] She then takes the idea further, reading the nostalgia for the maternal breast as a more fundamental symptom of the trauma provoked by separation from the maternal body: "... *dernière rupture de contiguïté matérielle avec l'intérieur du corps de la mère.*"[54]

For Irigaray, hunger for the breast is equated with hunger for the mother: "Il s'agirait d'une faim inavouable de dévorer la mère..."[55] For man this desire can be resolved by transferring it onto another woman (mother-substitute): "Alors, si l'on est garçon on désirera, dès que phallique, retourner à l'origine, se retourner vers l'origine. Soit: posséder la mère, entrer dans la mère, ce lieu originel, pour rétablir la continuité avec, et voir, et savoir, ce qui s'y passe. Et, encore, s'y reproduire."[56] The woman, however, has no way of resolving her *own* desire for origin and is reduced to becoming the site of *his desire* (for origin):

---

[53] Luce Irigaray, *Spéculum de l'autre femme*, p. 44.
[54] Ibid., p. 44.
[55] Ibid., p. 44.
[56] Ibid., p. 45.

In Dialogue with Irigaray: *Ombre sultane* 187

> ... elle ne (se) représentera pas "son" rapport à "son" origine; elle ne rentrera plus jamais dans la mère ... Laissée au *vide*, au *manque* de toute représentation ... de son désir (d')origine. Lequel en passera, dès lors, par le désir-discours-loi du désir de l'homme: *tu seras ma femme-mère, ma femme si tu veux, tu peux, être (comme) ma mère* = tu seras pour moi la possibilité de répéter-représenter-reproduire-m'approprier le (mon) rapport à l'origine.[57]

For Irigaray then, woman's inability to resolve her own desire for origin results in her substituting for the (man's) mother, inscribing herself into his desire, and alienating herself from her own desiring economy. Returning to *Ombre sultane*, we find Isma willingly responding to the male imperative: "Tu seras ma femme-mère." She too is willing and able to become "la femme-mère" in order to prise the unique place of the mother from her mother-in-law, in order to attain the unique position of *his* desire. Djebar describes the struggle between the two women in terms reminiscent of a tug of war:

> Dans l'antre maternel, nous nous réinstallons, moi, l'épouse aux antennes inaltérées, lui, le fils que je tire plus loin, plus loin... J'ai recréé sa naissance ou je l'ai engloutie, je ne sais. Mais je t'en ai dépouillée, ô mère devant laquelle je m'incline, à laquelle je me lie, mais que j'écarte enfin de mon amour. (pp. 62; 53)

> We make our home again in the mother's lair, I, the wife, as ever sensitive to every signal, he, the son, whom I draw further and further away ... Have I let him be reborn? or have I engulfed him? I cannot tell ... But I have stolen him away from you, O Mother, to whom I defer, to whom I am bound, but whom I finally separate from the man I love.

In this graphic illustration of the woman/wife taking on the role of "femme-mère", we find Isma enabling "l'homme" to re-enter the maternal womb, and allowing him to be born again in yet another act of substitution: "L'amour de la mère du côté féminin ne devrait ou ne pourrait s'exercer que sur le mode de la *substitution*? D'un prendre la place de? Inconsciemment teinté de haine?"[58]

According to Irigaray, the answer is yes. The mother occupies what she calls "a unique place", so to occupy that place is to depose the previous occupant, cutting off any possibility of relation with her.[59] The suffused hostility that, according to Irigaray, characterises the mother-daughter relation, resurfaces in Djebar's narrative. For while Isma's confrontation with her mother-in-law begins with Isma's declaration of love ("Tu es belle! Et je t'aime!" ['You are very

---

[57] Ibid., pp. 46, 47. [My emphasis]
[58] Luce Irigaray, *Éthique de la différence sexuelle*, p. 100.
[59] Ibid., p. 101.

beautiful! And I love you!'], pp. 61; 52), it ends with a recognition that her love is being withdrawn, precisely *because* she has won the battle, *because* she has substituted herself for her mother-in-law: "Mais je t'en ai dépouillée, ô mère devant laquelle je m'incline, à laquelle je me lie, mais que j'écarte enfin de mon amour" [But I have stolen him away from you, O Mother, to whom I defer, to whom I am bound, but whom I finally separate from the man I love] (pp. 62; 53).

The "Isma sections" present a whole landscape of reconciliations and ruptures, not only between Isma and her mother-in-law, but between Isma and "l'homme." Here there is a dance of desire and withdrawal, of pregnant intimacies and silent struggles, and the vagaries of physical passion that contrast starkly with the dark revelations of physical violence to follow in the combined narrative sections.

Combined narrative sections: A question of substitution

The last two chapters of Part 1 (XII and XIII) operate as a crossroads, as the two stories (Isma's and Hajila's) unite in time and space, and as first and second person narration start to alternate within (rather than between) chapters. Hajila and Isma's divergent personal histories also come to a meeting point here, as Hajila's present comes to repeat Isma's past. Tragically, this meeting-point is represented by a shared experience of violence, as we discover that Isma, like Hajila, has experienced physical abuse at the hands of "l'homme."

In these last two chapters we witness two battles, not only the physical confrontation between Hajila and "l'homme", but also a psychological struggle between Isma and Hajila. Although Isma's unconscious other is gradually being released (into the outside world), that other (Hajila) still exists as a projection of Isma's thoughts rather than a separate subjectivity in her own right. In order for that subjectivity to emerge, in order for the relation to move out of the sacrificial masculine economy, Isma first has to acknowledge the "founding act of sacrifice", in other words to acknowledge the fact that she has substituted Hajila in her place.

> C'est toujours moi qui te parle, Hajila. Comme si, en vérité, je te créais. Une ombre que ma voix lève. Une ombre-soeur? ... Plus les mots me devancent, plus mon présent se disperse; et ta forme s'impose. (pp. 91; 82)
>
> Here I am speaking to you again, Hajila. As, if in truth, I were causing you to exist. A phantom whom my voice has brought to life. A phantom-sister? ... The more my words outstrip me, the more my present existence dissolves; and your figure intrudes.

The opening words of Chapter XIII reveal that Isma is caught between two ways of relating to Hajila. On the one hand, she visualises Hajila as a projection of herself: "Comme si, en vérité, je te créais. Une ombre que ma voix lève" [As if, in truth, I were causing you to exist. A phantom whom my voice has brought to life] (pp. 91; 82). On the other hand, Isma is aware that change is taking place, and that, as her words take effect ("Plus les mots me devancent" [the more my words outstrip me]), the projection is starting to acquire a shape, a form or subjectivity of its own: "et ta forme s'impose" [and your figure intrudes]. In this sense, the relation is moving away from what Irigaray terms "une intuition de l'autre ... projective ou égoïste"[60] (in which the other is merely a projection of the self) towards a differentiated love that acknowledges the other's alterity: "[un] amour du même que moi, posé et maintenu hors de moi dans sa différence..."[61]

In the remainder of this chapter, Djebar describes the incident that provokes Isma to recognise that her relation with Hajila is based on an act of substitution. A series of events leads up to the act of recognition, starting with "l'homme" discovering Hajila's clandestine outings and subjecting her to an interrogation session.

As soon as "l'homme" starts interrogating Hajila, his words strike a chord in Isma. Memories of her own past flow into her consciousness, and, for the first time, she inserts herself directly into Hajila's story: "Comme toi, j'ai vécu cinquante débuts, cinquante instructions de procès, j'ai affronté cinquante chefs d'accusation!" [Like you, I have lived through fifty beginnings, fifty interrogations, I have faced fifty charges!] (pp. 94; 85). But it is not until "l'homme" is about to strike Hajila, it is not until she realises that history will repeat itself ("car il frappera" [for he will strike you], pp. 94, 85) that Isma realises the full consequence of her decision to substitute Hajila in her place.

At this point it is as if Isma suddenly makes a connection, not only between her ex-husband's past pattern of behaviour and his present conduct (as she senses the inevitability of the violence to come) but between her past life and Hajila's current predicament. It is now that Isma finally recognises the act of substitution, finally acknowledging that Hajila is suffering in her stead: "Le soleil te regarde, ô Hajila, toi qui me remplaces cette nuit" [The sun is watching you, O Hajila, as you stand in for me tonight] (pp. 94; 85). And, just as Isma makes this acknowledgement, the past does repeat itself before her very eyes:

---

[60] Ibid., p. 111.
[61] Ibid., p. 98.

Il interrogeait, procureur de la nuit et des autres ... "Qui allais-tu rejoindre dehors, avec qui parlais-tu dans les squares, quel inconnu, quel ami ancien ou nouveau t'accompagnait et dans quelles promenades? ... Quel fard choisissais-tu, quelle jupe sous le voile portais-tu et pourquoi, quelle robe de couleur violente?" (pp. 95; 85-86)

He began his interrogation, this prosecutor for the night and all the other nights ... 'Who did you go to meet, when you went out? Who did you talk to in the public gardens? What strange man, what old or new friend accompanied you on these walks? ... What make-up did you choose? What skirt did you wear under your veil, and why? What loud-coloured dress?'

Hajila's explanation strikes a raw nerve in "l'homme", and precipitates the first act of physical violence:

"J'aimais enlever le voile dans une ruelle, quand personne ne passait, ensuite marcher nue!"
Il a frappé au mot "nue." (pp. 95; 86)

'I liked to take off my veil in a narrow alley-way, when no one was passing, and then walk about naked!'
He struck at the word 'naked'.

Hajila's words also strike another chord in Isma. As if unable to contain herself, she reinserts herself once again into the narrative, her voice-over overriding the soundtrack, muffling Hajila's cries of pain: "Ô ma soeur des bidonvilles, ô ma suivante du malheur inextricable, quand, adolescente, j'ai rencontré cet homme, c'était 'nue' que je déambulais!" [O, my sister from the shantytown, who has followed my footsteps into this tangle of misfortune, I used to walk naked when, as an adolescent, I first met this man!] (pp. 95; 86). For the first time Isma addresses Hajila directly as sister, and, for the first time, her words do not report but echo Hajila's. So not only has Isma compelled Hajila to follow in her footsteps, but she has done so knowing (and now finally acknowledging) that tragedy would be inevitable: "... ô ma suivante du malheur inextricable" [O, my sister ... who has followed my footsteps into this tangle of misfortune] (pp. 95; 86).

It is this act of recognition that will enable the relationship between Isma and Hajila to be propelled out of the sacrificial masculine economy of relations into another mode of relations, a transition that will enable Hajila to step outside Isma's mind and emerge as a separate subjectivity "in its difference", a transition that will not take place until Part 3 (where Hajila's story is taken up again), but which is foreshadowed, in Part 2, in the relation between Schéhérazade and Dinarzade.

Towards a Feminine Economy of Relations

Both Irigaray and Djebar are concerned with the negative effect of the sacrificial patriarchal economy of relations on the relations between women, and both point the way to another, positive model of women-to-women relations. But whereas Irigaray presents us with a philosophical model of a female sociality, here in Part 2, Djebar presents us with a literary one. For Djebar's reinterpretation of the story of *Les Mille et Une Nuits* provides us with not a symbolic but a mythical horizon of sisterhood towards which women can aspire. In the first part of Part 2, I will compare Djebar's "horizon" of sisterhood with Irigaray's blueprint for relations between women.

Part 2 continues with Isma's narration, which alternates between her memories of her own childhood/adolescence, and her memories of the lives of other women. It is as if that having opened herself up to one "other" (Hajila), Isma now becomes open to all the "other others" of her past: "Deux décennies plus tard, l'amertume de ces femmes m'atteint enfin" [Two decades later, those women's bitterness finally overtakes me] (pp. 88; 79).

All the stories of women in Part 2 describe relations between women that reflect this bitterness, and that are characterised by rivalry and hatred, a theme that is familiar in Irigaray's writing. Before proceeding to the theme of rivalry, I will refer to Fatima Mernissi's work, *Sexe, idéologie, Islam,*[62] which examines the mechanics of repression in an Arab society, relating her conclusions both to Isma's stories of women, and to Irigaray's analysis of repression from a Western perspective. Meanwhile, we return to Djebar's variation on *Les Mille et Une Nuits.*

Sisterhood versus a female sociality

"It should not be assumed that the sacrificial is inevitable; it corresponds too closely to the male imaginary. An exploration of symbolic alternatives to sacrifice should be made."[63] In Part 2 of *Ombre sultane*, Djebar does not assume that the sacrificial economy, in which Isma and Hajila's relationship *first* operates, is inevitable –

---

[62] Fatima Mernissi, *Sexe, idéologie, Islam* (Paris: Tierce, 1983), trans. Diane Brower and Anne-Marie Pelletier, p. 9.
[63] Margaret Whitford, *Luce Irigaray: Philosophy in the Feminine*, p. 147. This quotation is taken from a list of what Whitford regards as "the main points of Irigaray's discussion on religion" (p. 147).

she, like Irigaray, believes that there is another, better way for women to relate to each other.[64]

The story of Schéhérazade provides a graphic illustration of the *sacrifice* of women in a patriarchal economy. Taking this idea of a female sacrifice to the very extreme, the women in the story find themselves literally suspended between life and death. The story of *Les Mille et Une Nuits* provides a mechanism for Djebar to expose the workings of patriarchy (based on the sacrifice of the other/woman/"sultane") and to illustrate another economy of relations which *challenges* the notion of sacrifice.

In Djebar's revision of the story of *Les Mille et Une Nuits*, the sultan fades into the background as Djebar highlights the relationship between the two women, and the role of the less famous sister, Dinarzade, in particular. Her aim, as she clearly states, is to reinstate the importance of Dinarzade's role: "Éclairer Dinarzade de la nuit!" [To throw light on the role of Dinarzade, as the night progresses!] (pp.104; 95).

Djebar opens Part 2 with an epigraph from Mardrus's translation of *Les Mille et Une Nuits*. The passage quoted in the epigraph then resurfaces immediately afterwards, in the first chapter of Part 2, but this time without quotation marks, and with a short insert of Djebar's own writing included. Appearing to mimic Irigaray's approach (mimicking her mimicry of the philosophers), Djebar weaves her own writing into the citation (now quoted without quotation marks) so that, as in the case of Irigaray's writing, it is difficult to tell where one begins and the other ends.

In the original passage (in quotation marks) Schéhérazade addresses Dinarzade directly, asking for help, but Dinarzade's reply is omitted – the story takes her assent for granted. In Djebar's version, she re-quotes the formal request for help but slips in a sentence which foregrounds Dinarzade's active participation in the plan and her eager willingness to help:
Original version:

> "Ma chère soeur, j'ai besoin de votre secours dans une affaire très importante; je vous prie de ne me le pas refuser. Mon père va me conduire chez le sultan pour être son épouse!...
> Dès que je serai devant le sultan, je le supplierai de permettre que vous couchiez dans la chambre nuptiale ..." (etc.) (pp. 101; 93)

---

[64] At the end of the novel, as we will see, Djebar revises her position vis-à-vis the patriarchal economy.

In Dialogue with Irigaray: *Ombre sultane*

> 'My dear sister, I need your help in a matter of great importance; I beg you not to refuse me this. My father is about to take me to the sultan, to be his bride!...
> As soon as I am in the sultan's presence, I shall beseech him to let you sleep in the bridal chamber...' (etc.)

Djebar's version:

> – Ma chère soeur, commence Schéhérazade, j'ai besoin de votre secours dans une affaire très importante. Mon père va me conduire chez le sultan pour être son épouse!
> *Et Dinarzade consent avant même que la demande s'explicite.*
> – Dès que je serai devant le sultan... (pp. 103, 95)

> 'My dear sister,' Scheherazade begins, 'I need your help in a matter of great importance ... My father is about to take me to the sultan, to be his bride!'
> *And Dinarzade agrees, even before the request is formulated.*
> 'As soon as I am in the sultan's presence'... [My emphasis]

So while Irigaray reads between the lines in order to pry out the repressed maternal-feminine, Djebar shines a torch between the lines ("Le féminin étant dès lors à déchiffrer comme inter-dit: dans les signes ou entre eux, entre des significations réalisées, entre les lignes..."[65]), in order to light up the forgotten sister figure who has been relegated to the shadow lands. Later in the passage, Djebar again shines her torch, this time under the sultan's bed, showing up the sister-figure :

> En tout cas, Dinarzade, la soeur, va veiller tout près: elle côtoiera l'étreinte; elle contemplera la fête sensuelle, ou du moins l'écoutera. Et la sultane sera sauvée pour un jour encore, pour un deuxième, parce qu'elle invente certes, mais d'abord parce que sa soeur a veillé et l'a réveillée. (pp. 103; 95)

> In any case, Dinarzade, the sister, will be keeping watch near at hand: she will be close by while they embrace; she will look on at their carnal feast, or at least give ear to it. And the sultan's bride will be reprieved for one day more, then for a second; to be sure, the tales she spins help save her, but first and foremost it is because her sister has kept watch and woken her in time.

Djebar thus shifts the emphasis from Schéhérazade's role in saving her (own) life, to Dinarzade's role in the "rescue operation." In Djebar's eyes, it is Dinarzade who has the starring role in the scene – Schéhérazade is saved "parce qu'elle invente certes, mais *d'abord* parce que sa soeur a veillé et l'a réveillée" [the tales she spins help

---

[65] Luce Irigaray, *Spéculum de l'autre femme*, p. 20.

save her, *but first and foremost* it is because her sister has kept watch and woken her in time] (pp. 103; 95).

Relating this story to that of Isma and Hajila, it first seems as if a clear parallelism can be drawn between Isma's role as Dinarzade (Isma the helper who comes to her sister Hajila's rescue, as Isma will do in Part 3) and Hajila's role as Schéhérazade (the new bride who needs to be rescued from a tragic destiny). This apparent parallelism is reinforced by Isma's subsequent resolve to help Hajila, which is inspired by Dinarzade's example: "Aujourd'hui, pour secourir une concubine, je m'imagine sous le lit; éveilleuse et solitaire, je déploie l'image proférée autrefois" [Today, to come to the rescue of a concubine, I imagine myself beneath the bed; alone, with the task of waking her, I revive the image offered long ago] (pp. 113; 103).

However, it becomes apparent that Isma not only identifies with Dinarzade but *also* identifies with Schéhérazade (as fellow narrator/storyteller), when she wonders whether her "paroles", like those of "la sultane", have the power to save: "Le récit de la sultane des aubes sauvera-t-il l'une de ces opprimées?" [Will the tale of the sultan's bride save one of these oppressed women?] (pp. 113; 103). So it seems that Isma identifies not only with the helper (Dinarzade) but also with the victim (Schéhérazade).

What Djebar is in fact showing is that there is no easy parallelism between Dinarzade/Isma and Schéhérazade/Hajila, helper/helped. For *both* Schéhérazade and Dinarzade contribute to the deferral of the "death sentence" (one by staying awake, the other by talking) and *both* women are potential victims. It is not only Schéhérazade's life that is at stake here, but also Dinarzade's, who is also a potential victim: "Pour le polygame, la consanguine de l'épouse est interdite, tout au moins tant que sa femme est vivante" [For the polygamist, any female blood relation of his wife is taboo, at least in the wife's lifetime] (pp. 103; 95). *Both* women help *each other* and *both women* need *each other's* help.

Both this idea of reciprocity (of both women helping each other), and the language used to express it, strongly resonates with Irigarayan undertones. Djebar sums up the message of the story in the last sentence of the chapter: "Et notre peur à toutes aujourd'hui se dissipe, puisque la sultane est double" [And all the fears haunting women today are dispelled, because of the two faces of the sultan's bride] (pp.104; 95). In "L'amour du même, l'amour de l'Autre", Irigaray outlines her idea of the necessary requirements for a positive relation between women, echoing Djebar's affirmation of reciprocal duality:

In Dialogue with Irigaray: *Ombre sultane* 195

> Pour établir, ou rendre possible l'amour d'elles, et du féminin entre elles, les femmes devraient nécessairement rejouer ou redoubler deux fois amoureusement ce qu'elles sont. Soit:
> – l'amour de *l'enveloppe nourrissante* externe et interne, interne et externe, en ses peaux et muqueuses;
> – l'amour du *corps*: et de ce corps qu'elles donnent et de ce corps qu'elles (se) redonnent.
> Il faut qu'elles s'aiment en tant que mères et d'un amour maternel, en tant que filles et d'un amour de fille. *Les deux*.[66]

What Irigaray is saying is that women should be both "the nourishing envelope" (nurturers), and the body (the nurtured body) – they should be both mothers (nurturers) and daughters (able to receive nurture) and "both of them" because *both* mothers and daughters should be able to *both* give and receive. Rather than competing with each other for the "unique place of the mother", rather than competing for the one, they should be two separate subjectivities, they should "play double." The paralysis created by them occupying the *one* place (of the object of man's desire) is displaced by the dynamics of relationality between the *two* (subjectivities).

For Irigaray freedom is double – both mother and daughter must be free in order for there to be a relation between the two: "En somme, nous libérer avec nos mères."[67] This need to achieve freedom *with the other* finds its echo in the relation between another mother-daughter couple, Isma and Mériem:

> J'avais voulu m'exclure pour rompre avec le passé. Ce fardeau, pendant mes errances dans les villes où j'étais de passage, s'était allégé. Mériem m'avait écrit. J'accourais; *je ne pouvais me libérer seule*. (pp. 90; 81)
>
> I had tried to keep my distance in order to break with the past. I had lightened my burden during my wanderings through cities. Meriem had written to me. I had hurried back; *I could not free myself on my own*. [My emphasis]

This last phrase also foreshadows the future relation between Isma and Hajila – because Isma will come to realise that she must not only liberate herself *with her daughter*, Mériem, but also *with her "sister"*, Hajila. Their relationship will then no longer conform to the substitutionary masculine economy based on the one's sacrifice of the other, but to a feminine economy based on the association or contiguity of the two.

---

[66] Luce Irigaray, *Éthique de la différence sexuelle*, p. 103.
[67] Luce Irigaray, *Le Corps-à-corps avec la mère* (Montréal: Editions de la pleine lune, 1981), p. 86.

Sexuality, repression and rivalry

In the rest of Part 2, we pass from the extremes of the sultan's sacrifice and the bonds of sisterhood to the norms of Islamic society, where repression no longer takes the form of a threatened death sentence, but of innumerable social prohibitions, and where the bonds of sisterhood are displaced by stories that parade bitter rivalries between women. With reference to the work of Fatima Mernissi, I will examine the origins and mechanics of sexual repression in Islamic culture. Then, using the example of "L'exclue" [The Outcast] (Chapter V of Part 2), I will show how this repression produces the conditions not only for negative relations *between the sexes* but also for the kind of rivalry *between women* that Irigaray denounces as *polemos*.

Mernissi refers to two ways of differentiating between Western and Islamic conceptions of sexuality. Some theories focus on the different ways in which Western and Islamic societies enforce sexual taboos; Western societies operate by "une forte intériorisation des interdits sexuels au cours du processus de socialisation", whereas Islamic societies operate by "des barrières de précautions extérieures telles que les règles de conduite ségrégationnistes" (such as veiling, seclusion, surveillance etc.).[68] Mernissi, however, believes that the contrast between Eastern and Western concepts of sexuality lies not so much between internalised ethics and external devices but between different conceptions of sexuality itself:

> Dans les sociétés où l'isolement et la surveillance des femmes prédominent, le concept de la sexualité de la femme est implicitement actif, mais là où ces méthodes de surveillance et de coercition du comportement de la femme n'existent pas, le concept de la sexualité de la femme est passif.[69]

Mernissi then qualifies the above statement, stating that Islamic society is in fact characterised by a "double theory" of sexual dynamics. On the one hand there is an *explicit assumption* of passive compliant female sexuality versus an active, aggressive masculine sexuality; on the other hand there is the *implicit assumption that female sexuality is active*.[70]

---

[68] Fatima Mernissi, *Sexe, idéologie, Islam*, p. 9.
[69] Ibid., p. 10.
[70] Ibid., p. 11. One could argue that Western society has also traditionally operated a double theory of feminine sexuality, a point which is reinforced by images of woman in Western literature: "But behind the angel lurks the monster: the obverse of the male idealisation of woman is the male fear of femininity". Quotation from Toril Moi, *Sexual/Textual Politics*, p. 58.

Mernissi focuses her attention on this implicit assumption, quoting from the writings of Islamic clerics, such as Al-Ghazali, to illustrate her point. Al-Ghazali presents us not only with a sexually active woman but also with sexually insatiable woman: "Si l'on n'a pas fixé avec précision ce que la femme peut exiger en matière de coït, c'est en raison de la difficulté de la présentation d'une pareille requête et de la satisfaction à lui accorder."[71]

For Mernissi these Islamic "images of women" stand in stark contrast to the images offered by Freud: "Par opposition à la passivité et la frigidité de la femme selon Freud, les exigences sexuelles de la femme selon Imam Ghazali semblent véritablement accablantes et la nécessité où est l'homme de les satisfaire devient un devoir social pressant."[72] Mernissi describes the Islamic conception of female sexuality as female aggression turned outwards (in contrast to Freud's masochistic female whose sexuality is turned inwards): "La nature de son agressivité est précisément sexuelle. La femme musulmane est dotée d'une attraction fatale qui érode la volonté de l'homme de lui résister et le réduit à un rôle passif et soumis."[73]

This Islamic theory of an active feminine sexuality creates a climate of suspicion around women who are branded as potential temptresses. The Muslim male, and by extension the Islamic social order, is threatened by this powerful female sexuality, and by the "fitna" or "chaos" that the temptress woman has the potential to provoke "en attirant d'autres hommes vers des relations sexuelles illicites."[74] This threat of "fitna" or sexual chaos in society is countered by a proliferation of external prohibitions imposed on women (such as veiling, surveillance, segregation, seclusion etc.), which exist to ensure that no forms of illicit sexual relationship ("zina") outside marriage take place.

So whether a society adopts an active *or* a passive theory of sexuality, the result in either case is that women find themselves in the position of being repressed. Echoing Irigaray's association of the female imaginary and the processes of the unconscious, Mernissi suggests that the dominant conceptualisation of the "Islamic" woman also offers the features of the unconscious, not in the sense of its

---

[71] Abu Hamid al-Ghazali (1058-1111), *The Revivification of Religious Sciences* (Cairo: al-Maktaba at-Tijariya al-Kubra, no date cited), p. 50. Quoted in Fatima Mernissi, *Sexe, idéologie, Islam*, p. 22.
[72] Fatima Mernissi, *Sexe, idéologie, Islam*, p. 22.
[73] Ibid., pp. 24-25.
[74] Ibid., p. 22.

fluidity or mobility, but in the sense of its indifference to the laws of social order:

> Il n'a pas le choix; il ne peut que céder à son attraction, d'où cette identification de la femme avec *fitna*, le chaos, avec les forces anti-sociales et anti-divines de l'univers.[75]

Here again the woman becomes the negative in the representation of sexual difference, not as in Freud's thinking because she is absence to his presence, but because she represents chaos to his (social) order. Here too we have echoes of Irigaray's critique of Plato's myth, as the feminine becomes synonymous not with the non-transcendental but with the "anti-divine": "La femme ressemble dans ce sens à Satan dans son incitation à faire le mal et à le rendre séduisant."[76]

Because man's first loyalty is to the divine, emotional attachment to women, (who are regarded as temptation away from the spiritual life), is discouraged, to the extent that Mernissi can speak of Muslim wariness of heterosexual involvement. By this she means that Islamic society is constructed in such a way as to undermine the possibility of a close male-female bond. Viewed from this vantage-point, many of the repressive features of Islamic society can be seen to conspire against male/female intimacy – "la ségrégation sexuelle et ses corollaires: le mariage arrangé, le rôle important que joue la mère dans la vie du fils et la fragilité du lien matrimonial (révélée par les institutions que sont la répudiation et la polygamie)."[77] Moreover, as Djebar's text confirms, the repressive features of Islamic society also conspire against intimacy between *women*.

Competition between women

The story of "l'exclue" [the outcast] illustrates how the image of the Islamic woman as sexually aggressive or as temptress leads to a climate of suspicion between women that recreates the conditions for Irigaray's *polemos*.

Irigaray believes that competition is the basic way that women relate to each other in a patriarchal society. The supposed traditional expressions of empathy between women, based on comparatives, are dismissed by Irigaray as evidence of a more insidious form of *competition*, which is rooted in their lack of subjectivity: "Ces *comme*

---

[75] Ibid., p. 25.
[76] Abu al-Hassan Muslim, *al-Jami as-Sahib* (Beirut: al Maktaba at-Tijariya, no date cited) Vol. III, Book of Marriage, p. 130. Quoted in Fatima Mernissi, *Sexe, idéologie, Islam*, p. 25.
[77] Fatima Mernissi, *Sexe, idéologie, Islam*, p. 30.

toi, moi aussi, moi plus (ou moins), comme tout le monde n'ont pas grand-chose à voir avec une éthique amoureuse. Ils sont les traces-symptômes du *polemos* entre femmes. Pas de *avec toi* dans cette économie."[78] This compulsive need to compare themselves to others deprives women of their own sense of self: "Ces harcelants calculs (inconscients, ou préconscients) paralysent la fluidité des affects. Par durcissement, emprunt, situation des bords de l'autre pour 'exister.' Preuves d'amour, ces comparatifs abolissent la possibilité d'un lieu entre femmes. Elles s'estiment en fonction de mesures qui ne sont pas les leurs et qui occupent sans habiter ce lieu possible de leur identité."[79]

Djebar's story of "l'exclue" [the outcast] and "la voyeuse" [feminine form of "voyeur"] provides an extreme example of the kind of rivalry that Irigaray describes, which literally results in the *exclusion of a woman* not from the symbolic order, but from her social environment, the village where she has grown up. Here is a graphic embodiment of what Irigaray describes as "living in the edge of the other", a story in which a woman, "la voyeuse", literally positions herself "on the edges of the other", by the window l/edge so that she can spy on others: "... elle trônait devant ses persiennes entrouvertes. Écran derrière lequel elle guettait chaque instant de chaque jour..." [... she sat enthroned at her half-open shutters. Behind this screen she kept watch every minute of every day...] (pp. 119; 110).

Lla Hajda becomes obsessed with the furtive glances exchanged between a young woman "mariée depuis l'âge de seize ans à un époux vieilli et malade" and a childhood friend of hers who has recently returned to the village [married at sixteen to a man now old and ailing] (pp. 123; 114). She maliciously wills the inevitable to happen, "l'inattendu ... ou le trop attendu!" [the unexpected happens ... or is it not to be expected?], and it is as if her evil intent hastens the day when the young girl braves "l'interdit" and exchanges a few whispered words with her old friend (pp. 124, 125; 115, 116).

Lla Hajda's response to this simple gesture is to spread salacious rumours about the young woman. Because of the assumption of the woman's sexual aggression, the young man's part in the incident is forgotten, while the finger of suspicion is pointed at the young woman: "Lla Hajda affirme que c'est la femme, la 'possédée du démon', 'la tentatrice', qui chuchote la première" [Lla Hadja declares that it is the woman 'possessed by the devil', 'the temptress' who

---

[78] Luce Irigaray, *Éthique de la différence sexuelle*, p. 102.
[79] Ibid., pp. 101-02.

whispers the first word] (pp. 124; 115). As the widow's diatribe against the "temptress and her sins" becomes more venomous, the nameless young woman is likened to the ultimate symbols of evil and temptation, and in the words of Mernissi, "d'où cette identification de la femme avec *fitna*, le chaos, avec les forces anti-sociales et anti-divines de l'univers",[80] a comparison echoed in Djebar's narrative: "Imaginez Satan. Ève" [Imagine Satan. Eve] (pp. 125; 115). Finally, false accusations are added to speculation to bolster the case against the hapless defendant: "Je l'affirme: elle a réussi à glisser une lettre à son amoureux! L'ensorceleuse, la stérile!" ['I can tell you, she managed to slip a letter to her lover! The sorceress! The barren wife! Poor, poor bed-ridden husband, whose wife has no pity!'] (pp. 125, 116). The consequences of these accusations for the young woman are tragic – she is ostracised by the community and is compelled by her own family to leave her village forever.

Irigaray's explanation as to how women have the capacity to destroy one another is based on her belief that women experience difficulties in differentiation. Because women situate themselves on the edges of the other, the edges of the self are blurred, and they cannot completely differentiate themselves from one another. Women thus represent a kind of undifferentiated magma, "Sorte de magma, de 'nuit où toutes les vaches sont noires'…"[81] and any woman who stands out from the crowd, who affirms her *own* identity, whose differentiated form rises up from the rest is regarded as a threat and destroyed:

> Sans le savoir ni le vouloir, le plus souvent, les femmes constituent le moyen le plus terrible de leur propre oppression: elles détruisent tout ce qui émerge de leur condition indifférenciée, se faisant l'agent de leur propre anéantissement, de leur réduction à un même qui n'est pas *leur* même.[82]

So it is that in Djebar's story, one woman destroys another woman, precisely because she has stepped out of line, because she has dared to take the smallest step out of the shadow of "l'interdit."

Rescuing negative images of women

The story of "l'exclue" [the outcast] and other stories in Part 2 reveal Djebar's view of relations between women (like that of Irigaray) to be extremely negative. Irigaray's writing can be

---

[80] Fatima Mernissi, *Sexe, idéologie, Islam*, p. 25.
[81] Luce Irigaray, *Éthique de la différence sexuelle*, p. 102.
[82] Ibid., p. 102.

interpreted as propagating caricatural stereotypes of women and of parading images illustrating "[the] hatred of the mother, rivalry between women, women as women's own worst enemies." All the negative stereotypes mentioned above in relation to Irigaray resurface in Part 2 of Djebar's text (for "hatred of the mother" see the story of Houria, pp. 141-44; 130-34).

In *Luce Irigaray: Philosophy in the Feminine*, Whitford explains how Irigaray rescues these negative images of women: "What she does do is to make a link between certain clichés of psychological or psychoanalytical descriptions ... and the symbolic order; thus she allows for the possibility that a different symbolization could have [positive] effects on women's relationships with each other."[83] I would like to show that a similar rescue operation takes place in Djebar's text. What *Djebar* does is to make a link between her negative images of women and a positive transformation in Isma's consciousness (which takes place at the end of Part 2) that will enable her to enter into positive relations with women, and with Hajila in particular.

In Part 1 of *Ombre sultane*, Isma opens herself up to the other (Hajila). In Part 2 she opens herself up to the "other others" of her past (the women of her childhood), and at the end of Part 2 she comes to realise that she too is part of that "otherness", of that repressed maternal world, as her first buried memory of paternal repression (and separation from childhood) is brought to the fore of her consciousness.

The transformation of Isma's consciousness takes the form of her retracing the moment of her separation from childhood, and her entry into the Law of The Father, a moment in which she is compelled to disown her own body and to place it under the Prohibition of the Father, the law of "l'interdit." This reliving of the moment of separation from the body and entry into the paternal culture represents a turning-point in Isma's life, which paves the way back towards her re-entry into the world of women.

The process of reliving the moment of separation (as a means of recovering a lost feminine identity) finds its echoes in Irigaray's article "Le mystère oublié des généalogies féminines"[84], where she too advocates a way for women to work their way back to the maternal by *retracing the moment of separation* (from the maternal, and entry into the paternal). I will first look at Irigaray's description of the process and then show how a similar process occurs in Djebar's text.

---

[83] Margaret Whitford, *Luce Irigaray: Philosophy in the Feminine*, p. 78.
[84] Luce Irigaray, *Le Temps de la différence*, pp. 101-23.

In "Le mystère oublié des généalogies féminines"[85], this process of tracing back the relation with the maternal is described with reference to a mythical mother-daughter relationship:

> Le plus bel exemple du devenir de la relation mère-fille est peut-être illustré par les mythes et rites relatifs à Déméter et Korè .... Mère et fille se retrouvent avec bonheur. Déméter demande à Perséphone de lui raconter tout ce qui lui est arrivé. Elle lui en fait le récit en commençant par la fin. *Elle remonte le temps en quelque sorte, comme doit le faire aujourd'hui toute femme qui tente de retrouver les traces de l'éloignement de sa mère.* C'est à cela que devrait lui servir le parcours psychanalytique, *à retrouver le fil de son entrée, et, si possible, de sa sortie des enfers.*[86]

Turning her attention from the mythical to the psychoanalytical, Irigaray refers to Freud's theoretical account of the turning away from the mother. Continuing the metaphor of the entry into patriarchy as Hades ("l'entrée et la sortie des enfers"), Freud now becomes the villain of the piece, the devil incarnate, pointing the way away from the mother figure into the hell-fires of patriarchy:

> Freud se conduit ici en prince des ténèbres par rapport à toutes les femmes. Il les entraîne dans l'ombre et la séparation d'avec leur mère et d'avec elles-mêmes pour l'établissement d'une culture de l'entre-hommes: Elle doit oublier son enfance, sa mère, elle doit s'oublier dans sa relation à la *philotès* d'Aphrodite.[87]

Turning to Djebar's narrative, the motifs of separation, loss of childhood/feminine identity, and the imposition of paternal culture resurface. In contrast to Irigaray's metaphor of the spiritual underworld, conjuring up images of eternal separation and torment, Djebar comes up with a more physical image of separation, that of "la mutilation originelle" [primal injury], conjuring up the trauma and lasting disfigurement of a violent amputation (pp. 145; 134).

In Chapter IX, Isma describes how the repressed memory of this separation/mutilation now flows back into her adult consciousness. The experience of mutilation is identified with a specific moment in time and space, an impromptu escapade to a fair that ends in recrimination. In her description of the incident, Djebar foregrounds the child's relation to her body, contrasting Isma's carefree enjoyment of physical sensations with the ambiguity later installed by paternal intervention.

---

[85] Ibid., pp. 101-23.
[86] Ibid., pp.112, 118. [My emphasis]
[87] Ibid., p. 121.

While playing with a cousin one day, the young Isma comes across a circus where she rides on a giant mechanical swing. The action of swinging serves to magnify the pleasures of occupying not only her body space, but also the airspace around her:

> Quand la mécanique, jusque-là à terre, fut soulevée dans le ciel, quand, assise tremblante mais émerveillée, les bras accrochés aux barres, je sentis mon corps s'élever et se rythmer en tanguant régulièrement, plus rien n'exista, ni la ville, ni la foule, ni le cousin, seuls l'espace mobile et mon propre balancement. (pp. 146; 135)

> Up till then the mechanism had been stationary; but when it was lifted up into the air, when, as I sat trembling but entranced, tightly gripping the bars, I felt my body rise and dance to the regular rhythm, nothing else existed, neither the town nor the crowds, nor my cousin, only the motion of space and myself swinging to and fro.

The pleasure of her experience is intensified as she lets herself go further into the air: "Pour mieux sentir la rafale du vent sur mes joues et aviver l'excitation qui me rendait légère, comme éparpillée dans le soir commençant, je m'étais dressée. Ma jupe plissée virevoltant, je m'amusais à plier les genoux, quand la balançoire commença à ralentir" [The better to feel the rush of the wind against my cheeks and quicken the excitement that was making me feel weightless, as if I was being scattered in pieces into the early evening, I had stood up. I was enjoying myself bending my knees and letting my pleated skirt whirl around me, when the swing began to slow down] (pp. 147; 135).

This carefree scene abruptly comes to an end when Isma's father unexpectedly turns up, discovers her in mid-flight and swiftly orders her to return home with him. The reason for this sudden withdrawal only dawns slowly on Isma. When he starts voicing his thoughts – his horror caused by "... le fait que 'sa fille, sa propre fille, habillée d'une jupe courte, puisse, au-dessus des regards des hommes, montrer ses jambes!'" [... the fact that 'his daughter, his own daughter, dressed in a short skirt, could show her legs to all those men staring up at her, down below!'] (pp. 147-48; 136), Isma, unable to comprehend his response, takes refuge in complete denial:

> Percevant enfin ses mots débités à voix basse, j'écoutais un inconnu, non, pas mon père; "pas mon père", me répétais-je. (pp. 147, 136)

> When I finally caught the words he was muttering, I found I was listening to a stranger, not my father; 'no, not my father' I kept telling myself.

What Isma has to come to terms with is that her body is no longer her own but has become the object of paternal censure. This incident not only represents a turning-point in Isma's attitude towards her father, and in her self-perception as an emancipated young girl, but more significantly, points to a traumatic experience of separation. This separation is described as expatriation, as banishment: *"Ce jour-là, je m'exilai de l'enfance"*, as propulsion into foreign territory, "les mots paternels m'avaient projetée ailleurs" [my father's words had projected me into another world], into an abyss "au plus profond d'un gouffre étrange" [into the depths of a strange abyss], an underworld which recalls Irigaray's Hades (pp. 148; 137). The foreign territory she has now consciously entered into is patriarchy, the country which, according to Irigaray, requires its women to leave their mothers, to disown their bodies, *and to forget their childhoods* in the name of its masculine culture: "Elle doit oublier son enfance, sa mère, elle doit s'oublier dans sa relation à la *philotès* d'Aphrodite."[88]

In a variation on Irigaray's "buried act of matricide", here we have "un père qui se présente en organisateur de précoces funéraires." This incident marks the "death" of Isma's childhood and her entry into masculine culture. But, as Irigaray suggests, the reliving of this kind of experience is the key to being liberated from its effects: C'est à cela que devrait lui servir le parcours psychanalytique, à retrouver le fil de son entrée, et, si possible, de sa sortie des enfers.[89]

Isma has recovered "les fils de son entrée dans les enfers" and now she will burrow her way out of the underworld, she will find the way out, not only for herself but also for Hajila: "L'enfance, ô Hajila! Te déterrer hors de ce terreau commun qui embourbe!" [Childhood, O Hajila! I must unearth you from this mouldering heap under which you have been buried] (pp. 149; 139). But even as the promise of liberation is whispered, the difficulty of the task, already foreshadowed in Irigaray's "si possible", is echoed in the final words of Part 2: "Éveilleuse pour quel désenchantement..." [To waken her sister to what disillusionment...] (pp. 149; 139).

The process of awakening and the transition to disillusionment is enacted in Part 3, where Isma finally comes face to face with Hajila.

Maternal Restoration or Paternal Revenge?

In Irigaray's work, the terms "*same*" and the "economy of the same" are normally used to refer to the self-reflexive masculine

---

[88] Ibid., p. 121.
[89] Ibid., p. 118.

economy. However, in "L'amour du même, l'amour de l'Autre"[90], Irigaray refers to "sameness" *not in relation to the economy of the same*, but in relation to the *maternal-feminine*. Here "sameness" is no longer associated with the reproduction of the same (as in the self-reflexive masculine economy of the same) but rather with a pre-subjective undifferentiated sameness (as in the undifferentiated maternal-feminine) from which the subject emerges as body.

These seemingly opposite connotations of sameness (first in relation to the masculine and them in relation to the feminine) are explained by Irigaray's belief that the original feminine sameness has come to be appropriated by the masculine. Man forgets his original undifferentiated state, his original feminine sameness, which he substitutes for a masculine sameness which he manufactures himself: "Là où était la germination, la naissance, la croissance selon l'économie naturelle, l'homme met l'instrument et l'oeuvre."[91]

So male production becomes a substitute for female reproduction. Production becomes his own "sameness", the origin to which he now relates, from which he creates his identity, while his real origin is forgotten: "Elle, au moins deux fois oubliée, demeure fond nocturne, sommeil létal à partir desquels il s'érige, et transparence imperceptible de l'entrée en présence."[92]

It is in this context that we read Irigaray's insistence on "the love of sameness":

> Aucun amour du même que moi, posé et maintenu hors de moi dans sa différence, ne peut avoir lieu sans interprétation de l'amour du même: maternel-féminin encore indifférencié, sous-sol de toute possibilité de détermination d'identité.[93]

Isma's identification with Hajila's suffering in Part 1 and her identification with the exclusion of women in Part 2 (which I have referred to up till now in terms of otherness) can now be interpreted as a return to the original sameness, a return to the feminine, an identification with the world of women. However, although Irigaray insists on the recognition of the feminine, on the love of sameness, she also argues that for a positive relation to emerge between two subjectivities, this love of sameness must be accompanied by a

---

[90] Luce Irigaray, "L'amour du même, l'amour de l'Autre", *Éthique de la différence sexuelle*, pp. 97-111.
[91] Ibid., p. 99.
[92] Ibid., p. 98.
[93] Ibid., p. 98.

recognition of difference: "... [un] amour du même que moi, posé et maintenu hors de moi dans sa différence ..."[94]

In Part 3 I will demonstrate how Hajila and Isma's relationship moves from the recognition of sameness to a recognition of difference. Before that I will refer to three chapters in *J'aime à toi*, "Toi qui ne seras jamais mien", "J'aime à toi", and "Dans un silence presque *absolu*", in which Irigaray communicates her vision of the coming into being of *a positive relation* between subjectivities as a result of the *recognition of difference*.

Love in the positive, love in the negative

In "Toi qui ne seras jamais mien", Irigaray claims that the only way for two subjects to relate to each other positively is for each of them to recognise each other's difference.

In the opening passage of the article, she opposes the two concepts of difference and sameness. Sameness in this context is associated with indifferentiation, with completeness and unity, in other words with the complete identification of one subjectivity with the other, resulting in one of the subjectivities being encircled or engulfed by the other. Difference, on the other hand, is the existence or creation of a gap between two subjectivities, each of which is separated and therefore guaranteed by this difference.

Difference as a "gap" between two subjectivities prevents them merging together, and being subsumed into one. This gap operates as a no-go area or protective zone around each subjectivity, so that the one becomes irreducible to the other: "Nous sommes insubstituables l'un à l'autre. Tu m'es transcendant(e), inaccessible en un sens..."[95]

Irigaray makes a distinction between knowing and identifying the other and knowing or identifying with the other *completely*. This complete knowing or identification with the other prevents the distance required for differentiation to be achieved, and, as such, should be resisted. Irigaray reformulates this idea in several ways: "Je ne peux *complètement* t'identifier, a fortiori m'identifier à toi ... Tu ne me seras jamais *totalement* visible."[96]

In "You who will never be mine", difference is articulated as a negative. The negative (gap) is what enables the positive interaction between subjectivities to take place: "La puissance d'un négatif

---

[94] Ibid., p. 98.
[95] Luce Irigaray, *J'aime à toi* (Paris: Grasset et Fasquelle: 1992), p. 161.
[96] Ibid. pp. 161, 163. [My emphasis]

demeure entre nous."[97] The power of this relational negative is reinforced linguistically by a whole string of negative verbal phrases, each of which stresses the essential elusiveness or impenetrability of the other: "…une liberté qui ne sera jamais mienne, une subjectivité qui ne sera jamais mienne, un mien qui ne sera jamais mien."[98]

In "J'aime à toi" Irigaray describes the same process of recognition, but this time using positive language structures. The gap expressed in the negative resurfaces linguistically as the preposition "to" which represents difference as mediation between two subjectivities: "I love to you." Without the "to" (i.e. in the phrase "I love you") Irigaray argues, the other person ("you") is reduced grammatically and relationally to an object: "Le 'à' empêche le rapport de transitivité sans irréductibilité de l'autre, et réciprocité possible … Le 'à' est le lieu de non-réduction de la personne à objet."[99]

For Irigaray, the "to" is a guarantor not only of the other's alterity but also of the other's intentionality: "Le 'à' est garant de deux intentionnalités: la mienne et la tienne."[100] The coming into being of two intentionalities is dependant on the subject's willingness to listen to the other: "Si je suis attentif(ve) à ton intentionnalité, à ta fidélité à toi-même et à son/ton devenir, il m'est permis d'imaginer si une durée peut exister entre nous, si nos intentionnalités peuvent s'accorder."[101]

Irigaray relates the act of listening with its corollary, the ability to keep silent. The attentive listener does not presume to "put words into the other's mouth" but allows for "… [le] non-encore codé, [le] silence, un lieu d'existence, d'initiative, d'intentionnalité libre, de soutien à ton devenir."[102] Silence challenges the preordained symbolic code of language, culture and relations, creating a sonic gap, a blank page upon which nothing is imposed or superimposed, a space that allows the other to be and to become: "Ce silence n'est pas hostile ni restrictif. Il est disponibilité que rien ni personne n'occupe, ne préoccupe."[103]

---

[97] Ibid., p. 161
[98] Ibid., p. 162.
[99] Ibid., pp. 171, 172.
[100] Ibid., p. 173.
[101] Ibid., p. 175.
[102] Ibid., p. 181.
[103] Ibid., p. 182.

Listening with mother

> T'écouter demande donc que je me rende disponible, que je sois encore et toujours capable de silence. Ce geste, jusqu'à un certain point, me libère moi-même.[104]

Irigaray's insistence on "availability" brings us back to Djebar's text and to the end of Part 2, where Isma wonders how to make herself available to Hajila ("je cherche comment me présenter à toi" [And I hunt for a way to introduce myself to you], pp. 149; 139). In the end, she decides to go to the family home and meet Hajila face to face. This initial encounter is followed by two subsequent meetings between Hajila and Isma, in the local *hammam*. These meetings are marked by *silence*, a silence that permits difference to come into being, and that enables Hajila to walk out of the shadowlands of Isma's unconscious and to finally emerge as a separate subjectivity.

The first time Isma meets Hajila, she turns up unannounced at her ex-husband's flat (and has to brave the hostility of Touma, Hajila's mother), only to find Hajila, weakened by her pregnancy, lying down on a bed:

> Je suis apparue sur le seuil. Devant toi, enfin. Pour la première fois. Toi, *ma fille et ma mère, ma consanguine*: ma blessure renouvelée (ainsi les mots ne mentent jamais). Te soutenant contre les murs, dans ta robe claire, bleu pâle, tu tentes de te tenir debout. J'aurais pu pleurer à la vue de ta défaillance. (pp. 157; 147)

> I appeared in the doorway. Standing before you, at last. For the first time. You, *my daughter and my mother, my half-sister*; my reopened wound (so words never lie). Supporting yourself against the wall, in you pale blue summer dress, you try to stand. I could have wept to see your weakness. [My emphasis]

Isma's reference to "mothers and daughters" is a pointer to the kind of reciprocal duality of relation that both Irigaray and Djebar believe in, echoing Irigaray's call to women to be double, to love one another both as mothers and as daughters[105], and foreshadowing the double gesture that will be enacted in the next meeting between Isma and Hajila. Moreover, the term "consanguine" recalls the contiguity that, for Irigaray, represents the ideal marker of the mother-daughter relation.

At the end of this first encounter, Isma hurriedly whispers to Hajila an arrangement for them to meet the following Friday. Significantly, the second meeting takes place in the *hammam*. Djebar foregrounds

---

[104] Ibid., pp. 183-84.
[105] Luce Irigaray, *Éthique de la différence sexuelle*, p. 103.

the symbolism of the *hammam* as womb, first implicitly "Retrouver chaleur, réconfort dans le bourdonnement d'échos sous des voûtes hautes" [To bask again in the warm solace of murmuring voices that reverberate in high vaulted chambers] and then explicitly "Je ne m'oublie que dans les brumes de vapeur brûlante, je ne m'abîme que dans l'eau mère: hier, celle de la volupté, aujourd'hui ruisseaux d'enfance remémorée" [Only in the clouds of scalding steam can I let go. I can only let myself be submerged in mother liquor: yesterday, that of sensual ecstasy, today the rivers of my remembered childhood] (pp. 158; 148). The *hammam* will be the space in which both women can "become", it will function like a narrative version of Irigaray's 'other of the other', a cave-womb-like space that woman can call her own, where "women [can be] among themselves, and where they can discover "love of the self on the side of women."[106]

In the second image proffered by Djebar, the *hammam*-womb merges into an inverted harem, where, as in Irigaray's maternal genealogy, feminine ritual (if not fertility) allows for transformation and renewal: "Chaque nuit, le bain maure, qui sert de dortoir aux ruraux de passage, devient un harem inversé, perméable – comme si, dans la dissolution des sueurs, des odeurs, des peaux mortes, cette prison liquide devenait lieu de renaissance nocturne. De transfusion. Là s'effectuent les passages de symbole, là jaillissent les éclairs de connivence, et leurs frôlements tremblés" [Every night the Turkish bath serves as a dormitory for country-folk in transit and so becomes a harem in reverse, accessible to all – as if, in the melting-pot of sweat, odours and dead skin, this liquid prison becomes a place of nocturnal rebirth] (pp. 158-59; 148).

As Isma and Hajila catch sight of each other, Djebar, like Irigaray, makes the link between the recognition of the other and the sounds of silence: "Lors de ce deuxième vendredi, tu es entrée. Tu m'as reconnue ... Nous n'avons pas parlé..." [On the second Friday, you came. You recognized me ... We didn't speak] (pp. 161; 151). This silence continues as Isma performs the ritual cleansing on Hajila: "En silence, j'ai empli d'eau chaude une tasse de cuivre; j'en déversai le jet sur tes épaules, puis sur ta chevelure" [Silently, I filled a copper cup with hot water and emptied it over your shoulders then your hair] (p161; 151). Rather than invading and overwhelming Hajila's world with her words (as she did incessantly in Part 1), Isma is now creating with her silence a gap, a space between herself and Hajila that allows her, in Irigaray's words, "to become."

---

[106] Margaret Whitford, *Luce Irigaray: Philosophy in the Feminine*, p. 104.

The silence is only broken when Hajila makes a gesture of appreciation towards Isma: "Continue! Que tu sois bénie! Cela me fait tant de bien ..." ['Go on! Bless you! That does me so much good ...'] (pp. 161; 151). And with a few perfunctory words they set the scene for their final encounter: "A vendredi prochain" ['I'll see you next Friday'] (pp. 161; 151).

The final planned meeting between the two women can be interpreted in the light of Irigaray's words on "wonder." Irigaray's discourse on wonder is yet another variation on the theme of difference. Difference can emerge not only as a result of silence but also as a result of wonder, which also creates space between subjectivities. Wonder is associated with surprise. It is that in the other which we did not presume to be there – the uncodified, unexpected, mysterious, elusive:

> Cet(te) autre devrait encore et encore nous *surprendre*, nous apparaître comme *nouveau, fort différent* de ce que nous connaissions ou que nous supposions qu'il devait être. Ce qui fait que nous le regarderions, nous arrêterions pour le regarder, nous interroger, nous approcher dans le questionnement. *Qui es-tu? Je suis* et *je deviens* grâce à cette question...[107]

Isma arrives early for their next meeting in the *hammam*, and in a build up to Hajila's entrance, the rituals of cleansing are performed with a deliberate slowness in the space symbolised as womb: "Dissoudre la touffeur de la claustration grâce à ce succédané du cocon maternel..." [This surrogate maternal cocoon providing an escape from the hothouse of cloistration...] (pp. 163; 152). When Hajila finally arrives, both women stand side by side: "Nous nous sommes lavées l'une à côté de l'autre" [We washed side by side] (pp. 163; 152). This image, of two subjectivities that are separate yet side by side, recalls the contiguity of Irigaray's maternal genealogy. The next image is of Hajila performing the ritual cleansings on Isma, followed by Isma doing the same for her, a double gesture, with which Djebar establishes a reciprocal duality between the two women: "... tu as proposé de me savonner les épaules et le dos, tu m'as aspergée de la dernière eau, la plus froide, celle du rinçage. A mon tour, j'ai fait pareil" [you offered to soap my shoulders and back; you sprinkled the last lot of water over me, the coldest used for rinsing. I then did the same for you] (pp. 163; 153).

This moment of peaceful intimacy is broken by Isma's voice offering Hajila the key to her escape from the life she abhors and the

---

[107] Luce Irigaray, *Éthique de la différence sexuelle*, p. 77.

child she did not wish to have: "Touma t'empêche de sortir ... Que tu gardes cet enfant dans ton ventre ou que tu le rejettes, c'est à toi d'en décider! Sors, consulte un médecin, une amie, qui tu veux. Sors, seulement pour sortir!" ['Touma prevents you going out, except for this weekly bath. It's up to you to decide whether you keep this child you're carrying, or whether you get rid of it. Get out of the house, go and consult a doctor or a friend, anyone you like. Get out for the sake of getting out!'] (pp. 163; 153). The offer of this gift to Hajila is followed by a moment of "wonder", where Isma looks at Hajila with new eyes:

> Tu me dévisageais, yeux grands ouverts, les bras ruisselants de vapeur. Dans cette pose de baigneuse un peu gauche, ton visage habité d'une hésitation enfantine, je perçois enfin ta grâce de femme; *ton secret*. (Et je me rappelle que, dans mon dialecte arabe, au-dessus de la beauté qu'on peut célébrer chez une femme, *c'est "le secret" qu'on loue, la trace insaisissable* qu'il laisse transparaître sur une face). (pp. 163-64; 153)
>
> You stared at me, eyes wide open, the moist steam dripping from your arms. As you stood awkwardly, with an expression of childish indecision on your face, I was finally aware of your grace as a woman; your secret. (And I remind myself that in my Arabic dialect, over and above the beauty that is celebrated in a woman, *she is mostly praised for her 'secret' – of which an elusive trace* momentarily flashes across her face. [My emphasis]

As Isma pauses in wonder before Hajila, as she recognises her "secret", her essential elusiveness, "la trace insaisissable" [the elusive trace], it is as if a protective ring has been formed around Hajila, a no-go area that Isma can no longer penetrate. It is at this moment that Isma finally lets go of Hajila, who is no longer "ombre" [shadow] but "forme" [figure], no longer a projection of Isma's unconsciousness, but a subjectivity, a separate and impenetrable consciousness all of her own. From now on Isma's words will no longer overwrite Hajila's, they will never capture her every movement. As we will see, Isma will no longer be able to enter Hajila's mind, she will no longer be able to read her every thought: "Je te reconnais suppose que je ne peux pas te voir de part en part. Tu ne me seras jamais totalement visible mais, grâce à cela, je te respecte comme différent(e) de moi."[108]

---

[108] Luce Irigaray, *J'aime à toi*, p. 163.

Future imperfect

> Je te donne du silence où le futur de toi – et peut-être de moi mais avec toi et non *comme* toi et *sans* toi – peut émerger et se fonder.[109]

What kind of future does Djebar envisage for Hajila and Isma? In the last two chapters we are presented with what may appear a confusing succession of unexpected narrative twists. These narrative twists can be interpreted in the light of the "symbolic" (in the conventional sense of the word) transformation of Hajila and Isma, who lose their own "specificity" and become symbolic representations of the two faces of Algerian womanhood, modern and traditional, both of whom have tasted liberation only to have it snatched away: "Éveilleuse pour quel désenchantement..." [To waken her sister to what disillusionment...] (pp. 149; 139).

The first "confusing" twist is Isma's seemingly unexplained and inexplicable decision to return to the traditional village and lifestyle of her youth, "... la cité rousse là-bas d'où ma mère ne sortit jamais? ... Je désire m'enfoncer, à mon tour. A ma manière, me revoiler... Reculer dans l'ombre; m'ensevelir" [... that distant red red-brown city that my mother never left? ... I too want to put down roots. To wear the veil again, in my own fashion ... To retreat into the shadows; bury myself] (pp. 165-66; 156). The decision and the reasons proffered for making it do not seem to be in keeping with the "intentionality" of an emancipated woman: "N'aimer nulle part, sinon en mon lieu d'origine, mon royaume. Je ne sais quel homme je choisirai de nouveau, je veux prévoir au moins les lieux où je pourrai aimer" [I must never fall in love again, except in the place of my birth, in my own kingdom. I don't know what man will be my next choice, but at least I want to anticipate the setting in which I may find love] (pp. 165; 155). Moreover it appears that this retreat into traditionalism is not a necessary compromise but a deliberate choice: "Je *désire* m'enfoncer, à mon tour" [I too *want* to put down roots] (pp. 166; 156) [My emphasis].

Hajila, on the other hand, more predictably, moves out into the outside world: "Or toi ... tu as vécu enfermée depuis l'enfance. A partir de ce lieu, tu cherches ta percée; tu quêtes ton échappée. Ville-vaisseau de ta première mobilité; de là, ta marche va commencer" [But you have lived cooped up all your life ... This is the place from which you are trying to escape; you are looking for a way out of this prison. This city is the ship on which you first cast yourself adrift; from here,

---

[109] Ibid., p. 117.

In Dialogue with Irigaray: *Ombre sultane* 213

your journey will begin] (pp. 166; 155-56). But Hajila's journey, as we will discover, will not be a slow walk to freedom but yet another journey into darkness.

As the two women walk in different directions, it is as if Isma herself catches a glimpse of the gap between them, the gap which now prevents her from seeing "right through" Hajila: "Ainsi je ne te crée plus, je ne t'imagine plus. Simplement je t'attends" [So I no longer call you into existence, I no longer have to imagine you. I merely wait for you] (pp. 166; 156). Isma, who once pre-empted Hajila's intentionality and who captured her every movement, can no longer read Hajila's thoughts, no longer knows her completely, no longer knows exactly when she is coming or going: "Tout au plus, je ne pensais pas que tu sortirais si tôt" [At the most, I had not thought you would go out so early] (pp. 167; 156-57). In order to know her movements she has to follow her, no longer in her mind, but in person: "Je t'ai suivie le dernier jour" [On the last day, I followed you] (pp. 167; 156).

The "last day" (the last time Isma follows Hajila) is to be transposed into an apocalyptic vision of near-death. The darkness of the last hour is prefigured at the end of chapter II of Part 3, as the point when Hajila and Isma leave the warm safety of the *hammam*: "nous nous mettons à craindre le dehors" [we dread the thought of the outside world] (pp.164; 154). In the final pages, the outside world, which had come to mean a place of escape and growth for Hajila, is now transformed into a threatening space, overwhelmed by men:

> Tour à tour, sur la scène du monde qui nous est refusée, dans l'espace qui nous est interdit, dans les flots de la lumière qui nous est retirée, tour à tour, toi et moi, fantômes et reflets pour chacune, nous devenons la sultane et sa suivante, la suivante et sa sultane! Les hommes n'existent plus, ou plutôt si, ils piétinent, ils encombrent. Ils espionnent, les yeux définitivement crevés! (pp. 168; 157-58)
>
> Turn and turn about on the world stage that is denied us, in the space we are forbidden to infringe, in the flooding light that is withdrawn from us, you and I, turn and turn about, ghost and mirror image of each other, we play both parts, sultan's bride and her attendant, attendant and her mistress! Men no longer exit or rather, they do exist, they stamp their feet, they are everywhere, obstructing our path. They spy on us endlessly with unseeing eyes!

The "last day" witnesses Hajila's brush with death as the drama of the car accident unfolds, leading to the death of Hajila's unborn child. As Isma rushes to the scene, there appears to be a sudden flashback to the kind of undifferentiated identification the narrative has been working against, undifferentiated not in the sense that Isma can see *through* Hajila again, but undifferentiated in the sense that she now sees herself *as* Hajila:

> Moi, j'ai regardé ton visage pâle. *J'ai vu le mien*, que je n'avais jamais pu voir, à ce même instant où l'aile de la mort vous caresse ... Mon visage que je n'ai pas trouvé" (pp. 168-69; 158-59)
>
> I gazed at your pale face. *I saw my own face*, as I had been, as I had never seen myself, at that same instant when death caresses you with his wing ... My own face that I never discovered. [My emphasis]

As the dark clouds of patriarchy invade the text, it is as if Hajila and Isma lose their individuality and become not separate beings, but joint victims, "fantômes et reflets pour chacune" [ghost and mirror image of each other] (pp. 168; 158), depersonalised and objectified by the world of men. Having struggled to present us with "deux femmes-sujets", the narrative abruptly retreats, leaving us with "deux femmes-objets", both at the mercy of the world of men.

Our hopes for both women are suddenly dashed. Isma, the emancipated woman, literally walks back into the darkness whereas Hajila, the newly freed woman, walks forward into the nightmare of prostitution, a transition which Djebar prefigures in the preface: "Là-bas, dans la capitale, tu dérivais, errante, mendiante, peut-être femme offerte aux passants ou aux voyageurs d'un jour. Nous voici toutes deux en rupture de harem, mais à ses pôles extrêmes: toi au soleil désormais exposée, moi tentée de m'enfoncer dans la nuit resurgie" [And back there, in the capital, you were adrift, wandering about like a beggar-woman, or maybe one who is offered for the day to passers-by or to be exposed henceforth to the sunlight, while I am tempted to plunge back into the night] (pp. 10; 2). We are left with two uncomfortable images, the slave-woman liberated only to turn to prostitution, the emancipated woman turning back to tradition. Just as Isma and Hajila appear to have tasted liberty, Djebar then sweeps that liberty from under their feet and transports them into unknown territory: "Sitôt libérées du passé, où sommes-nous?" [As soon as we women are freed from the past, where do we stand?] (pp. 171; 160).

Horizons of disillusionment

In the final chapter, "Luth", the themes of uncertainty and darkness form a leitmotif which comes to encompass not only the story of Hajila and Isma but which also doubles back to take hold of the story of *Les Mille et Une Nuits* and then spirals into the future and out of the narrative context of the story to extend over recent Algerian history.

First to be caught up in the whirlwinds of uncertainty is the story *Les Mille et Une Nuits*. The possibility of escape from death and the patriarchal economy, first foregrounded in this story, rapidly recedes as the hope of liberation is placed within the wider context of the story which uncovers the fragility of the two sisters' fates: "la reine des aubes, sur son estrade, n'espère survivre que jour après jour" [the queen of every dawn, on her dais, can only hope to survive for one day at a time] (pp. 171; 160). As their freedom recedes, so does the bright horizon of sisterhood. Their loss of liberty is then made to echo two deeper losses: the separation from the maternal (that of "l'enfance disparue" [our lost childhood]), and the separation from the bodily (that of "les mutilées de l'adolescence" [we who were mutilated in our adolescence], pp. 171; 160). As the losses reverberate and spiral into the emptiness, Isma's dream of saving her sister is revealed as illusory, its transitoriness cruelly resounding in Isma's doubts: "O ma soeur, j'ai peur, moi qui ai cru te réveiller" [O, my sister, I who thought to wake you] (pp. 171; 160).

Liberated only to be bound by tradition or blighted by prostitution, Isma and Hajila, the two faces of Algerian woman, modern and traditional, have both been awakened only to be hemmed in by the blackest of nights, their fates mirroring the fate of all the other "femmes d'Algérie":

> J'ai peur que toutes deux, que toutes trois, que toutes ... nous nous retrouvions entravées là, dans "cet occident de l'Orient", ce lieu de la terre où si lentement l'aurore a brillé pour nous que déjà, de toutes parts, le crépuscule vient nous cerner. (pp. 171-72; 160)
>
> I fear lest we all find ourselves in chains again, in 'this West in the Orient', this corner of the earth where day dawned so slowly for us that twilight is already closing in around us everywhere.

Conclusion

Ombre sultane is a narrative that works towards Irigaray's ideal of female subjectivity and sociality, only to abandon that ideal, in the face of the nightmare of political and social realities of Djebar's native Algeria. So whereas in the beginning we are slowly led towards the bright horizon of sisterhood and the possibility of female subjectivity, this hope of liberation is revealed to be transitory at the end of the novel, which offers little resistance to the forces of darkness and little hope for female subjectivity. So for Djebar, what starts off being an accessible idea – the liberation of woman thanks to the bonds of sisterhood – is revealed to be an *impossible dream*.

If I can compare the general direction of the novel with the general direction of Irigaray's thinking, it seems to me that the transition that operates in Djebar's novel is reversed in Irigaray's work. In her earlier works, Irigaray *starts off* by presenting female subjectivity and sociality as a utopian if not *impossible dream*, as a "blueprint for the future" that will take place "come the symbolic revolution." In her later writing, however, female subjectivity and sexual difference come to represent a more accessible idea, a reality that can be cultivated within the limitations of our *present* symbolic.

So both Djebar and Irigaray depart from the same starting-point – an interest in reclaiming *female subjectivity*. For Djebar, what starts off as a potential reality – female subjectivity – turns into an impossible ideal. For Irigaray, what starts off as an impossible ideal – female subjectivity – turns into a potential reality. So it is not only Hajila and Isma who go their separate ways, but also Djebar and Irigaray. For, as we watch Djebar, surrounded by her ghost women, chained and bound, "entravées là, dans 'cet Occident de l'Orient'", disappearing, with them, into the night, we can hear Irigaray's voice proclaiming "la réalité et la fécondité de la différence sexuelle"[110], as she advances towards a distant but bright horizon of hope.

---

[110] Ibid., p. 22.

# In Dialogue with Feminisms: *Loin de Médine*

The Forgotten Revolution

Loin de Médine is Assia Djebar's powerful reconstruction of pre-Islamic and Islamic Arabia, set around the time of the Prophet's death. In this novel, Djebar goes back to the roots of Islam and attempts to reclaim the religion for women, going so far as to say that the Islamic age heralded "une révolution féministe." By this statement alone, the novel enters into immediate dialogue with the work of other Arab feminist historical scholars, in an exchange that throws up the following questions: Can Islam be reclaimed for women? And can Djebar invent a "politically correct" Islam, palatable to both East and West? In examining Djebar's reworking of Islam, I will refer mainly to the historical research of the Arab feminist historian Leila Ahmed, but also to the work of Fatima Mernissi, as well as the revisionist approaches of Christian feminist theologians. Finally, a look at the principles of mainstream feminist historical scholarship will help to put Djebar's own approach in a broader perspective.

The Blank Page

A good framework for understanding *Loin de Médine* is Isak Dinesen's short story, "The Blank Page", which illustrates some of the principles and contradictions inherent in the text. The story, which has been passed down by generations of women, tells of a convent whose nuns, renowned for producing the finest flax in Portugal, act as the privileged suppliers of linen bridal sheets to the princesses of the royal household: "sheets which, blood-spotted, are hung on the balcony of the palace the morning after the wedding, as the Chamberlain of High Steward proclaims, 'Virginem eam tenemus' ('We declare her to have been a virgin')."[1] The nuns' privilege extends to maintaining a gallery, displaying a series of gilt frames, "each of them adorned with a coroneted plate of pure gold, on which is engraved the name of a princess." Each of the frames displays a square cut from a royal

---

[1] Gayle Greene and Coppélia Kahn, "Feminist scholarship and the social construction of woman", in Gayle Greene and Coppélia Kahn (eds), *Making a Difference: Feminist Literary Criticism* (London and New York: Routledge, 1985), p. 5.

wedding sheet bearing "the faded markings" of the wedding night; each frame that is except for one "... on this one plate no name is inscribed, and the linen within the frame is snow-white from corner to corner, a blank page."[2]

Gayle Greene and Coppélia Kahn point to the analogies Dinesen draws between bloodstained sheet and printed page, between female body and male authority, which "make[s] the story a critique of culture."[3] Furthermore, they creatively interpret "the contrast between the story told by the spotted bridal sheets and that which speaks in the silence of 'the blank page'" as a metaphor for the two major prongs of feminist scholarship: "deconstructing dominant male patterns of thought and social practice; and reconstructing female experience previously hidden or overlooked."[4]

In *Loin de Médine*, Djebar consciously reconstructs female experience in an era that has become the property of male historians writing male history from a male perspective. Her stated sources are respected historians from the eighth and ninth centuries AD (Ibn Hicham, Ibn Saad, Tabari) who, as Djebar puts it, are "transmetteurs certes scrupuleux, mais naturellement portés, par habitude déjà, à occulter toute présence féminine" [chroniclers, admittedly conscientious in recording the facts, but of course already habitually inclined to let any female presence be overshadowed].[5] Djebar takes on the task of filling in the blank pages, of sounding out the "silences" in these historians' accounts, which, according to William Montgomery Watt, are prone to "tendential shaping."[6]

Watt suggests that "tendential shaping", or the distortion of accounts of historical events, is a major problem in ninth century Islamic sources. He proposes that accounts of external acts are not the most likely subject of distortion, but rather the qualities and motivations attributed to the major actors in them. As far as Djebar is concerned, "tendential shaping" is at its most noticeable when it comes to the contributions of women, as the story of "la reine yéménite" [the Yemenite Queen] illustrates. The Yemenite queen, like

---

[2] Isak Dinesen, *Last Tales* (New York: Vintage, 1975), pp. 103, 104.
[3] Gayle Greene and Coppélia Kahn, "Feminist Scholarship and the Social Construction of Woman", p. 6.
[4] Ibid., p. 6.
[5] Assia Djebar, *Loin de Médine* (Paris: Albin Michel: 1991), Avant-propos, no page number, trans. Dorothy S. Blair, *Far from Madina* (London/New York: Quartet: 1994), p. xv. Unless stated otherwise, all subsequent quotations in English of *Loin de Médine* are drawn from Blair's translation.
[6] William Montgomery Watt, *Mohammed at Mecca* (Oxford: Oxford University Press, 1953), pp. xiii, xiv.

the anonymous princess of Dinesen's story, has been denied a name in the annals of history (pp. 17; 9), and this omission is compounded by the obscuring of her pivotal role as a historical agent. Djebar resuscitates her queen and gives her form: "La reine yéménite possède sans doute un corps frêle, des bras fragiles, des mains non de guerrière, mais de poupée. Peut-être ... Même si nous rêvons à d'autres formes physiques, pour la modeler là, devant nous, elle ne va pas elle-même résolument jusqu'au sang pour les autres" [The Yemenite queen probably has a frail body, weak arms, the hands not of a warrior-woman but of a doll. Perhaps ... But even if we imagine other physical models of her, to let her take shape before our eyes, she still does not have the firmness of purpose to go to the length of shedding blood for others] (pp. 26; 16).

As the story goes, Aswad, a "false prophet" of the Ans tribe, kills the queen's husband, seizes the queen and then proceeds to marry her. The account is framed by the prophetic words of Mohammed who foresees Aswad's imminent death. In Djebar's reconstruction of the story, the queen, "l'âme de la machination" [at the heart of the conspiracy] (pp. 20; 12), initiates and perpetrates the killing of her new husband, dreaming up the murder scenario, drawing the unsuspecting king to her bed, and allowing Fires, the ex-king's cousin, to accomplish the final deed. Tabari's account, however, points to two alternative reasons for the plot's success, each of which denies the queen's role as major actor. According to him, it is not the queen's "furia froide" [cold fury] (pp. 20; 12) that drives the murderous outcome, but Aswad's drunken stupor on the night, combined with the malediction of the Prophet: "La chronique préfère insister sur l'ivresse de l'homme, sur son péché d'avoir été maudit par le Prophète en personne. Comme si les voies qu'emprunte la comploteuse si assurée n'étaient que provisoires" [The chronicle prefers to insist on the man's intoxication, on his sin in having been cursed by the Prophet in person. As if the course taken by the conspirator – so sure of herself – was merely contingent] (pp. 21; 12).

Djebar wishes to restore "la reine yéménite" [The Yemenite queen] and her sisters to their proper place in the history, and to free them from the grip of "tendential shaping" to which Islamic history has succumbed in the hands of the male historian. This "tendential shaping" is evidenced on two counts: it is inscribed by an entrenched *Islamic* ideology that is set to reshape the pre-Islamic age or *Jahilia* in an Islamic mould, holding it up as an age of ignorance (*Jahilia* means "Ignorance") before the Golden Age of Islam, and it is inscribed by an entrenched *patriarchal* ideology only too ready to draw a veil over "la femme."

Djebar takes a stand against a monochrome vision of the past, with the monolithic force of Islam as its starting-point. Her reconstructed pages may be overshadowed by the black and white emblem of Islam, but they are framed by a multi-coloured, polyvalent surround, reflecting the diversity of race and religion that characterised the transitional period they cover, setting in motion the discovery of "une origine multiple, plurielle, et occultée par la réécriture phallique."[7]

Her eyes are drawn to the powerful women of the *Jahilia* whose autonomy she upholds, not as a threat to the incoming era of Islam, but as a celebration of the untamed spirit of womanhood. She resurrects the forgotten, neglected heroines of the past, women who have tasted freedom and who fear no man, mighty warriors and prophetesses, women like Selma who have known "la liberté bédouine" [Bedouin freedom] (pp. 33; 24) or Sajdah, the prophetess who represents "la menace d'une liberté incontrôlée" [... the threat of unrestrained freedom] (pp. 43; 33), or the fearless "chanteuse des satires" [the singer of satires] who comes to embody "une part de l'âme de résistance des siens" [the soul of her people's resistance][8] (pp. 131; 103). As in Dinesen's story, in *Loin de Médine* there is also a gallery of fame, and it is Djebar's project to reinstate her neglected heroines, both Muslim and non-Muslim, into successive frames, projecting technicolour images and quadraphonic sound onto each "blank page."

In her article "Ghostwriting", Gayatri Spivak visualises the reinstated heroines as ghosts and the novel itself in the genre of "ghostwriting." For Spivak, Djebar, by bringing to life the ghost-women of early Islam, joins the ranks of other "ghostwriters" such as Jacques Derrida, (who evokes the ghost of Karl Marx in *Spectres of Marx*).[9] Spivak also recalls another form of ghost art, ghost dancing, a religious ritual practised by the Sioux tribe, who claim to be haunted by their ancestors as they dance (the ancestors are therefore more than mere objects of ritual worship).[10] For Spivak, such rituals have limited

---

[7] Clarisse Zimra, "Comment peut-on être musulmane?", *Notre Librairie*, 118, Nouvelles Écritures Féminines 2: Femmes d'ici et d'ailleurs (July- September 1994), pp. 57-63, p. 61.
[8] Translation adapted.
[9] Gayatri Chakravorty Spivak, "Ghostwriting", *Diacritics*, 25: 2 (1995), pp. 64-84, p. 70. Jacques Derrida, *Spectres of Marx: The State of the Debt, the Work of Mourning and the New International*, trans. Peggy Kamuf (New York: Routledge, 1994).
[10] Ibid., p. 70.

uses because of their relationship to time: "Thus the 'end' of the ghost dance – if once can speak of such a thing – is to make the past a future, as it were – the future anterior, not a future present."[11] By reading *Loin de Médine* as a "ghost dance" situated in the future anterior, Spivak thus places the novel on a suspended time-axis, which eludes a linear conception of temporality.[12] Since the future anterior is the past of the future, Djebar's novel imposes a future that could have happened, creating a bridge between past and a possible future that bypasses the present. It is in this sense that Spivak can state that *Loin de Médine* does not function as "a blueprint" for the present or the future present.[13] Although for Spivak the novel therefore does not in any sense function as a model for modern day Islam, this does not, in her view, detract from the importance of rereading woman in the context of contemporary international Islam, a project which she compares to Derrida's rereading of Marx in post-Soviet Europe."[14]

Narrating Women

Djebar's desire to reconstruct women's experience can be discerned from the form of the novel, which she divides into three parts, containing three types of chapters (standard "narrative" chapters, chapters entitled "Rawiya", containing oral narratives of female storytellers, and chapters entitled "Voix" [Voice], expressing feminine voices). While the "Rawiya" sections function like new pages inserted into the annals of history, the "Voix" [Voice] sections enable women to speak out from between the lines of the blank pages of the male historians' writing, which in turn form the basis of an ironic commentary in the main "narrative" sections. And, just as Isak Dinesen's snow-white squares fire the imagination (Who was she? What happened?), so the blanks in "the réécriture phallique" fire that of Djebar (What was she really like? How would she have expressed herself?): "Dès lors la fiction, comblant les béances de la mémoire collective, s'est révélée nécessaire pour la mise en espace que j'ai tentée là, pour rétablir la durée de ces jours que j'ai désiré habiter..." [Consequently I found fiction – filling in the gaps in the collective memory – essential for me to be able to recreate those times in which I

---

[11] Ibid., p. 70.
[12] Ibid., p. 78.
[13] Ibid., p. 79.
[14] Ibid., p. 79.

wished to dwell, and to try to put those distant days into their context] (Avant-propos; Foreword).

In the first part of the work, the "Rawiyates" and "Voix" [Voice] sections have the effect of interrupting the main narrative sections. "Rawiya", singular of "rawiyates" is, as Djebar explains, the feminine form of "rawiy", a term denoting a storyteller within a specific Islamic context; namely one who invokes an incident in the life of the Prophet or of one of his Companions (Avant-propos; Foreword). The "Rawiyates" create a female chain of oral transmission that consciously mimics the "Isnad" or chain of transmission that must be established to authenticate a *hadith*. [15] As the words of both well-known and anonymous women in the "Rawiyates" and "Voix" proliferate, they open up "un univers d'oralité."[16] According to Greene and Kahn, again referring to Dinesen's tale, the traditional function of an oral culture is to subvert the dominant ideology:

> The complex, ambivalent relation of women to the patriarchy is suggested by Dinesen's tale, which concerns two types of 'communities of women' – both those that serve the dominant culture and those that subvert it. Each of these communities is the custodian of a tradition: the nuns, of the ancient craft of weaving; the storytellers, of the equally ancient art of narrative which has been handed down from one generation of women to the next. But though the nuns with their traditional 'frames'... serve the interests of patriarchy, the storytellers, keepers of another kind of record, comprise a counter-culture existing outside and as a challenge to it.[17]

Like Dinesen's storytellers, Djebar's "rawiyates" are keepers of another record, with their focus on women's experiences, and their manipulation of the spoken word challenging the historians' assumption that this era was the property of their infallible male writings. Nevertheless, their stories simultaneously serve the interests of what was fast becoming the dominant culture – Islam, as the central figure in all the "Rawiyates" is its leader – the Prophet Muhammad.

The third "rawiya" or storyteller is Oum Harem, who relates her own and her sister's encounters with the Prophet. Oum Harem strongly believes in women's responsibility to be "keepers of the

---

[15] Patricia Geesey, "Women's Worlds: Assia Djebar's *Loin de Médine*", in Kenneth W. Harrow (ed.), *The Marabout and the Muse: New Approaches to Islam in African Literature* (Portsmouth, NH: Heinemann, 1996), pp. 40-50, p. 40. The *Hadith* are sayings attributed to Muhammad and brief narratives about his life and those of his Companions, transmitted orally and then written down after the death of the Prophet.
[16] Clarisse Zimra, "Comment peut-on être musulmane?", p. 61.
[17] Gayle Greene and Coppélia Kahn, "Feminist Scholarship and the Social Construction of Woman", p. 21.

stories of the Prophet" and insistently confronts her sister's reluctance to take on that role. Oum Salem's reticence is attributed to her identity as mother, a role that this more timid sister believes to be incompatible with that of a "rawiya", because of its assumption of authority. She believes that only a man should be attributed the role of being the "official" transmitter of the stories of the Prophet, even if they are strictly speaking *her own* stories, words of the Prophet spoken to her:

> – Pourquoi ce ton de secret? Pourquoi ne pas parler ainsi, avec moi, avec toutes les femmes de Médine, Migrantes et 'Ançariyates? Pourquoi?
> Invariablement Oum Salem, après avoir baissé les yeux, répond;
> – Anas, mon fils, transmettra plus sûrement que moi-même!
> "Y a-t-il donc incompatibilité, pensai-je, entre se sentir rawiya et demeurer mère, mère fervente d'un fils tel que Anas ibn el Malik, devenu, malgré son jeune âge, un *fqih* si respectable? ... Et elle, Oum Salem?" (pp. 203; 161)

> 'Why this secretive tone? Why not speak out with me, with all the women of Madina, Migrants and wives of Ansars? Why?'
> Invariably Umm Salem would lower her eyes and reply, 'Anas, my son, will transmit more surely than I'
> 'So is there incompatibility?' I thought, 'between feeling oneself a *rawiya* and remaining a mother, the passionate mother of a son like Anas ibn al-Malik, who, despite his youth, is so respected a *faqih*? ... And she, Umm Salem?'

The "Rawiya" is characterised by a circular structure and repetitive patterns of speech, in which Oum Harem repeats herself and her identity throughout:

> "Je suis la soeur de celle qui a offert les palmiers au Prophète." (p. 200)
> "... oui, je suis la soeur de Oum Salem" (p. 200)
> "Oui, je suis la soeur de Oum Salem, la mère d'Anas" (p. 201)

> I am the sister of the woman who offered palm trees to the Prophet. (p. 159)
> ... yes I am the sister of Umm Salem (p. 159)
> Yes, I am the sister of Umm Salem, the mother of Anas ibn al-Malek (p, 159)

Whereas the form of the "rawiya's" self-presentation foregrounds the sororal relation, challenging the patriarchal order that sees women primarily as they relate to their male relations, the story itself points away from the two sisters towards the life of the Prophet, as Oum Harem tells of "les prévenances du Prophète à son [her sister's] égard" [all the consideration the Prophet showed her] (pp. 203; 161), recalling words of wisdom spoken by Muhammad to Oum Salem in the intimacy of her own home, words of prayer before a meal, multiplying the bread before their eyes, and words of blessing for her bereaved sister, being fulfilled by the birth of a son to replace the one she lost.

The "Voix" sections mainly express the voices of women, speaking in the first or third person and bringing the living word and the lived experience onto the page. These are voices which, by speaking for themselves, have escaped the objectifying hold of the historian's pen and his written word. These voices tell the story of history as it happened, or as it could have happened, recapturing its presence, not through the uniform, single, tuneless voice of Islamic historians writing history, but through the multiple, polyphonic voices of women speaking history.

The "Voix" sections rise out of the main narrative text, reinforcing or pre-empting the narrative sections they adjoin. Thematically, they are united by their demonstration of the power of the word, whether to heal or to destroy; stylistically, they are often compressed and intense, as if to reinforce that potency.

The voice of Esma bent Omaïs[18] can be heard in between two chapters dedicated to her: "La laveuse des morts" [She Who Lays Out the Dead], and "Celle aux mains tatouées." [She of the Tattooed Hands]. The first traces her symbolic role as the "laveuse" of the bodies of Fatima and Abou Bekr; the second goes back to her youth and charts her friendship with Fatima. Between these two narrative sections, the real Esma comes to life, her voice rising up in a heated debate with Omar ibn El Khattab, who has taken it upon himself to question her religious credentials. Omar denigrates Esma's role as Islamic "ambassador" to Abyssinia as trivial compared to that of the Muslims who stayed behind and suffered with the Prophet (Esma's first husband Djaffar, a cousin of the Prophet's, went to Abyssinia as one of the first ambassadors of Islam). Esma, the speaking subject, is indignant, quick to challenge the male rebuke, and impatient to take her case to a higher "authority":

> Je fais le serment le plus solennel que je ne goûterai à aucun mets, ni à aucune boisson, tant que je n'aurai pas raconté à l'Envoyé de Dieu ces paroles que je viens d'entendre, nous qui souffrions et qui étions en danger! Je veux dire tout cela au Prophète et lui demanderai, sur cela, son avis! (pp. 246; 194)

> I hereby swear the most solemn oath that I shall touch neither food nor drink until I have related to the Apostle of God the words I have just heard, we who suffered and were in danger! I wish I could tell all this to the Prophet and ask his opinion on this matter!

---

[18] In Dorothy S. Blair's translation, "Esma" is spelt "Asma."

The Prophet not only takes up Esma's cause, but bestows upon her sojourn in Abyssinia the status of a pilgrimage, honouring her and her like with the title of "deux fois Migrants" [twice over Migrants] (pp. 246, 195).

Djebar's use of "voices" can be evaluated in relation to her use of the historians' texts. The use of historical text as a reference-point, which is frequent in Section 1 (8 instances), becomes less frequent in Sections 2 and 3 (5 altogether) and then disappears in the final section. This diminishing number of references goes hand in hand with a corresponding increase in the number of "Voix" sections cutting through the narrative (2 in sections 1 and 2, 3 in sections 3, and 4 in section 4), as if the women of *Médine* are first liberated from the constricting grasp of the historian's pen, by being given form/shape, but then undergo a more dramatic liberation, by being given an autonomous voice which no longer needs to rely on the original written word for its existence. Like Cixous, Djebar allows her writing to be increasingly dominated by the immediacy and transparency of the voice: "La féminité dans l'écriture je la sens passer d'abord par: un privilège de la *voix*..."[19]

The act of reconstruction in the "narrative" sections, especially in Part 1, takes as its starting-point documented Islamic historical sources, lending a convincing historical weight to these accounts, which again mainly focus on the experiences of women. Transformed by Djebar's "imagination de cinéaste", the quick sketches provided by these historians are fleshed out, as Djebar creates for each unsung heroine a set, costumes and a script. Probing deeper still, Djebar proceeds to reach into the recesses of the minds of women such as Fatima, resurrecting them not only in body, but also in spirit.

The section dedicated to "la fille aimée" opens with Fatima's death at the age of twenty-eight. A historical sketch, short on detail, deliberately and ironically cites the impoverished accounts of the historians:

- On the day of her death: "Rien d'autre sur ce jour au soleil brûlant de Médine..." [We are told nothing more about this day in the burning Madina sun] (pp. 59; 46)
- On her daughter's upbringing: "Nous aurons droit alors à la brève précision: Oum Keltoum a été élevée d'une façon austère, à l'image de son père et de sa mère." [And then we are given one brief

---

[19] Hélène Cixous (in collaboration with Catherine Clément), *La Jeune née* (Paris: UGE, 10/18, 1975), p. 170.

detail about her: Umm Kulthum was brought up strictly, like her father and mother] (pp. 59; 46)
• On her marriage: "Rien de plus à ajouter, sinon que Fatima, au cours de sa vie conjugale, fut l'unique épouse de son cousin Ali." [There was nothing more to add, except that Fatima, during her marriage, was her cousin Ali's only wife] (pp. 59-60; 46)

Countering the dryness of these evocations of Fatima's life, Djebar attempts to capture her essence with a lyrical evocation of her sense of loss and emptiness after the death of her father. The emotional void gives way to the historical void, filled on a symbolic level by Djebar's accolade:

> Comme si la présence de la fille aimée, une fois son père mort, s'avérait un blanc, un creux, quasiment une faille... Qui durera six mois à peine. Fatima mise au tombeau, les descendants premiers du Prophète sont deux garçonnets, les quasi-jumeaux que Mohammed a si souvent tenus sur ses genoux!
> Mais pas une femme, si pure, si austère, si épouse unique fût-elle! (pp. 60; 47)

> As if the presence of the beloved daughter, once her father was dead, is evidence of a blank, an emptiness, little short of a flaw ... Which will last scarcely six months. With Fatima in her grave, the first descendants of the Prophet are two small boys, the 'virtual twins' whom Muhammad so often held on his knees!
> But there is no woman, however pure, however austere, however much a sole wife she may have been!

Whereas Virginia Woolf gives us "Shakespeare's sister"[20], Djebar here presents us with "Fatima's brother", or the son the Prophet never had: "Si Fatima avait été un fils" [If Fatima had been a son] (pp. 61; 47). Djebar proceeds to recall the scene of the Prophet's deathbed, a death that gave birth to the issue of succession, confused by Mohammed's lack of male heirs, and complicated further by his request for an unspecified scribe. Three were convoked (two fathers-in-law, later to be appointed Caliphs, and his cousin Ali, husband of Fatima): "Voyant trois personnes au lieu d'une seulement désirée, Muhammed détourne la tête et garde le silence. Quelque temps après, il meurt: sur-le-champ, l'incertitude sur la succession et sur son mode, sur la personne même du successeur, est présente" [Seeing three people instead of only one, as he wished, Muhammad turned his head away and kept silent. A short time afterwards, he died: there was immediate uncertainty over the succession and its mode, even over the identity of the successor] (pp. 61; 48).

---

[20] Virginia Woolf, *A Room of One's Own* (London: Penguin, 1945), p. 112.

The divided, multiple corpus of Islam seems to emanate from the divided, multiple loyalties of the Prophet: "Comme si le corps de l'Islam devait se diviser, enfanter par lui-même luttes civiles et querelles, tout cela en tribut payé à la polygamie du Fondateur" [It was as if the body of Islam had to break apart, itself to give birth to civil strife and quarrels, all this as a tribute payable for the Founder's polygamy] (pp. 61; 48). Djebar speculates that the whole history of Islam, beset by bitter and bloody civil wars because of the absence of an authoritative word from the Prophet on his succession, might have been different had a "male Fatima" existed, the son to whom the secret of succession would inevitably have been revealed.

The daughter of the Prophet in her public role is "au premier plan du théâtre islamique" [at the forefront of the Islamic stage] (pp. 62, 49), as mother of the three martyrs, yet Djebar wants to capture Fatima backstage, by herself, to discover Fatima the woman, rather than Fatima the daughter:

> Rêver à Fatima personnellement, en dehors de son père, de son époux, de ses fils, et se dire que peut-être – (qui l'a perçu, l'a écrit ou l'a transmis, osant par là même un péché de lèse-majesté...), – oui, peut-être que Fatima, dès sa nubilité ou en cours d'adolescence, s'est voulue garçon. Inconsciemment. A la fois Fille (pour la tendresse) et Fils (pour la continuité) de son père. (pp. 63; 49)

> Musing over Fatima personally, apart from her father, her husband, her sons, and thinking that perhaps (who has ever sensed this, written or transmitted it, daring thus to commit the sin of *lese-majesté*...) – yes, that perhaps ever since puberty, or during her adolescence, Fatima wished she were a boy. Subconsciously. To be both her father's Daughter (for the affection) and his Son (for the continuity).

The emotion of tenderness, which is symbolically extended to all the Prophet's relations to women in the novel, above all epitomises the portrayal of his relationship to Fatima. Djebar will take hold of this emotion, which in this novel will come to figure as the founding stone upon which Djebar will construct her presentation of the Prophet as the idealised father-figure. The terrible consequences of the succession vacuum are irrevocably and tragically linked to Fatima, both because she was not and could not be "le fils aimé" (the beloved son), and because her sons would be at the heart of its tragic development. But just as Fatima's desire to be male is not consciously voiced, Djebar too does not consciously challenge the male system of succession that underlies that desire. Nevertheless, later in the novel, she comes closer to that position, not by directly suggesting that Fatima should have been allowed to take on her father's political mantle, but by representing her as her father's *spiritual* heir.

Woman as Subject

If *Loin de Médine* thus appears to succeed in the feminist project of reconstructing female experience, to what extent does it meet the second objective of feminist scholarship, that of deconstructing male patterns of thinking and social practice? Does the novel take a stand against the patriarchal understanding of woman, which denies her subjectivity and her role in society? How far do Djebar's women escape the compulsive masculine force, which denies their constitution as a subject, providing "l'hypothèque garante de toute constitution irréductible d'objet: de représentation, de discours, de désir."[21]

Loin de Médine was written in the aftermath of the Algerian riots of 1988, which acted as catalyst for this act of repossession: "Les barbus m'ont conspuée. Une femme n'avait pas le droit d'écrire sur le Prophète... C'est une oeuvre de circonstance. J'ai eu besoin, devant ce sang qui coulait, de me porter témoin, de dire: 'cette religion n'appartient pas qu'à vous.'" [The bearded ones shouted me down. A woman did not have the right to write about the Prophet... It is a work of its time. With blood being shed around me, I needed to bear witness, to say: 'this religion does not belong exclusively to you'].[22] Yet can Islam be taken out of the hands of men and reclaimed for women? Can Djebar celebrate the subjectivity of women not only of the pre-Islamic age, but also of early Islam, an era which is traditionally seen as encroaching on their freedoms? Or are the women of early Islam in fact, as Djebar suggests, a liberated sex, who can be truly seen as the *subjects* of *Loin de Médine*?

According to Lerner, it is difficult to define the status of women within a given society, because no single criterion can be singled out (i.e. women's role in economics, or religion, or the family, or reproduction, or sexual life, etc.) as the determining factor of her position. Furthermore, losses in one area of life can mean, or can be accompanied by, gains in another.[23]

The world of *Médine* is one in which women have considerable status and power, defying the traditional separation of Islamic society into the "public" and "private" spheres. This is not a world where women are relegated to a domestic prison or where her childbearing

---

[21] Luce Irigaray, *Spéculum de l'autre femme* (Paris: Minuit, 1974), p. 165.
[22] Clarisse Zimra refers to this quotation of Djebar's made in January 1992 in "Comment peut-on être musulmane?", p. 57. My translation.
[23] Gerda Lerner, *The Majority Finds its Past: Placing Women in History* (Oxford: Oxford University Press, 1979*)*, pp. 81-82.

role "naturally" restricts her to the home. On the contrary, *Loin de Médine* takes a stand against a patriarchal understanding of woman that views her "not in terms of relationship – with other women and with men – but of difference and apartness ... as beings who *are* and have at all times been not actors but mere subjects of male action and female biology."[24] In evaluating Djebar's assessment of women's social status in this early Islamic age, to use Lerner's terms, the "criteria" I have selected here are women's role in warfare, religious life and sexuality.

Loin de Médine creates the impression of women in movement, fearlessly conquering "l'espace", and confidently taking possession of the outside world. The references in the novel to "femmes en mouvement" resonate with 1970s French feminist undertones, recalling the title of the magazine *Femmes en mouvement*, published by *des femmes*. For Clarisse Zimra, it is women's repossession of the outside world or "la question de l'espace", the founding theme in which the novel is firmly grounded, which forms the basis of the novel's continuity with all of Djebar's preceding works.[25]

The "space" which is most dramatically conquered in *Loin de Médine* is the battlefield. Participating in and even leading in battle, the women of *Loin de Médine* are included in the world of war, an arena that has traditionally been seen as the ultimate male prerogative, not only as the most exclusive of male activities, but as the activity that has "earned" man's superiority over women:

> Le guerrier pour augmenter le prestige de la horde, du clan auquel il appartient, met en jeu sa propre vie. Et par là il prouve avec éclat que ce n'est pas la vie qui est pour l'homme la valeur suprême mais qu'elle doit servir des fins plus importantes qu'elle-même. La pire malédiction qui pèse sur la femme c'est qu'elle est exclue de ces expéditions guerrières; ce n'est pas en donnant la vie, c'est en risquant la vie que l'homme s'élève au-dessus de l'animal; c'est pourquoi dans l'humanité la supériorité est accordée non au sexe qui engendre mais à celui qui tue.[26]

Both the pre-Islamic women and those converted in the early years of Islam (during the Prophet's life and until shortly after his death) were preserved from this "curse" of exclusion from the mainstay of manhood, and participated in war not just as nurse-maidens, but as

---

[24] Michelle Zimbalist Rosaldo, "The Use and Abuse of Anthropology: Reflections on Feminism and Cross-Cultural Understanding", *Signs* (Spring 1980), 5, 3, pp. 389-417, p. 409. Quoted in Gayle Greene and Coppélia Kahn, "Feminist Scholarship and the Social Construction of Woman", p. 16.
[25] Clarisse Zimra, "Comment peut-on être musulmane?", p. 58.
[26] Simone de Beauvoir, *Le Deuxième sexe 1* (Paris: Gallimard, 1949), p. 111.

battle-hungry warriors. Djebar recalls women such as Selma, daughter of Malik, chief of the Beni Ghatafan who, hearing of her brother's death by Islamic hands, takes up his mantle as "reine de clan", and sets out with her troops to avenge him: "La femme rebelle, abritée dans sa litière et installée au coeur même du danger, excite ses hommes de la voix" [The rebel, sheltered in her litter, in the very heart of the danger, urges on her men] (pp. 38; 28).

Other warrior-women emerge, such as Sajdah, from Mossoul, a woman of Christian origin, founder of a new religion, a heady cocktail of Islam and Christianity, who is impatient to impose her faith and her authority, to conquer "des terres en même temps que les consciences", with the aid of her four hundred soldiers. Khalid, leader of the Islamic armies, is confronted with a woman who has taken her destiny into her own hands, who bows to no earthly or spiritual authority but her own: "... la menace d'une liberté incontrôlée est concrétisée par une femme" [the threat of unrestrained freedom appears in the shape of a woman!] (pp. 43; 33).

Although Sajdah's story illustrates the acceptance of women as participants, and even leaders in battle in pre-Islamic Arabia, the position of the early converts to Islam is more complex. Djebar tells the story of Oum Hakim, who fights on the side of the Islamic armies in her youth and also in her later years. But in the intervening period, while she is married to Ikrima, she is forbidden by her husband to fight; while the object of Ikrima's authority, she can no longer act out her destiny.

Within her new faith, Oum Hakim is both free and forbidden to do battle, both fighting subject and object of male authority. Djebar makes the point that Islam did not prohibit women's right to fight and that Oum Hakim's temporary loss of freedom is the consequence of her husband's decree, not the consequence of Islamic law. However, I suggest that a direct link between this loss of autonomy and the impact of Islam can be established. For despite the fact that Oum Hakim was "technically" free to fight under the banner of Islam, her own temporary exclusion, and the general exclusion of women from war that was to follow, can be seen as the inevitable result of the new Islamic régime. For the hierarchical marriage system it instituted ensured that the decision-making process reverted to the male, and that it would only be a matter of time before the new patriarchs of Islam, following in the footsteps of Ikrima, would ban "their" women completely from war.

In a scene set in Médine shortly before the Prophet's death, Oum Hakim and her female companions remark that their participation in warfare has a profound effect on their husbands' conduct: "Nous, nous sortons avec nos hommes! intervint une Mecquoise que Oum Hakim ne reconnut pas. Nous les accompagnons, y compris au combat, et c'est pourquoi ils vont rarement vers les femmes de peu" ['We go out with our men!' intervened a Meccan woman whom Umm Hakim did not know. 'We accompany them, even into battle, and that is why they rarely go with women of little worth!'] (pp. 157; 123). Warfare, Djebar suggests, confers upon women a sense of subjectivity that, as Irigaray would have it, allows them to enter into subject-to-subject relations with the opposite sex. Moreover, she suggests that the desire for battle is not merely motivated by the desire to regain a lost sense of intimacy with her husband ("retrouver le passé et son rythme; savoir si une vie à deux restait possible, grâce au risque et à son ivresse" [to regain the past and its pace; to know if a shared life was still possible, thanks to the danger and its intoxication], pp. 157; 124), but by a desire is to "show them", the leaders of Médine (and by implication, the leaders of today), that women did, could and still should, move freely between the private and public worlds:

> Se battre. Se battre à cheval, ou à dos de chamelle, et pour l'Islam dorénavant. Leur montrer à eux, les chefs de Médine, les fameux Compagnons que, même du clan vaincu, ces femmes de La Mecque restaient des dames. A la fois des épouses, des maîtresses de maison, mais aussi des combattantes. (pp. 157; 124)

> To fight. To fight on horseback, or mounted on a camel, and for Islam now. To show the leaders from Madina, the famous Companions, that even in the clan of the defeated, these women of Mecca remained great ladies. Wives, mistresses of the home and also fighters.

Far from being relegated to the fringes of religious life, the women of *Loin de Médine* speak out loud and clear in the name of religion. The power of these women is exemplified in the prophetic authority of non-Muslim women of the time, but also, most strikingly, in the images of the two women closest to the Prophet, Fatima, his beloved daughter, and Aïcha, his favourite wife: "Parole donc de la contestation et, à l'autre extrême, parole de la transmission" [So, words of contention on the one hand and, at the other extreme, words transmitted] (pp. 337, 273). Djebar portrays both women as guardians of the true spirit of Islam, Fatima defending it, and Aïcha transmitting it to posterity.

Fatima is "Celle qui dit non à Médine" [The Woman Who Said No In Madina] (pp. 72; 57). The refusal that Fatima proclaims after her father's death is directed against his male successors, the new leaders of Islam, who want to deprive her of her inheritance, basing their argument on a "convenient" distortion of the following words of the

Prophet's: "Nous, les prophètes, aurait dit Mohammed un jour, on n'hérite pas de nous! Ce qui nous est donné nous est donné en don!" ['From us, the prophets,' Muhammad is said to have stated one day, 'no one shall inherit! What has been given to us, is given as a gift!'] (pp. 85; 67-8).

Actively resisting their attempt to disinherit her, proclaiming her "non" fearlessly, authoritatively and yet ultimately unsuccessfully, in a public space, and in front of Abou Bekr and the Companions, Fatima becomes one of the first victims of Islamic legalism, whose material loss is but a pale reflection of a far deeper wound, that of her spiritual disenfranchisement. Angered by their dismissal of her prophetic gift, Fatima becomes a symbol of "opposition féminine", opposed not to the faith of her beloved father, but to male distortion of the true spirit of Islam.

Aïcha too is a role model, a symbol of female religious authority, as her stories become part of the fabric of Islam. Djebar visualises her words as resisting the heavy formulaic prose of the Islamic writer, their lyricism liberating rather than imprisoning the true spirit of Islam: "Ce faisant, elle trouve les mots: les mots qui n'emmaillotent pas les jours d'hier, non, qui les dénudent. Les phrases qui ne durcissent pas en formules; qui restent poésie" [And as she does so, she finds the words: words that do not swaddle the past days, no, which strip them bare. Sentences that do not harden into formulas; which remain poetry] (pp. 339; 274).

Djebar foregrounds the importance of Aïcha's "parole" in her central role in transmitting the stories of the Prophet, linking that religious role with her symbolic role as mother of the children of Islam:

> Elle perçoit faiblement le sens de ces mots "mère des..." Soudain une aile d'archange semble frémir au-dessus d'elle. Elle a à nourrir les autres, elle a à entretenir le souvenir, le long ruban drapé des gestes, des mots, des soupirs et des sourires du Messager – que la grâce du Seigneur lui soit accordée! Vivre le souvenir pour "eux", les Croyants, tous les Croyants – oui, les vieux, les jeunes, les maigres, les pansus, les vertueux, les hésitants.
> Aïcha, "mère des Croyants" parce que première des rawiyates. (pp. 332; 267)
>
> She dimly detects the meaning of the words 'mother of the ...' Suddenly an archangel's wing seems to flutter above her. She must provide for others, she has to keep the memory alive, the long draped ribbon of the actions, words, sighs, smiles of the Messenger – may God's grace be granted him! Relive the memory for 'them', the Believers, all the Believers – yes the old, the young, the thin, the potbellied, the virtuous, the waverers.

Aisha, 'mother of the Believers' because the first of the rawiyat.

According to Leila Ahmed, it is significant that women, and Aïcha in particular, were important contributors to the oral texts of Islam, which were eventually transcribed into written form by men, contributing to the official history of Islam and the literature that established the normative practices of Islamic society – the *hadith*. For Ahmed, "the very fact of women's contribution to this important literature indicates that at least the first generation of Muslims, the generation closest to *Jahilia* days and *Jahilia* attitudes towards women – and their immediate descendants, had no difficulty accepting women as authorities."[27]

Djebar, using the examples of Fatima and Aïcha, also draws attention to the fact that the women of early Islam were accepted as religious authorities. For despite the fact that Fatima was ultimately disinherited by her father's successors, Djebar foregrounds her self-assurance in public and the power she wields over her audiences, demonstrating that she was a force to be reckoned with, and that she, like Aïcha, assumed a natural religious authority.

Other Arab women writers, such as Nawal El Saadawi, also pay special attention to Aïcha's assertiveness, putting the emphasis not so much on public authority but on personal contestation, citing her readiness to criticise the Prophet in conversation. She recounts an incident where one of the Prophet's close followers makes the following comment to Hafsa (another of Mohammed's wives): "You wish to criticise the Prophet like Aïsha does."[28] El Saadawi also reports an episode where Aïsha challenged the Prophet in relation to the inspiration of a Koranic verse: "When, in one of these verses, Allah permitted Mahomet to marry as many women as he wished, she [Aïsha] commented with heat: 'Allah always responds to *your* needs.'"[29]

---

[27] Leila Ahmed, *Women and Gender in Islam: Historical Roots of a Modern Debate* (New Haven and London: Yale University Press, 1992), p. 47.
[28] Muhammed Ibn Saad, *El Tabakat El Kobra*, Vol.8, (Cairo: Dar El Tahrir Publishers, 1970), p. 137, quoted in Nawal El Saadawi, *The Hidden Face of Eve* (London: Zed Books, 1985), p. 131.
[29] Ibid., p. 131. [My emphasis]. Saadawi quotes the original text from Mohammed Ibn Saad, *El Tabakat El Kobra*, pp. 140-41 in full: "The story, in the words of Mohammed Ibn Omar Ibn Ali Ibn Abi Talib, runs as follows: 'The Prophet of Allah, Allah's blessings and peace be upon him, did not die before Allah had bestowed upon him the right to have as many wives as he desired, and said unto him 'Take to yourself as many as you wish of them [women].' And when this verse descended, Aisha said: 'Indeed Allah responds immediately to your needs.'"

However, while Saadawi fails to clearly address the reasons behind the subsequent "closures" that were to ensue for women[30], Djebar and Ahmed come up with two differing interpretations as to why women's religious authority was gradually undermined. The example of Fatima in *Loin de Médine* foregrounds male misappropriation of the Koran as the reason behind Fatima's disinheritance, and, by implication, as the reason behind subsequent "closures." Ahmed, in contrast, views the losses of female autonomy not as the result of male exploitation of the true spirit of Islam but as the inevitable result of *the Islamic system itself*, which instituted a "hierarchical type of marriage", legitimising the husband's decisions to curtail his wife's freedoms.[31] She suggests that the autonomy and authority that women enjoyed in the early days of Islam are not, as Djebar implies, an inherent element of the new religion, but rather a residue of *pre-Islamic* freedoms.

The system of marriage that Islam established as the blueprint for sexual relationships ensured that the freedoms gained in the *Jahilia* age were slowly and inevitably eroded. Moreover, it is in the area of sexuality where it is most difficult not to relate the losses entailed for women to the new Islamic system rather than to subsequent misappropriations of the religion. The old system of "marriage" in pre-Islamic Arabia had granted women a degree of sexual autonomy that was clamped down upon by the new family structure imposed by Islam. This new structure was aimed at legalising male superiority, and protecting the interests of patriarchy: "La polygamie, la répudiation, l'interdiction de commettre *zina* [fornication, adultery] (qui concerne surtout les femmes, puisque les hommes avaient droit à plusieurs partenaires légitimes) et les garanties de paternité sont autant d'institutions qui ont contribué à favoriser la transition entre l'ancienne structure, où la famille reposait sur une certaine *auto-détermination* des femmes, et la nouvelle structure, où la famille repose sur le principe de la *suprématie masculine*."[32]

As in Dinesen's' tale, women under Islam became hostages to the concept of male honour. The cult of virginity, symbolised by Isak Dinesen's bloodstained sheets, and its corollary, the fear of *zina*, established the preservation of the honour of the male (father, husband, brother) as the new driving force behind the society of

---

[30] Saadawi refers rather vaguely to "a gradual, slow process related to the socio-economic changes taking place in society", which would lead to the curtailing of women's authority and independence. Ibid., p. 129.
[31] Leila Ahmed, *Women and Gender in Islam*, p. 63.
[32] Fatima Mernissi, *Sexe, idéologie, Islam* (Paris:Tierce, 1983), pp. 59-60. [My emphasis]

Islamic Arabia. The identity of women was now linked to their sexuality, which was henceforth to be perceived as a dangerous, uncontrolled force to be contained within a strict family structure.

Various theories exist as to the conception of pre-Islamic marriages at the time of the Prophet. All, however, attest to the coexistence of a variety of types of marriages, including both matrilineal and patrilineal. William Robertson Smith describes two of these as the "sadica" [friend, or marriage of friendship], and "ba'al" [property, or marriage of property] marriages.[33] In the "sadica" marriage, where the children and wife belonged to the *wife's* tribe, the wife could banish her husband at will. Physical paternity was not significant and women's chastity did not have a social function. In the patrilineal "ba'al" marriage, however, where the child belonged to the father's tribe, and where proof of physical paternity was paramount, women's chastity was required in establishing physical paternity.

A more complex but complementary account of pre-Islamic sexual unions emerges from the records of Al Buchtari, as transmitted by Aïcha, who cited four types of marriage prevalent in the pre-Islamic age. Two of these were polyandrous, the wife having as many husbands as she wanted. Although there is this evidence of polygyny before Islam, the type that the Prophet practiced, virilocal polygyny, was rare.[34] According to Mernissi, polygyny in the pre-Islamic matrilineal context probably entailed a husband visiting his different wives where they resided with their tribes, just as wives might have been visited by different husbands. In three out of four of "Aïcha's marriages", there is no emphasis on physical paternity, and therefore the notion of female chastity was absent.[35]

By transferring the rights to women's sexuality and her offspring from women and their tribes to men, and then by basing the new definition of marriage on that "proprietory male right", Islam changed the balance of power between the sexes: "Implicit in this new order was the male right to control women and to interdict their interactions with other men."[36] According to Ahmed, the ground was now prepared for the closures that would follow: "... women's exclusion from social activities in which they might have contact with men other than those with rights to their sexuality; their physical seclusion, soon to become the norm; and the institution of internal mechanisms of

---

[33] William Robertson Smith, *Kinship and Marriage in Early Arabia* (Boston: Beacon Press, 1903), p. 94.
[34] Leila Ahmed, *Women and Gender in Islam*, p. 44.
[35] Fatima Mernissi, *Sexe, idéologie, Islam*, p. 76.
[36] Leila Ahmed, *Women and Gender in Islam*, p. 62.

control, such as instilling the notion of submission as a woman's duty."[37]

Although the transition to Islamic mores was intended to "civilise" what Simone de Beauvoir calls "les hordes primitives", Mernissi points to the irony of such an assumption, and to the fundamental patriarchal bias which underlies it:

> ... ce qui est curieux dans la sexualité musulmane en tant que sexualité civilisée est la contradiction fondamentale entre la sexualité da la femme et celle de l'homme: s'il est vrai que promiscuité et laxisme sont la marque d'un certain barbarisme, alors la seule sexualité qui ait été civilisée par l'Islam est celle de la femme. La sexualité de l'homme est caractérisée par la promiscuité (du fait de la polygamie) et le laxisme (du fait de la répudiation).[38]

Within *Loin de Médine*'s multivalent framework, Djebar celebrates the sexual autonomy of pre-Islamic women, but also attempts to show that women in early Islamic marriages also had a certain autonomy. In the areas where autonomy was maintained (women, for example, had the right to initiate and refuse proposals of marriage[39]), this message is reinforced in *Loin de Médine*. In contrast, where her autonomy is stripped, *Loin de Medine* glosses over these "closures", obscuring the consequences they entailed for women rather than challenging the position of male authority.

So, rather than condemn Islam's endorsement of male polygyny, Djebar focuses on the fulfilment and intimacy of couples living within such polygamous relationships: "... l'expérience de l'amour conjugal – vécu sans doute en passion unique au coeur de la polygamie" [... conjugal love as they experienced it – doubtless an exclusive passion in a polygamous existence] (p. 238; 188). Djebar foregrounds the capacity for "une passion unique" within polygamous unions. Thus Esma, twice widowed, three times married to polygamous husbands, is "Esma, l'amoureuse. Esma à la vie pleine qui goûta trois vies de femme et qui, dans chacune, fut vraiment femme" [Asma, the loving wife, Asma with the full life, who enjoyed three women's lives and who, in each, was truly a woman] (pp. 267; 211). The positive emphasis on the physical intimacy of the couple within a polygamous union is achieved at the expense of any feminist critique of a practice

---

[37] Ibid., p. 62.
[38] Ibid., pp. 31-32.
[39] *Loin de Médine* offers examples of this practice: Oum Salama turns down Abou Bekr, second Caliph of Islam (p. 55), and the Prophet himself receives various offers of marriage, including that of an unnamed young girl (p. 122), suggesting that this custom overrode social status.

that gave the husband, but not the wife, the right to several sexual unions.

Similarly, the male prerogative on divorce is glossed over in the story of Oum Keltoum's second marriage to Zubeir, Ibn el Awwam. Here again the spiritual dimension of the story obscures the underlying problem of a system of divorce that privileges the husband at the expense of his wife. Oum Keltoum rebels against her new husband who ignores her repeated pleas for a divorce: "– Je désire que tu me répudies! finit-elle par dire à l'heure de la prière, un après-midi, à Zubeir entré chez elle. Il la regarda. Ne lui répondit rien" ['I want you to repudiate me!' she said at last when Zubair entered her room one day at the time of the afternoon prayer. He looked at her. Did not reply] (pp. 194; 154). Her release from marriage finally comes thanks to a moment of divine intervention, when she surprises her husband at the hour of prayer:

> Zubeir qui va s'adresser à Dieu, qui allège son esprit de ses soucis, de ses colères, de son désir hostile, Zubeir, surpris, s'est tourné vers elle; elle, la rétive. Encore habité de l'idée de Dieu, vers lequel humblement il désire s'approcher, il répond cette fois d'emblée, sans réfléchir:
> – Femme, par Dieu, tu es répudiée! (pp. 195; 155)
>
> Zubair is about to address God, who relieves the spirit of care, of anger, of hostile desires. Zubair turns to her – the rebellious one – in surprise. Still filled with the idea of God, whom he humbly wishes to approach, he replies this time immediately, without stopping to think, 'Woman, in God's name, you are repudiated!'

By foregrounding this instance of divine reprieve and female freedom, *Loin de Médine* distances itself from direct criticism of Islam's reductive divorce laws. The Islamic God, if not the Islamic laws, is on the side of women. In her desire to portray Islamic women as autonomous subjects, Djebar represses the patriarchal bias of Islam's marriage system.

The Prophet: the Real Subject or the Other Subject?

How does this desire to represent Islamic women as *subjects* relate to Djebar's portrayal of the Prophet as the author of Islam? Can her women be free if they are the objects of Prophetic authority? Djebar's treatment of the Prophet reveals an underlying tension within the work. Roland Barthes, describing the narrative practice of privileging one subject over another, states that the subject can also be double: "This dual is all the more interesting in that it relates to the subject of certain (very modern) games, in which two equal opponents try to gain possession of an object put into circulation by a referee."[40] The dual or duel being fought out in *Loin de Médine* is between the two competing subjects: *woman-as-subject* and the *Prophet-as-subject*. Is the subject of the novel the women who speak out from within the golden frame of Dinesen's tale, or is it the Prophet whose emblem, like that of the golden crown, adorns its golden plate, casting its objectifying shadow over the women contained within the frame?

Although the framework of *Loin de Médine* is polyvalent, encompassing the women of both pre-Islamic and Islamic Arabia, the emblem of Islam, in the shape of the person of the Prophet, is inscribed throughout the work, as the Prophet's voice both literally and metaphorically speaks throughout its pages. How can the woman-as-subject, the voice set free, the voice of freedom, coexist with the Prophet-as-subject, the Voice of authority?

In contrast to the portrayal of woman-as-subject in both the private and public domains, with the emphasis on the latter, the picture given of Mohammed is one that is very much concentrated on the private, the personal, and the spiritual. By elevating the voice of the Prophet to a mystical force, by foregrounding Islam's spiritual dimension, Djebar suppresses its pragmatic side, with its strong patriarchal bias, leaving behind a Voice that speaks with, for, and alongside women.

Ahmed explains the seemingly "inexplicable" contention made by many Muslim women, that Islam is not sexist, as a consequence of what she describes as the "two distinct voices within Islam, and the two competing understandings of gender, one expressed in the pragmatic regulations for society", based on a patriarchal notion of gender, and the other on "the articulation of an ethical vision", proclaiming an egalitarian conception of gender.[41] Ahmed notes that these tensions are contained within the Koran itself, which despite appearing to consolidate marriage as a hierarchical institution, contains verses that appear to qualify this position.[42] Also of considerable significance is the affirmation of women's right to inherit

---

[40] Roland Barthes, *Image Music Text*, trans. Stephen Heath (ed.), (London: Fontana Press, 1977), p. 108. From "Introduction à l'analyse structurale des récits", in Roland Barthes, *Oeuvres complètes*, tome 2 [1966-1973] (Paris:Seuil, 1994), p. 93.
[41] Leila Ahmed, *Women and Gender in Islam*, pp. 65-66.
[42] Ibid., p. 63. Ahmed points out specific Koranic verses that qualify marriage as a hierarchical institution – ie. verses proclaiming that women have corresponding rights to men (Sura 2: 229), verses directing men who wish to be polygamous to treat all their wives equally, but implying that this is an impossible ideal (such verses are open to being read to mean that men should not be polygamous), verses sanctioning divorce but which proceed to condemn it as being abhorrent to God.

In Dialogue with Feminisms: *Loin de Médine* 239

and control property and income without reference to male guardians, "a most crucial area with regard to personal autonomy, qualifying the institution of male control as an all-encompassing system."[43]

Ahmed goes so far as to say that "Islam's ethical vision, which is stubbornly egalitarian, including with respect to the sexes, is thus in tension with, and might even be seen to subvert, the hierarchical structure of marriage pragmatically instituted in the first Islamic society."[44]

So it is the ethical, egalitarian voice of Islam that speaks through Djebar's Prophet, a voice that rises above and drowns out the accusations of patriarchy directed at the pragmatic practices of Islam. In Djebar's representation of the Prophet, she foregrounds the private man, the Prophet at home with his family, who emerges as the idealised father-figure, both in relation to his beloved daughter Fatima, and in relation to the other daughters of Islam, to whom this relationship is symbolically extended. It is his voice, the Voice of the Father, rather than the voice of the Mother, which corresponds to Cixous's primeval song: "The voice in each woman, moreover is not only her own, but springs from the deepest layers of her psyche: her own speech becomes the echo of the primeval *song* she once heard, the voice the incarnation of the 'first voice of love which all women preserve alive ... in each woman sings the first nameless love'... the Voice of the Mother..."[45]

Loin de Médine's primeval song is the song of the Prophet, a song that resonates deep into the heart of its hearers, women such as Oum Hakim, whose story illustrates the mystical power of His voice. On the day of "le sermon de l'Adieu", Mohammed's last public appearance, Oum Hakim is drawn towards the thronging crowd, and then to the Voice. The Voice that transforms her life is compelling, drawing her to itself in an almost mystical way: "Elle sortit dans le matin ensoleillé. Elle se découvrait une hâte irraisonnée: dépasser ces rangées d'auditeurs, se rapprocher de quoi, sinon de la voix qui se gonflait maintenant, qui prenait de l'ampleur, qui s'éloignait puis revenait. Oum Hakim, comme dans un rêve, se dirigeait avec la même hâte vers l'avant" [She emerged into the sunlit morning. She found herself hurrying for no reason: the need to push past the rows of listeners, come closer – to what? Only that voice which now swelled, grew fuller, faded away and then returned. Umm Hakim hurried along

---

[43] Ibid., p. 63.
[44] Ibid., p. 63.
[45] Toril Moi, *Sexual/Textual Politics: Feminist Literary Theory* (London and New York: Routledge, 1985), p. 114.

as if in a dream] (pp. 161; 127). Despite herself, she is completely taken over by his presence: "Se rapprochant du lieu où *il* se tenait, Oum Hakim se sentait en état de ne plus rien entendre, de ne plus rien comprendre. Figée, tendue tout entière à regarder, à... (plus tard, elle songea sans oser le dire: 'à témoigner')" [Moving closer to the place where *he* was, Umm Hakim felt herself no longer capable of hearing anything, of understanding anything. She was rooted to the spot, concentrating all her attention on looking, on ... (later she thought, without daring to say it: 'on testifying')] (pp. 162; 128). And, as the Voice takes on a powerful intensity, she is carried onto a higher plane: "Oum Hakim percevait, comme voguant à travers d'autres sphères, la voix aérienne de Mohammed" [Umm Hakim caught Muhammad's light voice, as if it were sailing across other spheres] (p. 163; 128).

The representation of the Prophet foregrounds not only the impact of his spiritual power, but also by the emotion of tenderness which he bestows liberally on his daughter Fatima and to all the daughters of Islam. In *Loin de Médine,* the Prophet's communications with women are characterised not only by tenderness and compassion, but also by light-heartedness:

> Puis il rit, il rit ouvertement. Moi, bouleversée, j'ai répondu, des larmes dans la voix... [Then I laughed out loud. I was upset and replied, in a tearful voice...] (pp. 42; 31)

> Et la douceur de ses paroles illumina la face de la nouvelle adoptée. [And the sweetness of his words lit up the face of the newly adopted one] (pp. 101; 80) [conversation with Habiba]

> ... le Prophète resta les yeux baissés, comme s'il souffrait de l'émoi si vif de l'épouse de Djaffar ibn Abou Talib. [The Prophet remained with downcast eyes, as if he suffered at the deep emotion of the wife of Ja'far ibn Abi Talib] (pp. 246; 195)

The Prophet's relationship to women is, however, at its most striking in his spiritual "bonding" with Fatima. Djebar evokes their intense relationship, recreating a scene shortly before the Prophet's death, where Fatima finds him lost in a trance. The extremes of emotions portrayed reinforce the mystical intensity of the scene:

> Elle pleure, ployée en silence; elle se déchire, sans nulle réponse au père. Elle mêle seulement ses larmes contagieuses à celles du malade. Qui reprend toutefois son discours, qui murmure à nouveau une ou deux phrases.
> Alors Fatima brusquement consolée s'illumine; son visage encore en larmes s'éclaire d'une joie enfantine; elle sourit; elle rit. A nouveau penchée sur le père gisant, elle lui fait partager sa joie; et celui-ci de s'éclairer de cette volubilité filiale... Père et fille dans les larmes, puis dans l'égouttement pour ainsi dire du bonheur survenant, *fusant enfin de toutes parts.* (pp. 65; 51)

She weeps silently, quite overcome; she lacerates her flesh, while her father makes no response. She simply weeps, her tears flowing in sympathy with those of the sick man. Who nevertheless resumes his murmuring, again whispering a few sentences.

Then Fatima, suddenly comforted, brightens; her tear-stained face lights up with a childish joy; she smiles; she laughs. Stooping once more over her prostrate father, she lets him share her joy; and he is gladdened by the words that flow from her daughter's mouth ... Father and daughter in tears, then sharing in the unexpected happiness that seems to filter through and finally *fusing together everywhere.* [My emphasis][46]

In this portrayal of Mohammed, Djebar is in fact privileging what is perceived in traditional terms as the "feminine side" of the Prophet's character, the adjectives "doux" [gentle], "tendre" [tender], his ready capacity for emotions, his propensity for tears breaking down the hierarchical male/female opposition between them. But here it is not man but The Man, "Mohammed avec son auréole de dernier des Prophètes mais aussi sa présence toute humaine" [Muhammad, with his aura as last of the Prophets but also with his very human presence], the Prophet, who in his bonding/fusing with Fatima – "... fusant de toutes parts" [fusing together everywhere] – breaks down the divide, crosses out the bar, transcends the relationship of otherness, for a woman, if not all women "est une partie de [lui]-Même" [is a part of myself] – Fatima, not part of the eternal mother figure, forever linked in semiotic harmony, but Fatima the beloved daughter, eternally linked to the ideal father in a relationship of spiritual equality, defying the otherness that patriarchal Islam has since been trying to impose on its "second sex" (pp. 237; 187, 72; 57).

The dual/duel between the competing subjects of Médine, woman-as-subject and the Prophet-as-subject, is to some extent resolved by Djebar's obscuring the "difference' between the Prophet-as-man and Fatima-as-woman, by her refusing to oppose them in a power relationship of man/woman and by allowing them to relate as equal subjects bound by a mystical spiritual relationality.

Djebar presents us with a new non-hicrarchical Islam, not only by foregrounding the Prophet's relationship with Fatima, but also by the implication that the very authorship of Islam is shared by women, women who are the *mothers of Islam* – or "les femmes qui firent l'Islam."[47] The decision to present the personal side of the Prophet, the Messenger "at home", rather than "at work", serves to emphasise the influential role women had in his life, and by implication, in the

---

[46] Translation adapted.
[47] Clarisse Zimra, "Comment peut-on être musulmane?", p. 60.

formation of both the message and the future of Islam.[48] In *Loin de Médine*, women are seen to share the *authorship* of Islam, and, as such, retain a measure of their subjecthood. Their faith is not an exclusively male faith, with a single, all-powerful male Author, but a faith in which women shared in its beginnings, its creation, and in which the "mères des Croyants" gave birth to its future.

The concept of the shared authorship of Islam is communicated in *Loin de Médine* by stories showing how the Koran was inspired by the lives of individual women – women such as Oum Keltoum, "la fugueuse" [the runaway], who at the age of fifteen left her family at Mecca to join the Prophet and his followers at Médine Threatened by her brothers, this adolescent girl becomes the subject of prophetic inspiration, her brothers' attempts to recapture her prompting the *sura* protecting the lives of converted women who have to flee their families: "Des décennies durant, il suffira qu'une fugueuse répétât ces deux phrases du Prophète – rapportées par son épouse Aïcha – pour que, jeune ou vieille, forte ou faible, elle soit sauvegardée, mise sous protection islamique et, en aucun cas, renvoyée à un père, à des frères, à un mari..." [For many decades a runaway woman only had to repeat those two sentences of the Prophet – reported by his wife Aisha – for young or old, strong or weak, to be safe, under the protection of Islam, and in no case to be sent back to a father, brothers or husband ...] (pp. 187; 148-49).

Also lending weight to this concept of shared authorship is the image of an Islamic "family tree" of which women such as Oum Fadl, sister of Maïmouna, "mère des Croyants" [mother of the Believers], are the roots:

> Oum Fadl dont le premier fils, Fadl, s'est occupé de l'ensevelissement du Prophète avec Ali et Abbas, dont le second, Abdallah, deviendra plus tard un des plus célèbres commentateurs du Coran, Oum Fadl se sent peu à peu comme une première mémoire pour les Musulmanes. Au centre de la famille du Prophète – lui qui n'a pas eu de fils et dont presque toutes les filles sont mortes – Oum Fadl porte en elle tout un passé récent, brûlant comme une braise! (pp. 57-58; 45)

> Umm Fadl – whose eldest son, Fadl, together with Ali and Abbas, took charge of the Prophet's burial, and whose son, Abdallah, later becomes one of the most famous commentators on the Qur'an – Umm Fadl gradually feels she is like an original memory for the Muslims. In the centre of the Prophet's family – he who had no sons and whose daughters are nearly all dead – Umm Fadl bears within her a recent past, burning like a fiery coal!

---

[48] Although sources vary, the best substantiated evidence suggests that Muhammad had eleven wives and two concubines.

Islam's Empowered Heiresses

Despite the tributes to women, and to the "mères des Croyants", the role of motherhood in the relational (rather than the genealogical sense) is deliberately bypassed in *Loin de Médine*, as Djebar displaces the feminists' privileged mother-child relationship with the father-daughter bond. The mother-child relationship is absent, not only in the portrayal of the Prophet's family, but also in the portrayal of "les femmes insoumises" [the unsubdued women]. Their identity is as women, not as mothers; it is established in being actors, not in being "mere subjects of male action and female biology."[49] Those who have converted to Islam, "les soumises" [the subdued women], are, similarly, not represented within mother-daughter relationships but within husband-wife, and father-daughter configurations.

In the chapter entitled Esma, "La laveuse des morts" [She Who Lays Out The Dead], Esma bent Omaïs (who was to wash and embalm the body of Fatima, and in later years that of Abou Bekr) figures as part of a symbolic chain of relationships in which the role of motherhood is deliberately excluded, a chain that includes the Prophet himself, Fatima (daughter of the Prophet and friend of Esma), Abou Bekr (father of Aïcha, friend of the Prophet and first caliph of Islam), Aïcha (wife of the Prophet, daughter of Abou Bekr), and Esma (wife of Abou Bekr and friend of Fatima).

Djebar builds up a web of relationships, weaving in and out of the five figures, tightening "le fil invisible" around one and then the other, highlighting the bonds of intimacy between them, then loosening the thread, allowing the bond to be examined more closely. The invisible thread winds round and round the five figures in a configuration bringing together man with man by the intermediary of women – Esma, Fatima and Aïcha linking the Prophet and his caliph in multiple bonds of marriage, friendship and kinship: "Ainsi la mort pour le 'Nabi' [Prophet] et pour son vicaire deviendra vraiment fraternelle, rapprochant les deux hommes, si proches de leur vivant, par double, par triple intercession féminine" [Thus, death for the 'Nabi' and for his vicar will be in truth fraternal, linking the two men, so close in their lifetime, by the double, triple female intercession] (pp. 237; 187). It is as if the different threads of Islam are brought together by women, who relate to men not as mothers, but as daughters and wives.

---

[49] Michelle Zimbalist Rosaldo, "The Use and Abuse of Anthropology: Reflections on Feminism and Cross-Cultural Understanding", p. 409. Quoted in Gayle Greene and Coppélia Kahn, "Feminist Scholarship and the Social Construction of Woman", p. 16.

The thread that links these men and women is now transposed into another, more mystical plane, acquiring an almost dream-like quality, as the group of four is highlighted against the radiant Father-figure:

> Une sorte de jeu éclatant et abstrait, un mouvement intérieur translucide se lie et se délie autour de ce groupe de figures: Mohammed avec son auréole de dernier des Prophètes mais aussi sa présence tout humaine, Abou Bekr en face, et de l'autre côté Aïcha, jeune femme de dix-huit ans liée aux deux hommes, puis Fatima silhouette à la fois mélancolique et indomptable, sous l'éclat presque unique du Père, enfin, en arrière de celle-ci, dans son ombre, Esma les mains tendues vers Fatima, les yeux encore levés vers Abou Bekr qui va disparaître. (pp. 237: 187-88)
>
> A sort of bright, abstract interplay, inner translucent moving strands are tied and untied around this group of figures: Muhammad, with his aura as last of the Prophets, but also with his very human presence; facing him Abu Bakr; and on the other side eighteen-year-old Aisha, linked to both men; then Fatima, a figure both sad and indomitable, beneath the near unique radiance of the Father; and finally, behind her, in her shadow, Asma with hands outstretched to Fatima, her eyes still raised to Abu Bakr who will soon disappear. [50]

In this "tableau" or picture of "les hommes et les femmes qui firent l'Islam", now so closely linked and interwoven as to defy their "différence", and their differences, the light of Islam, "l'éclat du Père" is shining brightly onto the frame, radiating directly onto Fatima's face, light which is then diffused onto the surrounding figures. The stillness of these motionless, statue-like images contrasts with the inner movement incessantly weaving them together, as Esma, the symbol of a healing link, finally brings together Fatima and Abou Bekr, whose bitter alienation in life would be the catalyst for the bitter fracturation of Islam.

Djebar then shines her torch on the absent mother-figure, which she associates not with Islam, but with the cult of Mary, which, "shaped by pagan obsessions with fertility and chastity, has already made a fetish of virginity and motherhood."[51]

> Pour ces deux hommes dont le destin s'accomplit dans son ampleur à quarante ans et au-delà, la mère, toutefois, est absente. Ce rôle, de nos jours surévalué dans le vécu masculin musulman, était quasiment évacué.
>
> L'Islam, en son commencement, se contente d'adopter les valeurs de la maternité à travers Marie, mère de Jésus ... Le thème de la maternité a été tellement glorifié, célébré à satiété durant les sept

---

[50] Translation adapted
[51] "Mary, Mary, Once Contrary", *The Independent on Sunday*, (24 August 1997), p. 18.

In Dialogue with Feminisms: *Loin de Médine* 245

> siècles chrétiens qui ont précédé, qu'il semble normal de le voir alors reculer. (pp. 238: 188-89)
>
> For these two men, whose destiny reaches its complete fulfilment at the age of forty and beyond, the mother, however, is absent. This role, nowadays given too much significance in the life of a Muslim male, was, to all intents and purposes, unfilled.
> Islam in the beginning simply adopted the importance of motherhood from Mary, mother of Jesus ... The theme of motherhood had been so greatly extolled, celebrated *ad nauseam* during the seven Christian centuries that went before it, that it seemed normal to see it then lose ground.

In her criticism of the traditional perception of motherhood, Djebar's view conforms to that of feminists who view motherhood as the basis for women's oppression: "she [Kristeva] has claimed that it is not *woman* as such who is repressed by patriarchal society but *motherhood*."[52] But rather than viewing Islam as part of the problem of patriarchy, "the prevailing religion of the entire planet"[53], Djebar displaces the powerless Christian *femme-mère* onto the powerful Islamic *fille-héritière*. As the powerless "femme-mère" recedes into the background, the powerful female figures of Islam rise up: "Les femmes-épouses, les filles héritières se lèvent, elles, en cette aurore de l'Islam, dans une modernité neuve" [Wives, daughters, heiresses then take the stage in this dawn of Islam, in a new modernity] (pp. 238; 189). Thus, claims Djebar, women of Islam were not originally defined as "femmes-mères", in relationships of subservience to man and child, but as "femmes-épouses" in relationships of equality and love, or as "filles-héritières" in relationships of power, producing a sexual and economic revolution the world was not yet ready for, "l'insupportable révolution féministe de l'Islam en ce VIIe siècle chrétien!" [the intolerable feminist revolution of Islam in this seventh century of the Christian era!] (pp. 86; 68).

Ideological Collision?

Can Djebar thus really reclaim Islam for women, or is this a contradictory position to uphold? The ambiguity of her position is revealed in the structure of her language. In the "tableau" of the five figures, Fatima's silhouette is visualised "sous l'éclat *presque unique* du Père" [My emphasis]. Is it that the figure of Fatima is lit up *almost*

---

[52] Toril Moi, *Sexual/Textual Politics*, p. 167.
[53] Mary Daly, *Gyn/Ecology: The Metaethics of Radical Feminism* (Boston: Beacon Press, 1978), p. 39.

completely by the Father's radiant being, or is it the radiance itself, "l'éclat", which is not unique, but almost unique, the Truth or almost all the truth, the "almost" letting in the suggestion of otherness, of other realities, self-determined, subjective realities, self-determining, subject-women, grating against the uniqueness, the exclusiveness of objective, authoritative Islam.

For although Djebar overtly challenges a "closed" view of Islam, her acceptance of the Prophet as a figure of authority shows an adherence to a certain objective truth, conflicting with her celebration of plurality, of otherness, of women who have their own different versions of the truth, implying an understanding of truth as subjective. This conflict symbolises the meeting and clash of mutually exclusive ideologies, Islam and feminism, both of which have "interpellated" the author, neither of which she can wholly accept of reject.

However, some kind of resolution can be found in the form of a "politically correct Islam", its ideological fusion, if not its content, modelled along the lines of Christian feminism:

> What does it mean to these women to be called "Christian" feminists? Certainly it does not suggest anything distinctive or unique about Jesus Christ. Being Christian [for these Christian feminists] involves being religiously open; open to all other cultural and religious traditions where freedom for women is being sought, and open above all to the possibility that Christianity might be wrong. It means being prepared to allow experience to sift through the traditions in which we have previously seen ourselves and to work out a new hermeneutic which will make sense of this. In some cases it means being prepared to embrace a new paganism which will begin to incorporate the old female earth religions with a new non-patriarchal Christianity.[54]

Djebar too allows her feminist consciousness to sift through Islam in order "to work out a new 'hermeneutic' which will make sense of this." *Loin de Médine* too is "open to all other cultural and religious traditions", not, as in the case of Christian feminists, embracing a *new* paganism alongside a new non-patriarchal Christianity, but incorporating the *old* paganism of pre-Islamic Arabia with a new non-hierarchical Islam. For it is not only the special presence of the Prophet but also that of the non-Muslim heroines, "les insoumises", which radiates out from the pages of *Loin de Médine*, revealing his "éclat" as *not completely unique,* but rather as *shared* with these "others" who challenge both his pre-eminence and his monopoly on the Truth.

---

[54] Elaine Storkey, *Contributions to Christian Feminism* (London: Christian Impact, 1995), p. 13.

Djebar's openness to these "other" heroines is such that she celebrates their intelligence, courage and wit, even when these qualities are pitted against the might and mores of Islam, even when their "éclat" rivals that of the Prophet. The Prophet shares his "éclat" [radiance] with "la chanteuse des satires" [the singer of satires], the renowned poetess. This powerful woman uses her word as a subversive weapon against her enemies, the foremost of which is Mohammed himself:

> Avant le départ des chefs des Beni Kinda à Médine et donc avant leur islamisation, la poétesse avait été l'auteur de nombreuses diatribes poétiques contre Mohammed en personne ... C'est cet *éclat* même, c'est cette gloire acquise tôt dans la guerre verbale, qui dut ensuite retenir la chanteuse. Elle ne vint pas, c'est certain, à Médine; elle ne se trouva pas en présence de celui qui avait fait objet de sa verve acérée. Par fidélité à son art – une forme d'amour propre –, elle dut croire que ce serait se renier que de devenir musulmane. (pp. 132; 103-4)
>
> Before the Beni Kinda chiefs left for Madina, thus before their conversion to Islam, the poetess had composed many poetic diatribes against Muhammad in person ... It is this very *radiance*, this glory early acquired in the verbal war, which must have later restrained the singer. She did not come to Madina, that much is certain; she was never in the presence of the person she had made the target of her biting wit. Out of loyalty to her art – a form of *amour propre* – she must have thought that by turning Muslim she would be false to herself. [My emphasis][55]

Despite the fact that the poetess's distrust of religion is linked to its potential for stifling self-expression, this indirect indictment of Islam is counteracted by the suggestion that the poetess's fear of being muzzled is unfounded, and by the statement that art itself is nothing more than an expression of pride. Djebar thus celebrates the poetess's energy and art as a powerful life-force, while at the same time denouncing her spark of poetic genius as a dangerous expression of rebellion, "sa poésie-danger" [danger-poetry], and as a form of blind arrogance: "Tant que sa flamme la nourrissait, tant que son rôle polémique la parait aux yeux des siens d'une valeur rare, plus rare que la beauté, plus recherchée que l'attrait féminin ordinaire, elle n'éprouvait nul besoin de croire en Dieu. Quel Dieu? N'avait-elle pas en elle une étincelle divine?" [As long as her flame nourished her, as long as her role as a polemicist seemed precious in the eyes of her people, rarer than beauty, more sought after than ordinary female attractions, she felt no need to believe in God. What God? Did she not have within herself a divine spark?] (pp. 132; 103, 104).

---

[55] Translation adapted.

There is admiration for this "High Priestess of Poetry", but also a suggestion that her poetry is blasphemous and her religion false, its promise of immortality an illusion. The treatment the poetess receives at the hands of the Islamic military leader, Mohadjir ibn Ommayya, is horrific – her teeth are pulled out, her hands cut off. Her body, but not her soul, is cruelly crushed into submission: "– Je les maudirai avec mes mains, mes mains coupées! ... Mon chant leur restera insaisissable, tel l'épervier qu'ils n'atteignent pas!" ['I shall sing with my hands! I shall curse them with my hands, with my severed hands! ... My song will be inaudible to them, like a hawk they can never reach!'] (pp. 136; 107). Yet Djebar stresses that this barbaric act was condemned by the official representative of Islam, Abou Bekr ("Abou Bekr, mis au courant du châtiment subi par la poétesse, écrit une lettre de réprimandes véhémentes à Mohadjir..." [Abou Bekr, informed of the punishment inflicted on the poetess, writes to Muhajir, rebuking him severely] pp. 136; 107), and that, as such, can be seen to be a betrayal of the true spirit of Islam. So both the role of Islam as the perpetrator of evil, and the role of the poetess as the heroine are qualified. Islam is not the true "villain", neither is the poetess the perfect heroine.

"Kérama la Chrétienne" [Kerama, the Christian] also has a radiating presence: "On me disait belle dans ma jeunesse, certains le répètent encore comme s'ils avaient vu mon visage d'alors, alors qu'ils voyaient, j'en suis sûre, *l'éclat*, sur ma face, de mon espérance d'hier, de mon espérance d'aujourd'hui" [I was said to be beautiful in my youth, some still repeat this if they had seem my face of yore, whereas they saw, I am sure, my face *radiate* with my past hopes, my ever-present hopes] (pp. 141; 110) [My emphasis].[56] Kérama is an octogenarian nun whose legendary beauty convinces a simple Bedouin, attached to General Khalid's army, that she should be taken as a slave. Kérama's people rise to her defence, but because their position is precarious, and the whole situation so ridiculous, she offers to confront the old Bedouin herself rather than risk her people engaging in a doomed battle.

Again the official Islamic representative present in the story, General Khalid, is seen to distance himself from, and to be embarrassed by the whole episode: "tout en lui semblait regretter cette intervention" [his whole demeanour seemed to express regret for this intervention] (pp. 144; 112). He shows respect to her and to her people: "Retourne chez les tiens! Mon respect, notre respect pour toi

---

[56] Translation adapted.

et pour tous ceux du Livre t'accompagne. Que Dieu te garde!" ['Return to your people! My respect, the respect of us all for you and for all the people of the Book, goes with you. May God keep you!'] (pp. 146; 114).

As Khalid and Abou Bekr act as the representatives of the true spirit of Islam, a spirit which is open to the other, and which condemns the abuse of power, their messages reinforce the ideological agendas of the work. *Loin de Médine* presents an Islam that is open to the other, echoing the theology of Christian feminists. The novel also presents the true, non-hierarchical spirit of Islam as the Islam represented by the Prophet, and those closest to him. This second agenda is more in line with the thinking of evangelical "feminist" theology that seeks not to open up Christianity to the outside, but to expose an open or egalitarian spirit on the *inside*. But whereas not only Djebar, but also many *liberal* Christian feminists regard Mary, "la femme-mère", as unworthy of standing as a figure of liberation, ironically it is she who is cited by *evangelical* theologians as revealing an egalitarian spirit at the heart of Christianity, because of the focal point she occupies in biblical history: "It is a woman, rather than a man whom God chooses as the human vehicle which travels between the old and new covenants."[57]

The idea that *Loin de Médine* can be read as an apologia for the lost spirit of Islam is reinforced by an incident related about Omar ibn el Khattab, the second caliph, who recounts one of his last conversations with the Prophet, where they lament the passing of the golden age of Islam. The Prophet, finding Omar in tears, asks him why he is distressed:

> "Ce qui me fait pleurer, c'est que, jusqu'à présent, nous étions dans un accroissement constant dans notre religion, mais si, à présent, elle est achevée, il faut dire qu'il n'y a pas de choses qui atteignent leur plénitude sans que, par la suite, elles ne s'amoindrissent!" Et le Prophète, m'ayant écouté, a répondu après un long moment: "Certes, Omar, tu dis vrai!" (pp. 167; 132)

> "What makes me weep, is that, up till now, our religion has been in a state of continual growth, but if, at present, it is completed, it must be said that nothing reaches its plenitude without subsequently declining!" And the Prophet listened to me and then, after a long pause, replied, "Indeed, Umar, you speak truly!"'

The true spirit of Islam is rehabilitated not only as liberal, in the sense of being open, but also as liberating. "Islam, le contraire de la contrainte" are the words voiced by Oum Keltoum, and echoed

---

[57] Elaine Storkey, *Contributions to Christian Feminism*, p. 55.

repeatedly in the novel, as Djebar weaves stories into the text that challenge the traditional religious arguments used to justify "Islamic constraints" (such as the widespread imposition of veiling), and repressive measures taken against the freedom of artistic expression.[58] "L'Islam c'est le contraire de la contrainte!" ['Islam is the opposite of constraint!'] (pp. 193; 154). In Oum Keltoum's case it is her revulsion against her second husband that provokes her to utter these words, in her determination to be released from her marriage: "– Je suis musulmane! Si je désire encore partir, c'est parce que je n'accepte pas Zubeir comme époux! L'Islam, c'est le contraire de la contrainte! se réconforta-t-elle peu à peu" ['I am a Muslim! If I wish to leave, it is because I do not accept Zubair as a husband! Islam is the opposite of constraint!' so she gradually consoled herself] (pp. 193; 154). The hierarchy within their marriage is symbolically reversed, not by Islamic law, which upholds this hierarchy, but by the Prophet, the author of Islam, who when confronted by Zubeir's complaints about Oum Keltoum, upholds *the woman's* position in the spirit of egalitarian Islam and admonishes *the man* (alluding to a *sura* inspired by Oum Keltoum): "– Tu ne peux pas parler ainsi de cette femme, ô Zubeir. N'oublie pas que, pour cette Croyante, Dieu lui-même est intervenu! ... Tête baissée, le coeur humilié, il salua et quitta la pièce" ['You cannot speak in this way of this woman, O Zubair! Do not forget that God himself gave His ruling for this Believer!' ... With downcast head and humiliated heart, he took his leave] (pp. 197; 156).

The strong impulse towards freedom leads Djebar not only to look for it both outside and inside Islam, but also to extend it to the concept of faith itself. The freedom to question or doubt makes it possible for all the daughters of Islam, as it does for Oum Hakim, to come full circle and to freely choose the way of Islam. Like Djebar, Oum Hakim is simultaneously placed both at the heart and on the boundaries of faith. By selecting a woman of impeccable Islamic credentials as the subject of doubt (Oum Hakim's second marriage is to Omar ibn el Khattab, the second caliph), Djebar is presenting it as an acceptable facet of faith, rather than as a betrayal of the truth:

> Oum Hakim se savait musulmane d'emprunt, en quelque sorte. Non pas honteuse, non pas hypocrite, simplement "musulmane" ("soumise", comme ils spécifiaient parfois) parce que ainsi elle avait gardé, envers et contre tous, son époux ... Elle ne priait pas. (pp. 160; 126)

---

[58] See the discussions on veiling, pp. 156-57, and on entertainment at a wedding, pp. 138-40.

> Umm Hakin realized she was, in some respects, a sham Muslim. Not
> ashamed, not a hypocrite, simply 'a Muslim woman' ('submissive', as
> they sometimes specified) because in this way she had kept her
> husband, in spite of everyone ... She did not pray.

Djebar highlights ways in which Oum Hakim is a reluctant convert to Islam (she converts in order to save her husband, retains an attachment to the pagan statues of her childhood and refuses to pray), but also shows how this "hésitation intérieure" [inner hesitancy] is overcome, as Oum Hakim, inspired by her vision of the Prophet, goes on to distinguish herself on the Islamic battlefield and to gain religious prominence through her marriage to the caliph (pp. 170-72; 134-36).

Strategies of Feminist Historical Scholarship

On an ideological level, Djebar allows feminist consciousness to open her religion to the outside. At the same time she refuses to allow it to shine a torch on the problematic areas on the inside, revealing a profound ambiguity towards feminist ideology. But how far is Djebar's feminist consciousness in tune with another area of feminist scholarship – that of historical methodology? Reverting to Dinesen's tale, we note that Greene and Kahn see in the "Blank Page" a demonstration of the concerns of feminist historians:

> The nuns are entrusted with keeping the records, with preserving the
> histories of the royal women as recorded on their marriage sheets and
> then framed and displayed for the edification of future generations. In
> this respect they function like traditional historians whose focus has
> been the history of dynasties and who, if they have attended women at
> all, considered them within a domestic sphere and in relation to the
> ruling families.[59]

But Greene and Kahn point out that the nuns' records also tell a different story. For although the frames they display suggest the traditional way women have been contained in history, the blank page "implies other possibilities" suggesting a subtext which is subversive to the main text: "These two taken together represent the traditional paradigm and alternatives to it which are the dual concerns of feminist historians and literary critics."[60] They proceed to describe the elements of traditional historical scholarship, against which feminist historical scholarship should militate, as follows:

---

[59] Gayle Greene and Coppélia Kahn, "Feminist Scholarship and the Social Construction of Woman", p. 12.
[60] Ibid., p. 12.

The periodisation of history based on the concept of male achievement;
The focus on hierarchical power dynamics, exemplified in the prevalence of the "history of dynasties";
The traditional opposition between exclusively male and exclusively female history.[61]

How far does *Loin de Médine* avoid the traditional historical mould? Superficially, the novel's structure appears to mimic the periodisation of history based on the concept of male achievement. The prologue is centred on the Prophet in his dying moments at a time when the whole of Arabia was unified under the religion of Islam and its messenger. The book is then divided into two chronologically successive parts relating to the Caliphates of the Prophet's two successors, Abou Bekr (10e-13e année de l'hégire [10-13AH]), and Omar ibn el Khattab (13e-23e année de l'hégire [13-23 AH]).

The contents of the prologue, however, and the internal sections within the two main parts, undermine the "male" framework. The Prophet's dying moments show him not only as a figure of authority, as the divine messenger, but as a vulnerable figure in all his humanity. The opening scene also underlines one of the central tenets of *Loin de Médine*, which is that the Prophet was surrounded by, loved by, and dependent on women. Similarly, although the work is divided into two parts, based on two successive Caliphates, all the chapters they contain bear the title of a female subject who questions male authority. The main challenge to traditional periodisation is not, however, related to a concept of history based on *male* achievement, but to a concept of history limited to that of *Islamic* achievement. The swift movement between pre-Islamic and Islamic heroines, a movement which implies a common voice, a cry of sisterhood, defies the Islamic historian's tendency to cut off the pre-Islamic age, and to view the birth of Islam as the starting-point of history.

Nevertheless, Djebar, like Dinesen's nuns, appears to repeat the traditional paradigm, as she acts as the guardian not of the history of a royal dynasty but of the history of a religious dynasty, the Prophet's family. Although *Loin de Médine* provides an insight into the lives of both ordinary and extraordinary women, the text does (in contrast to *L'Amour, la fantasia*) privilege the "Greats" of history, the extraordinary women of the past, whether "soumises" or "insoumises." However, the political agenda that is the driving force

---

[61] Ibid., see section III, pp. 12-21.

behind the novel constrains Djebar to concentrate on "famous names" (and where the work does occasionally include "ordinary" people, their inclusion is subordinated to an ideological agenda which seeks to present Islam as an open religion[62]). Djebar does, however, use her extraordinary heroines to show how women of this transitional age functioned outside the "domestic sphere", and as such, challenges the traditional conception of women, and especially Muslim women, as being excluded from the public world.

Not only do feminist historians reject the privileging of the "Greats" of history, but they also denounce the privileging of female history over male history. As with feminist literary scholarship, feminist historical scholarship has come to reject the substitution of women's history (as opposed to women's literature) for mainstream history (as opposed to the canon) as reduplicating the central assumption – woman as the "other", separate and apart. As with early feminist literary criticism, which sought to *compensate* for the neglect of female writers by creating a female canon, early feminist historians also concerned themselves with *compensatory history* charting the lives of exceptional women and paying particular attention to women's contributions.

The trends of feminist literary criticism and feminist historical scholarship can be seen to mimic developments in feminist politics, which, according to Kristeva, progressed from this compensatory phase (as women demanded equal rights and strove to be accepted into the symbolic order) through a radical exclusive phase, where femininity is celebrated, towards a more inclusive relationship to the world of men.[63] Although the compensatory stage has been criticised for appending women to the symbolic order (or to history or to literature) as it has already been defined (while leaving the existing paradigm unchallenged), it can nevertheless be viewed as the valuable and necessary precursor to the more inclusive philosophy that succeeded it.

The compensatory stage to which *Loin de Médine* could itself be "appended" must be viewed in the same way as the compensatory

---

[62] Examples of "ordinary people" include Habiba, the errant woman who demonstrates Islam's acceptance of the marginalised, and Djamila, who demonstrates Islam's encouragement of the Arts (Habiba is the only entirely fictional main character in the work, see Djebar's comment p. 350).
[63] Julia Kristeva's analysis of the three stages in the development of the woman's movement is elaborated in "Women's time", trans. Alice Jardine and Harry Blake, *Signs* (1981), 7, 1, pp. 23-35, pp. 33-34. Discussed in Toril Moi, *Sexual/Textual Politics*, pp. 12-13.

phrase of the early Western feminist movement, namely as a necessary first step in the long road towards the possibility of a more inclusive perspective. Against the background of the Algeria of today, compared to that of the 1960s when the Anglo-American feminists were coming up with their compensatory histories, it is no mean feat for Djebar to ask "them", *les intégristes*, through the pages of *Loin de Médine*, however indirectly, not to be let into the symbolic order, the Nom-du-Père, but into the religion of the idealised Father, the order of Islam.

Conclusion

I have attempted to show the way in which Djebar's works are in constant dialogue with a variety of feminisms, highlighting the specific areas where this dialogue takes on a particular intensity, namely in the area of linguistic style, in the relation between woman and language, in the analysis of relations between women, and in the treatment of women in Islamic history.

Whereas elements of a writing style reminiscent of *écriture féminine* can be pinpointed throughout Djebar's work, demonstrated in outbursts of highly rhythmic language, in her privileging of voice, in her desire to incorporate "other experience", in the use of repetition and accumulation, and in the occasional fragmentation evident in her texts, the highly structured, consciously constructed "architectural" form of her novels evades the fluidity and openness to the processes of the unconscious which lie at the heart of Cixous's idea of feminine writing.

On the other hand, Kristeva's theory of language as a process, as interaction between semiotic and symbolic, provides a means of doing justice to the variety and mobility of the linguistic styles expertly manipulated by Djebar, in which the constant and dynamic balance between the semiotic and symbolic is played out within a wide spectrum of possibilities, with the balance between the two modalities shifting constantly. Paralleling the generic instability of the particular novel selected for its linguistic qualities (*L'Amour, la fantasia*), Djebar's language passes back and forth almost effortlessly from the defined boundaries of the historical symbolic, to the sensuous, limitless world of the semiotic, its dynamism marking her out as a writer of Kristevan credentials. But whether grounded in historical reality or in sensuous lyricism, Djebar uses language as a weapon that fiercely resists the colonial and patriarchal attempts to repress woman, whether figured as *l'Algérie-femme* or as *femmes d'Algérie*.

Cixous's idea of *écriture féminine* does nevertheless provide a key to Djebar's attitude to the relation between woman and language, if not to Djebar's stylistic disposition. For both Cixous and Djebar react against the sexual violence of patriarchal language and look for a language that woman can call her own. Despite the fundamental difference in their response to the problem of language, Djebar's *écriture des femmes*, as explored in *Vaste est la prison*, and Cixous's *écriture féminine* exhibit a surprising number of features in common, sharing a common starting-point of exclusion, a common engagement with the locus of the repressed, a common maternal source, and a common desire for resistance. But whereas Cixous's search leads to the possibility of a new freedom and transformation, Djebar's historical quest brings no such satisfaction. It is only by embracing a matrilineal writing, which rejoins Cixous in its desire to give voice to the other, that Djebar finds she can find the way to express the Maternal Voice silenced by patriarchal language.

Although the threat of male violence (whether colonial, political or domestic) threatens to overwhelm her texts, Djebar succeeds in subverting masculine power by either gradually phasing out masculine images from her text (as in *L'Amour, la fantasia*, which takes a sharp turn in the final stages towards the world of women) or by almost completely by-passing them (as in *Ombre sultane*). Here the only male character, who remains the anonymous "homme" throughout, is completely undeveloped, and gradually becomes irrelevant, as the two women take central stage.

The relation between Hajila and Isma provides the prototype for Djebar's images of sisterhood, which come surprisingly close to Irigaray's images of a female sociality – both being predicated on mutual reciprocity, both coming into being as a result of distance or difference, both being played out in silence, and both foregrounding a sense of wonder at the elusiveness of the other's subjectivity. Nevertheless, while Irigaray's later work comes to grips with the possibility of the coming into being of a relation between men *and* women, this consideration is largely absent in the works of Djebar studied in this work which concern themselves almost exclusively with the experience of women, and in the case of *Ombre sultane*, with restoring relations *between* women as a form of resistance to male power.

This "feminine exclusiveness" is also the hallmark of Djebar's treatment of Islam, in its primary focus on the experiences of women. While confirming her commitment to portraying positive images of women in Islam, her emphasis on woman's experience in *Loin de Médine* eschews current trends in feminist historical scholarship, which tend to demonstrate a more inclusive attitude towards *male* history. On the other hand, her approach to Islam conforms to the spirit of Christian feminist scholarship, which, like Djebar's work, also attempts to present a non-patriarchal religion. Ahmed's work, however, demonstrates the extent to which Djebar's desire to invent a "politically correct" Islam compels her to repress those pragmatic practices of Islam which reinforce its patriarchal/hierarchical bent, while foregrounding what she undeniably demonstrates to be the egalitarian spirit of Islam. Nevertheless, this exploration of the women at the dawn of Islam remains a powerful and courageous work of resistance to the trends of current fundamentalism.

What Djebar calls her "own kind of feminism"[1] is a feminism of exposure and resistance. As we have seen, many of her resistance strategies conform to those employed by the French feminists, whether she transgresses symbolic language with her semiotic rhythms, resists the Law of the Father by giving voice to the other/Mother, refuses the notion of woman as man's other, or revisits maternal genealogies.

But whereas it is possible to identify Djebar's resistance to "an unsatisfactory present"[2] and past, visions of a better future are notably absent from her work. This stands in marked contrast to the projects of Cixous and Irigaray in particular, whose blueprints for the future imply at least the possibility of the transformation of patriarchal codes, and therefore an underlying optimism. Djebar's novels, while demonstrating fierce resistance to patriarchal power-relations, are nevertheless increasingly overshadowed by the reality of the effect on these patriarchal power-relations on women in present-day Algeria.

As Algeria retreats into a Dark Age of fundamentalism, political intrigue and violence, the optimism of the early independence years is all but extinguished by the ever-worsening status and conditions of Algerian women. Nevertheless, while the will to resist and a certain fatalism hang in a precarious balance, it is the former that ultimately dominates in Djebar's oeuvre. Djebar herself identifies her writing as protest, quoting Mario Vargas Llhosa "In the heart of all fiction the flame of protest burns brightly."[3] At the same time she questions the effectiveness of writing in the face of extreme political circumstances, while expressing the hope that "my books can prolong the echo of the voices of so many other women..."[4] Despite her own doubts, it comes as no surprise that a woman who writes with such "unflinching

---

[1] Clarisse Zimra, "Woman's Memory Spans Centuries. An interview with Assia Djebar", Afterword to *Women of Algiers in their Apartment* (Charlottesville/London: University of Virginia Press, 1992). p. 175.
[2] Reference to previously cited quotation: "In all forms of feminism there is a tension between the critique of an unsatisfactory present and the requirement, experienced as psychological or political, for some blueprint, however sketchy, of the future." Margaret Whitford, *Luce Irigaray: Philosophy in the Feminine* (London and New York: Routledge, 1991), p. 18.
[3] Assia Djebar, "Neustadt Prize Acceptance Speech", *World Literature Today*, Autumn 1996, pp. 783-84, p. 784.
[4] Ibid., p. 784.

honesty and stately perseverance"[5] has been dubbed potentially "the most threatening person to Algeria's political chieftains, secular and religious."[6]

The final protest, not expressed by Assia Djebar but *on behalf* of her contribution to international literature, will be left to William Glass, who, in his encomium for Assia Djebar's 1996 Neustadt Prize, decried the label of "Women's Literature" attached to Djebar's work as profoundly disturbing, arguing that such labels, while being intrinsically reductive, are in the case of Djebar's work, a particular insult to the importance of her subject, her moral integrity, and perhaps most significantly, to her ability to write both beautifully and disturbingly: "Assia Djebar is not being celebrated here because she has brought us more bad news, or exotic treats, or even her eloquent imagination, worthy as much as that may be; we are lauding her here because she has given weeping its words and longing its lyrics."[7]

---

[5] Djelal Kadir, "Of Pencil Points and Petty Tyrants", *World Literature Today*, Autumn 1996, p. 777.
[6] Ibid., p. 777.
[7] William Glass, "Encomium for Assia Djebar, 1996 Neustadt Prize Laureate", *World Literature Today*, Autumn 1996, p. 782.

Bibliography

Primary Sources

Books

Djebar, Assia. *La Soif.* Paris: Julliard, 1957.
---. *Les Impatients.* Paris: Julliard, 1958.
---. *Les Enfants du nouveau monde.* Paris: Julliard, 1962.
---. *Les Alouettes naïves.* Paris: Julliard, 1967.
---. *Femmes d'Alger dans leur appartement.* Paris: des femmes, 1980. Trans. de Jager, Marjolijn. *Women of Algiers in their Apartment.* Charlottesville/London: University of Virginia Press, 1992.
---. *L'Amour, la fantasia.* Casablanca: EDDIF, 1992. First published 1985. Trans. Blair, Dorothy. S. *Fantasia: An Algerian Cavalcade.* London/New York: Quartet, 1988.
---. *Ombre sultane.* Paris: J.-C. Lattès, 1987. Trans. Blair, Dorothy S. *A Sister to Scheherazade.* London/New York: Quartet, 1988.
---. *Loin de Médine.* Paris: Albin Michel, 1991. Trans. Blair, Dorothy S. *Far from Madina.* London/New York: Quartet: 1994.
---. *Vaste est la prison.* Paris: Albin Michel, 1995. Trans. Wing, Betsy. *So Vast the Prison.* New York/Toronto/London: Seven Stories, 1988.
---. *Le Blanc de l'Algérie.* Paris: Albin Michel, 1996.
---. *Oran langue morte.* Paris: Actes Sud, 1997.
---. *Les Nuits de Strasbourg.* Paris: Actes Sud, 1997.
---. *Ces Voix qui m'assiègent.* Paris: Albin Michel, 1999.
---. *La Femme sans sépulture.* Paris: Albin Michel, 2002.
---. *La Disparition de la langue française.* Paris: Albin Michel, 2003.

Articles

Djebar, Assia. "Neustadt Prize Acceptance Speech", *World Literature Today*, Autumn 1996, pp. 783-84.

Secondary Sources

Books

Ahmed, Leila. *Women and Gender in Islam: Historical Roots of a Modern Debate*. New Haven and London: Yale University Press, 1992.
Al-Ghazali, Abu Hamid. *The Revivification of Religious Sciences*. Cairo: al-Maktaba at-Tijariya al-Kubra, no date cited.
Althusser, Louis. "Ideology and Ideological State Apparatuses". In *Lenin and Philosophy and Other Essays*. Trans. Brewster, Ben. London: NLB, 1971.
Barrett, Michèle. *Women's Oppression Today: Problems in Marxist Feminist Analysis*. London/New York: Verso, 1980. Revised edition. *Women's Oppression Today*: The Marxist/Feminist Encounter, 1988
Barthes, Roland. *Image Music Text*. Trans. Heath, Stephen (ed.). London: Fontana Press, 1977.
Barthes, Roland. *Oeuvres complètes*, tome 2 [1966-1973]. Paris: Seuil, 1994.
Beauvoir, Simone de. *Le Deuxième sexe 1*. Paris: Gallimard, 1949.
Blair, Dorothy S. Introduction to Djebar, Assia. *Fantasia: an Algerian cavalcade*. London/New York: Quartet, 1989.
Bouhdiba, Abdelwahab. *Sexuality in Islam*. Trans. Sheridan, Alan. London: Routledge and Kegan Paul, 1985.
Brahimi, Denise. Post-face à *L'Amour, la fantasia*. Casablanca: Editions EDDIF, 1992.
Budig-Markin, Valérie. "La Voix, l'historiographie: Les dernières oeuvres d'Assia Djebar". In Ginette Adamson, Jean-Marc Gouanvic (eds). *Francophonie Plurielle*. Quebec: Hurtubise HMH, 1995.
Cixous, Hélène. *L'Exil de James Joyce ou l'art du remplacement*. Paris: Grasset, 1969.
---. *Prénoms de personne*. Paris: Seuil, 1974.
---. *La Jeune née*. In collaboration with Catherine Clément. Paris: UGE, 10/18, 1975.
---. *Vivre l'orange*. Paris: des femmes, 1975.
---. *La*. Paris: Gallimard, 1976.
---. *La Venue à l'écriture*. In collaboration with Leclerc, Annie and Gignon, Madeleine. Paris: UGE, 10/18, 1977.
---. *Illa*. Paris: des femmes, 1980.

---. *(With) Ou l'art de l'innocence*. Paris: des femmes, 1981.
---. *Le Livre de Promethea*. Paris: Gallimard, 1983.
---. *L'Histoire terrible mais inachevée de Norodom Sihanouk, roi du Cambodge*. Paris: Théâtre du Soleil, 1985.
---. *L'Indiade ou L'Inde de leurs rêves*. Paris: Théâtre du Soleil, 1987.
---. "My Algeriance: In other words to depart not to arrive from Algeria". Trans. Prenowitz, Eric. In *Stigmata: Escaping Texts*. London/New York, Routledge, 1989.
---. "De la scène de l'inconscient à la scène de l'Histoire: Chemin d'une écriture". In Françoise van Rossum-Guyon, Myriam Díaz-Diocaretz (dir.). *Hélène Cixous, chemins d'une écriture*. St.-Denis: Presses Universitaires de Vincennes and Amsterdam/Atlanta: Rodopi, 1990.
---. *Three Steps on the Ladder of Writing*. Trans. Cornell, Sarah and Sellers, Susan. New York: Columbia University Press, 1993.
---. Hélène Cixous. *Les Rêveries de la femme sauvage*. Paris: Galilée, 2000.
Sellers, Susan (ed.). *The Hélène Cixous Reader*. London: Routledge, 1994.
Clerc, Jeanne-Marie. *Assia Djebar: écrire, transgresser, résister*. Paris: L'Harmattan, 1997.
Daly, Mary. *Gyn/Ecology: The Metaethics of Radical Feminism*. Boston: Beacon Press, 1978.
Déjeux, Jean. *Assia Djebar romancière algérienne, cinéaste arabe*. Québec: Naaman, 1984.
---. *La Littérature féminine de langue française au Maghreb*. Paris: Editions Karthala, 1994.
Delphy, Christine. *L'Ennemi principal*. Paris: Syllepse, 2001.
Derrida, Jacques. *Spectres of Marx: The State of the Debt, the Work of Mourning and the New International*. Trans. Kamuf, Peggy. New York: Routledge, 1994.
Diamond, Arlyn and Edwards, Lee R (eds). *The Authority of Experience*. Amherst: University of Massachusetts, 1977.
Dinesen, Isak. *Last Tales*. New York: Vintage, 1975.
Donovan, Josephine. *Feminist Theory*. New York: Continuum, 1993.
El Saadawi, Nawal. *The Hidden Face of Eve*. London: Zed Books, 1985.
Flaubert, Gustave. *Madame Bovary*. Paris: Garnier, 1971. First published 1857.
Fanon, Franz. *Peau noire, masques blancs*. Paris: Seuil, 1965.
Geesey, Patricia. "Women's Worlds: Assia Djebar's *Loin de Médine*". In Kenneth W. Harrow (ed.), *The Marabout and the Muse: New*

Approaches to Islam in African Literature. Portsmouth, NH: Heinemann, 1996.
Greene, Gayle and Kahn, Coppélia. "Feminist Scholarship and the Social Construction of Woman". In Greene, Gayle and Kahn, Coppélia (eds), *Making a Difference: Feminist Literary Criticism.* London and New York: Routledge, 1985.
Grosz, Elizabeth. *Sexual Subversions: Three French Feminists.* Sydney: Allen and Unwin, 1989.
---. *Jacques Lacan: A Feminist Introduction.* London: Routledge, 1990.
Hurtig, Marie-Claude, Kail, Michèle and Rouch, Hélène (dir.). *Sexe et genre: De la hiérarchie entre les sexes.* Paris: CNRS Editions, 2003.
Ibn Saad, Mohammed. *El Tabakat El Kobra, Vol.8.* Cairo: Dar El Tahrir Publishers, 1970.
Irigaray, Luce. *Spéculum de l'autre femme.* Paris: Minuit, 1974.
---. *Ce sexe qui n'en est pas un.* Paris: Minuit, 1977.
---. *Le Corps-à-corps avec la mère.* Montréal: Editions de la pleine lune, 1981.
---. *L'Oubli de l'air, chez Martin Heidegger.* Paris: Minuit, 1983.
---. *Éthique de la différence sexuelle.* Paris: Minuit, 1984.
---. *Parler n'est jamais neutre.* Paris: Minuit, 1985.
---. *Sexes et parentés.* Paris: Minuit, 1987.
---. *Le Temps de la différence.* Paris: Livre de Poche, 1989.
---. *J'aime à toi.* Paris: Grasset et Fasquelle, 1992.
JanMohamed, Abdul R. "The Economy of the Manichean Allegory". In Ashcroft, Bill, Griffiths, Gareth and Tiffin, Helen (eds). *The Post-colonial Studies Reader.* London: Routledge, 1994.
Jayyusi, Salma Khadra (ed.). *Modern Arabic Poetry: An Anthology.* New York: Columbia University Press, 1987.
Jefferson, Ann and Robey, David (eds). *Modern Literary Theory: A Comparative Introduction.* London: Batsford, 1982.
Johnson, Barbara. *A World of Difference.* Baltimore: John Hopkins University Press, 1987.
Johnstone, Barbara. *Repetition in Arabic Discourse: Paradigms, Syntagms, and the Ecology of language.* Amsterdam/ Philadelphia: John Benjamins, 1991.
Jong, Erica. *What Do Women Want?* London: Bloomsbury, 1999.
Kristeva, Julia. *La Révolution du langage poétique.* Paris: Editions du Seuil, 1974.
---. *Des Chinoises.* Paris: des femmes, 1974.
---. *Polylogue.* Paris: Editions du Seuil, 1977.

Lacan, Jacques. *Ecrits: A Selection.* Trans. Sheridan, Alan. London: Tavistock, 1977.
Lejeune, Philippe. *Le Pacte autobiographique.* Paris: Seuil, 1975.
Gerda Lerner. *The Majority Finds its Past: Placing Women in History.* Oxford: Oxford University Press, 1979.
Lodge, David. *The Modes of Modern Writing.* London: Edward Arnold, 1977.
Mernissi, Fatima. *Sexe, idéologie, Islam.* Paris: Tierce, 1983.
Minow-Pinkney, Makiko. *Virginia Woolf and the Problem of the Subject.* Brighton: The Harvester Press, 1987.
Moi, Toril. *Sexual/Textual Politics: Feminist Literary Theory.* London and New York: Routledge, 1985.
---. *The Kristeva Reader.* Blackwell: Oxford 1986.
Moreh, Shmuel. *Modern Arabic Poetry.* Leiden: E. J. Brill, 1976.
Morris, Pam. *Literature and Feminism.* Oxford: Blackwell, 1993.
Muslim, Abu al-Hassan. *al-Jami as-Sahib.* Beirut: al Maktaba at-Tijariya, no date cited.
Perelman, Chaim and Olbrechts-Tyteca, Lucie. *The New Rhetoric: A Treatise on Argumentation.* Trans. Wilkenson, John and Weaver, Purcell. Notre Dame, IN: The University of Notre Dame Press, 1969.
Robertson Smith, William. *Kinship and Marriage in Early Arabia.* Boston: Beacon Press, 1903.
Shiach, Morag. *Hélène Cixous: A Politics of Writing.* London and New York: Routledge, 1991.
Showalter, Elaine "Towards a Feminist Poetics". In Showalter, Elaine (ed.). *The New Feminist Criticism: Essays on Women, Literature and Theory.* London: Virago, 1985.
Spivak, Gayatri Chakravorty. "Acting Bits/Identity Talk". In Appiah, Kwame Anthony and Gates, Henry Louis Jr (eds), *Identities.* Chicago: University of Chicago Press, 1995.
---. "Three Women's Texts and Circumfession". In Hornung, Alfred and Ruhe, Ernstpeter (eds), *Postcolonialism and Autobiography.* Amsterdam/Atlanta: Rodopi, 1998.
Storkey, Elaine. *Contributions to Christian Feminism.* London: Christian Impact, 1995.
Todd, Loretto. "The English Language in West Africa". In Bailey, R. W. and Görlach, M. (eds), *English as a World Language.* Ann Arbor: University of Michigan Press, 1982.
Turkle, Sherry. *Psychoanalytical Politics: Freud's French Revolution.* London: Burnett, 1979.
Verdiglione, Armando. *Psychanalyse et Politique.* Paris: Seuil, 1974.

Warhol, Robyn R. and Price Herndl, Diane (eds). *Feminisms: An Anthology of Literary Theory and Criticism*. New Brunswick: Rutgers University Press, 1997.
Watt, William Montgomery. *Mohammed at Mecca*. Oxford: Oxford University Press, 1953.
Whitford, Margaret. *Luce Irigaray: Philosophy in the Feminine*. London and New York: Routledge, 1991
Woolf, Virginia. *A Room of One's Own*. London: Hogarth, 1967.
Zabus, Chantal. "Relexification". In Ashcroft, Bill, Griffiths, Gareth and Tiffin, Helen (eds). *The Post-colonial Studies Reader*. London: Routledge, 1994.
Zeghidour, Slimane. *Le Voile et la bannière*. Paris: Hachette, 1990.
Zimra, Clarisse. "Woman's Memory Spans Centuries: An Interview with Assia Djebar". Afterword to Djebar, Assia. *Women of Algiers in their Apartment*. Trans. de Jager, Marjolijn. Charlottesville/London: University of Virginia Press, 1992.

Articles

Accad, Evelyne. "Assia Djebar's Contribution to Arab Women's Literature: Rebellion, Maturity, Vision", *World Literature Today*, 70:4 (1996), pp. 801-12.
Assa-Rosenblum, Sonia. "M'introduire dans ton histoire: Entrée des narrateurs dans *L'Amour, la fantasia* d'Assia Djebar", *Etudes Francophones*, 12:2 (1977), pp. 67-80.
Cixous, Hélène. "Le Rire de la méduse", *L'Arc*, 61 (1975), pp. 39-54.
---. "Le Sexe ou la tête?", *Les Cahiers du GRIF*, 13 (1976), pp. 5-15.
---. "Mon algériance", *Les Inrockuptibles* 115. 20 August 1997. p. 70.
Gadant, Monique. "La Permission de dire 'je': Réflexions sur les femmes et l'écriture à propos d'un roman d'Assia Djebar, *L'Amour, la fantasia*", *Peuples Méditerranéens*, 48-49 (July-December 1989), pp. 93-105.
Gauvin, Lise. "Assia Djebar, territoires des langues: entretien", *Littérature – L'Écrivain et ses langues*, 101 (February 1996), pp. 73-87.
Glass, William. "Encomium for Assia Djebar", 1996 Neustadt Prize Laureate, *World Literature Today*, 70:4 (1996), p. 782.
Gracki, Katherine. "Writing Violence and the Violence of Writing in Assia Djebar's Algerian Quartet", *World Literature Today*, 70:4 (1996), pp. 835-43.

Hotte, Véronique. "Entretien avec Hélène Cixous", *Théâtre/Public*, 68 (1986), pp. 22-29.
Huughe, Laurence. "Ecrire comme un voile: The Problematics of the Gaze in the Work of Assia Djebar", *World Literature Today*, 70:4 (1996), pp. 867-76.
Kadir, Djelar. "Of Pencil Points and Petty Tyrants", *World Literature Today*, 70:4 (1996), p. 777.
Kristeva, Julia. "Women's time", trans. Jardine, Alice and Blake, Harry, *Signs* (1981), 7, 1, pp. 23-35.
Makward, Christiane. "Nouveau regard sur la critique féministe en France", *Revue de l'Université d'Ottowa*, 50:1 (1980), pp. 47-54.
Mortimer, Mildred. "Entretien avec Assia Djebar, écrivain algérien", *Research in African Literatures*, 19:2 (Summer 1988), pp. 197-205.
---. "Assia Djebar's Algerian Quartet: A Study in Fragmented Autobiography", *Research in African Literatures*, 28:2 (Summer 1997), pp. 102-117.
Murdoch, H. Adlai. "Rewriting Writing: Identity, Exile and Renewal in Djebar's *L'Amour, la fantasia*", *Yale French Studies*, 2:83 (1993), pp. 71-92.
Rosaldo, Michelle Zimbalist. "The Use and Abuse of Anthropology: Reflections on Feminism and Cross-Cultural Understanding", *Signs*, 5:3 (1980), pp. 389-417.
Spivak, Gayatri. "Ghostwriting", *Diacritics*, 25: 2 (1995), pp. 64-84.
Stevens, Christa. "Hélène Cixous, auteur en 'algériance'", *Expressions maghrébines*, 1: 1 (Summer 2002), pp. 77-97.
Stimpson, Catharine R. "Editorial", *Signs* 1:1 (1975), pp. v-viii.
Woodhull, Winifred. "Feminism and Islamic Tradition", *Studies in 20th century literature*, 17:1 (1993), pp. 27-44.
Zimra, Clarisse. "Writing Woman: The Novels of Assia Djebar", *Substance: A Review of Literary Criticism*, 21:3 (1992), pp. 68-84.
---. "When the Past Answers our Present: Assia Djebar Talks about *Loin de Médine*", *Callaloo*, 16:1 (1993), pp. 116-31.
---. "Comment peut-on être musulmane?", *Notre Librairie*, 118, Nouvelles Écritures Féminines 2: Femmes d'ici et d'ailleurs (July- September 1994), pp. 57-63.
---. "Disorienting the Subject in Djebar's *L'Amour, la fantasia*", *Yale French Studies*, 87 (1995), pp. 149-70.
---. "Introduction to Assia Djebar's *The White of Algeria*", *Yale French Studies*, 87 (1995), pp. 140-41.

Websites

Groden, Michael and Kreiswirth, Martin (eds), *The John Hopkins Guide to Literary Theory and Criticism*, 1997, http://www.press.jhu.edu/books/hopkins_guide_to_literary_theory/

---. Elam, Diane. "Feminist Theory and Criticism: 3. Poststructuralist Feminisms". In *The John Hopkins Guide to Literary Theory and Criticism* [Home page as above, restricted access].

---. Kime Scott, Bonnie. "Feminist Theory and Criticism: 2. Anglo-American Feminisms". In *The John Hopkins Guide to Literary Theory and Criticism* [Home page as above, restricted access].

---. Landry, Donna and MacLean, Gerald. "Feminist Theory and Criticism: 4. Materialist Feminisms". In *The John Hopkins Guide to Literary Theory and Criticism* [Home page as above, restricted access].

Table of Contents

Introduction — 7
  Dialogic Spaces — 7
  A Sister to Sagan? — 9
  Approaches to Djebar's Œuvre — 12
  Novelistic Choices and Theoretical Perspectives — 21
  Voices Searching amongst Open Graves — 22
  Matches Made in Heaven? — 27

In Dialogue with Kristeva: *L'Amour, la fantasia* — 35
  Ode to Beethoven — 35
  Identity and the Semiotic Continuum — 36
  Language as Signifying Process — 39
  A Kristevan Model — 40
  The Incredible Mobility of Being — 42
  The Symbolic Mode: Historical Orders and Disorders — 44
  The Symbolic Mode: Autobiographical Ambiguities — 55
  The Semiotic Mode: Desire in "Sistre" — 67
  Semiotic and Symbolic: A Permanent Alternation? — 76
  Conclusion — 92

In Dialogue with Cixous: *Vaste est la prison* — 95
  Patriarchal Prison-Houses — 95
  Cixous and the patriarchal value-system — 96
  A Subject is at Least a Thousand People — 99
  Writing's Silent Voice — 101
  The Problem of Segregation: All in a Word — 104
  Looking for a Way out — 108
  Ecriture des Femmes/Ecriture Féminine — 124
  A Sisterhood of Suffering — 147
  The Blood-Streams of Writing — 154
  Conclusion — 155

In Dialogue with Irigaray: *Ombre sultane*   159
The Repressed Maternal-Feminine   159
The Absent Sex: Irigaray and Symbolic Exclusion   160
A Double Take on the Novel   171
Moving away from a Masculine Economy of Relations   173
Towards a Feminine Economy of Relations   191
Maternal Restoration or Paternal Revenge?   204
Conclusion   215

In Dialogue with Feminisms: *Loin de Médine*   217
The Forgotten Revolution   217
The Blank Page   217
Narrating Women   221
Woman as Subject   228
The Prophet: the Real Subject or the Other Subject?   237
Islam's Empowered Heiresses   243
Ideological Collision?   245
Strategies of Feminist Historical Scholarship   251

Conclusion   255

Bibliography   259
Primary Sources   259
Secondary Sources   260